JOSEPH SMITH
TRANSLATION

JOSEPH SMITH TRANSLATION

Old & New Testaments

KENNETH AND LYNDELL LUTES

Previously published under the title
The Bible Corrected by Joseph Smith,
by Lutes International

First Printing in Paperbound 1998
First Printing in Hardbound 1999

Revised third edition.
Published by: Lutes Publishing

Distributed by:

Brigham Distributing
110 S 800 West, Brigham City, Utah 84302
435.723.6611

Cover Art by David Lindsley, used with permission

Cover Design: Kenneth Lutes Jr.
Page Layout and Design: Lyndell Lutes
Editing: Kenneth Lutes Sr.

ISBN: 978-1-56684-633-2

6th Printing, 2019

PRINTED IN THE UNITED STATES OF AMERICA

Joseph Smith Translation
also available at Amazon.com on Kindle
ISBN: 978-0-9891710-3-8

Other books by Kenneth and Lyndell Lutes:
Feast upon the Words of Christ
ISBN: 978-0-9891710-1-4
Feast upon the Words of Christ on Kindle
ISBN: 978-0-9891710-0-7

CONTENTS

Old Testament

New Testament

  * No revisions
** Not included in the Inspired Version

PREFACE

"Judge not, that ye be not judged" is a quote from the Bible we hear frequently (Matthew 7:1). But is it true? Joseph Smith's inspired translation of the Bible restores the original scripture as, "Judge not **unrighteously**, that ye be not judged**; but judge righteous judgment**" (Inspired Version, Matthew 7:**2**).

This is just one of thousands of inspired revisions that Joseph Smith made to the King James Version of the Bible. We can see in this example some of the "plain and precious things which have been taken away" (1 Nephi 13:40). No wonder the Lord directed Joseph Smith to translate the Bible: "Verily I say unto you, that it is my will that you should hasten to translate my scriptures . . . for the salvation of Zion" (D&C 93:53).

Joseph Smith considered the translation to be "part of his divine calling as a prophet of God."[1] He accomplished it in about three years, during 1830–1833, and spent the remaining eleven years of his life making improvements. Although he went through the entire Bible, he did not correct everything. However, he did intend to publish what he had done and in fact did print extracts from the translation.

The Community of Christ (Reorganized Church of Jesus Christ of Latter Day Saints) has published most of these vital restorations in the *Holy Scriptures*. However, in order for us to find the actual revisions and, therefore, the many very significant changes in meaning, we have to make word-for-word comparisons with the Bible.

The Holy Bible and the Pearl of Great Price, published by The Church of Jesus Christ of Latter-day Saints in 1979 and 1981, respectively, contain parts of the translation, but not all. These works do make it much easier to read some large, extracted portions of the translation and to find many of the corrections by checking the footnotes. However, it is rather tedious to check each verse of the Bible to see if there is a Joseph Smith translation for that verse and then, if it exists, to find it and mentally insert the correction.

As Robert J. Matthews wrote in his book, *"A Plainer Translation:" Joseph Smith's Translation of the Bible*, "to obtain maximum benefit from the New Translation one must read . . . in large segments, to catch the flavor and flow of the language . . . . Much is lost when one reads only isolated passages, or only from a commentary."[2] We agree and, therefore, have presented all of Joseph Smith's revisions so that they can be readily seen right in the Bible text.

We know that Joseph Smith's translation may not have been ready for publication, and that the Prophet may have continued the Bible restoration if he had lived longer. However, "since it is impossible for a man to be saved in ignorance of God and his laws,"[3] we feel it can be very profitable for one to read the corrections as far as they were completed. Elder Bruce R. McConkie wrote,

> Such Biblical revisions as have been made may be used with safety, and parts of these are now published by the Church in its standard works. . . . The fact that some changes were made in a particular passage or chapter does not mean that all needed corrections were given even in that portion of the Bible. Important changes were made in several thousand verses, but there are yet thousands of passages to be revised, clarified, and perfected.[4]

> The Joseph Smith Translation, or Inspired Version, is a thousand times over the best Bible now existing on earth.[5]

We relied heavily upon the more than 25 years of research by Robert J. Matthews, Ph.D. He studied the original manuscripts of the translation and compared them to what has been printed and the King James Version of the Bible. In his book, he has provided comprehensive lists of the verses with textual variants, as well as lists of publishing errors. Aside from those errors, he found that the various editions of the Inspired Version are true to Joseph Smith's translation. Since we have corrected all of the errors, you can read this work with confidence.

Some variations in versification will be noted. We have shown both verse numbers—the Inspired Version (IV) and the King James Version (KJV). If you compare various editions of the KJV or the IV, you will undoubtedly note variations in spelling, punctuation, choices of articles or prepositions, and the like. Generally, these variations were not made by the Prophet and can be attributed to scribal preferences or the particular edition of the KJV being used for comparison. For ease in reading, we elected to use the spellings consistent with modern usage in the United States. Differences in capitalization are noted when it could affect the meaning. For the most part, verses are not included where the only variant is said for saith, a for an, labor for labour, until for till, and such.

We have included, for convenience, the uncorrected verses of Genesis (through chapter 24) and all of Matthew, Mark, Luke, and John. This makes it possible to read the major portions of the Bible, that have been restored by the Lord, without having to refer to the KJV. And as the Spirit bears testimony of these revisions, the scriptures come alive with "new revelations" to the reader.

To make this book as complete as possible, we have made the corrections Matthews suggested in his book. We have also included some Bible corrections made by the Prophet that are not in the Joseph Smith Translation. Aside from the unavoidable inclusion of some IV editing (versification, spelling, punctuation, and the like), you will be reading as close as we can get to what the Prophet restored, corrected, and retranslated.

This book will be easy to read if you note the following:

- Deletions from the KJV are shown by ~~strikethrough~~.
- Additions to the KJV are in **bold type**.
- To read KJV, read the ~~strikethrough~~ but skip the **bold**.
- To read IV, read the **bold** but skip the ~~strikethrough~~.
- The symbol (˙) denotes a change based upon the 1991 IV.
- *Italics* are the same as used in the KJV.

At last, we have a companion book to the Bible, that allows us to easily read the scriptures with Joseph Smith's translation clearly indicated. Reflection upon the revisions can lead to significant improvements in our understanding of the Bible and, hopefully, the way we live. What could be more important as we approach the time of the Second Coming of our Lord and Savior, Jesus Christ?

If there are errors in this book, please do not let them detract from the marvelous work that the Prophet Joseph Smith accomplished. We hope you enjoy reading this, alongside your Bible, to obtain the additional insights provided through the Joseph Smith Translation. May Heavenly Father bless us to find the truth. As the Savior said, "Whoso treasureth up my words, shall not be deceived" (Matthew 24:**39**).

We testify that Joseph Smith is a prophet of God.

Kenneth and Lyndell Lutes

NOTES

1. Robert J. Matthews, *"A Plainer Translation:" Joseph Smith's Translation of the Bible, A History and Commentary* [1985], 3.

2. *Plainer*, 391.

3. Bruce R. McConkie, *Mormon Doctrine*, [1958], Preface.

4. *Mormon Doctrine*, 384.

5. Andrew C. Skinner, "Restored Light on the Savior's Last Week in Mortality," *Ensign*, June 1999, 21.

ANNOTATION KEY

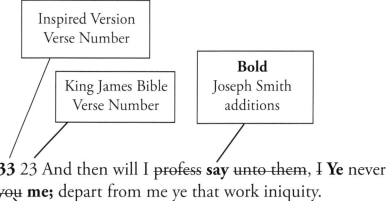

33 23 And then will I ~~profess~~ **say** ~~unto them~~, ~~I~~ **Ye** never knew ~~you~~ **me;** depart from me ye that work iniquity.

King James Version
Matthew 7:23

And then will I ~~profess~~ ~~unto them~~, ~~I~~ never knew ~~you~~; depart from me ye that work iniquity.

Inspired Version
Matthew 7:**33**

And then will I **say**, **Ye** never knew **me;** depart from me ye that work iniquity.

A Revelation
Given to Joseph the Seer
June A.D. 1830

1 The words of God which he spake unto Moses, at a time when Moses was caught up into an exceeding high mountain, and he saw God face to face, and he talked with him, and the glory of God was upon Moses; therefore Moses could endure his presence.

2 And God spake unto Moses, saying, Behold, I am the Lord God Almighty, and Endless is my name, for I am without beginning of days or end of years; and is not this endless?

3 And behold, thou art my son, wherefore, look, and I will show thee the workmanship of mine hands, but not all; for my works are without end, and also my words, for they never cease; wherefore, no man can behold all my works except he behold all my glory; and no man can behold all my glory, and afterwards remain in the flesh, on the earth.

4 And I have a work for thee, Moses, my son; and thou art in the similitude of mine Only Begotten; and mine Only Begotten is and shall be the Savior, for he is full of grace and truth; but there is no God beside me; and all things are present with me, for I know them all.

5 And now, behold, this one thing I show unto thee, Moses, my son; for thou art in the world, and now I show it unto thee.

6 And it came to pass, that Moses looked and beheld the world upon which he was created. And as Moses beheld the world, and the ends thereof, and all the children of men, which are and which were created; of the same he greatly marveled, and wondered. And the presence of God withdrew from Moses, that his glory was not upon Moses; and Moses was left unto himself; and as he was left unto himself, he fell unto the earth.

7 And it came to pass, that it was for the space of many hours before Moses did again receive his natural strength like unto man; and he said unto himself, Now, for this cause, I know that man is nothing, which thing I never had supposed; but now mine own eyes have beheld God; but not mine natural but my spiritual eyes, for mine natural eyes could not have beheld, for I should have withered and died in his presence; but his glory was upon me, and I beheld his face, for I was transfigured before him.

8 And now it came to pass, that when Moses had said these words, behold, Satan came tempting him, saying, Moses, son of man, worship me. And it came to pass that Moses looked upon Satan, and said, Who art thou, for behold I am a son of God, in the similitude of his Only Begotten; and where is thy glory, that I should worship thee? For, behold, I could not look upon God except his glory should come upon me, and I were transfigured before him. But I can look upon thee in the natural man. Is it not so surely?

9 Blessed be the name of my God, for his Spirit hath not altogether

withdrawn from me; or else where is thy glory, for it is darkness unto me, and I can judge between thee and God; for God said unto me, Worship God, for him only shalt thou serve. Get thee hence, Satan, deceive me not; for God said unto me, Thou art after the similitude of mine Only Begotten.

10 And he also gave unto me commandment, when he called unto me out of the burning bush, saying, Call upon God in the name of mine Only Begotten, and worship me.

11 And again, Moses said, I will not cease to call upon God. I have other things to inquire of him; for his glory has been upon me, and it is glory unto me; wherefore, I can judge between him and thee. Depart hence, Satan.

12 And now, when Moses had said these words, Satan cried with a loud voice, and wrent upon the earth, and commanded, saying, I am the Only Begotten, worship me.

13 And it came to pass, that Moses began to fear exceedingly; and as he began to fear, he saw the bitterness of hell; nevertheless, calling upon God he received strength, and he commanded, saying, Depart hence, Satan; for this one God only will I worship, which is the God of glory.

14 And now, Satan began to tremble, and the earth shook, and Moses received strength and called upon God in the name of his Son,[1] saying to Satan, Depart hence.

15 And it came to pass, that Satan cried with a loud voice, with weeping, and wailing, and gnashing of teeth, and he departed hence; yea, from the presence of Moses, that he beheld him not.

16 And now, of this thing Moses bore record; but because of wickedness, it is not had among the children of men.

17 And it came to pass, that when Satan had departed from the presence of Moses, that Moses lifted up his eyes unto heaven, being filled with the Holy Ghost, which beareth record of the Father and the Son; and calling upon the name of God, he beheld again his glory; for it rested upon him, and he heard a voice, saying, Blessed art thou, Moses, for I, the Almighty, have chosen thee, and thou shalt be made stronger than many waters; for they shall obey thy command even as if thou wert God.

18 And lo, I am with thee, even unto the end of thy days, for thou shalt deliver my people from bondage; even Israel my chosen.

19 And it came to pass, as the voice was still speaking, he cast his eyes and beheld the earth; yea, even all the face of it; and there was not a particle of it which he did not behold, discerning it by the Spirit of God. And he beheld also the inhabitants thereof, and there was not a soul which he beheld not, and he discerned them by the Spirit of God, and their numbers were great, even as numberless as the sand upon the seashore. And he beheld many lands, and each land was called earth; and there were inhabitants on the face thereof.

20 And it came to pass, that Moses called upon God, saying, Tell me, I pray thee, why these things are so, and by what thou madest them? And behold the glory of God was upon Moses, so that Moses stood in the presence of God, and he talked with him face to face.

21 And the Lord God said unto Moses, For mine own purpose have I made these things. Here is wisdom, and it remaineth in me. And by the word of my power have I created them, which is mine Only Begotten Son, who is full of grace and truth. And worlds without number have I created, and I also created them for mine own purpose; and by the Son I created them, which is mine Only Begotten. And the first man of all men have I called Adam, which is many. But only an account of this earth, and the inhabitants thereof, give I unto you; for behold, there are many worlds which have passed away by the word of my power; and there are many also which now stand, and numberless are they unto man; but all things are numbered unto me; for they are mine, and I know them.

22 And it came to pass, that Moses spake unto the Lord, saying, Be merciful unto thy servant, O God, and tell me concerning this earth, and the inhabitants thereof; and also the heavens, and then thy servant will be content.

23 And the Lord God spake unto Moses, saying, The heavens, they are many and they cannot be numbered unto man, but they are numbered unto me, for they are mine; and as one earth shall pass away, and the heavens thereof, even so shall another come; and there is no end to my works, neither to my words; for this is my work and my glory, to bring to pass the immortality and eternal life of man.

24 And now, Moses, my son, I will speak unto you concerning this earth upon which you stand; and you shall write the things which I shall speak. And in a day when the children of men shall esteem my words as naught, and take many of them from the book which you shall write, behold, I will raise up another like unto you, and they shall be had again among the children of men, among even as many as shall believe.

25 These words were spoken unto Moses in the mount, the name of which shall not be known among the children of men. And now they are spoken unto you. Amen.

The First Book of Moses, Called

GENESIS

1 And it came to pass, that the Lord spake unto Moses, saying, Behold, I reveal unto you concerning this heaven and this earth; write the words which I speak.

2 I am the Beginning and the End; the Almighty God. By mine Only Begotten I created these things.

3 1 **Yea,** in the beginning ~~God~~ **I** ~~created~~ **formed**[2] the heaven, and the earth **upon which thou standest.**

4 2 And the earth was ~~without form~~ **empty**, and ~~void~~ **desolate;**[3] and **I caused** darkness ~~was~~ **to come** upon the face of the deep.

5 2 And ~~the~~ **my** Spirit ~~of God~~ moved upon the face of the waters, **for I am God.**

6 3 And **I, God,** said, Let there be light, and there was light.

7 4 And **I, God,** saw the light, **and** that ~~it~~ **light** ~~was~~ good. And **I, God,** divided the light from the darkness.

8 5 And **I, God,** called the light day, and the darkness ~~he~~ **I** called night. **And this I did by the word of my power; and it was done as I spake.** And the evening and the morning were the first day.

9 6 And **again, I,** God, said, Let there be a firmament in the midst of the waters; **and it was so, even as I spake.** And **I said,** Let it divide the waters from the waters; **and it was done.**

10 7 And **I, God,** made the firmament, and divided the waters; **yea, the great waters** ~~which were~~ under the firmament, from the waters which *were* above the firmament; and it was so, **even as I spake.**

11 8 And **I, God,** called the firmament heaven. And the evening and the morning were the second day.

12 9 And **I, God,** said, Let the waters under the heaven be gathered together unto one place; **and it was so.** And **I, God, said,** Let ~~the~~ **there be** dry *land* ~~appear;~~ and it was so.

13 10 And **I, God,** called the dry *land* earth; and the gathering together of the waters called ~~he~~ **I the** ~~Seas~~ **sea.**

14 10 And **I, God,** saw that ~~it~~ **all things which I had made** ~~was~~ **were** good.

15 11 And **I, God,** said, Let the earth bring forth grass; the herb yielding seed; ~~and~~ the fruit tree yielding fruit after his kind; **and the tree yielding fruit,** whose seed ~~is~~ **should be** in itself, upon the earth; and it was so, **even as I spake.**

16 12 And the earth brought forth grass; ~~and~~ **every** herb yielding seed after his kind; and the tree yielding fruit, whose seed ~~was~~ **should be** in itself, after his kind.

17 12–13 And **I, God,** saw that ~~it~~ **all things which I had made** ~~was~~ **were** good. And the evening and the morning were the third day.

18 14–15 And **I, God,** said, Let there be lights in the firmament of the heaven, to divide the day from the night; and let them be for signs and for seasons, and for days and **for** years; and let them be for lights in the firmament of the heaven, to give light upon the earth; and it was so.

19 16 And **I, God,** made two great lights; the greater light to rule the day, and the lesser light to rule the night;

and the greater light was the sun, and the lesser light was the moon.

20 16–18 **And** ~~he made~~ the stars also **were made, even according to my word;** and **I**, God, set them in the firmament of the heaven, to give light upon the earth; and **the sun** to rule over the day, and **the moon to rule** over the night, and to divide the light from the darkness.

21 18–19 And **I**, God, saw that *it* **all things which I had made** ~~was~~ **were** good. And the evening and the morning were the fourth day.

22 20 And **I**, God, said, Let the waters bring forth abundantly, the moving creature that hath life, and fowl ~~that~~ **which** may fly above the earth, in the open firmament of heaven.

23 21 And **I**, God, created great whales, and every living creature that moveth, which the waters brought forth abundantly, after their kind; and every winged fowl, after his kind.

24 21–23 And **I**, God, saw that *it* **all things which I had created** ~~was~~ **were** good; and **I**, God, blessed them, saying, Be fruitful, and multiply, and fill the waters in the ~~seas~~ **sea**, and let fowl multiply in the earth. And the evening and the morning were the fifth day.

25 24 And **I**, God, said, Let the earth bring forth the living creature, after his kind; cattle and creeping ~~thing~~ **things**, and ~~beast~~ **beasts** of the earth, after ~~his~~ **their** kind; and it was so.

26 25 And **I**, God, made the ~~beast~~ **beasts** of the earth, after ~~his~~ **their** kind; and cattle after their kind; and everything ~~that~~ **which** creepeth upon the earth, after his kind. And **I**, God, saw that *it* **all these things** ~~was~~ **were** good.

27 26 And **I**, God, said **unto mine Only Begotten, which was with me from the beginning**, Let us make man in our image, after our likeness; **and it was so.**

28 26 And **I, God, said**, Let them have dominion over the ~~fish~~ **fishes** of the sea, and over the fowl of the air, and over the cattle, and over all the earth, and over every creeping thing that creepeth upon the earth.

29 27 ~~So~~ **And I**, God, created man in ~~his~~ **mine** *own* image, in the image of ~~God~~ **mine Only Begotten** created ~~he~~ **I** him; male and female created ~~he~~ **I** them.

30 28 And **I**, God, blessed them, and ~~God~~ said unto them, Be fruitful, and multiply, and replenish the earth, and subdue it; and have dominion over the fish of the sea, and over the fowl of the air, and over every living thing that moveth upon the earth.

31 29 And **I**, God, said **unto man**, Behold, I have given you every herb, bearing seed, which *is* upon the face of all the earth; and every tree in the which ~~is~~ **shall be** the fruit of a tree, yielding seed; to you it shall be for meat.

32 30 And to every beast of the earth, and to every fowl of the air, and to everything that creepeth upon the earth, wherein ~~there is~~ **I grant** life, *I* ~~have~~ **there shall be** *given* every ~~green~~ **clean** herb for meat; and it was so, **even as I spake.**

33 31 And **I**, God, saw everything that ~~he~~ **I** had made, and behold, *it* **all things which I had made** ~~was~~ **were** very good. And the evening and the morning were the sixth day.

CHAPTER 2

1 Thus the ~~heavens~~ **heaven** and the earth were finished, and all the host of them.

2 And on the seventh day, **I, God,** ended ~~his~~ **my** work, **and all things** which ~~he~~ **I** had made; and ~~he~~ **I** rested on the seventh day from all ~~his~~ **my** work; and **all things** which ~~he~~ **I** had made **were finished. And I, God, saw that they were good.**

3 And **I, God,** blessed the seventh day, and sanctified it, because that in it ~~he~~ **I** had rested from all ~~his~~ **my** work, which **I, God, had** created and made.

4 **4–5 And now, behold, I say unto you, that** these *are* the generations of the ~~heavens~~ **heaven,** and of the earth, when they were created in the day that I the LORD God made the ~~earth~~ **heaven** and the ~~heavens~~ **earth**, and every plant of the field before it was in the earth, and every herb of the field before it grew;

5 **For I, the Lord God, created all things of which I have spoken, spiritually, before they were naturally upon the face of the earth;** for I, the LORD God, had not caused it to rain upon **the face of** the earth.

6 **5 And I, the Lord God, had created all the children of men,** and ~~there was~~ not **yet** a man to till the ground, **for in heaven created I them, and there was not yet flesh upon the earth, neither in the water, neither in the air;**

7 **6 But I, the Lord God, spake, and** there went up a mist from the earth, and watered the whole face of the ground.

8 **7 And I, the** LORD **God,** formed man ~~of~~ **from** the dust of the ground, and breathed into **Adam** his ~~nostrils~~ **spirit** ~~the~~ **or**[4] breath of life; and man became a living soul; **the first flesh upon the earth, the first man also;**

9 **Nevertheless, all things were before created, but spiritually were they created and made, according to my word.**

10 8 And **I, the** LORD **God,** planted a garden eastward in Eden; and there ~~he~~ **I** put the man whom ~~he~~ **I** had formed.

11 9 And out of the ground, made **I, the** LORD **God,** to grow every tree **naturally,** that is pleasant to the sight **of man, and man could behold it, and it became also a living soul; for it was spiritual in the day that I created it; for it remaineth in the sphere in which I, God, created it; yea, even all things which I prepared for the use of man;** and **man saw that it was** good for food.

12 9 **And I, the Lord God, planted** the tree of life also, in the midst of the garden; and **also** the tree of knowledge of good and evil.

13 10 And **I, the Lord God, caused** a river ~~went~~ **to go** out of Eden, to water the garden; and from thence it was parted, and became into four heads.

14 11–12 **And I, the Lord God, called** the name of the first ~~is~~ Pison, ~~that is~~ **and** it ~~which~~ compasseth the whole land of Havilah, where ~~there is~~ **I, the Lord, created much** gold; and the gold of that land ~~is~~ **was** good, **and** there ~~is~~ **was** bdellium, and the onyx stone.

15 13 And the name of the second river ~~is~~ **was called** Gihon, the same ~~is it~~ that compasseth the whole land of Ethiopia.

16 14 And the name of the third river ~~is~~ **was** Hiddekel, that ~~is it~~ which goeth toward the east of Assyria.

17 14 And the fourth river ~~is~~ **was** Euphrates.

18 15 And **I, the** LORD **God,** took the man, and put him into the garden of Eden, to dress it, and to keep it.

19 16 And **I,** the LORD God, commanded the man, saying, Of every tree of the garden thou mayest freely eat;

20 17 But of the tree of the knowledge of good and evil, thou shalt not eat of it:

21 Nevertheless, thou mayest choose for thyself, for it is given unto thee; but remember that I forbid it;

22 17 For in the day that thou eatest thereof thou shalt surely die.

23 18 And **I,** the LORD God, said **unto mine Only Begotten**, that ~~it is~~ **was** not good that the man should be alone;

24 18 **Wherefore,** I will make ~~him~~ an help meet for him.

25 19 And out of the ground, **I** the LORD God, formed every beast of the field, and every fowl of the air; and ~~brought them~~ **commanded that they should come** unto Adam, to see what he would call them.

26 19 And **they were also living souls; for I, God, breathed into them the breath of life, and commanded that** whatsoever Adam called every living creature, that ~~was~~ **should be** the name thereof.

27 20 And Adam gave names to all cattle, and to the fowl of the air, and to every beast of the field; but **as** for Adam, there was not found an help meet for him.

28 21–22 And **I,** the LORD God, caused a deep sleep to fall upon Adam, and he slept, and ~~he~~ **I** took one of his ribs, and closed up the flesh ~~instead~~ **in the stead** thereof; and the rib, which **I,** the LORD God had taken from man, made ~~he~~ **I** a woman, and brought her unto the man.

29 23 And Adam said, This ~~is~~ **I know** now **is** bone of my bones, and

flesh of my flesh. She shall be called woman, because she was taken out of man.

30 24 Therefore shall a man leave his father and his mother, and shall cleave unto his wife: and they shall be one flesh.

31 25 And they were both naked, the man and his wife, and were not ashamed.

CHAPTER 3

1 And I, the Lord God, spake unto Moses, saying, That Satan whom thou hast commanded in the name of mine Only Begotten, is the same which was from the beginning;

2 And he came before me, saying, Behold I, send me, I will be thy Son, and I will redeem all mankind, that one soul shall not be lost, and surely I will do it; wherefore, give me thine honor.

3 But behold, my beloved Son, which was my beloved and chosen from the beginning, said unto me; Father, thy will be done, and the glory be thine forever.

4 Wherefore, because that Satan rebelled against me, and sought to destroy the agency of man, which I, the Lord God, had given him; and also that I should give unto him mine own power; by the power of mine Only Begotten I caused that he should be cast down, and he became Satan;

5 Yea, even the devil, the father of all lies, to deceive, and to blind men, and to lead them captive at his will, even as many as would not hearken unto my voice.

6 1 **And** now, the serpent was more ~~subtil~~ **subtle** than any beast of the field, which **I,** the LORD God, had made.

7 And Satan put it into the heart of the serpent, for he had drawn away many after him; and he sought also to beguile Eve, for he knew not the mind of God; wherefore, he sought to destroy the world.

8 1 And he said unto the woman, Yea, hath God said, Ye shall not eat of every tree of the garden. **And he spake by the mouth of the serpent.**

9 2–3 And the woman said unto the serpent, We may eat of the fruit of the trees of the garden; but of the fruit of the tree which ~~is~~ **thou beholdest** in the midst of the garden, God hath said, Ye shall not eat of it, neither shall ye touch it, lest ye die.

10 4–5 And the serpent said unto the woman, Ye shall not surely die; for God doth know, that in the day ye eat thereof, then your eyes shall be opened, and ye shall be as gods, knowing good and evil.

11 6 And when the woman saw that the tree *was* good for food, and that it ~~was~~ **became** pleasant to the eyes, and a tree to be desired to make ~~one~~ **her** wise, she took of the fruit thereof, and did eat; and gave also unto her husband with her, and he did eat.

12 7 And the eyes of them both were opened, and they knew that they ~~were~~ **had been** naked; and they sewed fig leaves together, and made themselves aprons.

13 8 And they heard the voice of the LORD God, **as they were** walking in the garden, in the cool of the day.

14 8 And Adam and his wife ~~hid~~ **went to hide** themselves from the presence of the LORD God, amongst the trees of the garden.

15 9–10 And **I, the** LORD God, called unto Adam, and said unto him, Where ~~art~~ **goest** thou? And he said, I heard thy voice, in the garden, and I

was afraid, because I **beheld that I** *was* naked, and I hid myself.

16 11 And ~~he~~ **I, the Lord God,** said **unto Adam,** Who told thee that thou *wast* naked? Hast thou eaten of the tree whereof I commanded thee that thou shouldest not eat, **if so thou shouldst surely die**?

17 12 And the man said, The woman whom thou gavest ~~to be~~ ~~with~~ me, **and commanded that she should remain with me,** she gave me of the **fruit of the** tree, and I did eat.

18 13 And **I,** the LORD God, said unto the woman, What *is* this **thing** ~~that~~ **which** thou hast done?

19 13 And the woman said, The serpent beguiled me, and I did eat.

20 14 And **I,** the LORD God, said unto the serpent, Because thou hast done this, thou ~~art~~ **shalt be** cursed above all cattle, and above every beast of the field; upon thy belly shalt thou go, and dust shalt thou eat all the days of thy life;

21 15 And I will put enmity between thee and the woman; and between thy seed and her seed; **and** ~~it~~ **he** shall bruise thy head, and thou shalt bruise his heel.

22 16 Unto the woman, ~~he~~ **I, the Lord God,** said, I will greatly multiply thy sorrow, and thy conception; in sorrow thou shalt bring forth children, and thy desire *shall be* to thy husband, and he shall rule over thee.

23 17 And unto Adam, ~~he~~ **I, the Lord God,** said, Because thou hast hearkened unto the voice of thy wife, and hast eaten **of the fruit** of the tree, of which I commanded thee, saying, Thou shalt not eat of it, cursed ~~is~~ **shall be** the ground for thy sake; in sorrow shalt thou eat *of* it all the days of thy life;

24 18 Thorns also and thistles shall

it bring forth to thee; and thou shalt eat the herb of the field;

25 19 ~~In~~ **By** the sweat of thy face shalt thou eat bread, ~~till~~ **until** thou **shalt** return unto the ground; **for thou shalt surely die;** for out of it wast thou taken; for dust thou ~~art~~ **wast**, and unto dust shalt thou return.

26 20 And Adam called his wife's name Eve, because she was the mother of all living; **for thus have I, the Lord God, called the first of all women, which are many.**

27 21 Unto Adam, ~~also~~ and **also** ~~to~~ **unto** his wife, did I, the Lord God, make coats of skins, and clothed them.

28 22 And **I,** the Lord God, said **unto mine Only Begotten**, Behold, the man is become as one of us, to know good and evil; and now, lest he put forth his hand, and ~~take~~ **partake** also of the tree of life, and eat, and live forever;

29 23 Therefore, I, the Lord God, ~~sent~~ **will send** him forth from the garden of Eden, to till the ground from whence he was taken;

30 For, as I, the Lord God, liveth, even so my words cannot return void, for, as they go forth out of my mouth, they must be fulfilled.

31 24 So ~~he~~ **I** drove out the man, and ~~he~~ **I** placed at the east of the garden of Eden, ~~Cherubims~~ **cherubim**, and a flaming sword, which turned every way, to keep the way of the tree of life.

32 (And these are the words which I spake unto my servant Moses. And they are true, even as I will.

33 And I have spoken them unto you. See thou show them unto no man, until I command you, except they that believe.) Amen.

Chapter 4

1 And it came to pass, that after I, the Lord God, had driven them out, that Adam began to till the earth, and to have dominion over all the beasts of the field, and to eat his bread by the sweat of his brow, as I, the Lord had commanded him; and Eve also, his wife, did labor with him.

2 And Adam knew his wife, and she bare unto him sons and daughters, and they began to multiply, and to replenish the earth.

3 And from that time forth, the sons and daughters of Adam began to divide, two and two, in the land, and to till the land, and to tend flocks; and they also begat sons and daughters.

4 And Adam called upon the name of the Lord, and Eve also, his wife; and they heard the voice of the Lord, from the way towards the garden of Eden, speaking unto them, and they saw him not; for they were shut out of his presence.

5 And he gave unto them commandments, that they should worship the Lord their God; and should offer the firstlings of their flocks for an offering unto the Lord.

6 And Adam was obedient unto the commandments of the Lord. And after many days, an angel of the Lord appeared unto Adam, saying, Why dost thou offer sacrifices unto the Lord? And Adam said unto him, I know not, save the Lord commanded me.

7 And then the angel spake, saying, This thing is a similitude of the sacrifice of the Only Begotten of the Father, which is full of grace and truth;

8 Wherefore, thou shalt do all that thou doest, in the name of the Son.

And thou shalt repent, and call upon God, in the name of the Son for evermore.

9 And in that day, the Holy Ghost fell upon Adam, which beareth record of the Father and the Son, saying, I am the Only Begotten of the Father from the beginning, henceforth and forever; that, as thou hast fallen, thou mayest be redeemed, and all mankind, even as many as will.

10 And in that day Adam blessed God, and was filled, and began to prophesy concerning all the families of the earth; saying, Blessed be the name of God, for because of my transgression my eyes are opened, and in this life I shall have joy, and again, in the flesh I shall see God.

11 And Eve, his wife, heard all these things and was glad, saying, Were it not for our transgression, we should never had seed, and should never had known good and evil,[5] and the joy of our redemption, and the eternal life which God giveth unto all the obedient.

12 And Adam and Eve blessed the name of God; and they made all things known unto their sons and their daughters.

13 And Satan came among them, saying, I am also a son of God, and he commanded them, saying, Believe it not. And they believed it not; and they loved Satan more than God. And men began from that time forth to be carnal, sensual and devilish.

CHAPTER 5 4

1 And the Lord God called upon men, by the Holy Ghost, everywhere, and commanded them that they should repent;

2 And as many as believed in the Son, and repented of their sins, should be saved. And as many as believed not, and repented not, should be damned. And the words went forth out of the mouth of God, in a firm decree, wherefore they must be fulfilled.

3 And Adam ceased not to call upon God; and Eve also his wife.

4 1 And Adam knew Eve his wife; and she conceived and bare Cain, and said, I have gotten a man from the LORD; wherefore he may not reject his words. But, behold, also Cain hearkened not, saying, Who is the Lord, that I should know him?

5 2 And she again conceived, and bare his brother Abel. And Abel hearkened unto the voice of the Lord. And Abel was a keeper of sheep, but Cain was a tiller of the ground.

6 3 And Cain loved Satan more than God. And Satan commanded him, saying, Make an offering unto the Lord. And in process of time it came to pass, that Cain brought of the fruit of the ground an offering unto the LORD.

7 4–5 And Abel, he also brought of the firstlings of his flock and of the fat thereof. And the LORD had respect unto Abel and to his offering: but unto Cain and to his offering he had not respect.

8 5 Now Satan knew this, and it pleased him. And Cain was very wroth, and his countenance fell.

9 6–7 And the LORD said unto Cain, Why art thou wroth? and Why is thy countenance fallen? If thou doest well thou shalt thou not be accepted, and if thou doest not well, sin lieth at the door; and Satan desireth to have thee, and except thou shalt hearken unto my commandments, I will deliver thee up, and it shall be unto

thee *shall be* **according to** his desire; and thou shalt rule over him**, for from this time forth thou shalt be the father of his lies.**

10 Thou shalt be called Perdition, for thou wast also before the world, and it shall be said in time to come, that these abominations were had from Cain, for he rejected the greater counsel, which was had from God; and this is a cursing which I will put upon thee, except thou repent.

11 And Cain was wroth, and listened not anymore to the voice of the Lord, neither to Abel his brother, who walked in holiness before the Lord.

12 And Adam also, and his wife, mourned before the Lord, because of Cain and his brethren.

13 And it came to pass, that Cain took one of his brother's daughters to wife, and they loved Satan more than God.

14 And Satan said unto Cain, Swear unto me by thy throat, and if thou tell it thou shalt die; and swear thy brethren by their heads, and by the living God, that they tell it not; for if they tell it they shall surely die; and this that thy father may not know it; and this day I will deliver thy brother Abel into thine hands.

15 And Satan swear unto Cain, that he would do according to his commands. And all these things were done in secret.

16 And Cain said, Truly I am Mahan, the master of this great secret, that I may murder and get gain. Wherefore Cain was called Master Mahan; and he gloried in his wickedness.**

17 8 **And Cain went into the field,** and Cain talked with Abel his brother;

and it came to pass, **that** ~~when~~ **while** they were in the field, ~~that~~ Cain rose up against Abel his brother, and slew him.

18 And Cain gloried in that which he had done, saying, I am free; surely the flocks of my brother falleth into my hands.

19 9 And the Lord said unto Cain, Where *is* Abel thy brother? And he said, I know not**,** *am* I my brother's keeper?

20 10 And ~~he~~ **the Lord** said, What hast thou done? The voice of thy brother's blood cries unto me from the ground.

21 11 And now**,** ~~art~~ thou **shalt be** cursed from the earth, which hath opened her mouth to receive thy brother's blood from thy hand**.**

22 12 When thou tillest the ground, it shall not henceforth yield unto thee her strength; a fugitive and a vagabond shalt thou be in the earth.

23 13 And Cain said unto the Lord, **Satan tempted me, because of my brother's flocks; and I was wroth also, for his offering thou didst accept, and not mine.**

24 13–14 My punishment *is* greater than I can bear! Behold, thou hast driven me out this day from the face of the ~~earth~~ **Lord,** and from thy face shall I be hid; and I shall be a fugitive and a vagabond in the earth; and it shall come to pass, *that* ~~every one~~ he that findeth me shall slay me**, because of mine iniquities, for these things are not hid from the Lord.**

25 15 And **I, the** Lord**,** said unto him, ~~Therefore~~ Whosoever slayeth ~~Cain~~ **thee**, vengeance shall be taken on him sevenfold**;** and **I, the** Lord**,** set a mark upon Cain, lest any finding him should kill him.

26 16 And Cain ~~went~~ **was shut** out

from the presence of the LORD, and **with his wife and many of his brethren,** dwelt in the land of Nod, on the east of Eden.

27 17 And Cain knew his wife, and she conceived and bare Enoch, **and he also begat many sons and daughters.** And he builded a city, and **he** called the name of the city after the name of his son Enoch.

28 18 And unto Enoch was born Irad, **and other sons and daughters,** and Irad begat Mehujael, **and other sons and daughters.**

29 18 And Mehujael begat Methusael, **and other sons and daughters.** And Methusael begat Lamech.

30 19 And Lamech took unto ~~him~~ **himself** two wives, the name of ~~the~~ one ~~was~~ **being** Adah, and the name of the other, Zillah.

31 20–21 And Adah bare Jabal; he was the father of such as dwell in tents, and ~~of such as have~~ **they were keepers of** cattle; and his brother's name *was* Jubal, ~~he~~ **who** was the father of all such as handle the harp and organ.

32 22 And Zillah, she also bare ~~Tubalcain~~ **Tubal Cain**, an ~~instructer~~ **instructor** of every artificer in brass and iron; and the sister of ~~Tubalcain~~ **Tubal Cain** *was* **called** Naamah.

33 23 And Lamech said unto his wives, Adah and Zillah, Hear my voice; ye wives of Lamech, hearken unto my speech: for I have slain a man to my wounding, and a young man to my hurt.

34 24 If Cain shall be avenged sevenfold, truly Lamech **shall be** seventy and sevenfold.

35 **For, Lamech having entered into a covenant with Satan, after the manner of Cain, wherein he became Master Mahan, master of that great secret which was administered unto Cain by Satan;**

36 **And Irad, the son of Enoch, having known their secret, began to reveal it unto the sons of Adam; wherefore, Lamech, being angry, slew him, not like unto Cain his brother Abel for the sake of getting gain; but he slew him for the oath's sake;**

37 **For, from the days of Cain, there was a secret combination, and their works were in the dark, and they knew every man his brother.**

38 **Wherefore the Lord cursed Lamech and his house, and all they that had covenanted with Satan; for they kept not the commandments of God. And it displeased God, and he ministered not unto them.**

39 **And their works were abominations, and began to spread among all the sons of men. And it was among the sons of men.**

40 **And among the daughters of men, these things were not spoken; because that Lamech had spoken the secret unto his wives, and they rebelled against him, and declared these things abroad, and had not compassion.**

41 **Wherefore Lamech was despised, and cast out, and came not among the sons of men, lest he should die.**

42 **And thus the works of darkness began to prevail among* the sons of men.**

43 **And God cursed the earth with a sore curse, and was angry with the wicked, with all the sons of men whom he had made, for they would not hearken unto his voice, nor believe on his Only Begotten Son, even him whom he declared should come in the meridian of time; who**

was prepared from before the foundation of the world.

44 And thus the gospel began to be preached from the beginning, being declared by holy angels, sent forth from the presence of God; and by his own voice, and by the gift of the Holy Ghost.

45 And thus all things were confirmed unto Adam by an holy ordinance; and the gospel preached; and a decree sent forth that it should be in the world until the end thereof; and thus it was. Amen.

CHAPTER **6** 4

1 And Adam hearkened unto the voice of God, and called upon his sons to repent.

2 25 And Adam knew his wife again, and she bare a son, and **he** called his name Seth.

3 25 **And Adam glorified the name of God,** for **he said**, God said she hath appointed me another seed instead of Abel whom Cain slew.

4 26 **And God revealed himself unto Seth, and he rebelled not, but offered an acceptable sacrifice like unto his brother Abel.** And to Seth to him also there was born a son, and he called his name Enos.

5 26 **And** then began **these** men to call upon the name of the LORD; **and the Lord blessed them; and a book of remembrance was kept in the which was recorded in the language of Adam, for it was given unto as many as called upon God, to write by the Spirit of inspiration;**

6 And by them their children were taught to read and write, having a language which was pure and undefiled.

7 Now this same priesthood which was in the beginning, shall be in the end of the world also.

8 Now this prophecy Adam spake, as he was moved upon by the Holy Ghost.

CHAPTER **6** 5

9 1–2 **And a genealogy was kept of the children of God. And** this is **was** the book of the generations of Adam, **saying,** In the day that God created man, (in the likeness of God made he him,) **in the image of his own body,** male and female created he them, and blessed them, and called their name Adam, in the day when they were created, **and became living souls, in the land, upon the footstool of God.**

10 3 And Adam lived an **one** hundred and thirty years, and begat *a son* in his own likeness, and after his **own** image, and called his name Seth.

11 4–5 And the days of Adam, after he had begotten Seth, were eight hundred **and seventy** years. And he begat **many** sons and daughters. And all the days that Adam lived were nine hundred and thirty **one thousand** years; and he died.[6]

12 6–7 And Seth lived an **one** hundred and five years, and begat Enos, **and prophesied in all his days, and taught his son Enos in the ways of God. Wherefore Enos prophesied also.** And Seth lived after he begat Enos, eight hundred and seven years, and begat **many** sons and daughters.

13 And the children of men were numerous upon all the face of the land. And in those days, Satan had great dominion among men, and raged in their hearts; and from thenceforth came wars and bloodshed.

14 8 And a man's hand was against his own brother in administering death, because of secret works, seeking for power. And all the days of

Seth were nine hundred and twelve years; and he died.

15 9 And Enos lived ninety years, and begat Cainan. **And Enos, and the residue of the people of God, came out from the land which was called Shulon, and dwelt in a land of promise, which he called after his own son, whom he had named Cainan.**

16 10–11 And Enos lived, after he begat Cainan, eight hundred and fifteen years, and begat **many** sons and daughters. And all the days of Enos were nine hundred and five years; and he died.

17 12 And Cainan lived seventy years, and begat Mahalaleel:

18 13–14 And Cainan lived after he begat Mahalaleel eight hundred and forty years, and begat sons and daughters: and all the days of Cainan were nine hundred and ten years: and he died.

19 15 And Mahalaleel lived ~~sixty and five~~ **sixty-five** years, and begat Jared.

20 16–17 And Mahalaleel lived after he begat Jared, eight hundred and thirty years, and begat sons and daughters. And all the days of Mahalaleel were eight hundred ~~and ninety~~ and ~~five~~ **ninety-five** years; and he died.

21 18 And Jared lived ~~an~~ **one** hundred ~~sixty~~ and ~~two~~ **sixty-two** years, and ~~he~~ begat Enoch.

22 19 And Jared lived, after he begat Enoch, eight hundred years, and begat sons and daughters. **And Jared taught Enoch in all the ways of God.**

23 And this is the genealogy of the sons of Adam, who was the son of God, with whom God himself conversed.

24 And they were preachers of righteousness, and spake and proph- esied, **and called upon all men everywhere to repent. And faith was taught unto the children of men.**

25 20 And **it came to pass, that** all the days of Jared were nine hundred ~~sixty~~ and ~~two~~ **sixty-two** years; and he died.

26 21 And Enoch lived ~~sixty and five~~ **sixty-five** years, and begat Methuselah. **And it came to pass that Enoch journeyed in the land, among the people; and as he journeyed the Spirit of God descended out of heaven, and abode upon him;**

27 And he heard a voice from heaven, saying, Enoch, my son, prophesy unto this people, and say unto them, Repent, for thus saith the Lord, I am angry with this people, and my fierce anger is kindled against them; for their hearts have waxed hard, and their ears are dull of hearing, and their eyes cannot see afar off.

28 And for these many generations, even since the day that I created them, have they gone astray, and have denied me, and have sought their own counsels in the dark; and in their own abominations have they devised murder, and have not kept the commandments which I gave unto their father Adam.

29 Wherefore, they have forsworn themselves, and by their oaths they have brought upon themselves death.

30 And an hell I have prepared for them, if they repent not;

31 And this is a decree which I have sent forth in the beginning of the world, from mine own mouth, from the foundation thereof; and by the mouths of my servants, thy fathers, have I decreed it; even as it

shall be sent forth in the world, unto the end thereof.

32 And when Enoch had heard these words, he bowed himself to the earth, before the Lord, and spake before the Lord, saying, Why is it that I have found favor in thy sight, and am but a lad, and all the people hate me, for I am slow of speech, wherefore am I thy servant?

33 And the Lord said unto Enoch, Go forth, and do as I have commanded thee, and no man shall pierce thee.

34 Open thy mouth, and it shall be filled, and I will give thee utterance; for all flesh is in my hands, and I will do as seemeth me good.

35 Say unto this people, Choose ye this day to serve the Lord God who made you.

36 Behold, my Spirit is upon you; wherefore all thy words will I justify, and the mountains shall flee before you, and the rivers shall turn from their course; and thou shalt abide in me, and I in you; therefore walk with me.

37 And the Lord spake unto Enoch, and said unto him, Anoint thine eyes with clay, and wash them, and thou shalt see; and he did so.

38 And he beheld the spirits that God had created, and he beheld also things which were not visible to the natural eye; and from thenceforth came the saying abroad in the land, A seer hath the Lord raised up unto his people.

39 And it came to pass, that Enoch went forth in the land, among the people, standing upon the hills, and the high places, and cried with a loud voice, testifying against their works.

40 And all men were offended because of him; and they came forth to hear him upon the high places, saying unto the tent-keepers, Tarry ye here and keep the tents, while we go yonder to behold the seer, for he prophesieth; and there is a strange thing in the land, a wild man hath come among us.

41 And it came to pass when they heard him, no man laid hands on him, for fear came on them all that heard him, for he walked with God.

42 And there came a man unto him, whose name was Mahijah, and said unto him, Tell us plainly who thou art, and from whence thou comest.

43 And he said unto them, I came out from the land of Cainan, the land of my fathers, a land of righteousness unto this day; and my father taught me in all the ways of God.

44 And it came to pass, as I journeyed from the land of Cainan by the sea east, I beheld a vision; and lo, the heavens I saw, and the Lord spake with me, and gave me commandment; wherefore for this cause, to keep the commandment, I speak forth these words.

45 And Enoch continued his speech, saying, The Lord which spake with me, the same is the God of heaven, and he is my God and your God, and ye are my brethren; and why counsel ye yourselves, and deny the God of heaven?

46 The heavens he made; the earth is his footstool, and the foundation thereof is his; behold, he laid it, and hosts of men hath he brought in upon the face thereof.

47 And death hath come upon our fathers; nevertheless, we know them,

and cannot deny, and even the first of all we know, even Adam; for a book of remembrance we have written among us, according to the pattern given by the finger of God; and it is given in our own language.

48 And as Enoch spake forth the words of God, the people trembled and could not stand in his presence.

49 And he said unto them, Because that Adam fell, we are; and by his fall came death, and we are made partakers of misery and woe.

50 Behold, Satan hath come among the children of men, and tempteth them to worship him; and men have become carnal, sensual, and devilish, and are shut out from the presence of God.

51 But God hath made known unto our fathers, that all men must repent.

52 And he called upon our father Adam, by his own voice, saying, I am God; I made the world, and men before they were* flesh.

53 And he also said unto him, If thou wilt, turn unto me and hearken unto my voice, and believe, and repent of all thy transgressions, and be baptized, even in water, in the name of mine Only Begotten Son, who is full of grace and truth, which is Jesus Christ, the only name which shall be given under heaven, whereby salvation shall come unto the children of men; and ye shall receive the gift of the Holy Ghost, asking all things in his name, and whatsoever ye shall ask it shall be given you.

54 And our father Adam spake unto the Lord, and said, Why is it that men must repent, and be baptized in water?

55 And the Lord said unto Adam, Behold, I have forgiven thee thy transgression in the garden of Eden.

56 Hence came the saying abroad among the people, that the Son of God hath atoned for original guilt, wherein the sins of the parents cannot be answered upon the heads of the children, for they are whole from the foundation of the world.

57 And the Lord spake unto Adam, saying, Inasmuch as thy children are conceived in sin, even so, when they begin to grow up sin conceiveth in their hearts, and they taste the bitter, that they may know to prize the good.

58 And it is given unto them to know good from evil; wherefore, they are agents unto themselves.

59 And I have given unto you another law and commandment; wherefore teach it unto your children, that all men, everywhere, must repent, or they can in no wise inherit the kingdom of God.

60 For no unclean thing can dwell there, or dwell in his presence; for, in the language of Adam, Man of Holiness is his name; and the name of his Only Begotten is the Son of Man, even Jesus Christ, a righteous judge, who shall come in the meridian of time.

61 Therefore I give unto you a commandment, to teach these things freely unto your children, saying, that by reason of transgression cometh the fall, which fall bringeth death; and inasmuch as ye were born into the world by water and blood, and the spirit, which I have made, and so become* of dust a living soul;

62 Even so ye must be born again, into the kingdom of heaven, of water, and of the Spirit, and be

cleansed by blood, even the blood of mine Only Begotten; that ye may* be sanctified from all sin; and enjoy the words of eternal life in this world, and eternal life in the world to come; even immortal glory.

63 For, by the water ye keep the commandment; by the Spirit ye are justified; and by the blood ye are sanctified.

64 Therefore it is given to abide in you, the record of heaven, the Comforter, the peaceable things of immortal glory, the truth of all things, that which quickeneth all things, which maketh alive all things, that which knoweth all things, and hath all power according to wisdom, mercy, truth, justice and judgment.

65 And now, behold, I say unto you, This is the plan of salvation unto all men, through the blood of mine Only Begotten, who shall come in the meridian of time.

66 And, behold, all things have their likeness; and all things are created and made to bear record of me; both things which are temporal, and things which are spiritual; things which are in the heavens above, and things which are on the earth, and things which are in the earth, and things which are under the earth, both above and beneath, all things bear record of me.

67 And it came to pass, when the Lord had spoken with Adam our father, that Adam cried unto the Lord, and he was caught away by the Spirit of the Lord, and was carried down into the water, and was laid under the water, and was brought forth out of the water; and thus he was baptized.

68 And the Spirit of God descended upon him, and thus he was born of the Spirit, and became quickened in the inner man.

69 And he heard a voice out of heaven, saying, Thou art baptized with fire and with the Holy Ghost; this is the record of the Father and the Son, from henceforth and forever;

70 And thou art after the order of him who was without beginning of days or end of years, from all eternity to all eternity.

71 Behold, thou art one in me, a son of God; and thus may all become my sons. Amen.

CHAPTER 7 5

1 And it came to pass, that Enoch continued his speech, saying, Behold, our father Adam taught these things, and many have believed, and become the sons of God; and many have believed not, and have perished in their sins, and are looking forth with fear, in torment, for the fiery indignation of the wrath of God to be poured out upon them.

2 And from that time forth, Enoch began to prophesy, saying unto the people, that, as I was journeying, and stood in the place Mahujah, and cried unto the Lord, there came a voice out of heaven, saying, Turn ye and get ye upon the mount Simeon.

3 And it came to pass, that I turned and went up on the mount; and as I stood upon the mount, I beheld the heavens open, and I was clothed upon with glory.

4 And I saw the Lord, and he stood before my face, and he talked with me, even as a man talketh one with another, face to face; and he said unto me, Look, and I will show unto

thee the world for the space of many generations.

5 And it came to pass, that I beheld in the valley of Shum, and, lo! a great people which dwelt in tents, which were the people of Shum.

6 And again the Lord said unto me, Look, and I looked towards the north, and I beheld the people of Canaan,[7] which dwelt in tents.

7 And the Lord said unto me, Prophesy; and I prophesied saying,

8 Behold, the people of Canaan[8] which are numerous, shall go forth in battle array against the people of Shum, and shall slay them, that they shall be utterly destroyed.

9 And the people of Canaan[9] shall divide themselves in the land, and the land shall be barren and unfruitful, and none other people shall dwell there, but the people of Canaan;[10] for, behold, the Lord shall curse the land with much heat, and the barrenness thereof shall go forth forever.

10 And there was a blackness came upon all the children of Canaan,[11] that they were despised among all people.

11 And it came to pass, that the Lord said unto me, Look, and I looked, and I beheld the land of Sharon, and the land of Enoch, and the land of Omner, and the land of Heni, and the land of Shem, and the land of Haner, and the land of Hanannihah, and all the inhabitants thereof.

12 And the Lord said unto me, Go forth to this people, and say unto them, Repent; lest I come out and smite them with a curse, and they die.

13 And he gave unto me a commandment, that I should baptize in the name of the Father, and of the Son, who is full of grace and truth, and the Holy Ghost which beareth record of the Father and the Son.

14 And it came to pass, that Enoch continued to call upon all the people, save it were the people of Canaan,[12] to repent.

15 And so great was the faith of Enoch, that he led the people of God, and their enemies came to battle against them, and he spake the word of the Lord, and the earth trembled, and the mountains fled, even according to his command.

16 And the rivers of water were turned out of their course, and the roar of the lions was heard out of the wilderness.

17 And all nations feared greatly, so powerful was the word of Enoch, and so great was the power of the language which God had given him.

18 There also came up a land out of the depths of the sea; and so great was the fear of the enemies of the people of God, that they fled and stood afar off, and went upon the land which came up out of the depths of the sea.

19 And the giants of the land also stood afar off; and there went forth a curse upon all the people which fought against God.

20 And from that time forth, there were wars and bloodshed among them; but the Lord came and dwelt with his people, and they dwelt in righteousness.

21 And the fear of the Lord was upon all nations, so great was the glory of the Lord which was upon his people.

22 And the Lord blessed the land, and they were blessed upon the mountains, and upon the high places, and did flourish.

23 And the Lord called his people, Zion; because they were of one heart and one mind, and dwelt in righteousness; and there were* no poor among them.

24 And Enoch continued his preaching in righteousness unto the people of God.

25 And it came to pass in his days, that he built a city that was called the city of Holiness, even Zion.

26 And it came to pass, that Enoch talked with the Lord, and he said unto the Lord, Surely, Zion shall dwell in safety forever. But the Lord said unto Enoch, Zion have I blessed, but the residue of the people have I cursed.

27 And it came to pass, that the Lord showed unto Enoch all the inhabitants of the earth, and he beheld, and lo! Zion in the process of time was taken up into heaven.

28 And the Lord said unto Enoch, Behold mine abode forever.

29 And Enoch also beheld the residue of the people which were the sons of Adam, and they were a mixture of all the seed of Adam, save it were the seed of Cain; for the seed of Cain were black, and had not place among them.

30 And after that Zion was taken up into heaven, Enoch beheld, and lo, all the nations of the earth were before him; and there came generation upon generation.

31 And Enoch was high and lifted up, even in the bosom of the Father, (and the Son of Man;) and, behold, the powers of Satan were upon all the face of the earth; and he saw angels descending out of heaven, and he heard a loud voice, saying, Woe! woe! be unto the inhabitants of the earth!

32 And he beheld Satan, and he had a great chain in his hand, and it veiled the whole face of the earth with darkness; and he looked up and laughed, and his angels rejoiced.

33 And Enoch beheld angels descending out of heaven, bearing testimony of the Father, and of the Son.

34 And the Holy Ghost fell on many, and they were caught up by the powers* of heaven into Zion.

35 And it came to pass, that Enoch looked upon the residue of the people, and wept; and he beheld and lo, the heavens wept also, and shed forth their tears as the rain upon the mountains. And Enoch said unto the Lord, How is it that thou canst weep, seeing thou art holy, and from all eternity to all eternity?[13]

36 And were it possible that man could number the particles of the earth, yea, and millions of earths like this, it would not be a beginning to the number of thy creations;

37 And thy curtains are stretched out still, and thou art there, and thy presence[14] is there; and also, thou art just, thou art merciful and kind forever;

38 Thou hast taken Zion to thine own bosom, from all thy creations, from all eternity to all eternity, and naught but peace, justice, and truth is the habitation of thy throne; and mercy shall go before thy face and have no end. How is it that thou canst weep?

39 The Lord said unto Enoch, Behold, these thy brethren, they are the workmanship of mine own hands, and I gave unto them their intelligence.[15]

40 And in the garden of Eden man had agency; and unto thy brethren have I said, and also gave commandment, that they should love one another; and that they should serve me their God.[16]

41 But, behold, they are without affection, and they hate their own blood; and the fire of mine indignation is kindled against them; and in my hot displeasure will I send in the floods upon them; for my fierce anger is kindled against them.

42 Behold, I am God; Man of Holiness is my name; Man of Counsel* is my name; and Endless and Eternal is my name also. Wherefore I can stretch forth my hands and hold all the creations which I have made, and mine eye can pierce them also.

43 And among all the workmanship of my hands there has not been so great wickedness as among thy brethren; but, behold, their sins shall be upon the heads of their fathers; Satan shall be their father, and misery shall be their doom; and the whole heavens shall weep over them, even all the workmanship of my hands.

44 Wherefore should not the heavens weep, seeing these shall suffer? But, behold, these which thine eyes are upon shall perish in the floods; and, behold, I will shut them up; a prison have I prepared for them, and he whom* I have chosen hath pleaded* before my face;

45 Wherefore he suffereth for their sins, inasmuch as they will repent, in the day that my chosen shall return unto me; and until that day they shall be in torment.

46 Wherefore for this shall the heavens weep, yea, and all the workmanship of my hands.

47 And it came to pass, that the Lord spake unto Enoch, and told Enoch all the doings of the children of men.

48 Wherefore Enoch knew and looked upon their wickedness, and their misery; and wept, and stretched forth his arms, and he beheld[17] eternity, and his bowels yearned, and all eternity shook.

49 And Enoch saw Noah also, and his family, that the posterity of all the sons of Noah should be saved with a temporal salvation.

50 Wherefore Enoch saw that Noah built an ark, and the Lord smiled upon it, and held it in his own hand; but upon the residue of the wicked came the floods and swallowed them up.

51 And as Enoch saw thus, he had bitterness of soul, and wept over his brethren, and said unto the heavens, I will refuse to be comforted.

52 But the Lord said unto Enoch, Lift up your heart and be glad, and look. And it came to pass, that Enoch looked, and from Noah he beheld all the families of the earth; and he cried unto the Lord, saying, When shall the day of the Lord come? When shall the blood of the righteous be shed, that all they that mourn may be sanctified, and have eternal life?

53 And the Lord said, It shall be in the meridian of time; in the days of wickedness and vengeance.

54 And, behold, Enoch saw the day of the coming of the Son of Man, even in the flesh; and his soul rejoiced, saying, The righteous is lifted up; and the Lamb is slain from the foundation of the world; and through faith I am in the bosom of the Father; and behold, Zion is with me!

55 And it came to pass, that Enoch looked upon the earth, and he heard a voice from the bowels thereof, saying, Woe! woe! is me, the mother of men! I am pained, I am weary, because of the wickedness of my children! When shall I rest, and be cleansed from the filthiness which has gone forth out of me? When will my Creator sanctify me, that I may rest, and righteousness for a season abide upon my face?

56 And when Enoch heard the earth mourn, he wept, and cried unto the Lord, saying, O Lord, wilt thou not have compassion upon the earth? wilt thou not bless the children of Noah?

57 And it came to pass, that Enoch continued his cry unto the Lord, saying, I ask thee, O Lord, in the name of thine Only Begotten, even Jesus Christ, that thou wilt have mercy upon Noah, and his seed, that the earth might never more be covered by the floods.

58 And the Lord could not withhold; and he covenanted with Enoch, and sware unto him with an oath, that he would stay the floods; that he would call upon the children of Noah; and he sent forth an unalterable decree, that a remnant of his seed should always be found among all nations, while the earth should stand.

59 And the Lord said, Blessed is he through whose seed Messiah shall come; for he saith, I am Messiah, the King of Zion, the Rock of Heaven,* which is broad as eternity; and whoso cometh in at the gate, and climbeth up by me shall never fall.

60 Wherefore blessed are they of whom I have spoken, for they shall come forth with songs of everlasting joy.

61 And it came to pass, that Enoch cried unto the Lord, saying, When the Son of Man cometh in the flesh shall the earth rest? I pray thee show me these things.

62 And the Lord said unto Enoch, Look; and he looked, and beheld the Son of Man lifted up on the cross, after the manner of men.

63 And he heard a loud voice, and the heavens were veiled; and all the creations of God mourned, and the earth groaned; and the rocks were rent; and the saints arose, and were crowned at the right hand of the Son of Man, with crowns of glory.

64 And as many of the spirits as were in prison came forth and stood on the right hand of God. And the remainder were reserved in chains of darkness until the judgment of the great day.

65 And again Enoch wept, and cried unto the Lord, saying, When shall the earth rest?

66 And Enoch beheld the Son of Man ascend up unto the Father; and he called unto the Lord, saying, Wilt thou not come again upon the earth? for inasmuch as thou art God, and I know thee, and thou hast sworn unto me, and commanded me that I should ask in the name of thine Only Begotten; thou hast made me, and given unto* me a right to thy throne, and not of myself, but through thine own grace; wherefore I ask thee if thou wilt not come again on the earth?

67 And the Lord said unto Enoch, As I live, even so will I come in the last days, in the days of wickedness and vengeance, to fulfill the oath

which I made unto you concerning the children of Noah.

68 And the day shall come that the earth shall rest. But before that day the heavens shall be darkened, and a veil of darkness shall cover the earth; and the heavens shall shake, and also the earth.

69 And great tribulations shall be among the children of men, but my people will I preserve; and righteousness will I send down out of heaven, and truth will I send forth out of the earth, to bear testimony of mine Only Begotten; his resurrection from the dead; yea, and also the resurrection of all men.

70 And righteousness and truth will I cause to sweep the earth as with a flood, to gather out mine own elect from the four quarters of the earth, unto a place which I shall prepare; an holy city, that my people may gird up their loins, and be looking forth for the time of my coming; for there shall be my tabernacle, and it shall be called Zion; a New Jerusalem.

71 And the Lord said unto Enoch, Then shalt thou and all thy city meet them there; and we will receive them into our bosom; and they shall see us, and we will fall upon their necks, and they shall fall upon our necks, and we will kiss each other;

72 And there shall be mine abode, and it shall be Zion, which shall come forth out of all the creations which I have made; and for the space of a thousand years shall the earth rest.

73 And it came to pass, that Enoch saw the day of the coming of the Son of Man, in the last days, to dwell on the earth, in righteousness, for the space of a thousand years.

74 But before that day, he saw great tribulation among the wicked; and he also saw the sea, that it was troubled, and men's hearts failing them, looking forth with fear for the judgment of the Almighty God, which should come upon the wicked.

75 And the Lord showed Enoch all things, even unto the end of the world. And he saw the day of the righteous, the hour of their redemption, and received a fullness of joy.

76 And all the days of Zion, in the days of Enoch, were three hundred and sixty-five years.

77 22 And Enoch **and all his people** walked with God ~~after he begat Methuselah three hundred years, and begat sons and daughters~~, **and he dwelt in the midst of Zion.**

78 23–24 And ~~Enoch walked with God: and~~ it came to pass, that ~~he~~ **Zion** *was* not, for God ~~took him~~ **received it up into his own bosom; and from thence went forth the saying, Zion is fled.** And all the days of Enoch were ~~three~~ **four** hundred ~~sixty and five~~ **and thirty** years.

79 And it came to pass, that Methuselah, the son of Enoch, was not taken, that the covenants of the Lord might be fulfilled which he made to Enoch; for he truly covenanted with Enoch, that Noah should be of the fruit of his loins.

80 And it came to pass, that Methuselah prophesied that from his loins should spring all the kingdoms of the earth; (through Noah,) and he took glory unto himself.

81 And there came forth a great famine into the land, and the Lord cursed the earth with a sore curse, and many of the inhabitants thereof died.

82 25–27 And **it came to pass, that** Methuselah lived ~~an~~ **one** hundred

eighty and seven **eighty-seven** years, and begat Lamech; and Methuselah lived after he begat Lamech, seven hundred eighty and two **eighty-two** years, and begat sons and daughters. And all the days of Methuselah were nine hundred sixty and nine **sixty-nine** years, and he died.

83 28–29 And Lamech lived an **one** hundred eighty and two **eighty-two** years, and begat a son, and he called his name Noah, saying, This same **son** shall comfort us concerning our work, and toil of our hands, because of the ground which the LORD hath cursed.

84 30–31 And Lamech lived after he begat Noah, five hundred ninety and five **ninety-five** years, and begat sons and daughters. And all the days of Lamech were seven hundred seventy and seven **seventy-seven** years; and he died.

85 32 And Noah was five **four** hundred **and fifty** years old, and Noah begat Shem, Ham, and Japheth, **and forty-two years afterwards, he begat Shem, of her who was the mother of Japheth, and when he was five hundred years old, he begat Ham.**

CHAPTER 8 6

1 And Noah and his sons hearkened unto the Lord, and gave heed; and they were called the sons of God.

2 1–2 And it came to pass when **these** men began to multiply on the face of the earth, and daughters were born unto them, That the sons of God **men** saw that the **their** daughters of men that they were fair, and they took them wives of all which **even as** they chose.

3 And the Lord said unto Noah, The daughters of thy sons have sold themselves, for behold, mine anger is kindled against the sons of men, for they will not hearken to my voice.

4 And it came to pass, that Noah prophesied, and taught the things of God, even as it was in the beginning.

5 3 And the LORD said **unto Noah,** My Spirit shall not always strive with man, for that he also is **shall know that all** flesh **shall die,** yet his days shall be an hundred and twenty years; **and if men do not repent, I will send in the floods upon them.**

6 4 **And in those days** there were giants in **on** the earth in those days, **and they sought Noah to take away his life;**

7 But the Lord was with Noah, and the power of the Lord was upon him; and the Lord ordained Noah after his own order, and commanded him that he should go forth and declare his gospel unto the children of men, even as it was given unto Enoch.

8 And it came to pass that Noah called upon the children of men, that they should repent, but they hearkened not unto his words.

9 4 And also, after that when **they had heard him, they came up before him, saying, Behold, we are** the sons of God; **have we not** came in **taken** unto **ourselves** the daughters of men? **and are we not eating and drinking, and marrying and given in marriage?** and they **our wives** bare **bear** unto us children to them, **and** the same became **are** mighty men, which were **are like unto them** of old, men of **great** renown. **And they hearkened not unto the words of Noah.**

10 5 And God saw that the wickedness of man was **had become** great in the earth; and that every **man was lifted up in the** imagination of the thoughts of his heart ~~was~~**; being** only evil continually.

11 And it came to pass, that Noah continued his preaching unto the people, saying, Hearken and give heed unto my words, believe and repent of your sins and be baptized in the name of Jesus Christ, the Son of God, even as our fathers did, and ye shall receive the Holy Ghost, that ye may have all things made manifest;

12 And if you do not this, the floods will come in upon you; nevertheless, they hearkened not.

13 6 And it repented ~~the LORD~~ **Noah, and his heart was pained,** that ~~he~~ **the Lord** had made man on the earth, and it grieved him at his heart.

14 7 And the LORD said, I will destroy man whom I have created**,** from the face of the earth**,** both man and beast, and the creeping ~~thing~~ **things**, and the fowls of the air**;**

15 7 For it repenteth ~~me~~ **Noah that I have created them, and** that I have made them**; and he hath called upon me, for they have sought his life.**

16 8–10 ~~But~~ **And thus** Noah found grace in the eyes of the LORD; ~~These are the generations of Noah~~ **for** Noah was a just man**,** *and* perfect in his ~~generations~~ **generation;** *and* ~~Noah~~ **he** walked with God, and ~~Noah begat~~ **also his** three sons, Shem, Ham, and Japheth.

17 11–12 The earth ~~also~~ was corrupt before God**;** and ~~the earth~~ **it** was filled with violence. And God looked upon the earth, and behold, it was corrupt**,** for all flesh had corrupted ~~his~~ **its** way upon the earth.

18 13 And God said unto Noah, The end of all flesh is come before me; for the earth is filled with violence ~~through them,~~ and behold, I

will destroy ~~them with~~ **all flesh from off** the earth.

19 14 Make thee **therefore,** an ark of gopher wood; rooms shalt thou make in the ark, and **thou** shalt pitch it within and without with pitch**;**

20 15 And ~~this is the fashion which thou shalt make it of~~ the length of the ark ~~shall be~~ **thou shalt make** three hundred cubits; the breadth of it fifty cubits; and the height of it thirty cubits.

21 16 ~~A~~ **And** ~~window~~ **windows** shalt thou make to the ark, and in a cubit shalt thou finish it above; and the door of the ark shalt thou set in the side thereof; ~~with~~ lower, second, and third ~~stories~~ **chambers** shalt thou make **in** it.

22 17 And behold, I, even I ~~do~~ **will** bring **in** a flood of ~~waters~~ **water** upon the earth, to destroy all flesh, wherein *is* the breath of life, from under heaven; *and* everything that ~~is in~~ **liveth on** the earth shall die.

23 18 But with thee will I establish my covenant**, even as I have sworn unto thy father Enoch, that of thy posterity shall come all nations.**

24 18 And thou shalt come into the ark, thou, and thy sons, and thy wife, and thy sons' wives with thee.

25 19 And of every living thing of all flesh, two of every ~~sort~~ **kind** shalt thou bring into the ark, to keep ~~them~~ alive with thee; they shall be male and female.

26 20 Of fowls after their kind, and of cattle after their kind, of every creeping thing of the earth after his kind**;** two of every ~~sort~~ **kind** ~~shall come unto thee~~ **shalt thou take into the ark,** to keep ~~them~~ alive.

27 21 And take thou unto thee of all food that is eaten, and thou shalt gather ~~it~~ **fruit of every kind** ~~to~~ **unto**

thee **in the ark,** and it shall be for food for thee, and for them.

28 22 Thus did Noah**,** according to all that God commanded him ~~so did he~~.

29 1 And the LORD said unto Noah, Come thou and all thy house**,** into the ark; for thee **only** have I seen righteous before me**,** in this generation.

30 2 Of every clean beast thou shalt take to thee by sevens, the male and his female: and of beasts that *are* not clean by two, the male and his female.

31 3 Of fowls also of the air**,** by sevens, the male and ~~the~~ **his** female; to keep seed alive upon the face of ~~all~~ the earth.

32 4 For yet seven days, and I will cause it to rain upon the earth forty days and forty nights; and every living substance that I have made will I destroy from off the face of the earth.

33 5–6 And Noah did according unto all that the LORD commanded him. And Noah *was* six hundred years old when the flood of waters was upon the earth.

34 7 And Noah went in, and his sons, and his wife, and his sons' wives with him, into the ark, because of the waters of the flood.

35 8–9 Of clean beasts, and of beasts that ~~are~~ **were** not clean, and of fowls, and of everything that creepeth upon the earth, there went in two and two, unto Noah into the ark, the male and the female, as God had commanded Noah.

36 10–12 And it came to pass**,** after seven days, that the waters of the flood were upon the earth. In the six hundredth year of Noah's life, in the second month, **and** the seventeenth day of the month, the same day were all the fountains of the great deep broken up, and the windows of heaven were opened**,** and the rain was upon the earth forty days and forty nights.

37 13–14 In the selfsame day entered Noah, and Shem, and Ham, and Japheth, the sons of Noah, and Noah's wife, and the three wives of his sons with them into the ark; they, and every beast after his kind, and all the cattle after their kind, and every creeping thing that creepeth upon the earth after his kind, and every fowl after his kind, every bird of every sort.

38 15–16 And they went ~~in~~ unto Noah**,** into the ark, two and two of all flesh, wherein *is* the breath of life**;** and they that went in, went in male and female of all flesh, as God had commanded him**,** and the LORD shut him in.

39 17 And the flood was forty days upon the earth**,** and the waters increased, and bare up the ark, and it was ~~lift~~ **lifted** up above the earth.

40 18 And the waters prevailed and ~~were~~ increased greatly upon the earth**,** and the ark went upon the face of the waters.

41 19–20 And the waters prevailed exceedingly upon **the face of** the earth**,** and all the high hills, ~~that were~~ under the whole ~~heaven~~ **heavens** were covered. Fifteen cubits **and** upward did the waters prevail; and the mountains were covered.

42 21 And all flesh died that moved upon **the face of** the earth, both of fowl, and of cattle, and of ~~beast~~ **beasts**, and of every creeping thing that creepeth upon the earth, and every man**.**

43 22 All in whose nostrils *was* **the Lord had breathed** the breath of life, of all that ~~was~~ **were** ~~in~~ **on** the dry land, died.

44 23 And every living substance

was destroyed, which was upon the face of the ground, both man, and cattle, and the creeping things, and the ~~fowl~~ **fowls** of the ~~heaven~~ **air**; and they were destroyed from the earth;

45 23 And Noah only remained ~~alive~~, and they that *were* with him in the ark.

46 24 And the waters prevailed ~~upon~~ **on** the earth ~~an~~ **one** hundred and fifty days.

CHAPTER 8

47 1 And God remembered Noah, and ~~every living thing, and~~ all ~~the cattle~~ that ~~was~~ **were** with him in the ark. And God made a wind to pass over the earth, and the waters ~~asswaged~~ **assuaged**.

48 2–3 The fountains also of the deep, and the windows of heaven were stopped, and the rain from heaven was restrained; and the waters returned from off the earth ~~continually~~.

49 3–4 And after the end of the hundred and fifty days, the waters were abated. And the ark rested in the seventh month, on the seventeenth day of the month, upon the ~~mountains~~ **mountain** of Ararat.

50 5 And the waters decreased ~~continually~~ until the tenth month; **and** in the tenth *month*, on the first *day* of the month, were the tops of the mountains seen.

51 6–7 And it came to pass at the end of forty days, that Noah opened the window of the ark which he had made: and he sent forth a raven, which went forth to and fro, until the waters were dried up from off the earth.

52 8–9 ~~Also~~ He **also** sent forth a dove from him, to see if the waters were abated from off the face of the ground; but the dove found no rest for the sole of her foot, and she

returned unto him into the ark, for the waters ~~were on~~ **had not receded from off** the face of the whole earth; then he put forth his hand and took her, and pulled her in unto him into the ark.

53 10–11 And he stayed yet other seven days, and again he sent forth the dove out of the ark, and the dove came in to him in the evening; and, lo, in her mouth ~~was~~ an olive leaf ~~pluckt~~ **plucked** off; so Noah knew that the waters were abated from off the earth.

54 12 And he stayed yet other seven days, and sent forth ~~the~~ **a** dove, which returned not again unto him anymore.

55 13 And it came to pass, in the six ~~hundredth~~ **hundred** and first year, in the first *month*, the first *day* of the month, the waters were dried up from off the earth.

56 13–14 And Noah removed the covering of the ark, and looked, and, behold, the face of the ground was dry. And in the second month, on the seven and twentieth day of the month, was the earth dried.

CHAPTER **9** 8

1 15–16 And God spake unto Noah, saying, Go forth **out** of the ark, thou and thy wife, and thy sons, and thy sons' wives with thee.

2 17 Bring forth with thee every living thing that *is* with thee, of all flesh, *both* of fowl, and of cattle, and of every creeping thing that creepeth upon the earth; that they may breed abundantly in the earth, and be fruitful, and multiply upon the earth.

3 18–19 And Noah went forth, and his sons, and his wife, and his sons' wives with him. **And** every beast, every creeping thing, and every fowl

~~*and* whatsoever creepeth~~ upon the earth, after their kinds, went forth out of the ark.

4 20 And Noah builded an altar unto the LORD**,** and took of every clean beast, and of every clean fowl, and offered burnt offerings on the altar**; and gave thanks unto the Lord, and rejoiced in his heart.**

5 21 **And the Lord spake unto Noah, and he blessed him.** And ~~the LORD~~ **Noah** smelled a sweet savor, and ~~the LORD~~ **he** said in his heart**;**

6 21–22 I will **call on the name of the Lord, that he will** not again curse the ground anymore for man's sake**,** for the imagination of man's heart *is* evil from his youth; ~~neither~~ **and that he** will ~~I~~ **not** again smite anymore everything living, as ~~I~~ **he** ~~have~~ **hath** done**,** while the earth remaineth**;**

7 22 **And**, **that** seed-time and harvest, and cold and heat, and summer and winter, and day and night, ~~shall~~ **may** not cease **with man.**

CHAPTER 9

8 1–2 And God blessed Noah and his sons, and said unto them, Be fruitful and multiply, and replenish the earth. And the fear of you and the dread of you shall be upon every beast of the earth, and upon every fowl of the air, upon all that moveth *upon* the earth, and upon all the fishes of the sea; into your hand are they delivered.

9 3 Every moving thing that liveth shall be meat for you; even as the green herb have I given you all things.

10 4 But**,** **the blood of all** flesh **which I have given you for meat, shall be shed upon the ground,** ~~with the~~ **which taketh** life thereof, ~~*which is*~~ **and** the blood ~~thereof~~ **ye** shall ~~ye~~ not eat.

11 5 And surely ~~your blood of your lives will I require; at the hand~~, **blood shall not be shed, only for meat, to save your lives; and the blood** of every beast will I require ~~it, and~~ at ~~the hand of man~~ **your hands** ~~at the hand of every man's brother will I require the life of man~~.

12 6 **And** whoso sheddeth man's blood, by man shall his blood be shed**;** for ~~in the image of God made he~~ **man shall not shed the blood of** man.

13 **For a commandment I give, that every man's brother shall preserve the life of man, for in mine own image have I made man.**

14 7 And **a commandment I give unto** you, Be ye fruitful, and multiply; bring forth abundantly ~~in~~ **on** the earth, and multiply therein.

15 8–9 And God spake unto Noah, and to his sons with him, saying, And I, behold, I **will** establish my covenant with you, ~~and with~~ **which I made unto your father Enoch, concerning** your seed after you.

16 10–11 And **it shall come to pass**, ~~with~~ **that** every living creature that *is* with you, of the fowl, **and** of the cattle, and of ~~every~~ **the** beast of the earth **that is** with you**,** ~~from all that~~ **which shall** go out of the ark, ~~to every beast of the earth~~ **shall not altogether perish:** neither shall all flesh be cut off anymore by the waters of a flood**:** neither shall there anymore be a flood to destroy the earth**.**

17 11 And I will establish my covenant with you, **which I made unto Enoch, concerning the remnants of your posterity.**

18 12 And God **made a covenant with Noah, and** said, This ~~*is*~~ **shall be** the token of the covenant ~~which~~ I make between me and you**,** and **for** every living creature ~~*that is*~~ with you,

and for perpetual generations;

19 13 I ~~do~~ **will** set my bow in the cloud; and it shall be for a token of a covenant between me and the earth.

20 14–15 And it shall come to pass, when I bring a cloud over the earth, that the bow shall be seen in the cloud; and I will remember my covenant, which ~~is~~ **I have made** between me and you, ~~and~~ **for** every living creature of all flesh. And the waters shall no more become a flood to destroy all flesh.

21 16 And the bow shall be in the cloud; and I will look upon it, that I may remember the everlasting covenant ~~between God and every living creature of all flesh that is upon the earth~~, **which I made unto thy father Enoch; that, when men should keep all my commandments, Zion should again come on the earth, the city of Enoch which I have caught up unto myself**.

22 And this is mine everlasting covenant, that when thy posterity shall embrace the truth, and look upward, then shall Zion look downward, and all the heavens shall shake with gladness, and the earth shall tremble with joy;

23 And the general assembly of the church of the firstborn shall come down out of heaven, and possess the earth, and shall have place until the end come. And this is mine everlasting covenant, which I made with thy father Enoch.

24 And the bow shall be in the cloud, and I will establish my covenant unto thee, which I have made between me and thee, for every living creature of all flesh that shall be upon the earth.

25 17 And God said unto Noah, This *is* the token of the covenant which I have established between me

and **thee; for** all flesh that *is* **shall be** upon the earth.

26 18–19 And the sons of Noah that went forth of the ark, were Shem, and Ham, and Japheth; and Ham ~~is~~ **was** the father of Canaan. These ~~are~~ **were** the three sons of Noah, and of them was the whole earth overspread.

27 20–21 And Noah began *to* **till the earth, and he** ~~be~~ **was** an husbandman; and he planted a vineyard, and he drank of the wine, and was drunken; and he was uncovered within his tent;

28 22–23 And Ham, the father of Canaan, saw the nakedness of his father, and told his ~~two~~ brethren without; and Shem and Japheth took a garment and laid *it* upon both their shoulders, and went backward and covered the nakedness of their father, ~~and their faces *were* backward~~ and they saw not their father's nakedness.

29 24–25 And Noah awoke from his wine, and knew what his ~~younger~~ **youngest** son had done unto him, and he said, Cursed *be* Canaan; a servant of servants shall he be unto his brethren.

30 26 And he said, Blessed *be* the Lord God of Shem; and Canaan shall be his servant, **and a veil of darkness shall cover him, that he shall be known among all men**.

31 27 God shall enlarge Japheth, and he shall dwell in the tents of Shem; and Canaan shall be his servant.

32 28–29 And Noah lived after the flood three hundred and fifty years. And all the days of Noah were nine hundred and fifty years: and he died.

Chapter 10

1 Now these ~~are~~ **were** the generations of the sons of Noah; Shem,

Ham, and Japheth; and unto them were sons born after the flood.

2 The sons of Japheth; Gomer, and Magog, and Madai, and Javan, and Tubal, and Meshech, and Tiras.

3 3–5 And **these are** the sons of Gomer; Ashkenaz, and Riphath, and Togarmah. And the sons of Javan; Elishah, and Tarshish, Kittim, and Dodanim. By these were the isles of the Gentiles divided in their lands; every one after ~~his~~ **the same** tongue, after their families, in their nations.

4 6–7 And the sons of Ham; Cush, and Mizraim, and Phut, and Canaan. And the sons of Cush; Seba, and Havilah, and Sabtah, and Raamah, and Sabtecha: and the sons of Raamah; Sheba, and Dedan.

5 8–9 And Cush begat Nimrod; he began to be a mighty one in the earth. He was a mighty hunter ~~before the Lord~~ **in the land.** Wherefore, it is said; Even as Nimrod, the mighty hunter ~~before the Lord~~ **in the land**.

6 10 **And he began a kingdom,** and the beginning of his kingdom was Babel, and Erech, and Accad, and Calneh, in the land of Shinar.

7 11–12 Out of that land went forth Asshur, and builded Nineveh, and the city Rehoboth, and Calah, and Resen between Nineveh and Calah; the same ~~is~~ **was** a great city.

8 13–14 And Mizraim begat Ludim, and Anamim, and Lehabim, and Naphtuhim, and Pathrusim, and Casluhim, (out of whom came Philistim,) and Caphtorim.

9 15–18 And Canaan begat Sidon, his firstborn, and Heth, and the Jebusite, and the Amorite, and ~~the Girgasite~~ **Girgashite**, and the Hivite, and the Arkite, and the Sinite, and the Arvadite, and the Zemarite, and the Hamathite; and afterward were the families of the Canaanites spread abroad.

10 19 And the ~~border~~ **borders** of the Canaanites ~~was~~ **were** from Sidon, as thou comest to Gerar unto Gaza; as thou goest unto Sodom and Gomorrah, and Admah, and ~~Zeboim~~ **Zeboiim,** even unto Lasha.

11 20 These ~~are~~ **were** the sons of Ham, after their families, after ~~their~~ **the same** ~~tongues~~ **tongue**, in their countries, *and* in their nations.

12 21 Unto Shem also, **which was the elder, children were born; and he was** the father ~~of all the children~~ of Eber, ~~the brother of Japheth the elder~~ **and** even to him were *children* born.

13 22 **And these are** the children of Shem; **Eber, and** Elam, and Asshur, and Arphaxad, and Lud, and Aram.

14 23 And **these were** the children of Aram; ~~Uz~~ **Us**, and Hul, and Gether, and Mash.

15 24–25 And Arphaxad begat Salah; and Salah begat Eber. And unto Eber were born two sons: the name of one, ~~was~~ Peleg, ~~and his brother's name was~~ **the other** Joktan.

16 25 **And Peleg was a mighty man,** for in his days was the earth divided.

17 26–29 And Joktan begat Almodad, and Sheleph, and Hazarmaveth, and Jerah, and Hadoram, and Uzal, and Diklah, and Obal, and Abimael, and Sheba, and ~~Ophir~~ **Ophar**, and Havilah, and Jobab; ~~all~~ **and** these *were* the sons of Joktan.

18 30 And their dwelling was from Mesha, as thou goest unto Sephar a mount of the east.

19 31 These ~~are~~ **were** the sons of Shem, after their families, after their tongues, in their lands, after their nations.

20 32 These ~~are~~ **were** the families of

the sons of Noah, after their generations, in their nations; and by these were the nations divided ~~in~~ **on** the earth, after the flood.

CHAPTER 11

1 1–2 And the whole earth was of ~~one~~ **the same** language, and of ~~one~~ **the same** speech. And it came to pass, **that many journeyed from the east, and** as they journeyed from the east, ~~that~~ they found a plain in the land of Shinar, and they dwelt there **in the plain of Shinar**.

2 3 And they said one to another, **Come,** go to, let us make brick, and burn them thoroughly. And they had brick for stone, and ~~slime~~ **they** had ~~they~~ **slime** for mortar.

3 4 And they said, **Come,** go to, let us build us a city, and a tower whose top ~~may~~ **will** ~~reach~~ **be high, nigh** unto heaven; and let us make us a name, lest we be scattered abroad upon the face of the whole earth.

4 5 And the LORD came down, ~~to see~~ **beholding** the city and the tower which the children of men ~~builded~~ **were building;**

5 6–8 And the LORD said, Behold, the people ~~is~~ **are** ~~one~~ **the same**, and they **all** have ~~all~~ **one** **the same** language; and this **tower** they begin to ~~do~~ **build,** and now, nothing will be restrained from them, which they have imagined ~~to do~~, **except I, the Lord,** ~~Go to, let us go down, and there~~ confound their language, that they may not understand one another's speech. So **I,** the LORD, ~~scattered~~ **will scatter** them abroad from thence, upon **all** the face of ~~all~~ the ~~earth~~ **land, and unto every quarter of the earth.**

6 8–9 **And they were confounded,** and ~~they~~ left off to build the city, **and they hearkened not unto the Lord,**

therefore**,** is the name of it called Babel**,** because the LORD **was displeased with their works, and** did there confound the language of all the earth; and from thence did the LORD scatter them abroad upon the face ~~of all the earth~~ **thereof**.

7 10–11 **And** these ~~are~~ **were** the generations of Shem. **And** Shem ~~was~~ **being** an hundred years old, ~~and~~ begat Arphaxad two years after the flood; and Shem lived after he begat Arphaxad five hundred years, and begat sons and daughters.

8 12–13 And Arphaxad lived five and thirty years, and begat Salah: and Arphaxad lived after he begat Salah four hundred and three years, and begat sons and daughters.

9 14–15 And Salah lived thirty years, and begat Eber: and Salah lived after he begat Eber four hundred and three years, and begat sons and daughters.

10 16–17 And Eber lived four and thirty years, and begat Peleg: and Eber lived after he begat Peleg four hundred and thirty years, and begat sons and daughters.

11 18–19 And Peleg lived thirty years, and begat Reu: and Peleg lived after he begat Reu two hundred and nine years, and begat sons and daughters.

12 20–21 And Reu lived two and thirty years, and begat Serug: and Reu lived after he begat Serug two hundred and seven years, and begat sons and daughters.

13 22–23 And Serug lived thirty years, and begat Nahor: and Serug lived after he begat Nahor two hundred years, and begat sons and daughters.

14 24–25 And Nahor lived nine and twenty years, and begat Terah: and Nahor lived after he begat Terah an hundred and nineteen years, and begat sons and daughters.

15 26 And Terah lived seventy years, and begat Abram, Nahor, and Haran.

16 27 Now these ~~are~~ **were** the generations of Terah; Terah begat Abram, Nahor, and Haran; and Haran begat Lot.

17 28 And Haran died before his father Terah in the land of his nativity, in Ur of the Chaldees.

18 29–30 And Abram and Nahor took them wives; **and** the name of Abram's wife *was* Sarai; and the name of Nahor's wife, Milcah, the daughter of Haran, the father of Milcah, and the father of Iscah; but Sarai was barren, **and** she ~~had~~ **bear** no child.

19 31 And Terah took Abram his son, and Lot the son of Haran, his son's son, and Sarai his daughter-in-law, his son Abram's wife; and ~~they~~ went forth with them from Ur of the Chaldees, to go into the land of Canaan; and they came unto Haran, and dwelt there.

20 32 And the days of Terah were two hundred and five years: and Terah died in Haran.

CHAPTER 12

1 Now the LORD had said unto Abram, Get thee out of thy country, and from thy kindred, and from thy father's house, unto a land that I will shew thee:

2 2–3 And I will make of thee a great nation, and I will bless thee, and make thy name great; and thou shalt be a blessing; and I will bless them that bless thee, and curse ~~him~~ **them** that ~~curseth~~ **curse** thee; and in thee shall ~~all~~ **the** families of the earth be blessed.

3 4 So Abram departed, as the LORD had spoken unto him; and Lot went with him: and Abram *was* seventy and

five years old when he departed out of Haran.

4 5 And Abram took Sarai his wife, and Lot, his brother's son, and all their substance that they had gathered, and the souls that they had gotten in Haran; and they went forth to go into the land of Canaan; and into the land of Canaan they came.

5 6 And Abram passed through the land unto the place of Sichem, ~~unto~~ **and** the plain of Moreh. And the ~~Canaanite~~ **Canaanites** ~~was~~ **were** then in the land.

6 7 And the LORD appeared unto Abram, and said, Unto thy seed will I give this land: and there builded he an altar unto the LORD, who appeared unto him.

7 8–9 And he removed from thence unto a mountain on the east of Beth-el, and pitched his tent, ~~having~~ **leaving** Beth-el on the west, and Hai **was** on the east. And there he builded an altar unto the LORD, and called upon the name of the LORD. And Abram journeyed, going on still toward the south.

8 10 And there was a famine in the land; and Abram went down into Egypt to sojourn there; for the famine ~~was~~ **became** grievous in the land.

9 11–13 And it came to pass, when he was come near to enter into Egypt, that he said unto Sarai his wife, Behold, now I know ~~that thou art~~ **thee to be** a fair woman to look upon; therefore it shall come to pass, when the Egyptians shall see thee, that they shall say, This *is* his wife; and they will kill me, but they will save thee alive; say I pray thee **unto them**, ~~thou~~ I ~~art~~ **am** ~~my~~ **his** sister; that it may be well with me for thy sake; and my soul shall live because of thee.

10 14 And it came to pass, that

when Abram was come into Egypt, the Egyptians beheld the woman that she *was* very fair.

11 15 The princes also of Pharaoh saw her, and ~~commended~~ **commanded** her **to be brought** before Pharaoh; and the woman was taken into Pharaoh's house.

12 16 And he entreated Abram well for her sake: and he had sheep, and oxen, and he asses, and menservants, and maidservants, and she asses, and camels.

13 17 And the Lord plagued Pharaoh and his house with great plagues because of Sarai, Abram's wife.

14 18–19 And Pharaoh called Abram, and said, What ~~is this that~~ **hast** thou ~~hast~~ done unto me **in this thing**? Why didst thou not tell me that she *was* thy wife? Why saidst thou, She *is* my sister? so I might have taken her ~~to~~ **unto** me to wife; now therefore, behold **I say unto thee, Take** thy wife ~~take her~~ and go thy way.

15 20 And Pharaoh commanded *his* men concerning him; and they sent him away, and his wife, and all that he had.

Chapter 13

1 1–2 And Abram went up out of Egypt, he, and his wife, and all that he had, and Lot with him, ~~into~~ **unto** the south. And Abram *was* very rich in cattle, in silver, and in gold.

2 3–4 And he went on his ~~journeys~~ **journey** from the south, even to Bethel, unto the place where his tent had been at the beginning, between Bethel and Hai; unto the place of the altar, which he had made there at the first; and there Abram called on the name of the Lord.

3 5 And Lot also, which went with Abram, had flocks, and herds, and tents.

4 6–7 And the land was not able to bear them, that they might dwell together; for their substance was great, so that they could not dwell together. And there was a strife between the herdmen of Abram's cattle, and the herdmen of Lot's cattle, **that they could not dwell together**.

5 7 And the Canaanite and the Perizzite dwelled then in the land

6 8 And Abram said unto Lot, Let there be no strife, I pray thee, between me and thee, and between my herdmen and thy herdmen; for we ~~be~~ **are** brethren.

7 9 *Is* not the whole land before thee? Separate thyself, I pray thee, from me; if *thou* ~~wilt take~~ **go to** the left hand, then I will go to the right; ~~or~~ if *thou* ~~depart~~ **go** to the right hand, then I will go to the left.

8 10 And Lot lifted up his eyes, and beheld all the plain of Jordan, that it *was* well watered everywhere, before the Lord destroyed Sodom and Gomorrah, ~~even~~ **like** as the garden of the Lord, like the land of Egypt ~~as thou comest unto Zoar~~.

9 11 Then Lot chose him all the plain of Jordan; and Lot journeyed east: and they separated themselves the one from the other.

10 12 Abram dwelled in the land of Canaan, and Lot dwelled in the cities of the plain, and pitched *his* tent toward Sodom.

11 13 But the men of Sodom ~~were~~ **becoming sinners, and exceedingly** wicked ~~and sinners~~ before the Lord ~~exceedingly~~, **the Lord was angry with them**.

12 14 And the Lord said unto Abram, after that Lot was separated from him, Lift up now thine eyes, and look from the place where thou art, northward, and southward, and eastward, and westward;

13 And remember the covenant which I make with thee; for it shall be an everlasting covenant; and thou shalt remember the days of Enoch thy father;

14 15–16 For all the land which thou seest, ~~to thee~~ will I give ~~it~~ **thee,** and to thy seed forever; and I will make thy seed as the dust of the earth; so that if a man can number the dust of the earth, ~~then shall~~ thy seed **shall** also be numbered.

15 17–18 Arise, walk through the land in the length of it and in the breadth of it; for I will give it unto thee. Then Abram removed *his* tent, and came and dwelt in the plain of Mamre, which *is* in Hebron, and built there an altar unto the LORD.

CHAPTER 14

1 And it came to pass**,** in the days of Amraphel king of Shinar, **and** Arioch king of Ellasar, **and** Chedorlaomer king of Elam, and Tidal king of nations;

2 *That these* **kings** made war with Bera king of Sodom, and with Birsha king of Gomorrah, Shinab king of Admah, and Shemeber king of Zeboiim, and the king of Bela, which is Zoar.

3 All these were joined together in the vale of Siddim, which is the salt sea.

4 Twelve years they served Chedorlaomer, and in the thirteenth year they rebelled.

5 5–6 And in the fourteenth year came Chedorlaomer, and the kings that *were* with him, and smote the Rephaims in Ashteroth Karnaim, and the Zuzims in Ham, and the Emims in Shaveh Kiriathaim, and the Horites in their mount Seir, unto El-paran, which ~~is~~ **was** by the wilderness.

6 7 And they returned and came to En-mishpat, which *is* Kadesh, and smote all the country of the Amalekites, and also the Amorites, ~~that dwelt~~ in Hazezon-tamar.

7 8 And there went out the king of Sodom, and the king of Gomorrah, and the king of Admah, and the king of Zeboiim, and the king of Bela, ~~the same~~ **which** *is* Zoar;

8 8–9 And they joined battle with them in the vale of Siddim; with Chedorlaomer ~~the~~ king of Elam, and with Tidal king of nations, and Amraphel king of Shinar, and Arioch king of Ellasar; four kings with five.

9 10 And the vale of Siddim *was* ~~full~~ **filled** ~~of~~ **with** slime pits; and the kings of Sodom and Gomorrah fled and fell there; and they that remained fled to the mountain **which was called Hanabal**.

10 11 And they took all the goods of Sodom and Gomorrah, and all their victuals, and went their way.

11 12 And they took Lot, Abram's brother's son, who dwelt in Sodom, and his goods, and departed.

12 13 And there came one that had escaped, and told Abram the Hebrew, **the man of God,** for he dwelt in the plain of Mamre the Amorite, brother of Eschol, and brother of Aner; and these *were* confederate with Abram.

13 14 And when Abram heard that **Lot,** his ~~brother~~ **brother's son,** was taken captive, he armed his trained ~~servants~~ **men, and they which were** born in his own house, three hundred and eighteen, and pursued ~~them~~ unto Dan.

14 15 And he divided himself against them, he and his ~~servants~~ **men,** by night, and smote them, and pursued them unto Hobah, which ~~is~~ **was** on the left hand of Damascus.

15 16 And he brought back ~~all the goods, and also brought again~~ **Lot,** his ~~brother Lot~~ **brother's son**, and **all** his goods, and the women also, and the people.

16 17 And the king of Sodom **also** went out to meet him after his return from the slaughter of Chedorlaomer, and of the kings that *were* with him, at the valley of Shaveh, which *is* **was** the king's dale.

17 18 And Melchizedek**,** king of ~~Salem~~ **Shalom,**[18] brought forth bread and wine**;** and **he brake bread and blest it; and he blest the wine,** he ~~was~~ **being** the priest of the most high God,

18 19 **And he gave to Abram,** and he blessed him, and said, Blessed ~~be~~ Abram**, thou art a man** of the most high God, possessor of heaven and **of** earth**;**

19 20 And blessed ~~be~~ **is** the **name of the** most high God, which hath delivered thine enemies into ~~thy~~ **thine** hand.

20 And ~~he~~ **Abram** gave him tithes of all **he had taken**.

21 And the king of Sodom said ~~unto~~ **to** Abram, Give me the persons, and take the goods to thyself.

22 And Abram said to the king of Sodom, I have ~~lift~~ **lifted** up ~~mine~~ **my** hand unto the LORD, the most high God, the possessor of heaven and earth**.**

23 **And have sworn** that I will not *take* **of thee** from a thread even to a shoelatchet, and that I will not take anything that *is* thine, (lest thou shouldest say, I have made Abram rich**;**)

24 Save only that which the young men have eaten, and the portion of the men which went with me, Aner, Eshcol, and Mamre; let them take their portion.

25 And Melchizedek* lifted up his voice and blessed Abram.

26 Now Melchizedek* was a man of faith, who wrought righteousness; and when a child he feared God, and stopped the mouths of lions, and quenched the violence of fire.

27 And thus, having been approved of God, he was ordained an high priest after the order of the covenant which God made with Enoch,

28 It being after the order of the Son of God; which order came, not by man, nor the will of man; neither by father nor mother; neither by beginning of days nor end of years; but of God;

29 And it was delivered unto men by the calling of his own voice, according to his own will, unto as many as believed on his name.

30 For God having sworn unto Enoch and unto his seed with an oath by himself; that everyone being ordained after this order and calling should have power, by faith, to break mountains, to divide the seas, to dry up waters, to turn them out of their course;

31 To put at defiance the armies of nations, to divide the earth, to break every band, to stand in the presence of God; to do all things according to his will, according to his command, subdue principalities and powers; and this by the will of the Son of God which was from before the foundation of the world.

32 And men having this faith, coming up unto this order of God, were translated and taken up into heaven.

33 And now, Melchizedek* was a priest of this order; therefore he obtained peace in Salem, and was called the Prince of peace.

34 And his people wrought righteousness, and obtained heaven, and sought for the city of Enoch which God had before taken, separating it from the earth, having reserved it unto the latter days, or the end of the world;

35 And hath said, and sworn with an oath, that the heavens and the earth should come together; and the sons of God should be tried so as by fire.

36 And this Melchizedek,˙ having thus established righteousness, was called the king of heaven by his people, or, in other words, the King of peace.

37 And he lifted up his voice, and he blessed Abram, being the high priest, and the keeper of the storehouse of God;

38 Him whom God had appointed to receive tithes for the poor.

39 Wherefore, Abram paid unto him tithes of all that he had, of all the riches which he possessed, which God had given him more than that which he had need.

40 And it came to pass, that God blessed Abram, and gave unto him riches, and honor, and lands for an everlasting possession; according to the covenant which he had made, and according to the blessing wherewith Melchizedek˙ had blessed him.

CHAPTER 15

1 And it came to pass, that after these things, the word of the LORD came unto Abram in a vision, saying;

2 1 Fear not, Abram; I am will be thy shield; and I will be thy exceeding great reward. And according to the blessings of my servant, I will give unto thee.

3 2 And Abram said, Lord GOD, what wilt thou give me, seeing I go childless, and Eliezer˙ of Damascus was made the steward of my house is this Eliezer of Damascus?

4 3 And Abram said, Behold, to me thou hast given no seed: and, lo, one born in my house is mine heir.

5 4 And, behold, the word of the LORD came unto him again, saying,

6 4 This shall not be thine heir; but he that shall come forth out of thine own bowels shall be thine heir.

7 5 And he brought him forth abroad, and he said, Look now toward heaven, and tell the stars, if thou be able to number them.

8 5 And he said unto him, So shall thy seed be.

9 And Abram said, Lord God, how wilt thou give me this land for an everlasting inheritance?

10 And the Lord said, Though thou wast dead, yet am I not able to give it thee?

11 And if thou shalt die, yet thou shalt possess it, for the day cometh, that the Son of Man shall live; but how can he live if he be not dead? he must first be quickened.

12 6 And it came to pass, that Abram looked forth and saw the days of the Son of Man, and was glad, and his soul found rest, and he believed in the LORD; and he the Lord counted it to unto him for righteousness.

13 7 And he the Lord said unto him, I am, the LORD, that brought thee out of Ur, of the Chaldees, to give thee this land to inherit it.

14 8–9 And he Abram said, Lord GOD, whereby shall I know that I shall inherit it? yet he believed God. And he the Lord said unto him, Take me an a heifer of three years old, and a she goat of three years old, and a ram of

three years old, and a turtledove, and a young pigeon.

15 10 And he took unto him all these, and **he** divided them in the midst, and **he** laid each piece one against ~~another~~ **the other;** but the birds divided he not.

16 11–12 And when the fowls came down upon the ~~carcases~~ **carcasses,** Abram drove them away. And when the sun was going down, a deep sleep fell upon Abram; and, lo, ~~an~~ **a great** horror of ~~great~~ darkness fell upon him.

17 13–14 **And the Lord spake,** and he said unto Abram, Know of a surety that thy seed shall be a stranger in a land ~~that~~ **which** ~~is~~ **shall** not **be** theirs, and shall serve ~~them~~ **strangers**; and they shall ~~afflict~~ **be afflicted, and serve** them four hundred years; and also that nation whom they shall serve will I judge; and ~~afterward~~ **afterwards** shall they come out with great substance.

18 15 And thou shalt **die, and** go to thy fathers in peace; thou shalt be buried in a good old age.

19 16 But in the fourth generation they shall come hither again: for the iniquity of the Amorites *is* not yet full.

20 17 And it came to pass, that when the sun went down, and it was dark, behold, a smoking furnace, and a burning lamp ~~that~~ **which** passed between those pieces **which Abram had divided**.

21 18 **And** in ~~the~~ **that** same day the LORD made a covenant with Abram, saying, Unto thy seed have I given this land, from the river of Egypt unto the great river ~~the river~~ Euphrates;

22 19–21 The Kenites, and the ~~Kenizzites~~ **Kenazites,** and the Kadmonites, and ~~the~~ Hittites, and the Perizzites, and the Rephaims, and the Amorites, and the Canaanites, and the Girgashites, and the Jebusites.

CHAPTER 16

1 Now Sarai Abram's wife bare him no children: and she had an handmaid, an Egyptian, whose name *was* Hagar.

2 And Sarai said unto Abram, Behold now, the LORD hath restrained me from bearing: I pray thee go, in unto my maid; it may be that I may obtain children by her. And Abram hearkened to the voice of Sarai.

3 And Sarai Abram's wife took Hagar her maid the Egyptian, after Abram had dwelt ten years in the land of Canaan, and gave her to her husband Abram to be his wife.

4 And he went in unto Hagar, and she conceived: and when she saw that she had conceived, her mistress was despised in her eyes.

5 And Sarai said unto Abram, My wrong ~~be~~ **is** upon thee; I have given my maid into thy bosom; and when she saw that she had conceived, I was despised in her eyes; the LORD judge between me and thee.

6 But Abram said unto Sarai, Behold, thy maid *is* in thy hand; do to her as it pleaseth thee.

7 6 And when Sarai dealt hardly with her, she fled from her face.

8 7 And ~~the~~ **an** angel of the LORD found her by a fountain of water in the wilderness, by the fountain in the way to Shur.

9 8 And he said, Hagar, Sarai's maid, whence camest thou? and whither wilt thou go? And she said, I flee from the face of my mistress Sarai.

10 9 And the angel of the LORD said unto her, Return to thy mistress, and submit thyself under her hands.

11 10 And the angel of the Lord said unto her, ~~I~~ **The Lord** will multiply thy seed exceedingly, **so** that it shall not be numbered for multitude.

12 11 And the angel of the Lord said unto her, Behold, thou *art* with child, and shalt bear a son, and ~~shalt~~ **shall** call his name Ishmael; because the Lord hath heard thy ~~affliction~~ **afflictions**.

13 12 And he will be a wild man; **and** his hand *will be* against every man, and every man's hand against him; and he shall dwell in the presence of all his brethren.

14 13 And she called the name of the **angel of the** Lord.

15 13 **And he** ~~that~~ spake unto her, **saying, Knowest** thou **that** God seest ~~me~~ **thee?**

16 13 ~~for~~ **And** she said, **I know that God seest me, for I** have ~~I~~ also here looked after him ~~that seeth me~~.

17 14 ~~Wherefore the~~ **And there was a** well ~~was called Beer-lahai-roi; behold, it is~~ between Kadesh and Bered**, near where Hagar saw the angel**.

18 And the name of the angel was Beer-la-hai-roi; wherefore the well was called Beer-la-hai-roi for a memorial.

19 15 And Hagar bare Abram a son: and Abram called his son's name, which Hagar bare, Ishmael.

20 16 And Abram *was* fourscore and six years old, when Hagar bare Ishmael to Abram.

Chapter 17

1 And when Abram was ninety ~~years old~~ and nine **years old**, the Lord appeared to Abram, and said unto him, I ~~am~~**,** the Almighty God**, give unto thee a commandment that thou shalt** walk **uprightly** before me, and be ~~thou~~ perfect.

2 And I will make my covenant between me and thee, and **I** will multiply thee exceedingly.

3 And **it came to pass, that** Abram fell on his face**, and called upon the name of the Lord.**

4 3 And God talked with him, saying, **My people have gone astray from my precepts, and have not kept mine ordinances, which I gave unto their fathers;**

5 And they have not observed mine anointing, and the burial, or baptism wherewith I commanded them;

6 But have turned from the commandment, and taken unto themselves the washing of children, and the blood of sprinkling;

7 And have said that the blood of the righteous Abel was shed for sins; and have not known wherein they are accountable before me.

8 4 **But** as for ~~me~~ **thee**, behold, **I will make** my covenant ~~is~~ with thee, and thou shalt be a father of many nations.

9 5 **And this covenant I make, that thy children may be known among all nations.** Neither shall thy name anymore be called Abram, but thy name shall be **called** Abraham; for**,** a father of many nations have I made thee.

10 6 And I will make thee exceeding fruitful, and I will make nations of thee, and kings shall come out of thee**, and of thy seed**.

11 7 And I will establish **a covenant of circumcision with thee, and it shall be** my covenant between me and thee**,** and thy seed after thee**,** in their generations ~~for an everlasting covenant, to be a God unto thee, and to thy seed after thee~~**; that thou mayest know forever that children are not**

accountable before me until they are eight years old.

12 And thou shalt observe to keep all my covenants wherein I covenanted with thy fathers; and thou shalt keep the commandments which I have given thee with mine own mouth, and I will be a God unto thee and thy seed after thee.

13 8 And I will give unto thee and ~~to~~ thy seed after thee, ~~the~~ a land wherein thou art a stranger; all the land of Canaan, for an everlasting possession; and I will be their God.

14 9 And God said unto Abraham, **Therefore,** thou shalt keep my covenant ~~therefore~~, thou and thy seed after thee**,** in their generations.

15 10 **And** this *is* **shall be** my covenant which ye shall keep between me and ~~you~~ **thee** and thy seed after thee; every man child among you shall be circumcised.

16 11 And ye shall circumcise the flesh of your foreskin; and it shall be a token of the covenant betwixt me and you.

17 12 And he that is eight days old shall be circumcised among you, every man child in your generations,

18 12 He that is born in the house, or bought with money of any stranger, which *is* not of thy seed.

19 13 He that is born in thy house, and he that is bought with thy money, must needs be circumcised: and my covenant shall be in your flesh for an everlasting covenant.

20 14 And the uncircumcised man child whose flesh of his foreskin is not circumcised, that soul shall be cut off from his people; he hath broken my covenant.

21 15 And God said unto Abraham, As for Sarai thy wife, thou shalt not call her name Sarai, but Sarah **thou** ~~shall~~ **shalt call** her name ~~be~~.

22 16 And I will bless her, and **I will** give thee a son ~~also~~ of her**;** yea, I will bless her, and she shall be **blessed,** *a* The *mother* of nations; kings ~~of~~ **and** people shall be of her.

23 17 Then Abraham fell upon his face and ~~laughed~~ **rejoiced**, and said in his heart, **There** shall *a child* be born unto him that is an hundred years old**,** and ~~shall~~ Sarah that is ninety years old **shall** bear**.**

24 18 And Abraham said unto God, O that Ishmael might live **uprightly** before thee!

25 19 And God said, Sarah thy wife shall bear thee a son ~~indeed,~~ and thou shalt call his name Isaac**;** and I will establish my covenant with him **also,** for an everlasting covenant ~~and~~ with his seed after him.

26 20 And as for Ishmael, I have heard thee: Behold, I have blessed him, and will make him fruitful, and will multiply him exceedingly;

27 20 Twelve princes shall he beget, and I will make him a great nation.

28 21 But my covenant will I establish with Isaac, which Sarah shall bear unto thee at this set time in the next year.

29 22 And he left off talking with him, and God went up from Abraham.

30 23 And Abraham took Ishmael his son, and all that were born in his house, and all that were bought with his money, every male among the men of Abraham's house; and circumcised the flesh of their foreskin in the selfsame day, as God had said unto him.

31 24 And Abraham *was* ninety ~~years old~~ and nine **years old** when he was circumcised in the flesh of his foreskin.

32 25 And Ishmael ~~his son~~ *was* thirteen years old when he was circumcised in the flesh of his foreskin.

33 26–27 In the selfsame day ~~was~~ Abraham **was** circumcised, and Ishmael his son; and all the men of his house **which were** born in ~~the~~ **his** house, and bought with money of ~~the~~ ~~stranger~~ **strangers**, were **also** circumcised with him.

CHAPTER 18

1 And the LORD appeared unto ~~him~~ **Abraham** in the plains of Mamre. And he sat in ~~the~~ **his** tent door in the heat of the day;

2 2–3 And he ~~lift~~ **lifted** up his eyes and looked, and lo, three men stood by him; and when he saw ~~them~~, he ran to meet them from his tent door, and bowed himself toward the ground, and said;

3 My ~~LORD~~ **brethren**, if now I have found favor in ~~thy~~ **your** sight, pass not away I pray ~~thee~~ **you** from thy servant.

4 4–5 Let a little water I pray you be fetched, and wash your feet, and rest yourselves under the tree, and I will fetch a morsel of bread, and comfort ye your hearts; after that ~~ye~~ **you** shall pass on; for therefore are ye come to your servant. And they said, So do, as thou hast said.

5 6 And Abraham hastened into the tent unto Sarah, and said, Make ready quickly three measures of fine meal, knead ~~it~~, and make cakes upon the hearth.

6 7 And Abraham ran unto the herd, and fetcht a calf tender and good, and gave *it* unto a young man; and he hasted to dress it.

7 8 And he took butter and milk, and the calf which he had dressed, and set ~~it~~ **them** before them, and he

stood by them under the tree, and they did eat.

8 9 And they said unto him, Where *is* Sarah thy wife? And he said, Behold, in the tent.

9 10 **And one of them blessed Abraham,** and he said, I will certainly return unto thee **from my journey, and lo,** according to the time of life, ~~and, lo,~~ Sarah thy wife shall have a son.

10 And Sarah heard ~~it~~ **him,** in the tent door ~~which was behind him~~.

11 **And** now Abraham and Sarah ~~were~~ **being** old, *and* ~~well~~ stricken in age; ~~and~~ **therefore** it **had** ceased to be with Sarah after the manner of women;

12 Therefore Sarah laughed within herself, saying, After I ~~am~~ **have** waxed old shall I have pleasure, my lord being old also?

13 13–14 And the **angel of the** LORD said unto Abraham, Wherefore did Sarah laugh, saying, Shall I of a surety bear a child, which am old? Is anything too hard for the LORD?

14 At the time appointed**, behold,** I will return unto thee **from my journey, which the Lord hath sent me; and** according to the time of life ~~and~~ **thou mayest know that** Sarah shall have a son.

15 Then Sarah denied, saying, I laughed not; for she was afraid. And he said, Nay; but thou didst laugh.

16 And the ~~men~~ **angels** rose up from thence, and looked toward Sodom; and Abraham went with them to bring them on the way.

17 17–18 And the **angel of the** LORD**,** said, Shall I hide from Abraham that thing which ~~I~~ **the Lord will** do **for him;** seeing that Abraham shall surely become a great and mighty nation, and all the nations of the earth shall be blessed in him?

18 19 For I know him, that he will command his children and his household after him, and they shall keep the way of the LORD, to do justice and judgment; that the LORD may bring upon Abraham that which he hath spoken of him.

19 20 And the **angel of the** LORD said **unto Abraham, The Lord said unto us,** Because the cry of Sodom and Gomorrah is great, and because their sin is very grievous**, I will destroy them.**

20 21 **And** I will **send you, and ye shall** go down now, and see ~~whether they~~ **that their iniquities are rewarded unto them.**

21 **And ye shall** have **all things** done altogether according to the cry of it, which is come unto me ~~and if not, I will know.~~

22 And if ye do it not, it shall be upon your heads; for I will destroy them, and you shall know that I will do it, for it shall be before your eyes.

23 22 And the ~~men~~ **angels which were holy men, and were sent forth after the order of God,** turned their faces from thence and went toward Sodom.

24 22 But Abraham stood yet before the LORD, **remembering the things which had been told him.**

25 23 And Abraham drew near **to Sodom,** and said **unto the Lord, calling upon his name, saying,** Wilt thou ~~also~~ destroy the righteous with the wicked? **Wilt thou not spare them?**

26 24 Peradventure there **may** be fifty righteous within the city**,** wilt thou also destroy and not spare the place for the fifty righteous that ~~are~~ **may be** therein?

27 25 **O may** that be far from thee to do after this manner, to slay the righteous with the wicked**;** and that the righteous should be as the wicked**.**

28 25 **O God, may** that be far from thee, **for** shall not the Judge of all the earth do right?

29 26 And the LORD said **unto Abraham,** If ~~I~~ **thou** ~~find~~ **findest** in Sodom, fifty righteous within the city, then I will spare all the place for their sakes.

30 27 And Abraham answered and said, Behold**,** now, I have taken upon me to speak unto the Lord, which ~~am but~~ **is able to destroy the city, and lay all the people in** dust and ashes**;**

31 28 **Will the Lord spare them** peradventure there ~~shall~~ lack five of the fifty righteous**;** wilt thou destroy all the city for ~~lack of~~ **their wickedness, if I find there forty and** five **righteous**?

32 28 And he said, ~~If I find there forty and five~~ I will not destroy ~~it~~, **but spare them.**

33 29 And he spake unto him ~~yet~~ again, and said, Peradventure there ~~shall~~ **should** be forty found there?

34 29 And he said, I will not ~~do~~ **destroy** ~~it~~ for forty's sake.

35 30 And he said **again** unto ~~him~~ **the Lord,** ~~Oh~~ **O,** let not the Lord be angry, and I will speak**;** Peradventure there shall thirty be found there?

36 30 And he said, I will not ~~do~~ **destroy** ~~it~~ **them** if ~~I~~ **thou shalt** find thirty there.

37 31 And he said, Behold now, I have taken upon me to speak unto the Lord**; wilt thou destroy them if** peradventure there shall ~~be~~ twenty **be** found there?

38 31 And he said, I will not destroy ~~it~~ **them** for twenty's sake.

39 32 And ~~he~~ **Abraham** said **unto the Lord,** ~~Oh~~ **O,** let not the Lord be angry, and I will speak yet but this once, Peradventure ten shall be found there?

40 32 And ~~he~~ **the Lord** said, I will not destroy ~~it~~ **them** for ten's sake. **And the Lord ceased speaking with Abraham.**

41 33 And ~~the Lord went his way~~ as soon as he had left communing with **the Lord,** Abraham **went his way.**

42 33 And **it came to pass that** Abraham returned unto his ~~place~~ **tent**.

CHAPTER 19

1 And **it came to pass, that** there came ~~two~~ **three** angels to Sodom ~~at even~~ **in the evening**; and Lot sat in the ~~gate~~ **door of his house, in the city** of Sodom.

2 1 And Lot, seeing ~~them~~ **the angels,** rose up to meet them; and he bowed himself with his face toward the ground;

3 2 And he said, Behold now, my lords, turn in, I pray you, into your servant's house, and tarry all night, and wash your feet, and ye shall rise up early, and go on your ways.

4 2 And they said, Nay; but we will abide in the street all night.

5 3 And he pressed upon them greatly; and they turned in unto him, and entered into his house; and he made them a feast, and did bake unleavened bread, and they did eat.

6 4 But before they lay down **to rest,** the men of the city ~~even the men~~ of Sodom compassed the house round, **even men which were** both old and young, ~~all~~ **even** the people from every quarter;

7 5 And they called unto Lot, and said unto him, Where *are* the men which came ~~in~~* ~~to~~ **unto** thee this night? bring them out unto us, that we may know them.

8 6–7 And Lot went out ~~at~~ **of** the door, unto them, and shut the door after him, and said, I pray you, brethren, do not so wickedly.

9 And they said **unto him,** Stand back. **And they were angry with him.**

10 9 And they said *again* **among themselves,** This one *fellow* **man** came in to sojourn **among us,** and he will needs **now make himself to** be a judge; now ~~will~~ we **will** deal worse with ~~thee~~ **him** than with them.

11 Wherefore they said unto the man, We will have the men, and thy daughters also; and we will do with them as seemeth us good.

12 Now this was after the wickedness of Sodom.

13 8 **And Lot said,** Behold now, I have two daughters which have not known man; let me, I pray you, **plead with my brethren that I may not** bring them out unto you; and **ye shall not** do ~~ye to~~ **unto** them as *is* **seemeth** good in your eyes;

14 8 **For God will not justify his servant in this thing; wherefore, let me plead with my brethren, this once** only, **that** unto these men ye do nothing, **that they may have peace in my house;** for therefore came they under the shadow of my roof.

15 9–10 And they ~~pressed sore upon the man, even~~ **were angry with** Lot and came near to break the door, but the ~~men~~ **angels of God, which were holy men,** put forth their hand and pulled Lot into the house to them, and shut the door.

16 11 And they smote the men ~~that were at the door of the house~~ with blindness, both small and great, **that they could not come at the door.**

17 11 **And they were angry,** so that they wearied themselves to find the door, **and could not find it**.

18 12 And ~~the~~ **these holy** men said unto Lot, Hast thou **any** here ~~any~~ besides **thy** ~~son in law~~ **sons-in-law**, and thy **sons'** * sons and thy daughters?

19 12–13 And **they commanded Lot, saying,** Whatsoever thou hast in the city, **thou shalt** bring ~~them~~ out of this place, for we will destroy this place;

20 13 Because the cry of them is waxen great, **and their abominations have come up** before the face of the Lord; and the Lord hath sent us to destroy it.

21 14 And Lot went out, and spake unto his sons in law, which married his daughters, and said, Up, get you out of this place; for the Lord will destroy this city.

22 14 But he seemed as one that mocked unto his sons in law.

23 15 And when the morning ~~arose~~ **came**, ~~then~~ the angels hastened Lot, saying, Arise, take thy wife, and thy two daughters which are here, lest thou be consumed in the iniquity of the city.

24 16 And while he lingered the ~~men~~ **angels** laid hold upon his hand, and upon the hand of his wife, and upon the hand of his two daughters; the Lord being merciful unto ~~him~~ **them;** and they brought ~~him~~ **them** forth, and set ~~him~~ **them down** without the city.

25 17 And it came to pass, when they had brought them forth abroad that ~~he~~ **they** said **unto them**, Escape for ~~thy~~ **your** ~~life~~ **lives**; look not behind ~~thee~~ **you**, neither stay ~~thou~~ **you** in all the plain; escape to the mountain lest ~~thou~~ **you** be consumed.

26 18–19 And Lot said unto **one of** them, Oh, not so my Lord! behold now, thy servant ~~hath~~ **has** found grace in thy sight, and thou hast magnified thy mercy which thou hast showed unto me in saving my life; and I cannot escape to the mountain, lest some evil ~~take~~ **overtake** me, and I die.

27 20 Behold now, **here is another city, and** this ~~city~~ *is* near to flee unto, and it *is* a little one; Oh, let me escape thither, ~~is it not a little one~~ **and may the Lord not** * **destroy it,** and my soul shall live.

28 21–22 And ~~he~~ **the angel** said unto him, See, I have accepted thee concerning this thing also, that I will not overthrow this city, for the which thou hast spoken; haste thee, escape thither, for I cannot do anything until thou be come thither.

29 22–23 ~~Therefore~~ **And** the name of the city was called Zoar. **Therefore** the sun was risen upon the earth when Lot entered into Zoar.

30 And the Lord did not destroy Sodom until Lot had entered into Zoar.

31 24 **And then, when Lot had entered into Zoar,** the Lord rained upon Sodom, and upon Gomorrah; **for the angels called upon the name of the Lord for** brimstone and fire from the Lord out of heaven.

32 25 And **thus** ~~he~~ **they** overthrew those cities and all the plain, and all the inhabitants of the cities, and that which grew upon the ground.

33 26 But **it came to pass, when Lot fled,** his wife looked back from behind him, and ~~she~~ became a pillar of salt.

34 27–28 And Abraham ~~gat~~ **got** up early in the morning to the place where he stood before the Lord; and he looked toward Sodom and Gomorrah, and toward all the land of the plain, and beheld, ~~and~~ lo, the smoke of the country went up as the smoke of a furnace.

35 29 And it came to pass, when God **had** destroyed the cities of the plain, that God **spake unto Abraham, saying, I have** remembered ~~Abraham~~ **Lot**, and sent ~~Lot~~ **him** out of the midst of the overthrow, **that thy brother might not be destroyed,** when ~~he~~ **I** overthrew the ~~cities~~ **city** in the which **thy brother** Lot dwelt.

36 30 **And Abraham was comforted.** And Lot went up out of Zoar, and dwelt in the mountain, and his two daughters with him; for he feared to dwell in Zoar. And he dwelt in a cave, he and his two daughters.

37 31 And the firstborn **dealt wickedly, and** said unto the younger, Our father ~~is~~ **has become** old, and ~~there is~~ **we have** not a man ~~in~~ **on** the earth to come in unto us, **to live with us** after the manner of all **that live on** the earth;

38 32 Therefore come, let us make our father drink wine, and we will lie with him, that we may preserve seed of our father.

39 33 And they **did wickedly, and** made their father drink wine that night; and the firstborn went in and lay with her father; and he perceived not when she lay down, nor when she arose.

40 34 And it came to pass on the morrow, that the firstborn said unto the younger, Behold, I lay yesternight with my father: let us make him drink wine this night also; and go thou in, *and* lie with him, that we may preserve seed of our father.

41 35 And they made their father drink wine that night also: and the younger arose, and lay with him; and he perceived not when she lay down, nor when she arose.

42 36 Thus were both the daughters of Lot with child by their father.

43 37 And the firstborn bare a son, and called his name Moab; ~~the same is~~ the father of the Moabites, **the same which are** unto this day.

44 38 And the younger, she also bare a son, and called his name Benammi; ~~the same is~~ the father of the children ~~of~~ **which are** ~~Ammon~~ **Ammonites; the same which are** unto this day.

1 And Abraham journeyed from thence toward the south country, and dwelled between Kadesh and Shur, and sojourned in Gerar.

2 And Abraham said **again** of Sarah his wife, She *is* my sister.

3 2–3 And Abimelech, king of Gerar, sent and took Sarah. But God came to Abimelech in a dream by night, and said to him, Behold, thou ~~art but a dead man for~~ **hast taken** ~~the~~ **a** woman which ~~thou hast taken~~ **is not thine own,** for she *is* ~~a man's~~ **Abraham's** wife.

4 **And the Lord said unto him, Thou shalt return her unto Abraham, for if thou do it not thou shalt die.**

5 4 ~~But~~ **And** Abimelech had not come near her; **for the Lord had not suffered him.**

6 4–5 And he said, Lord, wilt thou slay **me, and** also a righteous nation? **Behold,** said he not unto me, She *is* my sister? And she, even she herself said, He *is* my brother; **and** in the integrity of my heart, and innocency of my hands have I done this.

7 6 And God said unto him in a dream, Yea, I know that thou didst **do** this in the integrity of thy heart; for I also withheld thee from sinning against me; therefore suffered I **not** thee ~~not~~ to touch her.

8 7 Now, therefore, restore the ~~man~~ **man's** ~~his~~ wife **to him,** for he *is* a

prophet, and he shall pray for thee, and thou shalt live; and if thou restore *her* not **to him**, know thou that thou shalt surely die; thou and all that *are* thine.

9 8 Therefore, Abimelech rose early in the morning, and called ~~all~~ his servants, and told all these things in their ears; and the men were sore afraid.

10 9 Then Abimelech called Abraham, and said unto him, What hast thou done unto us? and **in** what have I offended thee, that thou hast brought on me and on my kingdom a great sin?

11 9–10 Thou hast done ~~deeds~~ **things** unto me that ought not to be done. And Abimelech said unto Abraham, What sawest thou, that thou hast done this thing?

12 11 And Abraham said, Because I thought ~~Surely~~ **assuredly** the fear of God *is* **was** not in this place, and they ~~will~~ **would** slay me for my wife's sake.

13 12 And yet indeed *she* ~~is~~ **was** my sister; she ~~is~~ **was** the daughter of my father, but not the daughter of my mother; and she became my wife.

14 13 And it came to pass, when God caused me to wander from my father's house, that I said unto her, This ~~is~~ **shall be** thy kindness which thou shalt show unto me, at every place whither we shall come, say of me, He *is* my brother.

15 14 And Abimelech took sheep and oxen, and menservants, and womenservants, and gave *them* unto Abraham, and restored **unto** him Sarah his wife.

16 15 And Abimelech said, Behold, my land ~~is~~ **lieth** before thee; dwell where it pleaseth thee.

17 16 And unto Sarah he said, Behold, I have given thy brother a thousand *pieces* of silver; behold, he ~~is~~

shall give ~~to~~ **unto** thee a covering of the eyes, **and it shall be a token** unto all that ~~are with thee, and with all other~~ **thou mayest not be taken again from Abraham thy husband. And** thus she was reproved.

18 17 So Abraham prayed unto God; and God healed Abimelech, and his wife, and his maidservants; and they bare **unto him** *children*.

19 18 For **because of Sarah, Abraham's wife,** the LORD had fast closed up all the wombs of the house of Abimelech ~~because of Sarah Abraham's wife~~.

CHAPTER 21

1 1–2 And the LORD visited Sarah as he had said, and the LORD did unto Sarah as he had spoken **by the mouth of his angels;** for Sarah conceived and ~~bare~~ **bear** Abraham a son in his old age, at the set time of which **the angels of** God had spoken to him.

2 3 And Abraham called the name of his son that was born unto him, whom Sarah bare to him, Isaac.

3 4 And Abraham circumcised his son Isaac, **he** being eight days old, as God had commanded him.

4 5 And Abraham was an hundred years old, when his son Isaac was born unto him.

5 6 And Sarah said, God hath made me to ~~laugh~~ **rejoice**, ~~so that~~ **and also** all that ~~hear~~ **know me** will ~~laugh~~ **rejoice** with me.

6 7 And she said **unto Abraham**, Who would have said ~~unto Abraham~~ that Sarah should have given children suck? For **I was barren, but the Lord promised, and** I have borne ~~him~~ **unto Abraham** a son in his old age.

7 8–9 And the child grew, and was weaned. And **the day that Isaac was weaned,** Abraham made a great feast ~~the same day that Isaac was weaned,~~

and Sarah saw the son of Hagar the Egyptian, which ~~she~~ **Hagar** had borne unto Abraham, mocking; **and she was troubled.**

8 10 Wherefore she said unto Abraham, Cast out this bondwoman and her son; for the son of this bondwoman shall not be heir with my son, ~~even with~~ Isaac.

9 11 And ~~the~~ **this** thing was very grievous ~~in~~ **unto** ~~Abraham's~~ **Abraham** ~~sight~~ because of his son.

10 12 And God said unto Abraham, Let it not be grievous in thy sight because of the lad, and because of thy bondwoman; in all that Sarah hath said unto thee, hearken unto her voice; for in Isaac shall thy seed be called.

11 13 And also of the son of the bondwoman will I make a nation, because he *is* thy seed.

12 14 And Abraham rose up early in the morning, and took bread, and a bottle of water, and gave *it* unto Hagar, ~~putting it on her shoulder~~ and **she took** the child, and **he** sent her away; and she departed, and wandered in the wilderness of Beer-sheba.

13 15–16 And **it came to pass that** the water was spent in the bottle, and she cast the child under one of the shrubs, and she went and sat her down over against ~~him~~ **the child**, a good way off, as it were a bowshot; for she said, Let me not see the death of the child.

14 16 And she sat over against ~~him~~ **the child**, and ~~lift~~ **lifted** up her voice and wept.

15 17 And God heard the voice of the lad; and the angel of ~~God~~ **the Lord** called to Hagar out of heaven, and said unto her;

16 17–18 What aileth thee, Hagar? fear not, for God hath heard the voice of the lad where he ~~is~~ **lieth**; arise, lift

up the lad, and hold him in thine hand, for I will make **of** him a great nation.

17 19 And God opened her eyes, and she saw a well of water; and she went, and filled the bottle with water, and gave the lad drink.

18 20–21 And God was with the lad; and he grew, and dwelt in the wilderness, and became an archer; and he dwelt in the wilderness of Paran, **he** and his mother.

19 21 **And he** took him a wife out of the land of Egypt.

20 22 And it came to pass at that time, that Abimelech and ~~Phichol~~ **Phicol** the chief captain of his host spake unto Abraham, saying, God *is* with thee in all that thou doest.

21 23 Now therefore, swear unto me here, **that,** by **the help of** God ~~that~~ thou wilt not deal falsely with me, nor with my son, nor with my son's son; *but,* **that** according to the kindness that I have ~~done~~ **shown** unto thee, thou shalt do unto me, and to the land wherein thou hast sojourned.

22 24 And Abraham said, I will swear.

23 25 And Abraham reproved Abimelech because of a well of water, which Abimelech's servants had ~~violently~~ **recently** taken away.

24 26 And Abimelech said, **Thou didst not tell me; and** I ~~wot~~ **know** not who hath done this thing; ~~neither didst thou tell me~~ neither yet **have I** heard ~~I of~~ **that** *it* **was done** ~~but~~ **until** ~~to~~ **this** day.

25 27 And Abraham took sheep and oxen, and gave them unto Abimelech; and both of them made a covenant.

26 28 And Abraham set seven ewe lambs of the flock by themselves.

27 29 And Abimelech said unto

Abraham, What ~~mean~~ **wilt thou do with** these seven ewe lambs which thou hast set by themselves?

28 30 And he said, ~~For these~~ Seven ewe lambs shalt thou take ~~of~~ **at** my hand, that they may be a witness unto me that I have digged this well.

29 31 **And because they sware, both of them,** wherefore he called that place Beer-sheba ~~because there they sware both of them;~~

30 32 **And** thus they made a covenant at Beer-sheba.

31 32–33 Then Abimelech ~~rose up,~~ and ~~Phichol~~ **Phicol,** the chief captain of his ~~host~~ **hosts, rose up, and they planted a grove in Beer-sheba, and called there on the name of the Lord;** and they returned ~~into~~ **unto** the land of the Philistines.

32 33–34 And *Abraham* ~~planted a grove in Beer-sheba, and called there on the name of the~~ Lord **worshiped** the everlasting God, and ~~Abraham~~ sojourned in **the land of** the ~~Philistines'~~ **Philistines** ~~land~~ many days.

Chapter 22

1 And it came to pass after these things, that God did ~~tempt~~ **try** Abraham and said unto him, Abraham; and ~~he~~ **Abraham** said, Behold, *here I am* **I**.

2 And ~~he~~ **the Lord** said, Take now thy son, thine only ~~son~~ Isaac, whom thou lovest, and get thee into the land of Moriah; and offer him there for a burnt offering, upon one of the mountains which I will tell thee ~~of~~.

3 And Abraham rose up early in the morning, and saddled his ass, and took two of his young men with him, and Isaac his son,

4 3 And clave the wood for the burnt offering, and rose up, and went unto the place of which God had told him.

5 4 Then on the third day Abraham lifted up his eyes, and saw the place afar off.

6 5 And Abraham said unto his young men, Abide ~~ye~~ **you** here with the ass, and I and the lad will go yonder and worship, and come ~~again~~ to you **again**.

7 6 And Abraham took the wood of the burnt offering, and laid *it* upon ~~Isaac~~ his ~~son~~ **back**; and he took the fire in his hand, and a knife, **and Isaac his son;** and they went both of them together.

8 7 And Isaac spake unto Abraham his father, and said, My father: and he said, Here *am* I, my son.

9 7 And he said, Behold the fire and the wood: but where *is* the lamb for a burnt offering?

10 8–9 And Abraham said, My son, God will provide himself a lamb for a burnt offering. So they went both of them together; and they came to the place **of** which God had told him ~~of~~.

11 9 And Abraham built an altar there, and laid the wood in order, and bound Isaac his son, and laid him on the altar upon the wood.

12 10 And Abraham stretched forth his hand, and took the knife to slay his son.

13 11 And the angel of the Lord called unto him out of heaven, and said, Abraham! Abraham! And ~~he~~ **Abraham** said, Here *am* I.

14 12 And ~~he~~ **the angel** said, Lay not thine hand upon the lad, neither do thou anything unto him;

15 12 For now I know that thou fearest God, seeing thou hast not withheld thy son, thine only ~~son~~ **Isaac** from me.

16 13 And Abraham lifted up his eyes and looked, and behold, behind ~~him~~ **a thicket, there was** a ram caught in ~~a thicket~~ **it** by his horns.

17 13 And Abraham went and took the ram, and offered him up for a burnt offering in the stead of his son.

18 14 And Abraham called the name of that place Jehovah-jireh: as it is said ~~to~~ **unto** this day, In the ~~mount~~ **mountain** of the Lord it shall be seen.

19 15 And the angel of the Lord called unto Abraham out of heaven the second time, **and said,**

20 16 ~~And said~~ **Thus saith the Lord,** ~~By myself~~ I have ~~I~~ sworn **by myself,** ~~saith the Lord, for~~ **that*** because thou hast done this thing, and hast not withheld thy son, thine only ~~son~~ **Isaac from me;**

21 17 That in blessing I will bless thee; and in multiplying I will multiply thy seed as the stars of ~~the~~ heaven, and as the sand ~~which is~~ upon the seashore.

22 17–18 And thy seed shall possess the gate of his enemies; and in thy seed shall all the nations of the earth be blessed; because thou hast obeyed my voice.

23 19 So Abraham returned unto his young men, and they rose up and went ~~together~~ to Beer-sheba; and Abraham dwelt at Beer-sheba.

24 20 And it came to pass after these things, that it was told Abraham, saying,

25 20–21 Behold, Milcah, she hath also ~~born~~ **borne** children unto thy brother Nahor; Huz **is** his firstborn, and Buz **is** his brother,

26 21–22 And Kemuel **is** the father of Aram, and Chesed, and ~~Hazo~~ **Haza**, and ~~Pildash~~ **Bildash**, and Jidlaph, and Bethuel;

27 23 And Bethuel begat Rebekah:

28 23–24 These eight Milcah did bear to Nahor, Abraham's brother; and his concubine, whose name *was*

Reumah, she bare also Tebah, and Gaham, ~~and~~ Thahash, and Maachah.

CHAPTER 23

1 And Sarah was an hundred and ~~seven and twenty~~ **twenty-seven** years old, **and she died;** ~~these were~~ **and thus ended** the years of the life of Sarah.

2 And Sarah died in Kirjath-arba; the same *is* **now called** Hebron, in the land of Canaan.

3 2 And Abraham came to mourn for Sarah, and to weep for her, **his wife which was dead.**

4 3–4 And Abraham stood up from before his dead, and spake unto the sons of Heth, saying, I *am* a stranger and a sojourner with you: give me a possession of a buryingplace with you, that I may bury my dead out of my sight.

5 5–6 And the children of Heth answered Abraham, saying unto him, Hear us, my lord; thou *art* a mighty prince among us; in the ~~choice~~ **choicest** of our sepulchres bury **thou** thy dead; none of us shall withhold from thee his sepulchre, but that thou mayest bury thy dead.

6 7–8 And Abraham stood up, and bowed himself to the people of the land, ~~even~~ **and** to the children of Heth; and he communed with them, saying,

7 8–9 If it be your mind that I should bury my dead out of my sight, hear me, and entreat ~~for me to~~ Ephron the son of Zohar **for me**, that he may give me the cave of Machpelah, which he hath ~~which is~~ in the end of his field;

8 9 For, as much money as it is worth **he shall have, if** he ~~shall~~ **will** give it me for a possession of a buryingplace ~~amongst~~ **among** you.

9 10 And Ephron dwelt among the children of Heth:

10 And Ephron, the Hittite answered Abraham in the audience of the children of Heth, ~~even~~ of **among** all **of them** that went in at the ~~gate~~ **gates** of ~~his~~ **the** city, saying,

11 ~~Nay~~ **Hearken**, my lord, **and** hear me; the field **I** give ~~I~~ thee, and the cave that *is* therein; I give it thee in the presence of the sons of my people; **and I** give ~~I~~ it thee; **therefore,** bury thy dead.

12 12–13 And Abraham bowed ~~down~~ himself **down** before the people of the land, and he spake unto Ephron in the audience of the people of the land, saying, ~~But if thou *wilt give it*~~ I pray thee, hear me;

13 **If thou wilt take it of me,** I will give thee money for the field, ~~take *it* of me~~ and I will bury my dead there, **but I will give thee money for it**.

14 14–15 And Ephron answered Abraham, saying unto him, My lord, hearken unto me; the land ~~*is worth*~~ **thou shalt have for** four hundred shekels of silver; what ~~*is*~~ **shall** that **be** betwixt me and thee? Bury therefore thy dead.

15 16 And Abraham hearkened unto Ephron; and Abraham weighed ~~to~~ **unto** Ephron the silver which he had named in the audience of the sons of Heth, four hundred shekels of silver, **which was** current ~~*money*~~ with the merchant.

16 17–18 And the field of Ephron, which *was* in Machpelah, which *was* before Mamre; the field, and the cave which *was* therein, and all the trees that *were* in the field, that *were* in all the borders round about, were made sure unto Abraham for a possession, in the presence of the children of Heth, before all that went in at the gate of ~~his~~ **the** city.

17 19 And after this, Abraham buried Sarah his wife in the cave of the field of Machpelah, **which is** before Mamre; the same *is* **called** Hebron, in the land of Canaan.

18 20 And the field and the cave that ~~*is*~~ **was** therein, were made sure unto Abraham for a possession of a buryingplace by the sons of Heth.

Chapter 24

1 And now Abraham was old, ~~and~~ **being** well stricken in age; and the Lord had blessed Abraham in all things.

2 2–4 And Abraham said unto his eldest servant of his house, that ruled over all that he had; Put **forth** I pray thee thy hand under my ~~thigh~~ **hand,** and I will make thee swear ~~by~~ **before** the Lord, the God of heaven, and the God of the earth, that thou shalt not take a wife unto my son, of the daughters of the Canaanites among whom I dwell; but thou shalt go unto my country, and to my kindred and take a wife unto my son Isaac.

3 5 And the servant said unto him, ~~Peradventure~~ **Perhaps** the woman will not be willing to follow me unto this land, **then I** must ~~I~~ needs bring thy son again unto the land from whence thou camest.

4 6 And Abraham said unto him, Beware thou that thou bring not my son thither again.

5 7 The Lord God of heaven which took me from my father's house, and from the land of my kindred, and which spake unto me, and that sware unto me, saying, Unto ~~thy seed~~ **thee** will I give this land;

6 7 He shall send his angel before thee, and thou shalt take a wife unto my son from thence.

7 8 And if the woman will not be willing to follow thee, then thou shalt

be clear from this ~~my~~ **thine** oath, only bring not my son thither again.

8 9 And the servant put his hand under the ~~thigh~~ **hand** of Abraham his master, and sware to him concerning that matter.

9 10 And the servant took ten camels ~~of the camels~~ of his master, and departed; for all the goods of his master *were* in his hand**.**

10 And he arose, and went to Mesopotamia, unto the city of Nahor.

11 And he made his camels to kneel down without the city**,** by a well of water**,** at ~~the time of the~~ evening, *even* the time that women go out to draw *water*.

12 And he said, O LORD God of my master Abraham, I pray thee ~~send me good speed~~ this day, ~~and~~ **that thou wouldst** show kindness unto my master Abraham**, and send me good speed**.

13 Behold, I stand ~~here~~ by the well of water**,** and the daughters of the men of the city come out to draw water**;**

14 And let it come to pass, that the damsel to whom I shall say, Let down thy pitcher I pray thee, that I may drink; and she shall say, Drink, and I will give thy camels drink also**;** *let the same* **her** *be* ~~she~~ **the one** ~~that~~ **whom** thou hast appointed for thy servant Isaac; and thereby shall I know that thou hast showed kindness unto my master.

15 And it came to pass, before he had done speaking, that, behold, Rebekah came out, who was born to Bethuel, son of Milcah, the wife of Nahor, Abraham's brother, with her pitcher upon her shoulder.

16 And the damsel **being a virgin,** ~~was~~ very fair to look upon, ~~a virgin~~ **such as the servant of Abraham had**

not seen, neither had any man known **the like unto** her; and she went down to the well, and filled her pitcher, and came up.

17 And the servant ran to meet her, and said, Let me, I pray thee, drink a little water of thy pitcher.

18 And she said, Drink, my lord: and she hasted, and let down her pitcher upon her hand, and gave him drink.

19 And when she had done giving him drink, she said, I will draw ~~water~~ for thy camels also, until they have done drinking.

20 And she hasted, and emptied her pitcher into the trough, and ran again unto the well to draw ~~water~~, and drew for all his camels.

21 And the man**,** wondering at her**,** held his peace, ~~to wit~~ **pondering in his heart** whether the LORD had made his journey prosperous or not.

22 22–23 And it came to pass, as the camels had done drinking, that the man took a golden earring of half a shekel weight, and two bracelets for her hands of ten *shekels* weight of gold**,** and said, Whose daughter *art* thou? tell me, I pray thee**; and** is there room *in* thy father's house for us to lodge in?

23 24 And she said unto him, I *am* the daughter of Bethuel the son of Milcah, which she bare unto Nahor.

24 25 She said moreover unto him, We have both straw and provender enough, and room to lodge in.

25 26 And the man bowed down his head, and worshipped the LORD.

26 27 And he said, Blessed ~~be~~ **is** the LORD God of my master Abraham, who hath not left ~~destitute~~ my master **destitute** of his mercy and his truth**; and when** I ~~being~~ **was** in the way, the LORD led me to the house of my master's brethren.

27 28 And the damsel ran **to the house**, and told ~~them of~~ her ~~mother's~~ **mother** ~~house~~ these things.

28 29 And Rebekah had a brother, ~~and his~~ **whose** name *was* Laban; and Laban ran out unto the man, unto the well.

29 30 And it came to pass when he saw the ~~earring~~ **earrings,** and bracelets upon his sister's hands, and when he heard the words of Rebekah his sister, saying, Thus spake the man unto me, ~~that~~ **and** ~~he~~ **I** came unto the man, and behold, he stood by the camels at the well.

30 31 And he said, Come in, thou blessed of the LORD; wherefore standest thou without? for I have prepared the house, and room for the camels.

31 32 And the man came into the house:

32 And he ~~ungirded~~ **unburdened** his camels, and gave straw and provender for the camels, and water to wash his feet, and the men's feet that ~~were~~ **came** with him.

33 And there was set ~~meat~~ **food** before him to eat; but he said, I will not eat until I have told mine errand.

34 33–34 And ~~he~~ **Laban** said, Speak on. And he said, I *am* Abraham's servant;

35 And the LORD hath blessed my master greatly; and he is become great: and he hath given him flocks, and herds, and silver, and gold, and menservants, and maidservants, and camels, and asses.

36 And Sarah my master's wife bare a son to my master when she was old: and unto him hath he given all that he hath.

37 And my master made me swear, saying, Thou shalt not take a wife to my son of the daughters of the Canaanites, in whose land I dwell:

38 But thou shalt go unto my father's house, and to my kindred, and take a wife unto my son.

39 And I said unto my master, ~~Peradventure~~ **Perhaps** the woman will not follow me.

40 And he said unto me, The LORD, before whom I walk, will send his angel with thee, and **he will** prosper thy way;

41 40–41 And thou shalt take a wife for my son, of my kindred, and of my father's house; then shalt thou be clear ~~from~~ **of** ~~this~~ my oath.

42 41 When thou comest to my kindred, and if they give **thee** not ~~thee one~~ **a wife for my son**, thou shalt be clear from my oath.

43 42 And I came this day unto the well, and said, O LORD God of my master Abraham, if now thou ~~do~~ **wilt** prosper my way which I go;

44 43 Behold, I stand by the well of water; and it shall come to pass, that when the virgin cometh forth to draw *water*, and I say to her, Give me, I pray thee, a little water of thy pitcher to drink;

45 44 And **if** she say to me, Both drink thou, and I will also draw for thy camels; ~~let~~ the same ~~be~~ **is** the woman whom the LORD hath appointed out for my master's son.

46 45 And before I had done speaking in mine heart, behold, Rebekah came forth with her pitcher on her shoulder; and she went down unto the well, and drew *water*:

47 45 And I said unto her, Let me drink, I pray thee.

48 46 And she made haste, and let down her pitcher from her *shoulder*, and said, Drink, and I will give thy camels drink also: so I drank, and she made the camels drink also.

49 47 And I asked her, and said,

Whose daughter *art* thou?

50 47 And she said, The daughter of Bethuel, Nahor's son, whom Milcah bare unto him:

51 47 And I ~~put~~ **gave** the ~~earring~~ **earrings** ~~upon~~ **unto** her ~~face,~~ **to put into her ears,** and the bracelets upon her hands.

52 48 And I bowed down my head, and worshiped the Lord, and blessed the Lord God of my master Abraham, which had led me in the right way to take my master's brother's daughter unto his son.

53 49 And now if ye will deal kindly and truly with my master, tell me: and if not, tell me; that I may turn to the right hand, or to the left.

54 50 Then Laban and Bethuel answered and said, The thing proceedeth from the Lord: we cannot speak unto thee bad or good.

55 51 Behold, Rebekah *is* before thee, take *her*, and go, and let her be thy master's son's wife, as the Lord hath spoken.

56 52 And it came to pass, that, when Abraham's servant heard ~~their~~ **these** words, he worshiped the Lord, *bowing himself* to the earth.

57 53 And the servant brought forth jewels of silver, and jewels of gold, and raiment, and gave ~~them~~ to Rebekah. He gave also to her brother**,** and to her mother**,** precious things.

58 54 And they did eat and drink, he and the men that *were* with him, and tarried all night;

59 54 And they rose up in the morning, and he said, Send me away unto my master.

60 55 And her brother**,** and her mother**,** said, Let the damsel abide with us ~~a few days~~ at the least ten **days;** after that she shall go.

61 56 And he said unto them,

Hinder me not, seeing the Lord hath prospered my way; send me away that I may go to my master.

62 57 And they said, We will call the damsel, and enquire at her mouth.

63 58 And they called Rebekah, and said unto her, Wilt thou go with this man?

64 58–59 And she said, I will go. And they sent away Rebekah their sister, and her nurse, and Abraham's servant, and his men.

65 60 And they blessed Rebekah, and said unto her, **O** thou ~~art,~~ our sister, be thou ~~the mother~~ **blessed** of thousands—of millions**;** and let thy seed possess the gate of those ~~which~~ **who** hate them.

66 61 And Rebekah arose, and her damsels, and they rode upon the camels, and followed the man: and the servant took Rebekah, and went his way.

67 62 And Isaac came from the way of the well Lahai-roi; for he dwelt in the south country.

68 63 And Isaac went out to meditate in the field at eventide**;** and he lifted up his eyes, and saw, and behold the camels ~~were~~ coming.

69 64–65 And Rebekah lifted up her eyes, and when she saw Isaac, she lighted off the camel**;** for she ~~had~~ said unto the servant, What man *is* this that walketh in the field to meet us?

70 65 And the servant ~~had~~ said, It *is* my master: therefore she took a ~~vail~~ **veil**, and covered herself.

71 66 And the servant told Isaac all things that he had done.

72 67 And Isaac brought her into his mother Sarah's tent, and took Rebekah, and she became his wife; and he loved her:

73 67 And Isaac was comforted after his mother's *death.*

[Only verses with number or text revisions are included in the remainder of the Old Testament.]

CHAPTER 25

7 And these *are* the ~~days~~ **number** of the years of Abraham's life**,** which he lived, ~~an~~ **a** hundred threescore and fifteen years.

17 And these *are* **the number of** the years of the life of Ishmael, ~~an~~ **a** hundred and thirty and seven years**;** and he gave up the ghost and died**,** and was gathered unto his people.

21 And Isaac entreated the LORD for his wife, **that she might bare children,** because she *was* barren**.** And the LORD was entreated of him, and Rebekah his wife conceived.

22 And the children struggled together within her **womb**; and she said, If ~~it be so~~ **I am with child**, why ~~am~~ **is** ~~I~~ **it** thus **with me**? And she went to inquire of the LORD.

32 And Esau said, Behold, I *am* at the point ~~to die~~ **of dying;** and what ~~profit~~ shall this birthright ~~do to~~ **profit** me?

CHAPTER 26

7 And the men of the place asked *him* ~~of~~ **concerning** his wife; and he said, She *is* my sister**;** for he feared to say, *She is* my wife; lest, ~~said he~~ the men of the place should kill ~~me~~ **him** for **to get** Rebekah; because she *was* fair to look upon.

9 And Abimelech called Isaac, and said, Behold, of a surety ~~she~~ **Rebekah** *is* thy wife**;** and how saidst thou she *is* ~~my~~ **thy** sister? And Isaac said unto him, **I said it** because I ~~said~~ **feared** lest I die for her.

CHAPTER 28

12 And he dreamed, and behold a ladder set up on the earth, and the top of it reached to heaven; and behold the angels of God ascending and descending ~~on~~ **upon** it.

22 And **the place of** this stone which I have set *for* a pillar, shall be **the place of** God's house**;** and of all that thou shalt give me I will surely give the tenth unto thee.

CHAPTER 29

4 And Jacob said unto them, My brethren, **from** whence ~~be~~ **are** ye? And they said, ~~Of~~ **From** Haran ~~are we~~.

21 And Jacob said unto Laban, Give ~~me~~ **unto me** my wife, **that I may go and take her,** for my days **of serving thee** are fulfilled ~~that I may go in unto her.~~

22 And Laban **gave her to Jacob, and** gathered together all the men of the place, and made a feast.

23 And it came to pass in the evening, that he took Leah his daughter, and brought her to ~~him~~ **Jacob**, and ~~he~~ **she** went in ~~unto her~~ **and slept with him**.

24 And Laban gave unto his daughter Leah**,** Zilpah, his ~~maid~~ **handmaid**, ~~for~~ **to be** ~~an~~ **a** handmaid **for her**.

30 And he went in also ~~unto~~ **and slept with** Rachel, and he loved **Rachel** also ~~Rachel~~, more than Leah, and served with ~~him~~ **Laban** yet seven other years.

CHAPTER 30

3 And she said, Behold my maid Bilhah, go in ~~unto~~ **and lie with** her; and she shall bear upon my knees, that I may also have children by her.

4 And she gave him Bilhah her handmaid to wife**;** and Jacob went ~~in unto~~ **and lay with** her.

9 When Leah saw that she had left bearing, she took Zilpah her maid, and gave her **unto** Jacob to wife.

16 And Jacob came out of the field

in the evening, and Leah went out to meet him, and said, Thou must come in ~~unto~~ **and lie with** me; for surely I have hired thee with my son's mandrakes. And he lay with her that night.

CHAPTER 31

22 And it was told Laban on the third day, that Jacob ~~was~~ **had˚** fled.

CHAPTER 32

11 Deliver me, I pray thee, from the hand of my brother, from the hand of Esau; for I fear him, lest he will come and smite me, *and* the ~~mother~~ **mothers** with the children.

CHAPTER 37

2 **And** ~~These~~ **this** *are* **is the history of** the generations of Jacob. Joseph, *being* seventeen years old, was feeding the flock with his brethren; and the lad *was* with the sons of Bilhah, and with the sons of Zilpah, his father's wives; and Joseph brought unto his father their evil report.

CHAPTER 38

2 And Judah saw there a daughter of a certain Canaanite, whose name *was* Shuah; and he took her, and went in ~~unto~~ **and˚ lay with** her.

8 And Judah said unto Onan, Go ~~in unto~~ **and marry** thy brother's wife, ~~and marry her~~ and raise up seed ~~to~~ **unto** thy brother.

9 And Onan knew that the seed should not be his; and it came to pass, when he ~~went in unto~~ **married** his brother's wife, that he ~~spilled *it* on the ground~~ **would not lie with her**, lest ~~that~~ he should ~~give~~ **raise up** seed ~~to~~ **unto** his brother.

16 And he turned unto her by the way, and said, Go to, I pray thee, let me come ~~in unto~~ **and lie with** thee;

(for he knew not that she *was* his daughter-in-law;) and she said, What wilt thou give me, that thou mayest come ~~in unto~~ **and lie with** me?

18 And he said, What pledge shall I give thee? And she said, Thy signet, and thy bracelets, and thy staff that *is* in thine hand. And he gave *it* her, and came ~~in unto~~ **and slept with** her, and she conceived by him.

CHAPTER 39

8 But he refused, and said unto his master's wife, Behold, my master ~~wotteth~~ **knoweth** not what *is* with me in the house, and he hath committed all that he hath to my hand;

22 And the keeper of the prison committed to Joseph's hand all the prisoners that *were* in the prison; and whatsoever they did there, he was the ~~doer~~ **overseer** *of it*.

CHAPTER 44

15 And Joseph said unto them, What deed *is* this that ye have done? ~~wot~~ **knew** ye not that such a man as I can certainly divine?

CHAPTER 45

1 Then Joseph could not refrain himself before ~~all~~ them **all** that stood by him; and he cried, Cause every man to go out from me. And there stood no man with him, while Joseph made himself known unto his brethren.

CHAPTER 48

1 And it came to pass after these things, that ~~one~~ **it was** told Joseph, **saying,** Behold, thy father *is* sick; and he took with him his two sons, Manasseh and Ephraim.

2 And ~~one~~ **it was** told Jacob, ~~and said~~ **saying, Look, and** behold, thy son Joseph cometh unto thee; and

Israel strengthened himself, and sat upon the bed.

4 And said unto me, Behold, I will make thee fruitful, and multiply thee, **saith the Lord,** and I will make of thee a multitude of people; and will give this land to thy seed after thee, *for* an everlasting possession.

5 And now, **of** thy two sons, Ephraim and Manasseh, which were born unto thee in the land of Egypt, before I came unto thee into Egypt; **behold, they** *are* mine, **and the God of my fathers shall bless them; even** as Reuben and Simeon they shall be **blessed, for they are** mine; **wherefore they shall be called after my name. (Therefore they were called Israel.)**

6 And thy issue which thou begettest after them, shall be thine, *and* shall be called after the name of their brethren in their inheritance, **in the tribes; therefore they were called the tribes of Manasseh and of Ephraim.**

7 **And Jacob said unto Joseph, When**[*] **the God of my fathers appeared unto me in Luz, in the land of Canaan; he sware unto me, that he would give unto me, and unto my seed, the land for an everlasting possession.**

8 **Therefore, O my son, he hath blessed me in raising thee up to be a servant unto me, in saving my house from death;**

9 **In delivering my people, thy brethren, from famine which was sore in the land; wherefore the God of thy fathers shall bless thee, and the fruit of thy loins, that they shall be blessed above thy brethren, and above**[*] **thy father's house;**

10 **For thou hast prevailed, and thy father's house hath**[*] **bowed down unto thee, even as it was shown unto**

thee, before thou wast[*] **sold into Egypt by the hands of thy brethren; wherefore thy brethren shall bow down unto thee, from generation to generation, unto the fruit of thy loins forever;**

11 **For thou shalt be a light unto my people, to deliver them in the days of their captivity, from bondage; and to bring salvation unto them, when they are altogether bowed down under sin.**

12 7 And **therefore,** as for me, when I came from Padan, Rachel died by me in the land of Canaan, in the way when **we were** yet ~~there was~~ but a little way to come unto Ephrath; and I buried her there in the way of Ephrath; the same *is* **called** Bethlehem.

13 8 And Israel beheld Joseph's sons, and said, Who *are* these?

14 9 And Joseph said unto his father, They *are* my sons, whom God hath given me in this ~~place~~ **land.**

15 9 And he said, Bring them, I pray thee, unto me, and I will bless them.

16 10 Now the eyes of Israel were dim for age, *so that* he could not see **well.** And he brought them near unto him; and he kissed them, and embraced them.

17 11 And Israel said unto Joseph, I had not thought to see thy face: and, lo, God hath shewed me also thy seed.

18 12 And Joseph brought them out from between his knees, and he bowed himself with his face to the earth.

19 13 And Joseph took them both, Ephraim in his right hand toward Israel's left hand, and Manasseh in his left hand toward Israel's right hand, and brought *them* near unto him.

20 14 And Israel stretched out his right hand, and laid *it* upon Ephraim's

head, who *was* the younger, and his left hand upon Manasseh's head, guiding his hands wittingly; for Manasseh *was* the firstborn.

21 15 And he blessed Joseph, and said, God, before whom my fathers Abraham and Isaac did walk, the God which fed me all my life long unto this day,

22 16 The Angel which redeemed me from all evil, bless the lads; and let my name be named on them, and the name of my fathers Abraham and Isaac; and let them grow into a multitude in the midst of the earth.

23 17 And when Joseph saw that his father laid his right hand upon the head of Ephraim, it displeased him: and he held up his father's hand, to remove it from Ephraim's head unto Manasseh's head.

24 18 And Joseph said unto his father, Not so, my father: for this *is* the firstborn; put thy right hand upon his head.

25 19 And his father refused, and said, I know *it*, my son, I know *it*: he also shall become a people, and he also shall be great: but truly his younger brother shall be greater than he, and his seed shall become a multitude of nations.

26 20 And he blessed them that day, saying, In thee shall Israel bless, saying, God make thee as Ephraim and as Manasseh: and he set Ephraim before Manasseh.

27 21 And Israel said unto Joseph, Behold, I die: but God shall be with you, and bring you again unto the land of your fathers.

28 22 Moreover I have given to thee one portion above thy brethren, which I took out of the hand of the Amorite with my sword and with my bow.

CHAPTER 49

1 And Jacob called unto his sons, and said, Gather yourselves together, that I may tell you ~~that~~ ~~which~~ **what** shall befall you in the last days.

13 Zebulun shall dwell at the haven of the sea; and ~~he~~ *shall be* for ~~an~~ **a** haven of ships; and his border *shall be* unto Zidon.

CHAPTER 50

24 And Joseph said unto his brethren, I die, **and go unto my fathers; and I go down to my grave with joy. The God of˙ father Jacob be with you, to deliver you out of affliction in the days of your bondage; for the Lord hath visited me, and I have obtained a promise of the Lord, that out of the fruit of my loins, the Lord God will raise up a righteous branch out of my loins; and unto thee, whom my father Jacob hath named Israel, a prophet; (not the Messiah who is called Shilo;) and this prophet shall deliver my people out of Egypt in the days of thy bondage.**

25 And it shall come to pass that they shall be scattered again; and a branch shall be broken off, and shall be carried into a far country; nevertheless they shall be remembered in the covenants of the Lord, when the Messiah cometh, for he shall be made manifest unto them in the latter days, in the Spirit of power; and shall bring them out of darkness into light; out of hidden darkness, and out of captivity unto freedom.

26 A seer shall the Lord my God raise up, who shall be a choice seer unto the fruit of my loins.

27 Thus saith the Lord God of my fathers unto me, A choice seer will I raise up out of the fruit of thy loins, and he shall be esteemed highly

among the fruit of thy loins; and unto him will I give commandment* that he shall do a work for the fruit of thy loins, his brethren.*

28 And he shall bring them to the knowledge of the covenants which I have made with thy fathers;* and he shall do whatsoever work I shall command him.

29 And I will make him great in mine eyes, for he shall do my work; and he shall be great like unto him whom I have said I would raise up unto you, to deliver my people, O house of Israel, out of the land of Egypt; for a seer will I raise up to deliver my people out of the land of Egypt; and he shall be called Moses. And by this name he shall know that he is of thy house; for he shall be nursed by the king's daughter, and shall be called her son.

30 And again, a seer will I raise up out of the fruit of thy loins, and unto him will I give power to bring forth my word unto the seed of thy loins; and not to the bringing forth of my word only, saith the Lord, but to the convincing them of my word, which shall have already gone forth among them in the last days;

31 Wherefore the fruit of thy loins shall write, and the fruit of the loins of Judah shall write; and that which shall be written by the fruit of thy loins, and also that which shall be written by the fruit of the loins of Judah, shall grow together unto the confounding of false doctrines, and laying down of contentions, and establishing peace among the fruit of thy loins, and bringing them to a knowledge of their fathers in the latter days; and also to the knowledge of my covenants, saith the Lord.

32 And out of weakness shall he be made strong, in that day when my work shall go forth among all my people, which shall restore them, who are of the house of Israel, in the last days.

33 And that seer will I bless, and they that seek to destroy him shall be confounded; for this promise I give unto you; for I will remember you from generation to generation; and his name shall be called Joseph, and it shall be after the name of his father; and he shall be like unto you; for the thing which the Lord shall bring forth by his hand shall bring my people unto salvation.

34 And the Lord sware unto Joseph, that he would preserve his seed forever, saying, I will raise up Moses, and a rod shall be in his hand, and he shall gather together my people, and he shall lead them as a flock, and he shall smite the waters of the Red Sea with his rod.

35 And he shall have judgment, and shall write the word of the Lord. And he shall not speak many words, for I will write unto him my law by the finger of mine own hand. And I will make a spokesman for him, and his name shall be called Aaron.

36 24 And it shall be done unto thee in the last days also, even as I have sworn. Therefore, Joseph said unto his brethren, and God will surely visit you, and bring you out of this land, unto the land which he sware to unto Abraham, and to unto Isaac, and to Jacob.

37 25 And Joseph confirmed many other things unto his brethren, and took an oath of the children of Israel, saying unto them, God will surely visit you, and ye shall carry up my bones from hence.

38 26 So Joseph died ~~being~~ **when he was** an hundred and ten years old; and they embalmed him, and ~~he was~~ **they** put **him** in a coffin in Egypt; **and he was kept from burial by the** children of Israel, that he might be carried up and laid in the sepulchre with his father. And thus they remembered the oath which they sware unto him.

The Second Book of Moses, Called
EXODUS

CHAPTER 1

1 Now these *are* the names of the children of Israel, which came into Egypt; every man ~~and~~ **according to** his household **who** came with Jacob.

CHAPTER 3

2 And **again,** the ~~angel~~ **presence** of the LORD appeared unto him**,** in a flame of fire ~~out of~~ **in** the midst of a bush; and he looked, and, behold, the bush burned with fire, and the bush *was* not consumed.

3 And Moses said, I will now turn aside, and see this great sight, why the bush is not ~~burnt~~ **consumed**.

CHAPTER 4

21 And the LORD said unto Moses, When thou goest to return into Egypt, see that thou do all those wonders before Pharaoh, which I have put in thine hand**, and I will prosper thee;** but ~~I~~ **Pharaoh** will harden his heart, that he ~~shall~~ **will** not let the people go.

24 And it came to pass**, that the Lord appeared unto him as he was** ~~by~~ **in** the way, ~~in~~ **by** the inn. ~~that~~ The LORD ~~met~~ **was angry with** ~~him~~ **Moses,** and ~~sought~~ **his hand was about to fall upon him**, to kill him; **for he had not circumcised his son.**

25 Then Zipporah took a sharp stone and ~~cut off the foreskin of~~ **circumcised** her son, and cast ~~it~~ **the stone** at his feet, and said, Surely **thou art** a bloody husband ~~art thou~~ unto me.

26 ~~So~~ **And** ~~he~~ **the Lord spared Moses and** let him go**, because Zipporah, his wife, circumcised the child.** ~~then~~ **And** she said, **Thou art** a bloody husband ~~thou art~~ ~~because of the circumcision~~. **And Moses was ashamed, and hid his face from the Lord, and said, I have sinned before the Lord.**

27 And the LORD said ~~to~~ **unto** Aaron, Go into the wilderness to meet Moses**,** and he went and met him**,** in the mount of God; **in the mount where God appeared unto him;** and **Aaron** kissed him.

CHAPTER 5

4 And the king of Egypt said unto them, Wherefore do ye, Moses and Aaron, ~~let~~ **lead** the people from their works? get you unto your burdens.

11 Go ye, get ~~you~~ **your** straw where ye can find it; yet not ~~ought~~ **aught** of your work shall be diminished.

CHAPTER 6

3 And I appeared unto Abraham, unto Isaac, and unto Jacob**.** ~~by the name of~~ **I am the Lord** God Almighty; ~~but by my name~~ **the Lord** JEHOVAH.

And was ~~I~~ not **my name** known ~~to~~ **unto** them?

4 **Yea,** and I have also established my covenant with them, **which I made with them,** to give them the land of Canaan, the land of their pilgrimage, wherein they were strangers.

8 And I will bring you in unto the land, concerning the which I did swear to give it to Abraham, to Isaac, and to Jacob; and I will give it you for ~~an~~ **a** heritage; I ~~am~~ the LORD **will do it.**

12 And Moses spake before the LORD, saying, Behold, the children of Israel have not hearkened unto me; how then shall Pharaoh hear me, who ~~am~~ **is** of uncircumcised lips?

14 These ~~be~~ **are** the heads of their fathers' houses; The sons of Reuben the firstborn of Israel; Hanoch, and Pallu, Hezron, and Carmi; these ~~be~~ **are** the families of Reuben.

26 These *are* **the sons of Aaron, according to their families. And all these are the names of the children of Israel according to the heads of their families,** that ~~Aaron and Moses, to whom~~ the LORD said **unto Aaron and Moses, they should** bring **up** out ~~the children of Israel from~~ **of** the land of Egypt, according to their armies.

27 These *are* they ~~which~~ **concerning whom the Lord** spake to Pharaoh, king of Egypt, **that he should let them go. And he sent Moses and Aaron** to bring out the children of Israel from Egypt ~~these are that Moses and Aaron.~~

28 **28–29** And it came to pass, on the day ~~when~~ the LORD spake unto Moses, in the land of Egypt, that the LORD ~~spake unto~~ **commanded** Moses ~~saying, I am the LORD~~ **that he should** speak ~~thou~~ unto Pharaoh, king of Egypt, **saying, I, the Lord, will do unto Pharaoh, king of Egypt,** all that I say unto thee.

29 30 And Moses said, before the LORD, Behold, I *am* of ~~uncircumcised~~ **stammering** lips, **and slow of speech;** ~~and~~ how shall Pharaoh hearken unto me?

CHAPTER 7

1 And the LORD said unto Moses, See, I have made thee a ~~god~~ **prophet** to Pharaoh; and Aaron thy brother shall be thy ~~prophet~~ **spokesman.**

2 Thou shalt speak **unto thy brother** all that I command thee; and Aaron thy brother shall speak unto Pharaoh, that he send the children of Israel out of his land.

3 And ~~I~~ **Pharaoh** will harden ~~Pharaoh's~~ **his** heart, **as I said unto thee;** and **thou shalt** multiply my signs, and my wonders, in the land of Egypt.

4 But Pharaoh shall not hearken unto you, ~~that~~ **therefore** I ~~may~~ **will** lay my hand upon Egypt, and bring forth mine armies, ~~and~~ my people, the children of Israel, out of the land of Egypt by great judgments.

9 When Pharaoh shall speak unto you, saying, Show a miracle ~~for~~ **that I may know** you; then thou shalt say unto Aaron, Take thy rod, and cast *it* before Pharaoh, *and* it shall become a serpent.

13 And ~~he~~ **Pharaoh** hardened ~~Pharaoh's~~ **his** heart, that he hearkened not unto them; as the LORD had said.

CHAPTER 9

12 And ~~the LORD~~ **Pharaoh** hardened ~~the~~ **his** heart ~~of Pharaoh~~, and he hearkened not unto them; as the LORD had spoken unto Moses.

17 **Therefore speak unto Pharaoh the thing which I command thee,**

who as yet exaltest ~~thou thyself against my people~~ **himself** that ~~thou~~ **he** ~~wilt~~ **will** not let them go**.**

CHAPTER 10

1 And the LORD said unto Moses, Go in unto Pharaoh**;** for ~~I~~ **he** ~~have~~ **hath** hardened his heart, and the ~~heart~~ **hearts** of his servants, ~~that~~ **therefore** I ~~might~~ **will** show these my signs before him**;**

20 But ~~the LORD~~ **Pharaoh** hardened ~~Pharaoh's~~ **his** heart, so that he would not let the children of Israel go.

27 But ~~the LORD~~ **Pharaoh** hardened ~~Pharaoh's~~ **his** heart, and he would not let them go.

CHAPTER 11

8 And all these ~~thy~~ **the** servants **of Pharaoh** shall come down unto me, and bow ~~down~~ themselves **down** unto me saying, Get thee out, and all the people that follow thee**;** and after that I will go out. ~~And he went out from Pharaoh in a great anger.~~

9 And the LORD said unto Moses, Pharaoh ~~shall~~ **will** not hearken unto you**;** ~~that~~ **therefore** my wonders ~~may~~ **shall** be multiplied in the land of Egypt.

10 And Moses and Aaron did all these wonders before Pharaoh**, and they went out from Pharaoh, and he was in a**[19] **great anger.** And ~~the LORD~~ **Pharaoh** hardened ~~Pharaoh's~~ **his** heart, so that he would not let the children of Israel go out of his land.

CHAPTER 12

33 And the Egyptians were urgent upon the people, that they might send them out of the land in haste; for they said, We ~~be~~ **have found our firstborn** all dead ~~men~~**; therefore get ye out of the land lest we die also**.

37 And the children of Israel journeyed from Rameses to Succoth, about six hundred thousand **men** on foot ~~that were~~ ~~men~~, ~~beside~~ **besides**[*] **women and** children.

CHAPTER 14

4 And ~~I~~ **Pharaoh** will harden ~~Pharaoh's~~ **his** heart, that he shall follow after them; and I will be honored upon Pharaoh, and upon all his host; that the Egyptians may know that I *am* the LORD. And they did so.

8 And ~~the LORD~~ **Pharaoh** hardened ~~the~~ **his** heart ~~of Pharaoh king of Egypt~~, and he pursued after the children of Israel**;** and the children of Israel went out with ~~an~~ **a** high hand.

17 And I ~~behold, I will harden~~ **say unto thee that**[*] the hearts of the Egyptians **shall be hardened**, and they shall follow them**;** and I will get me honor upon Pharaoh, and upon all his host, upon his chariots, and upon his horsemen.

20 And it came between the camp of the Egyptians and the camp of Israel; and it was a cloud and darkness *to them* **the Egyptians**, but it gave light by night *to these* **the Israelites,** so that the one came not near the other all the night.

CHAPTER 15

16 Fear and dread shall fall upon them; by the greatness of thine arm they shall be *as* still as a stone; till ~~thy~~ **the** people pass over, O LORD, till the people pass over, *which* thou hast purchased.

CHAPTER 18

1 When Jethro, the **high** priest of Midian, Moses' father-in-law, heard of all that God had done for Moses, and for Israel his people, *and* that the LORD had brought Israel out of Egypt;

Chapter 20

23 Ye shall not make ~~with me~~ **unto you** gods of silver, neither shall ye make unto you gods of gold.

Chapter 21

6 Then his master shall bring him unto the judges; he shall also bring him to the door, or unto the door post; and his master shall bore his ear through with an ~~aul~~ **awl**; and he shall serve him forever.

8 If she please not her master, who hath **not** betrothed her to himself, then shall he let her be redeemed; **not** to sell her unto a strange nation; he shall have no power **to do this**, seeing he hath dealt deceitfully with her.

20 And if a man smite his servant, or his maid, with a rod, and he die under his hand; he shall be surely ~~punished~~ **put to death**.

21 Notwithstanding, if he continue a day or two, **and recover,** he shall not be ~~punished~~ **put to death**, for he *is* his ~~money~~ **servant**.

Chapter 22

18 Thou shalt not suffer a ~~witch~~ **murderer** to live.

28 Thou shalt not revile ~~the gods~~ **against God**, nor curse the ruler of thy people.

Chapter 23

3 Neither shalt thou countenance a ~~poor~~ **wicked** man in his cause.

Chapter 27

8 Hollow with boards shalt thou make it; as it was showed thee in the mount, so shall ~~they~~ **thou** make *it*.

Chapter 31

10 And the ~~cloths~~ **clothes** of service, and the holy garments ~~for~~ **of** Aaron the priest, and the garments of his sons, to minister in the priest's office,

Chapter 32

1 And when the people saw that Moses delayed to come down out of the mount, the people gathered themselves together unto Aaron, and said unto him, Up, make us gods, which shall go before us; for *as for* this Moses, the man that brought us up out of the land of Egypt, we ~~wot~~ **know** not what is become of him.

12 Wherefore should the Egyptians speak, and say, For mischief did he bring them out, to slay them in the mountains, and to consume them from the face of the earth? Turn from thy fierce wrath. ~~and~~ **Thy people will** repent of this evil; **therefore come thou not out** against ~~thy people~~ **them.**

14 And the LORD **said unto Moses, If they will** ~~repented~~ **repent of the evil which they have done, I will spare them, and turn away my fierce wrath; but, behold, thou shalt execute** judgment upon **all that will not repent of this evil this day. Therefore, see thou do this thing that I have commanded thee, or I will execute all that** which ~~he~~ **I** had thought to do unto ~~his~~ **my** people.

23 For they said unto me, Make us gods, which shall go before us; for *as for* this Moses, the man that brought us up out of the land of Egypt, we ~~wot~~ **know** not what is become of him.

35 And the LORD plagued the people, because they ~~made~~ **worshiped** the calf, which Aaron made.

Chapter 33

1 And the LORD said unto Moses, Depart, *and* go up hence, thou and

the people which thou hast brought up out of the land of Egypt, unto **a land flowing with milk and honey,** the land which I sware unto Abraham, to Isaac, and to Jacob, saying, Unto thy seed will I give it**;**

20 And he said **unto Moses,** Thou canst not see my face **at this time, lest mine anger be kindled against thee also, and I destroy thee, and thy people;** for there shall no man **among them** see me **at this time**, and live, **for they are exceeding sinful. And no sinful man hath at any time, neither shall there be any sinful man at any time, that shall see my face and live.**

21 And the LORD said,˙ Behold, ~~there is~~ ~~a place by me and~~ thou shalt stand upon a rock**, and I will prepare a place by me for thee**.

22 And it shall come to pass, while my glory passeth by, that I will put thee in a ~~clift~~ **cleft** of ~~the~~ **a** rock, and ~~will~~ cover thee with my hand while I pass by**.**

23 And I will take away mine hand, and thou shalt see my back parts**,** but my face shall not be seen, **as at other times; for I am angry with my people Israel**.

CHAPTER 34

1 And the LORD said unto Moses, Hew thee two **other** tables of stone, like unto the first**,** and I will write upon ~~these~~ ~~tables~~ **them also,** the words **of the law,** ~~that~~ **according as they** were **written** ~~in~~ **at** the first **on the** tables which thou brakest**; but it shall**

not be according to the first, for I will take away the priesthood out of their midst; therefore my holy order, and the ordinances thereof, shall not go before them; for my presence shall not go up in their midst, lest I destroy them.

2 **But I will give unto them the law as at the first, but it shall be after the law of the carnal commandment; for I have sworn in my wrath, that they shall not enter into my presence, into my rest, in the days of their pilgrimage. Therefore do as I have commanded thee,** and be ready in the morning, and come up in the morning unto mount Sinai, and present thyself there to me**,** in the top of the mount.

4 And ~~he~~ **Moses** hewed two tables of stone like unto the first; and ~~Moses~~ **he** rose up early in the morning, and went up unto mount Sinai, as the LORD had commanded him, and took in his hand the two tables of stone.

7 Keeping mercy for thousands, forgiving iniquity and transgression and sin, and that will by no means clear *the* ~~guilty~~ **rebellious**; visiting the iniquity of the fathers upon the children, and upon the children's children, unto the third and to the fourth *generation*.

14 For thou shalt worship no other god**;** for the LORD, whose name *is* ~~Jealous~~ **Jehovah**, *is* a jealous God**.**

35 And the children of Israel saw the face of Moses, that the skin of Moses' face shone**;** and Moses put the ~~vail~~ **veil** upon his face again, until he went in to speak with ~~him~~ **the Lord.**

The Third Book of Moses, Called
LEVITICUS

CHAPTER 12
3 And in the eighth day, the ~~flesh of his foreskin~~ **man child** shall be circumcised.

4 And she shall then continue in the ~~blood~~ **time** of her purifying **which shall be** three and thirty days; she shall touch no hallowed thing, nor come into the sanctuary, until the days of her purifying be fulfilled.

5 But if she bear a maid child, ~~then~~* she shall be unclean two weeks, as in her separation; and she shall continue in the ~~blood~~ **time** of her purifying threescore and six days.

CHAPTER 21
1 And the LORD said unto Moses, Speak unto the priests the sons of Aaron, and say unto them, There shall none be defiled ~~for~~ **with** the dead among his people;

11 Neither shall he go in to **touch** any dead body, nor defile himself for his father, or ~~for~~ his mother;

CHAPTER 22
9 They shall therefore keep mine ordinance, lest they bear sin for it, and die; therefore, if they profane ~~it~~ **not mine ordinances,** I the LORD ~~do~~ **will** sanctify them.

CHAPTER 25
29 And if a man sell ~~a~~ **his** dwelling-house in a walled city, then he may redeem it within a whole year after it is sold; *within* a full year may he redeem it.

The Fourth Book of Moses, Called
NUMBERS

CHAPTER 16
10 And he hath brought thee near *to him*, and all thy brethren the sons of Levi with thee; and seek ye the **high** priesthood also?

CHAPTER 22
20 And God came unto Balaam at night, and said unto him, If the men come to call thee, rise up, ~~and~~ **if thou wilt** go with them; but yet the word which I shall say unto thee, ~~that~~ shalt thou ~~do~~ **speak.**

The Fifth Book of Moses, Called

DEUTERONOMY

CHAPTER 2

30 But Sihon king of Heshbon would not let us pass by him; for ~~the Lord thy God~~ **he** hardened his spirit, and made his heart obstinate, that ~~he~~ **the Lord thy God** might deliver him into thy hand, as ~~appeareth~~ **he hath done** this day.

CHAPTER 10

1 At that time the LORD said unto me, Hew thee two other tables of stone like unto the first, and come up unto me ~~into~~ **upon** the mount, and make thee an ark of wood.

2 And I will write on the tables the words that were ~~in~~ **on** the first tables, which thou brakest, **save the words of the everlasting covenant of the holy priesthood,** and thou shalt put them in the ark.

CHAPTER 14

21 Ye shall not eat *of* anything that dieth of itself; thou shalt **not** give it unto the stranger that *is* in thy gates, that he may eat it; or thou mayest **not** sell it unto an alien; for thou *art* ~~an~~ **a** holy people unto the LORD thy God. Thou shalt not seethe a kid in his mother's milk.

CHAPTER 16

22 Neither shalt thou set thee up *any* **graven** image; which the LORD thy God hateth.

CHAPTER 34

6 ~~And~~ **For** ~~he buried~~ **the Lord took** him **unto his fathers,** in a valley in the land of Moab, over against Beth-peor; ~~but~~ **therefore** no man knoweth of his sepulchre unto this day.

The Book of

JOSHUA

CHAPTER 11

20 For it was of the LORD to **destroy them utterly, because they** ~~harden~~ **hardened** their hearts, that they should come against Israel in battle; that ~~he~~ **they** ~~might destroy them utterly, and~~ that they might have no favor, ~~but~~ that ~~he~~ **they** might destroy them **in battle**, as the LORD commanded Moses.

CHAPTER 17

5 And there fell ten portions to Manasseh, ~~beside~~ **besides** the land of Gilead and Bashan, which *were* on the other side Jordan;

The Book of
JUDGES

CHAPTER 2

18 And when the LORD raised them up judges, then the LORD was with the judge, and delivered them out of the hand of their enemies all the days of the judge; for ~~it repented~~ the LORD **hearkened** because of their groanings by reason of them that oppressed them and vexed them.

The First Book of
SAMUEL

CHAPTER 15

11 ~~It repenteth me that~~ I have set up Saul *to be* king**, and he repenteth not that he hath sinned,** for he is turned back from following me, and hath not performed my commandments. And it grieved Samuel; and he cried unto the LORD all night.

35 And Samuel came no more to see Saul until the day of his death; nevertheless**,** Samuel mourned for Saul**;** and the LORD ~~repented~~ **rent the kingdom from Saul** ~~that~~ **whom** he had made ~~Saul~~ king over Israel.

CHAPTER 16

14 But the Spirit of the LORD departed from Saul, and an evil spirit ~~from~~ **which was not of** the LORD troubled him.

15 And Saul's servants said unto him, Behold now, an evil spirit ~~from~~ **which is not of** God troubleth thee.

16 Let our lord now command thy servants, *which are* before thee, to seek out a man, *who is* a cunning player on a harp; and it shall come to pass, when the evil spirit**,** ~~from~~ **which is not of** God, is upon thee, that he shall play with his hand, and thou shalt be well.

23 And it came to pass, when the *evil* spirit**,** ~~from~~ **which was not of** God, was upon Saul, that David took ~~an~~ **a** harp, and played with his hand**;** so Saul was refreshed, and was well, and the evil spirit departed from him.

CHAPTER 18

10 And it came to pass on the morrow, that the evil spirit ~~from~~ **which was not of** God came upon Saul, and he prophesied in the midst of the house**;** and David played with his hand, as at other times**;** and *there was* a javelin in Saul's hand.

CHAPTER 19

9 And the evil spirit ~~from~~ **which was not of** the LORD was upon Saul, as he sat in his house with his javelin in his hand**;** and David played with *his* hand.

CHAPTER 28

9 And the woman said unto him, Behold, thou knowest what Saul hath done, how he hath cut off those that have familiar spirits, and the wizards, out of the land**;** wherefore then layest

thou a snare for my life, to cause me to die **also, who hath not a familiar spirit?**

11 Then said the woman, **The word of** whom shall I bring up unto thee? And he said, Bring me up **the word of** Samuel.

12 And when the woman saw **the words of** Samuel, she cried with a loud voice; and the woman spake to Saul, saying, Why hast thou deceived me? for thou *art* Saul.

13 And the king said unto her, Be not afraid; for what sawest thou? And the woman said unto Saul, I saw ~~gods~~ **the words of Samuel** ascending out of the earth. **And she said, I saw Samuel also.**

14 And he said unto her, What form *is* he of? And she said, **I saw** an old man ~~cometh~~ **coming** up, ~~and he *is*~~ covered with a mantle. And Saul perceived that it *was* Samuel, and he stooped, *his* face to the ground, and bowed himself.

15 And **these are the words of** Samuel ~~said to~~ **unto** Saul, Why hast thou disquieted me, to bring me up? And Saul answered, I am sore distressed; for the Philistines make war against me, and God is departed from me, and answereth me no more, neither by prophets, nor by dreams; therefore I have called thee, that thou mayest make known unto me what I shall do.

The Second Book of
SAMUEL

CHAPTER 12
13 And David said unto Nathan, I have sinned against the LORD. And Nathan said unto David, The LORD also hath **not** put away thy sin **that** thou shalt not die.

CHAPTER 22
48 It *is* God that avengeth me, and that bringeth down the people ~~under~~ **unto** me,

CHAPTER 24
16 And when the angel stretched out his hand upon Jerusalem to destroy it, the LORD ~~repented him of the evil, and~~ said ~~to~~ **unto** ~~the angel that destroyed the people~~ **him,** ~~It is enough~~ Stay now thine hand, **it is enough; for the people repented, and the Lord stayed the hand of the angel, that he destroyed not the people**. And the angel of the LORD was by the ~~threshingplace~~ **threshing floor** of Araunah, the Jebusite.

17 ~~And~~ **For** David spake unto the LORD when he saw the angel that smote the people, and said, Lo, I have sinned, and I have done wickedly; but these sheep, what have they done? let thine hand, I pray thee, be against me, and against my father's house.

The First Book of the
KINGS

CHAPTER 3

1 And **the Lord was not pleased with** Solomon, **for he** made affinity with Pharaoh, king of Egypt, and took Pharaoh's daughter **to wife**, and brought her into the ~~city~~ **house** of David until he had made an end of building his own house, and the house of the LORD, and the wall of Jerusalem round about. **And the Lord blessed Solomon for the people's sake only.**

2 ~~Only~~ **And** the people sacrificed in high places, because there was no house built unto the name of the LORD, until those days.

3 And **because the Lord blessed** Solomon ~~loved the LORD~~ **as he was** walking in the statutes of David, his father, **he began to love the Lord,** ~~only~~ **and** he sacrificed and burnt incense in high places, **and he called on the name of the Lord.**

4 And the king went to Gibeon to sacrifice there, for ~~that~~ Gibeon *was* **in** ~~the~~ **a** great high place; **and Solomon offered upon that altar, in Gibeon,** a thousand burnt offerings ~~did Solomon offer upon that altar~~.

5 ~~In Gibeon~~ **And** the LORD **God hearkened unto Solomon, and** appeared ~~to~~ **unto** ~~Solomon~~ **him** in a dream by night, and ~~God~~ said, Ask what I shall give thee.

6 And Solomon said, Thou hast showed unto thy servant David, my father, great ~~mercy~~ **things** according **to thy mercy,** ~~as~~ **when** he walked before thee in truth, and in righteousness, and in uprightness of heart with thee; and thou hast kept for him this great kindness, that thou hast given him a son to sit on his throne ~~as it is~~ this day.

7 And now, O LORD my God, thou hast made thy servant king, instead of David, my father, **over thy people.**

8 7–8 And ~~I am but a little child~~ I know not *how* **to lead them,** to go out, or come in **before them,** and **I,*** thy servant, ~~is~~ **am as a little child,** in the midst of thy people ~~which~~ **whom** thou hast chosen, a great people that cannot be numbered, nor counted for multitude.

9 Give therefore thy servant an understanding heart to judge thy people, that I may discern between good and bad; for who is able to judge this thy ~~so great a~~ people, **so great a people?***

12 Behold, I have done according to thy ~~words~~ **word;** lo, I have given thee a wise and an understanding heart; so that there was none **made king over Israel** like **unto** thee before thee, neither after thee shall any arise like unto thee.

14 And if thou wilt walk in my ways to keep my statutes, and my commandments, **then I will lengthen thy days, and thou shalt not walk in unrighteousness,** as ~~did~~ thy father David ~~did walk, then I will lengthen thy days~~.

CHAPTER 11

4 For it came to pass, when Solomon was old, ~~that~~ his wives turned away his heart after other gods; and his heart was not perfect with the LORD his God, ~~as was~~ **and it became as** the heart of David his father.

6 And Solomon did evil in the sight of the LORD, **as David his father,** and

went not fully after the LORD ~~as did David his father~~.

33 Because that they have forsaken me, and have worshiped Ashtoreth the goddess of the Zidonians, Chemosh the god of the Moabites, and Milcom the god of the children of Ammon, and have not walked in my ways, to do *that which is* right in mine eyes, and ~~to keep~~ my statutes, and my judgments, **and his heart is become as David his father; and he repenteth not** as *did* David his father, **that I may forgive him**.

34 Howbeit, I will not take the whole kingdom out of his hand, but I will make him prince all the days of his life, for David my servant's sake, whom I chose, because he kept my commandments and my statutes **in that day.**

35 35–36 But I will take the kingdom out of his son's hand, and will give ~~it~~ unto thee, ~~even~~ ten tribes. And unto his son will I give one tribe.

36 That David my servant may have a light ~~alway~~ **always** before me in Jerusalem, the city which I have chosen me to put my name there.

37 And I will take thee, and thou shalt reign according to all that thy soul desireth, and ~~shalt~~ **shall** be king over Israel.

38 And it shall be, if thou wilt hearken unto all that I command thee, and wilt walk in my ways, and do ~~that is~~ right in my sight, to keep my statutes and my commandments, as David my servant did **in the day that I blessed him;** ~~that~~ I will be with thee, and build thee a sure house as I built for David, and will˙ give Israel unto thee.

39 **And for the transgression of David, and also for the people, I have rent the kingdom,** and **for this** I will afflict the seed of David, but not forever.

CHAPTER 13

18 He said unto him, I *am* a prophet also**, even** as thou ~~art,~~ and an angel spake unto me by the word of the LORD, saying, Bring him back with thee into thine house, that he may eat bread and drink water**, that I may prove him;** ~~But~~ **and** he lied **not** unto him.

26 And when the prophet that brought him back from the way heard *thereof,* he said, It *is* the man of God, who was disobedient unto the word of the LORD; therefore the LORD hath delivered him unto the lion, which hath torn him, and slain him, according to the word of the LORD, which he spake unto ~~him~~ **me**.

CHAPTER 14

8 And rent the kingdom away from the house of David and gave it thee**, because he kept not my commandments.** ~~and~~ **But** ~~yet~~ thou hast not been as my servant David, ~~who kept my commandments, and who~~ **when he** followed me with all his heart **only** to do ~~that~~ ~~only~~ ~~which was~~ right in mine eyes**.**

CHAPTER 15

3 And he walked in all the sins of his father, which he had done before him**;** and his heart was not perfect with the LORD his God, as the ~~heart of~~ **Lord commanded** David his father.

5 Because David did ~~that which was~~ right in the eyes of the LORD, and turned not aside from ~~any thing~~ **all** that he commanded him**, to sin against the Lord; but repented of the evil** all the days of his life, save only in the matter of Uriah the Hittite**, wherein the Lord cursed him.**

11 And Asa did ~~that which was~~ right in the eyes of the Lord, as ~~did~~ **he commanded** David his father.

12 And he took away the sodomites out of the land, and removed all the idols that his fathers had made; **and it pleased the Lord.**

The Second Book of the
KINGS

Chapter 1

10 And Elijah answered and said to the captain of fifty, If I *be* a man of God, then let fire come down ~~from~~ **out of** heaven, and consume thee and thy fifty. And there came down fire ~~from~~ **out of** heaven, and consumed him and his fifty.

12 And Elijah answered and said unto them, If I *be* a man of God, let fire come down ~~from~~ **out of** heaven, and consume thee and thy fifty. And the fire of God came down ~~from~~ **out of** heaven, and consumed him and his fifty.

14 Behold, there came fire down ~~from~~ **out of** heaven, and burnt up the two captains of the former fifties with their fifties; therefore let my life now be precious in thy sight.

Chapter 18

37 Hear me, O Lord, hear me, that this people may know that thou *art* the Lord God, and ~~that~~ thou ~~hast mayest~~ **mayest** ~~turned~~ **turn** their heart back again.

Chapter 8

10 And Elisha said unto him, **Thou wilt** go, **and** say unto him, Thou mayest certainly recover; howbeit, the Lord hath showed me that he shall surely die.

Chapter 18

33 Hath any of the gods of the nations delivered at all ~~his~~ **this** land out of the hand of the king of Assyria?

Chapter 19

35 And it came to pass that night, that the angel of the Lord went out, and smote in the camp of the Assyrians ~~an~~ **a** hundred fourscore and five thousand; and when they **who were left** arose early in the morning, behold, they *were* all dead corpses.

The First Book of the
CHRONICLES

Chapter 6

69 And ~~Aijalon~~ **Ajalon** with her suburbs, and Gath-rimmon with her suburbs;

Chapter 10

13 So Saul died for his transgression which he committed against the Lord, ~~even~~ **or** against the word of the

LORD, which he kept not, and also for asking **for** *counsel* of *one that had* a familiar spirit, to inquire *of it*;

CHAPTER 17

20 O LORD, *there is* none like thee, neither *is there any* God ~~beside~~ **besides** thee, according to all that we have heard with our ears.

CHAPTER 21

15 And God sent an angel unto Jerusalem to destroy it. And ~~as he~~ **the angel** ~~was destroying~~ **stretched forth his hand unto Jerusalem to destroy it;** ~~the LORD beheld, and he repented~~ ~~him of the evil~~ and **God** said to the angel ~~that destroyed, It is enough,~~ Stay now thine hand, **it is enough; for as he was destroying, the Lord beheld Israel, that he repented him of the evil; therefore the Lord stayed the angel that destroyed,** ~~And~~ as ~~the angel of the LORD~~ **he** stood by the threshing floor of Ornan the Jebusite.

20 **Now Ornan was threshing wheat, and his four sons with him;** and Ornan turned back and saw the angel, and ~~his four sons with him~~ **they** hid themselves. ~~Now Ornan was threshing wheat.~~

The Second Book of the
CHRONICLES

CHAPTER 2

3 And Solomon sent to Huram the king of Tyre, saying, As thou didst deal with David my father, and didst send him cedars to build him a house to dwell therein, **therefore** *even so deal with me.*

4 Behold, I build ~~an~~ **a** house to the name of the LORD my God, to dedicate *it* to him, *and* to burn before him sweet incense, and for the continual showbread, and for the burnt offerings morning and evening, on the sabbaths, and on the new moons, and on the solemn feasts of the LORD our God. **And** this ~~is an~~ ordinance ~~for ever to~~ **shall be kept in** Israel **forever.**

5 And the house which I build ~~is~~ **shall be a** great **house;** for great *is* **the Lord** our God above all gods.

7 Send me now therefore a man cunning to work in gold, and in silver, and in brass, and in iron, and in purple, and crimson, and blue, and that ~~can~~ **has*** skill to grave with the cunning men that *are* with me in Judah and in Jerusalem, whom David my father did provide.

8 Send me also cedar trees, fir trees, and algum trees, out of Lebanon; for I know that thy servants ~~can~~ **have** skill to cut timber in Lebanon; and, behold, **I will send** my servants ~~shall be~~ with thy servants,

18 And he set threescore and ten thousand of them *to be* bearers of burdens, and fourscore thousand *to be* hewers in the mountain, and three thousand and six hundred overseers to set the people ~~a~~ **at*** work.

CHAPTER 4

8 He made also ten tables, and placed *them* in the temple, five on the right side, and five on the left. And he made ~~an~~ **a** hundred ~~basons~~ **basins** of gold.

CHAPTER 6

17 Now then, O LORD God of Israel, let ~~thy~~ **the** word be verified, which thou hast spoken unto thy servant David.

CHAPTER 7

22 And it shall be answered, Because they forsook the LORD God of their fathers, which brought them forth out of the land of Egypt, and laid hold on other gods, and worshiped them, and served them; therefore hath he brought ~~all this~~ evil upon them.

CHAPTER 9

14 ~~Beside~~ **Besides** *that which* chapmen and merchants brought. And all the kings of Arabia and governors of the country brought gold and silver to Solomon.

CHAPTER 12

3 With twelve hundred chariots, and threescore thousand horsemen; and the people *were* without number that came with him out of Egypt; the ~~Lubims~~ **Lubim**, the ~~Sukkiims~~ **Sukkiim**, and the Ethiopians.

CHAPTER 13

3 And Abijah set the battle in array with an army of valiant men of war, *even* four hundred thousand chosen men; Jeroboam also set the battle in array against him with eight hundred thousand ~~chosen~~ men, *being* mighty men of valor.

CHAPTER 16

8 Were not the Ethiopians and the ~~Lubims~~ **Lubim** a huge host, with very many chariots and horsemen? yet, because thou didst rely on the LORD, he delivered them into thine hand.

CHAPTER 18

20 Then there came out **of them** a lying[20] spirit, and stood before the LORD, and said, I will entice him. And the LORD said unto him, Wherewith?

21 And he said, I will go out, and be a lying spirit in the mouth of all his prophets. And *the* LORD said, Thou shalt entice *him*, and thou shalt also prevail; go out, and do *even* so; **for all these have sinned against me**.

22 Now therefore, behold, the LORD hath ~~put~~ **found** a lying spirit in the mouth of these thy prophets, and the LORD hath spoken evil against thee.

CHAPTER 20

2 Then there came some that told Jehoshaphat, saying, There cometh a great multitude against thee from beyond the sea on this side Syria; and, behold, they ~~be~~ **are** in Hazazon-tamar, which ~~is~~ **was called** En-gedi.

6 And said, O LORD God of our fathers, ~~art not~~ thou God **who art** in heaven; and rulest ~~not thou~~ over all the kingdoms of the heathen; and in ~~thine~~ **thy** hand ~~is there not~~ **thou hast** power and might, so that none is able to withstand thee;

7 ~~Art not~~ Thou our God ~~who~~ didst drive out the inhabitants of this land before thy people Israel, and gavest it to the seed of Abraham thy friend forever.

11 Behold, ~~I say, how~~ they reward us **not**, ~~to~~ **but have** come to cast us out of thy possession, which thou hast given us to inherit.

17 Ye shall not ~~need~~ **go** to fight in this ~~battle~~ **day**; set yourselves, stand ye *still*, and see the salvation of the LORD with you, O Judah and Jerusalem; fear not, nor be dismayed; tomorrow go out against them; for the LORD *will be* with you.

CHAPTER 22

2 ~~Forty~~ **Two** and ~~two~~ **twenty** years old *was* Ahaziah when he began to

reign, and he reigned one year in Jerusalem. His mother's name also *was* Athaliah the daughter of Omri.

CHAPTER 24

9 And they made a proclamation through Judah and Jerusalem, to bring in to the LORD the collection ~~that~~ **of** Moses the servant of God ~~laid~~ upon Israel in the wilderness.

22 Thus Joash the king remembered not the kindness which Jehoiada his father had done to him, but slew his son. And when he died he said, The LORD look upon ~~it~~ **me**, and require ~~it~~ **me.**

CHAPTER 25

18 And Joash king of Israel sent to Amaziah king of Judah, saying, The

thistle that ~~was~~ **grew** in Lebanon sent to the cedar that ~~was~~ **grew** in Lebanon, saying, Give thy daughter to my son to wife; and there passed by a wild beast that *was* in Lebanon, and trode down the thistle.

CHAPTER 33

10 And the LORD spake to Manasseh, and to ~~his~~ **the*** people; but they would not hearken.

CHAPTER 34

16 And Shaphan carried the book to the king, and brought **the word of** the king ~~word~~ back again, saying, All that was committed to thy servants, they do ~~it~~.

The Book of
NEHEMIAH

CHAPTER 6

11 And I said, Should such a man as I flee? and who *is* ~~there~~ **mine enemy**, that ~~being~~ **such a man** as I ~~am~~ would go into the temple to save his life? I will not go in.

13 Therefore ~~was~~ he hired, ~~that I~~ should **I** be afraid **of him he hired,** and do so **as he said,** and sin; and *that* they might have ~~matter~~ **me** for an evil report, that they might reproach me?

CHAPTER 7

10 The children of Arah, ~~six~~ **seven** hundred ~~fifty~~ **seventy** and ~~two~~ **five.**

11 The children of Pahath-moab, of the children of Jeshua and Joab, two thousand and eight hundred *and* ~~eighteen~~ **twelve.**

13 The children of Zattu, ~~eight~~ **nine*** hundred forty and five.

15 The children of ~~Binnui~~ **Bani**, six hundred forty and ~~eight~~ **two.**

16 The children of Bebai, six hundred twenty and ~~eight~~ **three.**

17 The children of Azgad, ~~two~~ **a** thousand ~~three~~ **two** hundred twenty and two.

18 The children of Adonikam, six hundred ~~threescore~~ **sixty** and ~~seven~~ **six.**

19 The children of Bigvai, two thousand ~~threescore~~ **fifty** and ~~seven~~ **six.**

20 The children of Adin, ~~six~~ **four** hundred fifty and ~~five~~ **four.**

22 The children of Hashum, ~~three~~ **two** hundred twenty and ~~eight~~ **three.**

23 The children of Bezai, three hundred twenty and ~~four~~ **three.**

24 The children of ~~Hariph~~ **Jorah**, ~~an~~ **a** hundred and twelve.

32 The men of Beth-el and Ai, ~~an~~ **two** hundred twenty and three.

37 The children of Lod, Hadid, and Ono, seven hundred twenty and ~~one~~ **five**.

38 The children of Senaah, three thousand ~~nine~~ **six**[*] hundred and thirty.

44 The singers **of** the children of Asaph, ~~an~~ **a** hundred ~~forty~~ **twenty** and eight.

45 The porters; the children of Shallum, the children of Ater, the children of Talmon, the children of Akkub, the children of Hatita, the children of Shobai, ~~an~~ **a** hundred thirty and ~~eight~~ **nine**.

62 The children of Delaiah, the children of Tobiah, the children of Nekoda, six hundred ~~forty~~ **fifty** and two.

Chapter 10

29 They clave to their brethren, their nobles, and entered into ~~a curse, and into~~ an oath, ~~to~~ **that a curse should come upon them if they did not** walk in God's law, which was given by Moses the servant of God, and to observe and do all the commandments of the Lord ~~our Lord~~ **their God**, and his judgments and his statutes.

30 And that ~~we~~ **they** would not give ~~our~~ **their** daughters unto the people of the land, nor take ~~their~~ **the** daughters **of the people** for ~~our~~ **their** sons.

The Book of
JOB

Chapter 1

6 Now there was a day when the ~~sons~~ **children** of God came to present themselves before the Lord, and Satan came also among them.

Chapter 2

1 Again there was a day when the ~~sons~~ **children** of God came to present themselves before the Lord, and Satan came also among them to present himself before the Lord.

The Book of
PSALMS

Psalm 10

6 **For** he hath said in his heart, I shall not be moved, ~~for I shall~~ never ~~be~~ in adversity.

7 His mouth is full of cursing and deceit; and **his heart is full of** fraud; **and** under his tongue *is* mischief and vanity.

10 He croucheth **to the strong ones,** *and* humbleth himself, that the poor may fall by his ~~strong ones~~ **devices**.

13 ~~Wherefore doth~~ The wicked contemn God**; wherefore** he ~~hath~~ **doth** ~~said~~ **say** in his heart, Thou wilt not require ~~it~~ **iniquity at my hand**.

14 **O Lord,** thou hast seen ~~it~~ **all this,** for thou beholdest mischief and spite, to requite *it* with thy hand**.** The poor committeth himself unto thee; thou art the helper of the fatherless.

15 ~~Break~~ **O Lord,** thou **wilt break** the arm of the wicked, and **of** the evil ~~man~~**; and** seek out his wickedness ~~till~~ **until** thou find none **that remain**.

16 **And** the LORD ~~is~~ **shall be** King forever and ever **over his people; for** the ~~heathen~~ **wicked** ~~are~~ **shall** ~~perished~~ **perish** out of his land.

PSALM 11

1 In ~~the~~ **that day thou shalt come, O Lord; and I will** put ~~I~~ **my trust in thee. Thou shalt say unto thy people, for mine ear hath heard thy voice;** ~~how~~ **thou shalt** say ~~ye to~~ **unto** ~~my~~ **every** soul, Flee ~~as a bird to~~ **unto** ~~your~~ **my** mountain**; and the righteous shall flee like a bird that is let go from the snare of the fowler.**

2 For ~~lo~~ the wicked bend *their* bow; **lo,** they make ready their arrow upon the string, that they may privily shoot at the upright in heart**, to destroy their foundation.**

3 ~~If~~ **But** the foundations **of the wicked shall** be destroyed, **and** what can ~~the righteous~~ **they** do?

4 **For** the LORD, ~~is in~~ **when he shall come into** his holy temple, **sitting upon** ~~the Lord's~~ **God's** throne ~~is~~ in heaven, his eyes **shall pierce the wicked**.

5 4–5 Behold his eyelids **shall** try the children of men, ~~The LORD trieth the righteous~~ **and he shall redeem the righteous, and they shall be tried. The Lord loveth the righteous,**

but the wicked**,** and him that loveth violence**,** his soul hateth.

6 Upon the wicked he shall rain snares, fire**,** and brimstone, and ~~an~~ **a** horrible tempest**,** ~~this shall be~~ the portion of their cup.

PSALM 12

1 **In that day thou shalt** help, **O** LORD**, the poor and the meek of the earth.** For the godly man **shall** ~~ceaseth~~ **cease to be found,** ~~for~~ **and** the faithful fail from among the children of men.

2 They **shall** speak vanity everyone with his neighbor**;** *with* flattering lips, ~~and~~ with a double heart do they speak.

3 **But** the LORD shall cut off all flattering lips, ~~and~~ the tongue that speaketh proud things:

4 Who have said, With our tongue will we prevail; our lips *are* our own, who ~~is~~ **shall be** lord over us?

5 **Therefore, thus saith the Lord, I will arise in that day, I will stand upon the earth, and I will judge the earth** for the oppression of the poor, for the sighing of the needy**; and their cry hath entered into mine ear.** ~~now will I arise, saith the LORD; I will~~

6 5–6 **Therefore the Lord shall sit in judgment upon all those who say in their hearts, We all** ~~set~~ **sit** ~~him~~ in safety**;** ~~from him that~~ **and** puffeth at him. **These are** the words of the LORD; **yea,** ~~are~~ pure words, ~~as~~ **like** silver tried in a furnace of earth, purified seven times.

7 Thou shalt ~~keep~~ **save** ~~them~~ **thy people,** O LORD**; thou shalt keep them;** thou shalt preserve them from **the wickedness of** ~~this~~ **their** generation forever.

8 The wicked walk on every side, ~~when~~ **and** the vilest men are exalted;

but in the day of their pride thou shalt visit them.

PSALM 13

1 How long, **O Lord, wilt thou withdraw thyself from me? How long wilt thou hide thy face from me, that I may not see thee?** Wilt thou forget me, ~~O Lord~~ **and cast me off from thy presence** forever ~~how long wilt thou hide thy face from me~~?

2 How long shall I take counsel in my soul, ~~having sorrow~~ **sorrowing** in my heart daily? How long shall mine enemy be exalted over me?

3 3–4 Consider ~~and hear~~ me, O LORD; **and hear my cry, O** my God; **and** lighten mine eyes, lest I ~~sleep the sleep of~~ **the** death **of the ungodly;** lest mine enemy say, I have prevailed against him**.**

4 ~~and~~ Those that trouble me, rejoice when I am moved**;**

PSALM 14

1 The fool hath said in his heart, *There is* no **man that hath seen** God. **Because he showeth himself not unto us, therefore there is no God. Behold,** they are corrupt; they have done abominable works, ~~there is~~ **and** none **of them** ~~that~~ doeth good.

2 **For** the LORD looked down from heaven upon the children of men, **and by his voice said unto his servant, Seek ye among the children of men,** to see if there ~~were~~ **are** any that ~~did~~ **do** understand ~~and seek~~ God. **And he opened his mouth unto the Lord, and said, Behold, all these who say they are thine.**

3 **The Lord answered, and said,** They are all gone aside, they are ~~all~~ together become filthy, ~~there is~~ **thou canst behold** none **of them*** that ~~doeth~~ **are doing** good, no, not one.

4 **All they** have ~~all the~~ **for their teachers are** workers of iniquity**, and there is** no knowledge **in them. They are they** who eat up my people. ~~as~~ They eat bread and call not upon the LORD.

5 **They** ~~There were~~ **are** ~~they~~ in great fear, for God ~~is~~ **dwells** in the generation of the righteous. **He is the counsel of the poor, because they are ashamed of the wicked, and flee unto the Lord for their refuge.**

6 ~~Ye~~ **They** ~~have~~ **are** ~~shamed~~ **ashamed of** the counsel of the poor because the LORD ~~is~~ his refuge.

7 Oh that **Zion were established out of heaven,** the salvation of Israel ~~were come out of~~. **O Lord, when wilt thou establish** Zion? When the LORD bringeth back the captivity of his people, Jacob shall rejoice, ~~and~~ Israel shall be glad.

PSALM 15

1 LORD, who shall abide in thy tabernacle? who shall dwell in thy holy hill **of Zion**?

4 In whose eyes a vile person is contemned; but he honoreth them that fear the LORD; ~~He that~~ sweareth **not falsely** to ~~his own~~ hurt **any man**, and changeth not.

PSALM 16

2 ~~O my soul~~ Thou hast said unto ~~the LORD~~ **me, that** thou *art* ~~my~~ **the** Lord **my God, and,** My goodness ~~extendeth not~~ **is extended** ~~to~~ **unto** thee;

3 ~~But~~ **And** to **all** the saints that ~~are~~ **dwell** in the earth, and ~~to~~ the excellent, in whom *is* all my delight.

4 **And the wicked, there is no delight in them;** their sorrows shall be multiplied **upon all those** ~~that~~ **who** hasten ~~after~~ **for to seek** another *god*; their drink offerings of blood will I not ~~offer~~ **accept**, nor take up their names into my lips.

5 ~~The~~ **Therefore thou,** Lord, ~~is~~ **art** the portion of mine inheritance, and of my cup; thou maintainest my lot.

PSALM 17

1 ~~Hear the~~ **Give me** right **words**, O Lord; **speak, and thy servant shall hear thee;** attend unto my cry, give ear unto my prayer. ~~that goeth~~ **I come** not **unto thee** out of feigned lips.

3 3–4 Thou hast proved mine heart; thou hast visited *me* in the night; thou hast tried me; ~~and~~ thou shalt find nothing **evil in me, for** I am purposed ~~that~~ my mouth shall not transgress concerning the works of men.

4 By the word of thy lips I have kept ~~me from~~ **out of** the paths of the destroyer.

6 I have called upon thee, for thou wilt hear, ~~me~~* O God, **my speech; and** incline thine ear unto me ~~and hear~~ my speech.

7 Show thy marvelous loving-kindness, O thou that savest ~~by thy right hand~~ them which put their trust *in thee*, **by thy right hand** from those that rise up ~~against them~~.

9 ~~From the wicked that oppress me, from~~ My deadly enemies ~~who~~ compass me about;

14 13–14 Deliver my soul from the wicked ~~which is~~ **by** thy* sword; from men ~~which are~~ **by** thy **strong** hand. **Yea,** O Lord, from men of the world; ~~which have~~ **for** their portion **is** in ~~this~~ **their** life, and whose belly thou fillest with thy ~~hid treasure~~ **good things;** they are full of children, and **they die and** leave the rest of their ~~substance~~ **inheritance** to their babes.

PSALM 18

3 I will call upon the Lord, for ~~who~~ **he** *is worthy* to be praised; so shall I be saved from mine enemies.

30 ~~As for~~ **O** God, ~~his~~ **thy** ~~way~~ **ways** ~~is~~ **are** perfect; the word of the Lord is tried; he *is* a buckler to all those ~~that~~ **who** trust in him.

32 ~~It is~~ **Our** God that girdeth me with strength, and maketh my way perfect?

41 They cried, but ~~there was~~ **found** none to save ~~them;~~ ~~even~~ unto the Lord, but he answered them not.

PSALM 19

3 ~~There is~~ No speech nor language ~~where~~ **can be**, **if** their voice is not heard.

13 Keep back thy servant also from presumptuous ~~sins~~ **acts;**[21] let them not have dominion over me; then shall I be upright, and I shall be innocent from the great transgression.

PSALM 22

1 My God, ~~my God~~ why hast thou forsaken me? **My God, hear the words of my roaring;** ~~why art~~ thou **art** ~~so~~ far from helping me ~~and from the words of my roaring~~.

2 O my God, I cry in the daytime, but thou ~~hearest~~ **answereth** not; and in the night season, and am not silent.

3 But thou *art* holy ~~O thou~~ that inhabitest **the heavens; thou art worthy of** the praises of Israel.

6 But I, ~~am~~ a worm, ~~and~~ **am loved of** no man; a reproach of men, and despised of the people.

10 I was cast upon thee from the womb; thou ~~art~~ **wast** my God from my mother's ~~belly~~ **breasts**.

12 Many ~~bulls~~ **armies** have compassed me; strong ~~bulls~~ **armies** of Bashan have beset me ~~round~~ **around**.

13 They gaped upon me ~~with~~ their mouths, ~~as~~ **like** a ravening and a roaring lion.

21 Save me from the lion's mouth, for thou hast heard me **speak** from **the secret places of the wilderness, through** the horns of the unicorns.

31 They shall come, and shall declare his righteousness unto a people that shall be born, ~~that~~ **what** he hath done ~~this~~.

Psalm 24

7 7–8 Lift up your heads, O ye ~~gates~~ **generations of Jacob**; and be ye ~~lift~~ **lifted** up; ~~ye everlasting doors~~ and the **Lord strong and mighty; the Lord mighty in battle, who is the** King of glory, shall ~~come in~~ **establish you forever**. ~~Who *is* this King of glory? The Lord strong and mighty, the Lord mighty in battle.~~

8 And he will roll away the heavens; and will come down to redeem his people; to make you an everlasting name; to establish you upon his everlasting rock.

9 Lift up your heads, O ye ~~gates~~ **generations of Jacob**; ~~even~~ lift ~~*them*~~ up **your heads**, ye everlasting ~~doors~~ **generations,** and the ~~King~~ **Lord** of ~~glory shall come in~~ **hosts, the king of kings;**

10 ~~Who is~~ **Even** ~~this~~ **the** King of glory ~~The Lord of hosts, he *is* the King of glory~~ **shall come unto you; and shall redeem his people, and shall establish them in righteousness.** Selah.

Psalm 27

3 Though an host should encamp against me, my heart shall not fear; though war should rise against me, in this ~~*will*~~ I ~~*be*~~ **am** confident.

13 ~~*I had fainted*~~ Unless I had believed to see the goodness of the Lord in the land of the living, **thou wouldst deliver my soul into hell.**

14 **Thou didst say unto me,** Wait on the Lord, be of good courage, and he shall strengthen ~~thine~~ **thy** heart; wait, I say, on the Lord.

Psalm 30

5 For his anger ~~*endureth but*~~ **kindleth against the wicked; they repent, and in** a moment **it is turned away, and they are** in his favor ~~*is*~~**, and he giveth them** life**; therefore,** weeping may endure for a night, but joy *cometh* in the morning.

9 ~~What profit *is there* in my blood~~ When I go down to the pit, **my blood shall return to the dust.** ~~Shall the dust~~ **I will** praise thee; **my soul** shall ~~it~~ declare thy truth; **for what profit am I, if I do it not?**

12 To the end that *my* ~~glory~~ **soul** may **give glory to thy name, and** sing praise to thee, and not be silent. O Lord my God, I will give thanks unto thee forever.

Psalm 32

1 Blessed ~~*is he*~~ **are they** *whose* ~~transgression~~ **transgressions** ~~*is*~~ **are** forgiven, **and** ~~*whose*~~ **who have no** ~~sin~~ **sins** ~~*is*~~ **to be** covered.

3 When I kept silence, **my spirit failed within me; when I opened my mouth,** my bones waxed old through my ~~roaring~~ **speaking** all the day long.

4 For day and night thy ~~hand~~ **Spirit** was heavy upon me; my moisture is turned into the drought of summer. Selah.

8 **Thou hast said,** I will instruct thee and teach thee in the way which thou shalt go; I will guide thee with mine eye.

Psalm 33

1 Rejoice in the Lord, O ye righteous; ~~*for*~~ **to** praise **the Lord** is comely for the upright **in heart.**

2 Praise the LORD with ~~harp~~ **thy voice;** sing unto him with the psaltery *and* **harp,** an instrument ~~of~~ **with** ten strings.

4 For the word of the LORD *is* **given to the** ~~right~~ **upright**; and all his works *are done* in truth.

9 For he spake, and it was ~~done~~ **finished**; he commanded, and it stood fast.

12 Blessed ~~is~~ **are** the ~~nation~~ **nations*** ~~whose God is the LORD~~ *and* the people *whom* ~~he~~ **the Lord God** hath chosen for his own inheritance.

19 To deliver their soul from death, and to keep them alive in **a time of** famine.

PSALM 35
12 They rewarded me evil for good, ~~to~~ **for the purpose of** the spoiling of my soul.

PSALM 36
1 The ~~transgression of the~~ wicked, **who live in transgression,** saith ~~within~~ **in** ~~my~~ **their** ~~heart~~ **hearts,** *that* ~~There is~~ **no condemnation; for there is** no fear of God before ~~his~~ **their** eyes.

2 For ~~he~~ **they** flattereth ~~himself~~ **themselves** in ~~his~~ **their** own eyes, until ~~his~~ **their** ~~iniquity~~ **iniquities** ~~be~~ **are** found to be hateful.

3 The words of ~~his~~ **their** mouth *are* **full of** iniquity and deceit. ~~he~~ **The wicked man** hath left off to be wise, *and* to do good;

4 He deviseth mischief upon his bed; he setteth himself in a way *that is* not good ~~he abhorreth not evil.~~

5 ~~Thy mercy~~ O LORD, **thou** ~~is~~ **art** in the heavens; ~~and thy faithfulness reacheth unto~~ **they are full of thy mercy. And the thoughts of a righteous man ascendeth up unto thee whose throne is far above** the clouds.

6 **He is filled with** thy righteousness ~~is~~ like the great mountains**, and with** thy judgments ~~are~~ **like** a great deep. O LORD, thou preservest man and beast.

12 ~~There~~ **They** are the workers of iniquity ~~fallen~~ **and shall fall;** they ~~are~~ **shall be** cast down, and shall not be able to rise.

PSALM 37
38 But the transgressors shall be destroyed together**;** the end of the wicked shall **come, and they will*** be cut off.

PSALM 38
7 For my loins are filled with a loathsome ~~disease~~ **distress;** and ~~there is~~ no soundness **is found** in my flesh.

8 I am feeble**,** and ~~sore~~ broken**, and very sore.** I have ~~roared~~ **wept** by reason of the disquietness of my heart.

11 My lovers and my friends stand aloof ~~from~~ **because of** my sore; and my kinsmen stand afar off.

PSALM 39
9 I was dumb, ~~I~~ **and** opened not my mouth; because thou didst ~~it~~ **chasten me.**

10 Remove thy stroke away from me, **or** I ~~am~~ **shall be** consumed by the blow of ~~thine~~ **thy** hand.

PSALM 41
3 The LORD will strengthen him upon the bed of languishing; thou wilt make all his **pains to cease, when he is laid in his** bed ~~in his~~ **of** sickness.

PSALM 42
2 My soul thirsteth for **to see** God, for **to see** the living God; when shall I come and appear before **thee, O** God?

3 My tears have been ~~my meat~~

poured out unto thee day and night, while ~~they~~ **mine enemies** continually say unto me, Where *is* thy God?

4 When I remember these ~~things~~ **mine enemies**, I pour out my soul ~~in~~ **unto** ~~me~~ **thee;** for I had gone with the multitude, I **also** went with them to the house of God, with the voice of joy and praise, with ~~a~~ **the** multitude that kept holyday.

Psalm 46

1 God *is* our refuge and strength, a ~~very~~ present help in trouble.

2 Therefore **we** will not ~~we~~ fear, though the earth **shall** be removed, and though the mountains **shall** be carried into the midst of the sea;

3 ~~Though~~ **And** the waters thereof roar, ~~and~~ ~~be~~ **being** troubled, ~~though~~ **and** the mountains shake with the swelling thereof. ~~Selah.~~

4 **Yet** *there* ~~is~~ **shall be** a river, the streams whereof shall make glad the city of God, the holy *place** of the ~~tabernacles~~ **tabernacle** of the Most High.

5 **For Zion shall come, and** God ~~is~~ **shall be** in the midst of her; she shall not be moved; God shall help her ~~and~~ ~~that~~ right early.

6 The heathen **shall be** ~~raged~~ **enraged, and** ~~the~~ **their** kingdoms ~~were~~ **shall be** moved, **and** ~~he~~ **the Lord shall** ~~uttered~~ **utter** his voice, **and** the earth **shall be** melted;

7 The Lord of hosts **who** ~~is~~ **shall be** with us, the God of Jacob ~~is~~ our refuge. Selah.

8 Come, behold the works of the Lord, what desolations he ~~hath~~ **shall** ~~made~~ **make** in the earth **in the latter days**.

9 He maketh wars to cease unto the end of the earth; he breaketh the bow, and cutteth the spear in sunder; he

burneth the chariot in the fire, **and saith unto the nations,**

11 The Lord of hosts ~~is~~ **shall be** with us; the God of Jacob ~~is~~ our refuge. Selah.

Psalm 49

7 None ~~of them~~ can by any means redeem his brother;

8 7–8 Nor give to God a ransom for him **that he should still live forever, that it ceaseth not forever to see corruption.**

9 8 For the redemption of their ~~soul~~ **souls** *is* **through God, and** precious ~~and it ceaseth for ever~~.

10 For he seeth ~~that~~ wise men die; likewise the fool and the brutish person perish, and leave their wealth to others;

11 Their inward thought ~~is, that~~ **of** their houses ~~shall continue~~ forever; ~~and~~ their dwelling places, to all generations. **Lands** they ~~call~~ **called after** *their* ~~lands after their~~ own names, **and they are honorable**.

12 Nevertheless, man ~~being~~ in honor abideth not; he is **also** like the beasts *that* perish.

13 This **I speak of them who walk in** their way, **and forsaketh the Almighty** ~~is~~ **in** their folly; yet their posterity approve their sayings. Selah.

Psalm 50

21 These *things* hast thou done, and I kept silence; thou thoughtest that I was altogether *such* ~~an~~ **a** one as thyself; but I will reprove thee, and set ~~them~~ **covenants** in order before thine eyes.

22 Now consider this, ye that forget God, lest I tear *you* in pieces, and ~~there~~ ~~be~~ none ~~to~~ **can** deliver.

Psalm 52

7 Lo, ~~this~~ ~~is~~ the man ~~that~~ **who** made not God his strength; but trusted in

the abundance of his riches, *and* strengthened himself in his wickedness.

9 I will praise thee forever, because thou hast done ~~it~~ **wonderful works;** ~~and~~ I will wait on thy name; for ~~it~~ **thou** ~~is~~ **art** good before thy saints.

PSALM 53

1 The fool hath said in his heart, *There is* no God. **Such are** corrupt ~~are they~~, and **they** have done abominable iniquity**.** *There* ~~is~~ **are** none that doeth good.

4 ~~Have~~ The workers of iniquity **have** no knowledge**;** ~~who~~ **they** eat up my people *as* they eat bread**;** they have not called upon God.

5 3,5 *There is* none that doeth good, no not one. ~~There were~~ They **were** in great fear ~~where no fear was~~, for God hath scattered the bones of him that encampeth *against* ~~thee~~ **him.**

6 5–6 **O Lord,** thou hast put ~~them~~ to shame **those who have said in their hearts there was no fear,** because ~~God~~ **thou** ~~hath~~ **hast** despised them.

7 6 Oh that ~~the salvation of Israel~~ **Zion** *were come*, **the salvation of Israel; for** out of Zion **shall they be judged,** when God bringeth back the captivity of his people. **And** Jacob shall rejoice**;** ~~and~~ Israel shall be glad.

PSALM 55

12 For *it was* not an enemy *that* reproached me**,** ~~then I could have borne it~~ neither ~~was it~~ he that hated me *that* did magnify *himself* against me; **if so,** then I ~~would~~ **could** have **borne it; I would have** hid myself from him**;**

13 But *it was* ~~thou~~ a man**,** mine equal, my guide, and mine acquaintance.

20 ~~He~~ **They** ~~hath~~ **have** put forth ~~his~~ their hands against such as be at peace with ~~him~~ **them;** ~~he~~ **they** ~~hath~~ **have** broken ~~his~~ **the Lord's** covenant.

21 *The words* of ~~his~~ **their** mouth were smoother than butter, but war *was* in ~~his~~ **their** heart**.** ~~his~~ **Their** words were softer than oil, yet ~~were~~ they **have** drawn swords.

PSALM 56

3 What**!** ~~time I~~ am **I** afraid? I will trust in thee.

PSALM 82

2 How long will ye **suffer them to** judge unjustly, and accept the persons of the wicked? Selah.

PSALM 90

13 Return **us**, O LORD. How long **wilt thou hide thy face from thy servants?** and let ~~it~~ **them** repent ~~thee~~ **of all their hard speeches they have spoken** concerning **thee** ~~thy servants~~.

PSALM 92

13 Those that ~~be~~ **he** planted in the house of the LORD shall flourish in the courts of our God.

PSALM 102

18 This shall be written for the generation to come**;** and the people which shall be ~~created~~ **gathered** shall praise the LORD.

PSALM 104

1 Bless the LORD, O my soul. O LORD my God, thou art very great; thou art clothed with ~~honor~~ **power** and majesty.

26 There go the ships**;** ~~there is that~~ **and thou hast made** leviathan ~~whom thou hast made~~ to play therein.

PSALM 105

42 For he remembered his holy

promise, ~~and~~ **unto** Abraham his servant.

Psalm 106

4 Remember me, O Lord, with the favor ~~that thou bearest unto~~ **of** thy people; O visit me with thy salvation;

7 Our fathers understood not thy wonders in Egypt; they remembered not the multitude of thy mercies; but provoked ~~him~~ **thee** at the sea, ~~even~~ at the Red sea.

45 And he remembered for them his covenant, and ~~repented~~ **spared his people** according to the multitude of his mercies.

Psalm 107

11 Because they rebelled against the ~~words~~ **works** of God, and contemned the counsel of the Most High;

Psalm 109

3 They compassed me about ~~also;~~ **they spake against me also,** with words* of hatred; and fought against me without a cause.

4 ~~For~~ **And, notwithstanding** my love, they are my adversaries; ~~but~~ **yet** I ~~give myself unto~~ **will continue in** prayer **for them**.

6 Set thou a wicked man over ~~him~~ **them;** and let Satan stand at his right hand.

7 When ~~he~~ **they** shall be judged, let ~~him~~ **them** be condemned; and let ~~his~~ **their** prayer become sin.

8 Let ~~his~~ **their** days be few; ~~and~~ let another take ~~his~~ **their** office.

9 Let ~~his~~ **their** children be fatherless, and ~~his~~ **their** ~~wife~~ **wives** ~~a widow~~ **widows.**

10 Let ~~his~~ **their** children be continually vagabonds, and beg; let them seek ~~their bread~~ also out of their desolate places.

11 Let the extortioner catch all that ~~he~~ **they** ~~hath~~ **have**; and let the ~~strangers~~ **stranger** spoil ~~his~~ **their** labor.

12 Let there be none to extend mercy unto ~~him~~ **them,** neither let there be any to favor ~~his~~ **their** fatherless children.

13 Let ~~his~~ **their** posterity be cut off ~~and~~ in the generation following; let their ~~name~~ **names*** be blotted out.

14 Let the iniquity of ~~his~~ **their** fathers be remembered ~~with~~ **before** the Lord; and let not the sin of ~~his~~ **their** ~~mother~~ **mothers** be blotted out.

16 Because ~~that he~~ **they** remembered not to show mercy, but persecuted the poor and needy man, that ~~he~~ **they** might even slay the broken in heart.

17 As ~~he~~ **they** loved cursing, so let it come upon ~~him~~ **them;** as ~~he~~ **they** delighted not in blessing, so let it be far from ~~him~~ **them.**

18 As ~~he~~ **they** clothed ~~himself~~ **themselves** with cursing like as with ~~his~~ **their** ~~garment~~ **garments,** so let it come into ~~his~~ **their** bowels like water, and like oil into ~~his~~ **their** bones.

19 Let it be unto ~~him~~ **them** as ~~the~~ **a** garment *which** covereth ~~him~~ **them,** and for a girdle wherewith ~~he~~ **they** ~~is~~ **are** girded continually.

20 ~~Let~~ **This** **shall** ~~be~~ the reward of mine adversaries, from the Lord; and of them ~~that~~ **who** speak evil against my soul.

21 But do thou ~~for~~ **deliver** me, O ~~God the~~ Lord **my God,** for thy name's sake; because thy mercy *is* good, **therefore** deliver thou me.

Psalm 110

6 He shall judge among the heathen, he shall fill ~~the places~~ **their streets** with ~~the~~ **their** dead bodies; he shall

wound the heads over many countries.

PSALM 112

1 Praise ye the LORD. Blessed *is* the man ~~that~~ **who** feareth the LORD, ~~that~~ **and** delighteth greatly in his commandments.

8 His heart *is* established, he shall not be afraid, until he see ~~his desire~~ **judgment executed** upon his enemies.

PSALM 115

1 Not unto us, O LORD, not unto us, but unto thy name ~~give~~ **be** glory, for thy mercy, *and* for thy truth's sake.

9 O Israel, trust thou in the LORD; he *is* ~~their~~ **thy** help and ~~their~~ **thy** shield.

10 O house of Aaron, trust in the LORD; he *is* ~~their~~ **thy** help and ~~their~~ **thy** shield.

11 Ye that fear the LORD, trust in the LORD; he *is* ~~their~~ **your** help and ~~their~~ **your** shield.

PSALM 119

15 I will meditate ~~in~~ **upon** thy precepts, and have respect unto thy ways.

20 My ~~soul~~ **heart** breaketh**,** for ~~the my soul~~ ~~longing~~ **longeth** ~~that it hath unto~~ **after** thy judgments at all times.

21 Thou hast rebuked the proud; ~~that~~ **they** *are* cursed who do err from thy commandments.

33 Teach me, O LORD, the way of thy statutes; and I shall keep it ~~unto~~ **to** the end.

48 My hands also will I lift up unto thy commandments, which I have loved; and I will meditate ~~in~~ **upon** thy statutes.

78 Let the proud be ashamed; for they dealt perversely with me without

a cause; *but* I will meditate ~~in~~ **upon** thy precepts.

109 My soul *is* continually in ~~my~~ **thy** hand; ~~yet~~ **and** I do ~~I~~ not forget thy law.

126 ~~It is~~ **And the** time ~~for thee~~, O LORD, **for me** to work; *for* they have made void thy law.

130 The entrance of thy words giveth light; ~~it~~ **they** ~~giveth~~ **give** understanding unto the simple.

PSALM 121

3 4 Behold, he that keepeth Israel shall neither slumber nor sleep.

4 3 He will not suffer thy foot to be moved: he that keepeth thee will not slumber.

PSALM 124

1 1–3 **Now may Israel say,** If ~~it had not been~~ the LORD ~~who~~ was **not** on our side ~~now may Israel say; If it had not been the LORD who was on our side~~ when men rose up against us, then they had swallowed us up quick when their wrath was kindled against us.

2 4 Then the waters had overwhelmed us, the stream had gone over our soul:

3 5 Then the proud waters had gone over our soul.

4 6 Blessed *be* the LORD, who hath not given us *as* a prey to their teeth.

5 7 Our soul is escaped as a bird out of the snare of the fowlers: the snare is broken, and we are escaped.

6 8 Our help *is* in the name of the LORD, who made heaven and earth.

PSALM 125

1 They that trust in the LORD ~~shall be as~~ **in** mount Zion, ~~which~~ cannot be removed, *but* ~~abideth~~ **abide** forever.

4 Do good, O LORD, unto ~~those that~~

be **the** good, and ~~to them that are~~ **unto the** upright in their hearts.

PSALM 135

14 For the LORD will judge his people, and he will **not** repent himself concerning his servants.

21 Blessed be the LORD out of Zion; **Blessed be the Lord** ~~which dwelleth at~~ **out of** Jerusalem. Praise ye the LORD.

PSALM 137

5 If I forget thee, O Jerusalem, let my right hand forget ~~her~~ **its** *cunning*.

PSALM 138

2 I will worship toward thy holy temple, and praise thy name for thy loving-kindness and for thy truth; for ~~thou~~ **that** hast magnified thy word above all thy name.

8 The LORD will perfect ~~that~~ **me** ~~which~~ **in knowledge,** ~~concerneth~~ **concerning** ~~me~~ **his kingdom.** ~~thy mercy~~ **I will praise thee** O LORD, ~~en~~

~~dureth~~ forever; **for thou art merciful, and wilt not** forsake ~~not~~ the works of thine own hands.

PSALM 139

16 Thine eyes did see my substance, yet being unperfect; and in thy book all *my members* were written, *which* in continuance were fashioned, when *as* yet **I** ~~there was~~ **knew** none of them.

PSALM 141

5 ~~Let~~ **When** the righteous smite me **with the word of the Lord** *it* ~~shall be~~ **is** a kindness; and ~~let~~ **when** ~~him~~ **they** reprove me, *it shall be* an excellent oil, **and** ~~which~~ shall not ~~break~~ **destroy** my ~~head~~ **faith**; for yet my prayer also *shall be* **for them. I delight not** in their calamities.

PSALM 143

3 For the enemy hath persecuted my soul; he hath smitten my life down to the ground; he hath made me to dwell in darkness, as those that have **long** been ~~long~~ dead.

The Book of
PROVERBS

CHAPTER 11

1 A false balance *is* **an** abomination to the LORD; but a just weight *is* his delight.

20 They that are of a froward heart *are* **an** abomination to the LORD; but *such as are* upright in *their* way *are* his delight.

CHAPTER 16

29 A violent man enticeth his neighbor, and leadeth him into ~~the~~ **a** way *that is* not good.

CHAPTER 18

22 *Whoso* findeth a **good** wife ~~findeth a good~~ *thing,* and **hath** ~~obtaineth~~ **obtained** favor of the LORD.

CHAPTER 22

12 The eyes of the LORD preserve knowledge; ~~and~~ **but** he overthroweth the words of the transgressor.

CHAPTER 30

30 A lion, *which is* strongest among beasts and turneth not away ~~for~~ **from** any;

ECCLESIASTES
or, the Preacher

CHAPTER 3

1 To every *thing there is* a season, and a time to every purpose under ~~the~~ heaven;

The Book of the Prophet
ISAIAH

CHAPTER 1

16 Wash ~~you~~ **ye**, make you clean; put away the evil of your doings from before mine eyes; cease to do evil;

CHAPTER 2

2 And it shall come to pass in the last days, *that* **when** the mountain of the LORD's house shall be established in the top of the mountains, and shall be exalted above the hills, and all nations shall flow unto it;

5 O house of Jacob, come ye, and let us walk in the light of the LORD; **yea, come, for ye have all gone astray, everyone to his wicked ways.**

6 Therefore, **O Lord,** thou hast forsaken thy people the house of Jacob, because they be replenished from the east, and ~~are~~ **hearken unto the** soothsayers like the Philistines, and they please themselves in the children of strangers.

9 And the mean man boweth **not** down, and the great man humbleth himself **not;** therefore forgive them not.

10 **O ye wicked ones,** enter into the rock, and hide ~~thee~~ **ye** in the dust; for

the fear of the LORD and ~~for the glory of~~ his majesty **shall smite thee**.

11 **And it shall come to pass that** the lofty looks of man shall be humbled, and the haughtiness of ~~men~~ **man** shall be bowed down, and the LORD alone shall be exalted in that day.

12 For the day of the LORD of hosts ~~shall be~~ **soon cometh upon all nations; yea, upon everyone; yea,** upon ~~every one that is~~ **the** proud and lofty, and upon every *one* ~~that~~ **who** *is* lifted up, and he shall be brought low.

13 **Yea,** and **the day of the Lord shall come** upon all the cedars of Lebanon, **for** ~~that~~ **they** *are* high and lifted up; and upon all the oaks of Bashan;

14 And upon all the high mountains, and upon all the hills, **and upon all the nations** ~~that~~ **which** *are* lifted up;

15 And upon every **people, and upon every** high tower, and upon every fenced wall,

16 **And upon all the ships of the sea,** and upon all the ships of Tarshish, and upon all pleasant pictures.

19 And they shall go into the holes of the rocks, and into the caves of the

earth, for **the** fear of the Lord **shall come upon them,** and ~~for~~ the glory of his majesty **shall smite them**, when he ariseth to shake terribly the earth.

20 In that day a man shall cast his idols of silver, and his idols of gold, which ~~they~~ **he hath** made ~~each one~~ for himself to worship, to the moles and to the bats;

21 To go into the clefts of the rocks, and into the tops of the ragged rocks, for **the** fear of the Lord **shall come upon them**, and ~~for~~ the ~~glory of his~~ majesty **of the Lord shall smite them**, when he ariseth to shake terribly the earth.

Chapter 3

1 For, behold, the Lord, the Lord of hosts, doth take away from Jerusalem and from Judah the stay and the staff, the whole ~~stay~~ **staff** of bread, and the whole stay of water,

4 And I will give children **unto them** *to be* their princes, and babes shall rule over them.

6 When a man shall take hold of his brother of the house of his father, ~~saying~~ **and shall˙ say**, Thou hast clothing, be thou our ruler, and *let* **not** this ruin ~~be~~ **come** under thy hand;

7 In that day shall he swear, saying, I will not be ~~an~~ **a** healer; for in my house **there** *is* neither bread nor clothing; make me not a ruler of the people.

8 For Jerusalem is ruined, and Judah is fallen; because their ~~tongue~~ **tongues** and their doings ~~are~~ **have been** against the Lord, to provoke the eyes of his glory.

9 The show of their countenance doth witness against them; and ~~they~~ **doth** declare their sin **to be even** as Sodom, they **cannot** hide *it* ~~not~~. Woe unto their ~~soul~~ **souls**! for they have rewarded evil unto themselves.

10 Say ~~ye to~~ **unto** the righteous, that *it ~~shall be~~* **is** well *~~with him~~* **them;** for they shall eat the fruit of their doings.

11 Woe unto the wicked! **for** *~~it~~* **they** *shall ~~be~~* ~~ill~~ *~~with him~~* **perish**; for the reward of ~~his~~ **their** hands shall be ~~given~~ **upon** ~~him~~ **them**.

12 **And** *as for* my people, children *are* their oppressors, and women rule over them. O my people, they ~~which~~ **who** lead thee cause *thee* to err, and destroy the way of thy paths.

14 The Lord will enter into judgment with the ancients of his people, and the princes thereof; for ye have eaten up the vineyard; **and** the spoil of the poor *is* in your houses.

15 What mean ye? ~~that~~ ye beat my people to pieces, and grind the faces of the poor, saith the Lord God of hosts.

18 In that day the Lord will take away the bravery of *~~their~~* tinkling ornaments *~~about their feet~~*, and ~~their~~ cauls, and ~~their~~ round tires like the moon,

24 And it shall come to pass, ~~that~~ instead of sweet smell there shall be stink; and instead of a girdle a rent; and instead of well set hair, baldness; and instead of a stomacher a girding of sackcloth; ~~and~~ burning instead of beauty.

26 And her gates shall lament and mourn; and she *~~being~~* **shall be** desolate, **and** shall sit upon the ground.

Chapter 3 4

27 1 And in that day seven women shall take hold of one man, saying, We will eat our own bread, and wear our own apparel; only let us be called by thy name, to take away our reproach.[22]

Chapter 4

1 2 In that day shall the branch of the Lord be beautiful and glorious, and the fruit of the earth *shall be* excellent and comely ~~for~~ **to** them that are escaped of Israel.

2 3 And it shall come to pass, ~~that he~~ **they** *that* ~~is~~ **are** left in Zion, and *he that* remaineth in Jerusalem, shall be called holy, *even* everyone that is written among the living in Jerusalem;

3 4 When the Lord shall have washed away the filth of the daughters of Zion, and shall have purged the blood of Jerusalem from the midst thereof by the spirit of judgment, and by the spirit of burning.

4 5 And the Lord will create upon every dwelling place of mount Zion, and upon her assemblies, a cloud and smoke by day, and the shining of a flaming fire by night; for upon all the glory **of Zion** *shall be* a defense.

5 6 And there shall be a tabernacle for a shadow in the daytime from the heat, and for a place of refuge, and for a covert from storm and from rain.

Chapter 5

1 ~~Now~~ **And then** will I sing to my wellbeloved a song of my beloved touching his vineyard. My wellbeloved hath a vineyard in a very fruitful hill;

4 What could have been done more to my vineyard, that I have not done in it? wherefore, when I looked that it should bring forth grapes, **it** brought ~~it~~ forth wild grapes.

5 And now go to; I will tell you what I will do to my vineyard: I will take away the hedge thereof, and it shall be eaten up; *and* **I will** break down the wall thereof, and it shall be trodden down;

8 Woe unto them that join house to house, *that* lay field to field, till *there* **can** *be* no place, that they may be placed alone in the midst of the earth!

9 In mine ears *said* the Lord of hosts, Of a truth many houses shall be desolate, ~~even~~ **and** great and fair **cities** without inhabitant.

11 Woe unto them that rise up early in the morning, *that* they may follow strong drink**, and*** that continue until night, ~~till~~ **and** wine inflame them!

21 Woe unto ~~them that are~~ **the** wise in their own eyes, and prudent in their own sight!

22 Woe unto ~~them that are~~ **the** mighty to drink wine, and men of strength to mingle strong drink;

28 28–29 Whose arrows ~~are~~ **shall be** sharp, and all their bows bent, **and** their horses' hooves shall be counted like flint, and their wheels like a whirlwind; their roaring *shall be* like a lion**.**

29 They shall roar like young lions; yea, they shall roar, and lay hold of the prey, and shall carry ~~it~~ away safe, and none shall deliver ~~it~~.

30 And in that day they shall roar against them like the roaring of the sea; and if ~~one~~ **they** look unto the land, behold darkness *and* sorrow; and the light is darkened in the heavens thereof.

Chapter 6

7 And he laid *it* upon my mouth, and said, Lo, this ~~hath~~ **has** touched thy lips; and thine iniquity is taken away, and thy sin purged.

9 And he said, Go, and tell this people, Hear ye indeed, but **they** ~~understand~~ **understood** not; and see ye indeed, but **they** ~~perceive~~ **perceived** not.

10 Make the heart of this people fat, and make their ears heavy, and shut their eyes; lest they see with their eyes, and hear with their ears, and understand with their ~~heart~~ **hearts**, and convert, and be healed.

11 Then said I, Lord, how long? And he ~~answered~~ **said**, Until the cities be wasted without inhabitant, and the houses without man, and the land be utterly desolate.

12 And the Lord have removed men far away, ~~and~~ **for** *there* **shall** *be* a great forsaking in the midst of the land.

13 But yet in it **there** *shall be* a tenth, and ~~it~~ **they** shall return, and shall be eaten; as a teil tree, and as an oak, whose substance *is* in them, when they cast *their leaves; so* the holy seed *shall be* the substance thereof.

CHAPTER 7

6 Let us go up against Judah, and vex it, and let us make a breach therein for us, and set a king in the midst of it, **yea,** *even* the son of Tabeal;

14 Therefore the Lord himself shall give you a sign; Behold, a virgin shall conceive, and **shall** bear a son, and shall call his name Immanuel.

15 Butter and honey shall he eat, that he may know to refuse the evil, and **to** choose the good.

23 And it shall come to pass in that day ~~that~~ every place shall be, where there were a thousand vines at a thousand silverlings, ~~it~~ **which** shall ~~even~~ be for briers and thorns.

CHAPTER 8

1 Moreover **the word of** the Lord said unto me, Take thee a great roll, and write in it with a man's pen concerning Maher-shalal-hash-baz.

4 For behold, the child shall **not** have knowledge to cry, My father, and my mother, **before** the riches of Damascus and the spoil of Samaria shall be taken away before the king of Assyria.

CHAPTER 9

1 Nevertheless the dimness *shall* not be such as *was* in her vexation, when at the first he lightly afflicted the land of Zebulun, and the land of Naphtali, and afterward did more grievously afflict *her by* the way of the **Red** sea, beyond Jordan, in Galilee of the nations.

3 Thou hast multiplied the nation, *and* ~~not~~ increased the joy; **and**[*] they joy before thee, according to the joy in harvest, *and* as *men* rejoice when they divide the spoil.

7 Of the increase of *his* government and peace *there* ~~shall be~~ **is** no end, upon the throne of David, and upon his kingdom, to order it, and to establish it with judgment and with justice from henceforth even forever. The zeal of the Lord of hosts will perform this.

8 The Lord sent ~~a~~ **his** word ~~into~~ **unto** Jacob, and it hath lighted upon Israel.

17 Therefore the Lord shall have no joy in their young men, neither shall have mercy on their fatherless and widows; for everyone **of them** *is* ~~an~~ **a** hypocrite and an evildoer, and every mouth speaketh folly. For all this his anger is not turned away, but his hand *is* stretched out still.

CHAPTER 10

7 Howbeit he meaneth not so, neither doth his heart think so; but ~~it is~~ in his heart **it is** to destroy and cut off nations not a few.

10 As my hand hath ~~found~~ **founded** the kingdoms of the idols, and whose graven images did excel them of Jerusalem and of Samaria;

11 Shall I not, as I have done unto Samaria and her idols, so do to Jerusalem and **to** her idols?

13 For he saith, By the strength of my hand ~~I have done it~~, and by my wisdom **I have done these things**; for

I am prudent, and I have ~~removed~~ **moved** the ~~bounds~~ **borders** of the people, and have robbed their treasures, and I have put down the inhabitants like a valiant *man.*

23 For the Lord GOD of hosts shall make a consumption, even determined, in ~~the midst of~~ all the land.

CHAPTER 13

2 Lift ye up ~~a~~ **my** banner upon the high mountain, exalt the voice unto them, shake the hand, that they may go into the gates of the nobles.

3 I have commanded my sanctified ones, I have also called my mighty ones, for mine anger **is not upon** ~~even~~ them that rejoice in my highness.

4 The noise of the multitude in the mountains, like as of a great people; a tumultuous noise of the kingdoms of nations gathered together; the LORD of hosts mustereth the ~~host~~ **hosts** of the battle.

5 They come from a far country, from the end of heaven, **yea,** ~~even~~ the LORD, and the weapons of his indignation, to destroy the whole land.

15 Everyone that is ~~found~~ **proud** shall be thrust through; and everyone that is joined ~~unto~~ **to** ~~them~~ **the wicked** shall fall by the sword.

22 And the wild beasts of the islands shall cry in their desolate houses, and dragons in *their* pleasant palaces; and her time *is* near to come, and her days shall not be prolonged; **for I will* destroy her speedily; yea, for I will be merciful unto my people, but the wicked shall perish.**

CHAPTER 14

2 And the people shall take them, and bring them to their place; **yea, from far, unto the end of the earth, and they shall return to their land of** promise, and the house of Israel shall possess them in the land of the LORD for servants and handmaids; and they shall take them captives, whose captives they were; and they shall rule over their oppressors.

3 And it shall come to pass in ~~the~~ **that** day that the LORD shall give thee rest from thy sorrow and from thy fear, and from the hard bondage wherein thou wast made to serve,

4 **And it shall come to pass in that day** that thou shalt take up this proverb against the king of Babylon, and say, How hath the oppressor ceased! the golden city ceased!

5 The LORD hath broken the staff of the wicked, *and* the ~~sceptre~~ **scepters** of the rulers.

8 Yea, the fir trees rejoice at thee, *and* **also** the cedars of Lebanon, *saying,* Since thou art laid down, no feller is come up against us.

16 They that see thee shall narrowly look upon thee, *and* **shall*** consider thee, ~~saying~~ **and shall say,** *Is* this the man that made the earth to tremble, that did shake kingdoms;

17 ~~That~~ **And** made the world as a wilderness, and destroyed the cities thereof; ~~that~~ **and** opened not the house of his prisoners?

18 All the kings of the nations, **yea** ~~even~~ all of them, lie in glory, everyone **of them*** in his own house.

19 But thou art cast out of thy grave like an abominable branch, *and* ~~as~~ the ~~raiment~~ **remnant** of those that are slain, thrust through with a sword, that go down to the stones of the pit; as a ~~carcase~~ **carcass** trodden under feet.

21 Prepare slaughter for his children for the ~~iniquity~~ **iniquities** of their fathers; that they do not rise, nor possess the land, nor fill the face of the world with cities.

32 What shall ~~one~~ then answer the messengers of the nation? That the LORD hath founded Zion, and the poor of his people shall trust in it.

CHAPTER 16
6 We have heard of the pride of Moab; **of his haughtiness and his pride, for** *he is* very proud; ~~even of his haughtiness, and his pride~~ and his wrath, ~~but~~ his lies ~~shall not be so,~~ **and all his evil works**.

CHAPTER 21
1 The burden of the desert of the sea. As whirlwinds in the south pass through; *so* it cometh from the desert, from ~~a~~ **the** terrible land.

CHAPTER 23
10 Pass through thy land as a river, O daughter of Tarshish; *there is* no more strength **in thee**.

CHAPTER 29
2 Yet I will distress Ariel, and there shall be heaviness and sorrow; **for thus hath the Lord said unto me,** ~~and~~ It shall be unto ~~me as~~ Ariel;

3 ~~And~~ **That** I **the Lord** will camp against ~~thee~~ **her** round about, and will lay siege against ~~thee~~ **her** with a mount, and I will raise forts against ~~thee~~ **her**.

4 And ~~thou~~ **she** ~~shalt~~ **shall** be brought down, *and* ~~shalt~~ **shall** speak out of the ground, and ~~thy~~ **her** speech shall be low out of the dust; and ~~thy~~ **her** voice shall be as of one that hath a familiar spirit, out of the ground, and ~~thy~~ **her** speech shall whisper out of the dust.

5 Moreover the multitude of ~~thy~~ **her** strangers shall be like small dust, and the multitude of the terrible ones *shall be* as chaff that passeth away; yea, it shall be at an instant suddenly.

6 ~~Thou~~ **For they** ~~shalt~~ **shall** be visited of the LORD of hosts with thunder, and with earthquake, and great noise, with storm and tempest, and the flame of devouring fire.

8 **Yea,** it shall ~~even~~ be **unto them even** as ~~when~~ **unto** ~~an~~ **a** hungry *man* **who** dreameth, and behold, he eateth, but he awaketh and his soul is empty; or ~~as~~ **like** ~~when~~ **unto** a thirsty man **who** dreameth, and behold, he drinketh, but he awaketh, and behold, *he is* faint, and his soul hath appetite. **Yea, even** so shall the multitude of all the nations be that fight against mount Zion.

9 **For, behold, all ye that do iniquity,** stay yourselves, and wonder; **for ye shall** cry ~~ye~~ out, and cry; **yea,** ~~they~~ **ye** ~~are~~ **shall be** drunken, but not with wine; ~~they~~ **ye shall** stagger, but not with strong drink.

10 For, **behold,** the LORD hath poured out upon you the spirit of deep sleep. ~~and~~ **For, behold,** ye ~~hath~~ **have** closed your eyes**, and ye have rejected** the prophets**,** and your rulers; **and** the seers hath he covered **because of your iniquities**.

11 **And it shall come to pass, that the Lord God shall bring forth unto you the words of a book; and they shall be the words of them which have slumbered.**

12 **And behold, the book shall be sealed; and in the book shall be a revelation from God, from the beginning of the world to the ending thereof.**

13 **Wherefore because of the things which are sealed up, the things which are sealed shall not be delivered in the day of the wickedness and abominations of the people. Wherefore, the book shall be kept from them.**

14 But the book shall be delivered unto a man, and he shall deliver the words of the book, which are the words of those who have slumbered in the dust; and he shall deliver these words unto another, but the words that are sealed he shall not deliver, neither shall he deliver the book.

15 For the book shall be sealed by the power of God, and the revelation which was sealed shall be kept in the book until the own due time of the Lord, that they may come forth; for, behold, they reveal all things from the foundation of the world unto the end thereof.

16 And the day cometh, that the words of the book which were sealed shall be read upon the housetops; and they shall be read by the power of Christ; and all things shall be revealed unto the children of men which ever have been among the children of men, and which ever will be, even unto the end of the earth.

17 Wherefore, at that day when the book shall be delivered unto the man of whom I have spoken, the book shall be hid from the eyes of the world, that the eyes of none shall behold it, save it be that three witnesses shall behold it by the power of God, besides him to whom the book shall be delivered; and they shall testify to the truth of the book and the things therein.

18 And there is none other which shall view it, save it be a few according to the will of God, to bear testimony of his word unto the children of men; for the Lord God hath said, that the words of the faithful should speak as it were from the dead.

19 Wherefore, the Lord God will proceed to bring forth the words of the book; and in the mouth of as many witnesses as seemeth him good will he establish his word; and woe be unto him that rejecteth the word of God.

20 11 And the vision of all is become unto you as the words of a book that is sealed, which men But, behold, it shall come to pass, that the Lord God shall say unto him to whom he shall deliver the book, Take these words which are not sealed and deliver them to another, that he may show them to unto one that is the learned, saying, Read this, I pray thee.

21 11 And the learned shall say, Bring hither the book and I will read them; and now because of the glory of the world, and to get gain will they say this, and not for the glory of God. And he the man shall saith say, I cannot bring the book for it is sealed. Then shall the learned say, I cannot read it.

22 12 And the book is delivered Wherefore it shall come to pass, that the Lord God will deliver again the book and the words thereof to him that is not learned; saying, Read this, I pray thee and he the man that is not learned shall saith say, I am not learned. Then shall the Lord God say unto him, The learned shall not read them, for they have rejected them, and I am able to do mine own work; wherefore thou shalt read the words which I shall give unto thee.

23 Touch not the things which are sealed, for I will bring them forth in mine own due time; for I will show unto the children of men that I am able to do mine own work.

24 Wherefore, when thou hast read the words which I have commanded thee, and obtained the witnesses which I have promised unto

thee, then shalt thou seal up the book again, and hide it up unto me, that I may preserve the words which thou hast not read until I shall see fit in mine own wisdom to reveal all things unto the children of men.

25 For behold, I am God; and I am a God of miracles; and I will show unto the world that I am the same, yesterday, today, and forever; and I work not among the children of men, save it be according to their faith.

26 13–14 ~~Wherefore~~ **And again it shall come to pass, that** the Lord **shall** ~~said~~ **say unto him that shall read the words that shall be delivered him,** Forasmuch as this people draw near **unto** *me* with their mouth, and with their lips do honor me, but have removed their ~~heart~~ **hearts** far from me, and their fear toward me is taught by the ~~precept~~ **precepts** of men, therefore ~~behold~~ I will proceed to do a marvelous work among this people; **yea,** ~~even~~ a marvelous work and a wonder; for the wisdom of their wise ~~men~~ **and learned** shall perish, and the understanding of their prudent ~~men~~ shall be hid.

27 15–16 **And** woe unto them that seek deep to hide their counsel from the Lord. And their works are in the dark; and they say, Who seeth us and who knoweth us? **And they also say,** Surely, your turning of things upside down shall be esteemed as the potter's clay.

28 16 **But behold, I will show unto them, saith the Lord of hosts, that I know all their works.** For, shall the work say of him that made it, He made me not? or shall the thing framed say of him that framed it, He had no understanding?

29 17 **But behold, saith the Lord of hosts, I will show unto the children**

of men, that it *is* ~~it~~ not yet a very little while, and Lebanon shall be turned into a fruitful field; and the fruitful field shall be esteemed as a forest.

30 18–19 And in that day shall the deaf hear the words of the book; and the eyes of the blind shall see out of obscurity and out of darkness; **and** the meek also shall increase, **and** *their* joy **shall be** in the Lord; and the poor among men shall rejoice in the Holy One of Israel.

31 20–21 For, **assuredly as the Lord liveth, they shall see that** the terrible one is brought to naught, and the scorner is consumed, and all that watch for iniquity are cut off, **and they** that make a man an offender for a word, and lay a snare for him that reproveth in the gate, and turn aside the just for a thing of naught.

32 22–24 Therefore, thus saith the Lord who redeemed Abraham concerning the house of Jacob, Jacob shall not now be ashamed, neither shall his face now wax pale; but when he seeth his children, the work of ~~mine~~ **my** hands, in the midst of him, they shall sanctify my name, and sanctify the Holy One of Jacob, and shall fear the God of Israel. They also that erred in spirit shall come to understanding, and they that murmured shall learn doctrine.

CHAPTER 32

14 Because the palaces shall be forsaken; the ~~multitude~~ **houses** of the city shall be left **desolate**; the forts and towers shall be for dens forever, a joy of wild asses, a pasture of flocks;

CHAPTER 33

2 O Lord, be gracious unto us; we have waited for thee; be thou their arm every morning, ~~our~~ **their** salvation also in the time of trouble.

18 Thine heart shall meditate **in**˙ terror. Where *is* the scribe? where *is* the receiver? where *is* he that counted the towers?

Chapter 34

7 And the ~~unicorns~~ **reem**˙ shall come down with them, and the bullocks with the bulls; and their land shall be soaked with blood, and their dust made fat with fatness.

16 Seek ye out of the book of the Lord, and read **the names written therein;** no one of these shall fail; none shall want ~~her~~ **their** mate; for my mouth it hath commanded, and ~~his~~ **my** Spirit it hath gathered them.

17 And ~~he~~ **I** ~~hath~~ **have** cast the lot for them, and ~~his hand~~ **I** ~~hath~~ **have** divided it unto them by line; they shall possess it forever; from generation to generation **they** shall ~~they~~ dwell therein.

Chapter 35

8 And ~~an~~ **a** highway shall be there, ~~and~~ **for** a way **shall be cast up,** and it shall be called the way of holiness. The unclean shall not pass over **upon** it; but it *shall be* **cast up** for those **who are clean, and** the wayfaring men, though **they are accounted** fools, shall not err *therein.*

Chapter 36

5 I say, ~~sayest thou, but they~~ **thy words** *are but* vain ~~words~~ **when thou sayest,** *I have* counsel and strength for war. Now, on whom dost thou trust that thou rebellest against me?

Chapter 37

17 Incline thine ear, O Lord, and hear; open thine eyes, O Lord, and see; and hear all the words of Sennacherib, which **he** hath sent to reproach the living God.

32 For out of Jerusalem shall go forth a remnant; and they that escape out of **Jerusalem shall come up upon** mount Zion; the zeal of the Lord of hosts shall do this.

36 Then the angel of the Lord went forth, and smote in the camp of the Assyrians a hundred and fourscore and five thousand, and when they **who were left** arose, early in the morning, behold, they *were* all dead corpses.

Chapter 38

15 What shall I say? he hath both spoken unto me, and himself hath ~~done it~~ **healed me**. I shall go softly all my years, **that I may not walk** in the bitterness of my soul.

16 O Lord, ~~by these *things men* live, and in all these *things is*~~ **thou who art** the life of my spirit, **in whom I live;** so wilt thou recover me, and make me to live; **and in all these things I will praise thee.**

17 Behold, ~~for peace~~ I had great bitterness **instead of peace,** but thou hast in love to my soul, ~~*delivered it*~~ **saved me** from the pit of corruption; for thou hast cast all my sins behind thy back.

Chapter 39

2 And Hezekiah was glad of them, and showed them the house of his precious things, the silver, and the gold, and the spices, and the precious ointment, and all the house of his armor, and all that was found in his treasures; there was nothing in his house, nor in all his dominion, that Hezekiah showed ~~them~~ **him** not.

Chapter 41

28 For I beheld, and *there was* no man; even among ~~them~~ **men**, and *there was* no counselor, that, when I asked of them, could answer a word.

CHAPTER 42

19 ~~Who *is* blind, but~~ **For I will send** my servant ~~or deaf, as my messenger~~ ~~*that* I sent~~ **unto you** who *is* **are** blind ~~as *he that is* perfect, and blind as the~~ ~~L<small>ORD</small>'s servant~~; **yea, a messenger to open the eyes of the blind, and unstop the ears of the deaf;**

20 And they shall be made perfect notwithstanding their blindness, if they will hearken unto the messenger, the Lord's servant.

21 20 **Thou art a people,** seeing many things, but thou observest not; opening the ears **to hear**, but ~~he~~ **thou** ~~heareth~~ **hearest** not.

22 21 The L<small>ORD</small> is **not** well pleased **with such a people, but** for his righteousness' sake he will magnify the law and make *it* honorable.

23 22 ~~But this~~ **Thou** *is* **art** a people robbed and spoiled; ~~*they are*~~ **thine enemies,** all of them, **have** snared **thee** in holes, and they ~~*are*~~ **have** hid **thee** in prison houses; they ~~*are*~~ **have taken thee** for a prey, and none delivereth; for a spoil, and none saith, Restore.

24 23–24 Who among ~~you~~ **them** will give ear ~~to~~ **unto** ~~this~~ **thee, or** ~~who will~~ hearken and hear **thee** for the time to come? **and** who gave Jacob for a spoil, and Israel to the robbers? did not the L<small>ORD</small>, he against whom ~~we~~ **they** have sinned?

25 24–25 For they would not walk in his ways, neither were they obedient unto his law; therefore he hath poured upon ~~him~~ **them** the fury of his anger, and the strength of battle; and ~~it~~ **they** ~~hath~~ **have** set ~~him~~ **them** on fire round about, yet ~~he~~ **they** knew not, and it burned ~~him~~ **them**, yet ~~he~~ **they** laid *it* not to heart.

CHAPTER 43

13 Yea, before the day *was* I *am* he;

and *there is* none that can deliver out of my hand: I will work, and who shall ~~let~~ **hinder*** it?

CHAPTER 49

23 And kings shall be thy nursing fathers, and their queens thy nursing mothers; they shall bow down to thee with *their* ~~face~~ **faces** toward the earth, and lick up the dust of thy feet; and thou shalt know that I *am* the L<small>ORD</small>; for they shall not be ashamed that wait for me.

25 But thus saith the L<small>ORD</small>; Even the captives of the mighty shall be taken away, and the prey of the terrible shall be delivered; for **the mighty God shall deliver his covenant people. For thus saith the Lord,** I will contend with ~~him~~ **them** that ~~contendeth~~ **contend** with thee, and I will save thy children.

CHAPTER 50

1 **Yea, for thus saith the Lord, Have I put thee away, or have I cast thee off forever? For** thus saith the L<small>ORD</small>, Where *is* the bill of your mother's divorcement? **To** whom ~~I~~ have **I** put **thee** away, **or to** which of my creditors ~~*is it*~~ **have I sold you; yea,** to whom ~~I~~ have **I** sold you?

2 1–2 Behold, for your iniquities have ye sold yourselves, and for your transgressions is your mother put away; wherefore, when I came ~~was~~ *there* **was** no man; when I called ~~was~~ *there* **was** none to answer. **O house of Israel,** is my hand shortened at all, that it cannot redeem; or have I no power to deliver?

3 2–3 Behold, at my rebuke I dry up the sea, I make ~~the~~ **their** rivers a wilderness; **and** their fish ~~stinketh~~ **to stink**, because ~~there is no water~~ **the waters are dried up**, and **they** ~~dieth~~

die ~~for~~ **because of** thirst. I clothe the heavens with blackness, and I make sackcloth their covering.

4 The Lord GOD hath given me the tongue of the learned, that I should know how to speak a word in season ~~to~~ **unto** ~~him~~ **thee, O house of Israel,** ~~that~~ **when ye** ~~is~~ **are** weary. He ~~wakeneth~~ **waketh** morning by morning, he ~~wakeneth~~ **waketh** mine ear to hear as the learned.

5 5–8 The Lord GOD hath ~~opened~~ **appointed** mine ~~ear~~ **ears,** and I was not rebellious, neither turned away back. I gave my back to the smiters, and my cheeks to them that plucked off the hair. I hid not my face from shame and spitting, for the Lord GOD will help me; therefore shall I not be confounded; therefore have I set my face like a flint, and I know that I shall not be ashamed, **and** ~~He~~ **the Lord** *is* near ~~that~~ **and he** justifieth me.

6 8–9 Who will contend with me? let us stand together. Who *is* mine adversary? let him come near ~~to~~ me, **and I will smite him with the strength of my mouth;** ~~Behold~~ **for** the Lord GOD will help me; ~~who~~ ~~is~~ **and all** ~~he~~ **they** ~~that~~ **which** shall condemn me, ~~lo~~ **behold all** they ~~all~~ shall wax old as a garment, **and** the moth shall eat them up.

8 11 Behold all ye that ~~kindle~~ **kindleth** ~~a~~ fire, that compass *yourselves* about with sparks; walk in the light of your fire, and in the sparks ~~that~~ **which** ye have kindled; this shall ye have of mine hand, ye shall lie down in sorrow.

CHAPTER 51

1 Hearken ~~to~~ **unto** me, ye that follow after righteousness; ye that seek the LORD, look unto the rock **from** *whence* ye were hewn, and to the hole of the pit **from** *whence* ye are digged.

7 Hearken unto me, ye that know righteousness, the people in whose heart ~~is~~ **I have written** my law; fear ye not the reproach of men, neither be ye afraid of their revilings.

11 Therefore the redeemed of the LORD shall return, and come with singing unto Zion; and everlasting joy **and holiness** *shall be* upon their ~~head~~ **heads;** they shall obtain gladness and joy; *and* sorrow and mourning shall flee away.

12 I ~~even I~~ *am* he, **yea, I am he** that comforteth you; **behold,** who *art* thou, that thou shouldest be afraid of a man *that* shall die, and of the son of man *which* shall be made *as* grass;

16 And I have put my words in thy mouth, and I have covered thee in the shadow of mine hand, that I may plant the heavens, and lay the foundations of the earth, and say unto Zion, **Behold,** thou *art* my people.

18 **And** *there is* none to guide her among all the sons *whom* she hath brought forth; neither *is there any* that taketh her by the hand of all the sons *that* she hath brought up.

19 These two ~~things~~ **sons** are come unto thee; ~~who~~ **they** shall be sorry for thee, **thy** desolation, and destruction, and the famine, and the sword; **and** by whom shall I comfort thee?

20 Thy sons have fainted **save these two,** they lie at the head of all the streets, as a wild bull in a net; they are full of the fury of the LORD, the rebuke of thy God.

CHAPTER 52

6 Therefore, my people shall know my name; ~~therefore~~ **yea, in that day** *they shall know* ~~in that day~~ that I *am* he that doth speak; behold, *it is* I.

7 **And then shall they say,** How beautiful upon the mountains are the feet of him that bringeth good tidings

unto them, that publisheth peace; that bringeth good tidings **unto them** of good, that publisheth salvation; that saith unto Zion, Thy God reigneth!

15 So shall he ~~sprinkle~~ **gather** many nations; the kings shall shut their mouths at him; for *that* which had not been told them shall they see; and *that* which they had not heard shall they consider.

Chapter 54

10 For the mountains shall depart, and the hills be removed; but my kindness shall not depart from thee, neither shall the covenant of my ~~peace~~ **people** be removed, saith the Lord that hath mercy on thee.

Chapter 57

5 Inflaming yourselves with idols under every green tree, slaying the children in the valleys under the ~~clifts~~ **clefts** of the rocks?

Chapter 60

22 A little one shall become a thousand, and a small one a strong nation; I the Lord will hasten it in ~~his~~ **my** time.

Chapter 62

4 Thou shalt no more be termed Forsaken; neither shall thy land anymore be termed Desolate; but thou shalt be called ~~Hephzi-bah~~ **Delightful**, and thy land ~~Beulah~~ **Union;** for the Lord delighteth in thee, and thy land shall be married.

5 For *as* a young man marrieth a virgin, *so* shall thy ~~sons~~ **God** marry thee; and *as* the bridegroom rejoiceth over the bride, *so* shall thy God rejoice over thee.

Chapter 63

17 O Lord, why hast thou ~~made~~ **suffered** us to err from thy ways; *and*

to harden our heart from thy fear? Return for thy servants' sake, the tribes of thine inheritance.

Chapter 64

5 Thou meetest him that ~~rejoiceth and~~ worketh righteousness, **and rejoiceth** ~~those~~ **him** *that* ~~remember~~ **remembereth** thee in thy ways; ~~behold, thou art wroth; for we have sinned~~ in ~~those~~ **righteousness there** is continuance, and ~~we~~ **such** shall be saved.

6 But **we have sinned;** we are all as an unclean *thing*, and all our righteousnesses *are* as filthy rags; and we all do fade as a leaf; and our iniquities, like the wind, have taken us away.

Chapter 65

1 I am ~~sought~~ **found** of *them* ~~that~~ **who**[*] ~~asked not~~ **seek** ~~for~~ after *me*, I **give unto all them that ask of me;** I am **not** found of *them that* sought me not, **or that inquireth not after me.**

2 1–2 I said **unto my servant**, Behold me, ~~behold~~ **look upon** me; **I will send you** unto a nation *that* ~~was~~ **is** not called ~~by~~ **after** my name, **for** I have spread out my hands all the day ~~unto~~ **to** a ~~rebellious~~ people ~~which~~ **who** walketh **not** in ~~a~~ **my** ~~way~~ **ways, and** ~~that~~ **their works** ~~was~~ **are evil and** not good, **and they walk** after their own thoughts.

4 Which remain among the graves, and lodge in the monuments; which eat swine's flesh, and broth of abominable ~~things~~ **beasts, and** ~~is in~~ **pollute** their vessels;

20 **In those days** there shall be no more thence an infant of days, nor an old man that hath not filled his days; for the child shall **not** die, **but shall live to be** an hundred years old; but the sinner, ~~being~~ **living to be** an hundred years old, shall be accursed.

The Book of the Prophet
JEREMIAH

CHAPTER 2

24 A wild ass used to the wilderness, *that* snuffeth up the wind at her pleasure; in her occasion who can turn her away? all they that seek her will ~~not~~˙ weary themselves; in her month they shall **not** find her.

CHAPTER 3

2 Lift up thine eyes unto the high places, and see where thou hast not been ~~lien~~ **lain** with. In the ways hast thou sat for them, as the Arabian in the wilderness; and thou hast polluted the land with thy whoredoms and ~~with thy~~ wickedness.

3 Therefore ~~the~~ **thy** showers have been withholden, and there hath been no latter rain; and thou hadst a whore's forehead, thou refusedst to be ashamed.

CHAPTER 5

19 And it shall come to pass, when ye shall say, Wherefore doeth the LORD our God all these *things* unto us? then shalt thou answer them, Like as ye have forsaken me, and served strange gods in your land, so shall ye serve strangers in ~~a~~ **the** land *that is* not yours.

CHAPTER 7

5 For if ye thoroughly amend your ways and your doings; if ye ~~throughly~~ **thoroughly** execute judgment between a man and his neighbor;

CHAPTER 12

5 If thou hast run with ~~the~~ **our** footmen, and they have wearied thee, then how canst thou contend with horses? and *if* in the land of peace, *wherein*

thou trustedst, *they wearied thee*, then how wilt thou do in the swelling of Jordan?

CHAPTER 17

5 Thus saith the LORD; Cursed *be* the man that trusteth in man, and maketh flesh his arm; and **the man** whose heart departeth from the LORD.

CHAPTER 18

8 If that nation, against whom I have pronounced, turn from their evil, I will ~~repent~~ **withhold** ~~of~~ the evil that I thought to do unto them.

10 If it do evil in my sight, that it obey not my voice, then I will ~~repent~~ **withhold** ~~of~~ the good, wherewith I said I would benefit them.

14 Will ~~a man~~ **you not** leave the snow **of the fields**˙ of Lebanon ~~which cometh from the rock of the field~~; *or* shall **not** the cold flowing waters that come from another place **from the rock,** be forsaken?

CHAPTER 25

31 A noise shall come *even* to the ends of the earth; for the LORD hath a controversy with the nations; he will plead with all flesh; he will give ~~them that are~~ **the**˙ wicked to the sword, saith the LORD.

CHAPTER 26

3 If so be they will hearken, and turn every man from his evil way, **and repent,** ~~that~~ I ~~may repent me of~~ **will turn away** the evil which I purpose to do unto them because of the evil of their doings.

5 To hearken to the words of my servants, the prophets, whom I sent unto

you, **commanding** ~~both~~ **them to** ~~ris-ing~~ **rise** up early, and sending *them*; ~~but ye have not hearkened~~

6 Then will I make this house like Shiloh, and will make this city a curse to all the nations of the earth; **for ye have not hearkened unto my servants the prophets**.

13 Therefore now, amend your ways and your doings, and obey the voice of the Lord your God, **and repent,** and the Lord will ~~repent him of~~ **turn away** the evil that he hath pronounced against you.

18 Micah the Morasthite prophesied in the days of Hezekiah king of Judah, and spake to all the people of Judah, saying, Thus saith the Lord of hosts; Zion shall be plowed *like* a field, and Jerusalem shall become heaps, and the mountain of the house **of the Lord** as the high places of a forest.

19 Did Hezekiah, king of Judah, and all Judah put him at all to death? Did he not fear the Lord and ~~be-sought~~ **beseech** the Lord **and repent?** and the Lord ~~repented him of~~ **turned away** the evil which he had pronounced against them? Thus **by putting Jeremiah to death we** might ~~we~~ procure great evil against our souls.

20 And there was ~~also~~ a man **among the priests,** ~~that prophesied in the name of the Lord~~ **rose up and said, that,** Urijah the son of Shemaiah of Kirjath-jearim, **prophesied in the name of the Lord,** who **also** prophesied against this city, and against this land, according to all the words of Jeremiah;

Chapter 27

7 And all nations shall serve him, and his son, and his son's son, until the very time of ~~his land~~ **their end** come; and ~~then~~ **after that** many nations and great kings shall serve themselves of ~~him~~ **them**.

11 But the nations that bring their neck under the yoke of the king of Babylon, and serve him, those will I let **still** remain ~~still~~ in their own land, saith the Lord; and they shall till it, and dwell therein.

Chapter 29

12 Then shall ye call ~~upon~~ **unto** me, and ye shall go and pray unto me, and I will hearken unto you.

19 Because they have not hearkened to my words, saith the Lord, which I sent unto them by my servants the prophets, **commanding them** to ~~rising~~ **rise** ~~up~~ early, and sending *them*; but ye would not hear, saith the Lord.

Chapter 30

12 For thus saith the Lord, Thy bruise *is* **not** incurable, ~~and~~ **although** thy ~~wound~~ **wounds** ~~is~~ **are** grievous.

13 ~~There~~ *Is* **there** none to plead thy cause, that thou mayest be bound up; ~~thou~~ Hast **thou** no healing medicines?

14 **Have** all thy lovers ~~have~~ forgotten thee; **do** they **not** seek thee ~~not~~? For I have wounded thee with the wound of an enemy, with the chastisement of a cruel one, for the multitude of thine ~~iniquity~~ **iniquities;** *because* thy sins ~~were~~ **are** increased.

15 Why criest thou for thine affliction, **is** thy sorrow ~~is~~ incurable? **It was** for the multitude of thine ~~iniquity~~ **iniquities, and** *because* thy sins ~~were~~ **are** increased I have done these things unto thee.

16 ~~Therefore~~ **But** all they that devour thee shall be devoured; and all thine adversaries, everyone of them, shall go into captivity; and they that spoil thee shall be a spoil, and all that prey upon thee will I give for a prey.

CHAPTER 33

11 The voice of joy, and the voice of gladness, the voice of the bridegroom, and the voice of the bride, the voice of them that shall say, Praise the LORD of hosts; for the LORD *is* good; for his mercy *endureth* forever ~~and of~~ **unto** them that shall bring the sacrifice of praise into the house of the LORD. For I will cause to return the captivity of the land, as at the first, saith the LORD.

CHAPTER 34

15 ~~And~~ **But** ye were now turned, and had done right in my sight, in proclaiming liberty every man to his neighbor; and ye had made a covenant before me in the house which is called by my name.

CHAPTER 35

14 The words of Jonadab the son of Rechab, that he commanded his sons not to drink wine, are performed; for unto this day they drink none, but obey their father's commandment; notwithstanding I have spoken unto you, **commanding you to** ~~rising~~ **rise** early, and speaking **to you,** but ye hearkened not unto me.

15 I have sent also unto you all my servants the prophets, **commanding them to** ~~rising~~ **rise** up early, and sending *them,* saying, Return ye now every man from his evil way, and amend your doings, and go not after other gods to serve them, and ye shall dwell in the land which I have given to you and to your fathers; but ye have not inclined your ear, **nor hearkened unto me**.

CHAPTER 36

30 Therefore thus saith the LORD ~~of~~ **unto** Jehoiakim king of Judah; He shall have none to sit upon the throne of David; and his dead body shall be cast out in the day to the heat, and in the night to the frost.

CHAPTER 37

16 ~~When~~ **And** Jeremiah was entered into the dungeon, and into the cabins, and ~~Jeremiah~~ **he had** remained there many days.

CHAPTER 42

10 If ~~ye~~ **you** will still abide in this land, then will I build you, and not pull ~~you~~ down; ~~and~~ I will plant you, and not pluck ~~you~~ up; ~~for I repent me of~~ **and I will turn away** the evil that I have done unto you.

14 Saying, No; but we will go into the land of Egypt, where we shall see no war, nor hear the sound of the trumpet, nor have hunger **for want** of bread; and there will we dwell;

21 And *now* I have this day declared ~~it~~ to you; ~~but~~ **that** ye have not obeyed the voice of the LORD your God, nor any *thing* for the which he hath sent me unto you.

CHAPTER 44

4 Howbeit I sent unto you all my servants the prophets, **commanding them to** ~~rising~~ **rise** early, and sending *them,* saying, Oh, do not this abominable thing that I hate.

The Book of the Prophet
EZEKIEL

CHAPTER 14

9 And if the prophet be deceived when he hath spoken a thing, I the LORD have **not** deceived that prophet; and **therefore** I will stretch out my hand upon him, and will destroy him from the midst of my people Israel.

CHAPTER 18

32 For I have no pleasure in the death of him that dieth, saith the Lord GOD; wherefore turn ~~yourselves~~ **ye**, and live ~~ye~~.

CHAPTER 19

10 Thy mother *is* like a vine in ~~thy~~ **my*** blood, planted by the waters; she was fruitful and full of branches by reason of many waters.

CHAPTER 20

30 Wherefore say unto the house of Israel; Thus saith the Lord GOD; ~~Are~~ **Ye are** polluted after the manner of your fathers, and **ye** commit ~~ye~~ whoredom after their abominations.

CHAPTER 23

17 And the Babylonians came to her into the bed of love, and they defiled her with their whoredom, and she was polluted with them, and her mind was alienated from **me by** them.

22 Therefore, O Aholibah, thus saith the Lord GOD; Behold, I will raise up thy lovers against thee, ~~from~~ **by** whom thy mind is alienated **from me**, and I will bring them against thee on every side;

28 For thus saith the Lord GOD; Behold, I will deliver thee into the hand *of them* whom thou hatest, into the hand *of them* ~~from~~ **by** whom thy mind is alienated;

CHAPTER 35

6 Therefore, *as* I live, saith the Lord GOD, I will prepare thee unto blood, and blood shall pursue thee; ~~sith~~ **since** thou hast not hated blood, even blood shall pursue thee.

CHAPTER 36

36 Then the heathen that are left round about you shall know that I the LORD build the ruined *places, and* plant that ~~that~~ **which** was desolate; I the LORD have spoken *it*, and I will do *it*.

CHAPTER 40

31 And the arches thereof *were* toward the ~~utter~~ **outer** court; and palm trees *were* upon the posts thereof; and the going up to it *had* eight steps.

37 And the posts thereof *were* toward the ~~utter~~ **outer** court; and palm trees *were* upon the posts thereof, on this side, and on that side; and the going up to it *had* eight steps.

CHAPTER 42

1 Then he brought me forth into the ~~utter~~ **outer** court, the way toward the north; and he brought me into the chamber that *was* over against the separate place, and which *was* before the building toward the north.

3 Over against the twenty *cubits* which *were* for the inner court, and over against the pavement which *was* for the ~~utter~~ **outer** court, *was* gallery against gallery in three *stories*.

7 And the wall that *was* without over against the chambers, toward the ~~utter~~ **outer** court on the forepart of the chambers, the length thereof *was* fifty cubits.

8 For the length of the chambers that *were* in the ~~utter~~ **outer** court *was* fifty cubits; and, lo, before the temple *were* ~~an~~ **a** hundred cubits.

9 And from under these chambers *was* the entry on the east side, as one goeth into them from the ~~utter~~ **outer** court.

14 When the priests enter therein, then shall they not go out of the holy *place* into the ~~utter~~ **outer** court, but there they shall lay their garments wherein they minister; for they *are* holy; and shall put on other garments, and shall approach to *those things* which *are* for the people.

CHAPTER 44

19 And when they go forth into the ~~utter~~ **outer** court, *even* into the ~~utter~~ **outer** court to the people, they shall put off their garments wherein they ministered, and lay them in the holy chambers, and they shall put on other garments; and they shall not sanctify the people with their garments.

CHAPTER 46

20 Then said he unto me, This *is* the place where the priests shall boil the trespass offering and the sin offering, where they shall bake the meat offering; that they bear *them* not out into the ~~utter~~ **outer** court, to sanctify the people.

21 Then he brought me forth into the ~~utter~~ **outer** court, and caused me to pass by the four corners of the court; and, behold, in every corner of the court *there was* a court.

CHAPTER 47

2 Then brought he me out of the way of the gate northward, and led me about the way without unto the ~~utter~~ **outer** gate by the way that looketh eastward; and, behold, there ran out waters on the right side.

CHAPTER 48

35 *It was* round about eighteen thousand *measures*; and the name of the city from *that* day *shall be* **called, Holy; for** the LORD *is* **shall be** there.

The Book of
DANIEL

CHAPTER 5

28 ~~PERES~~ **UPHARSIN**; Thy kingdom is divided, and given to the Medes and Persians.

CHAPTER 10

11 And ~~he~~ said unto me, O Daniel, a man greatly beloved, understand the words that I speak unto thee, and stand upright; for unto thee am I now sent. And when he had spoken this word unto me, I stood trembling.

HOSEA

CHAPTER 11

8 How shall I give thee up, Ephraim? *how* shall I deliver thee, Israel? how shall I make thee as Admah? *how* shall I set thee as Zeboim? ~~mine~~ **My** heart is turned ~~within~~ **toward** ~~me~~ **thee, and** my ~~repentings~~ **mercies** are ~~kindled~~ **extended** ~~together~~ **to gather thee.**

JOEL

CHAPTER 1

6 For a nation is come up upon my land, strong, and without number, whose teeth *are* **as** the teeth of a lion, and he hath the cheek teeth of a great lion.

CHAPTER 2

13 And rend your heart, and not your garments, **and repent,** and turn unto the LORD your God; for he *is* gracious and merciful, slow to anger, and of great kindness, and ~~repenteth him of~~ **he will turn away** the evil **from you.**

14 **Therefore repent, and** who knoweth ~~if~~ **but** he will return ~~and repent~~ and leave a blessing behind him; **that you may offer** ~~even~~ a meat offering, and a drink offering, unto the LORD your God?

AMOS

CHAPTER 3

6 Shall a trumpet be blown in the city, and the people not be afraid? shall there be evil in a city, and the LORD hath not ~~done~~ **known** ~~it~~?

7 Surely the Lord GOD will do nothing, ~~but~~ **until** he revealeth ~~his~~ **the** secret unto his servants the prophets.

CHAPTER 4

3 And ye shall go out at the breaches, every ~~cow at that which is~~ **one** before ~~her~~ **his** enemy; and ye shall **be** cast ~~them into~~ **out of** ~~the~~ **your** ~~palace~~ **palaces,** saith the LORD.

5 And offer a sacrifice of thanksgiving with leaven, and proclaim *and* publish the free offerings; for ~~this~~ **thus** ~~liketh~~ **do** ~~you~~ **ye,** O ye children of Israel, saith the Lord GOD.

6 ~~And~~ **Therefore** I also have given you cleanness of teeth in all your cities, and want of bread in all your places; yet have ye not returned unto me, saith the LORD.

CHAPTER 6

10 And a man's uncle shall take him up, and he that burneth him, to bring out the bones out of the house, and ~~shall~~ **that** say unto him that *is* by the sides of the house, *Is there* yet *any* with thee? and he shall say, No. Then shall he say, Hold thy tongue; for we may not make mention of the name of the LORD.

CHAPTER 7

3 **And** the LORD **said, concerning Jacob, Jacob shall** ~~repented~~ **repent** for this, ~~It shall not be~~ **therefore I will not utterly destroy him**, saith the LORD.

6 **And** the LORD **said, concerning Jacob, Jacob shall** ~~repented~~ **repent** ~~for~~ **of** ~~this~~ **his wickedness;** ~~This also shall not be~~ **therefore I will not utterly destroy him**, saith the Lord GOD.

CHAPTER 8

2 And he said, Amos, what seest thou? And I said, A basket of summer fruit. Then said the LORD ~~unto~~ **with** me, The end is come upon my people of Israel; I will not again pass by them anymore.

CHAPTER 9

8 Behold, the eyes of the Lord GOD *are* upon ~~the~~ **a** sinful kingdom, and I will destroy it from off the face of the earth; saving that I will not utterly destroy the house of Jacob, saith the LORD.

JONAH

CHAPTER 3

9 Who can tell, *if* ~~God~~ **we** will ~~turn and~~ repent, and **turn unto God, but he will** turn away from **us** his fierce anger, that we perish not?

10 And God saw their works that they turned from their evil way and ~~God~~ repented ~~of~~; **and God turned away** the evil that he had said ~~that~~ he would ~~do~~ **bring** ~~unto~~ **upon** them ~~and he did it not.~~

ZECHARIAH

CHAPTER 4

10 For who hath despised the day of small things? for they shall rejoice, and shall see the plummet in the hand of Zerubbabel *with* those seven; they *are* the ~~eyes~~ **servants** of the LORD, which run to and fro through the whole earth.

14 Then said he, These *are* the two anointed ones, that stand ~~by~~ **before** the Lord of the whole earth.

CHAPTER 6

5 And the angel answered and said unto me, These *are* the four ~~spirits~~ **servants** of the heavens, which go forth from standing before the Lord of all the earth.

7 And the bay went forth, and sought to go that they might walk to and fro through the earth; and he said, Get ~~you~~ **ye** hence, walk to and fro through the earth. So they walked to and fro through the earth.

CHAPTER 8

7 Thus saith the LORD of hosts; Behold, I will ~~save~~ **gather** my people

from the east country, and from the west country;

13 And it shall come to pass, *that* as ye were a curse among the heathen, O house of Judah, and house of Israel; so will I ~~save~~ **gather** you, and ye shall be a blessing; fear not, *but* let your hands be strong.

MALACHI

CHAPTER 4

6 And he shall ~~turn~~ **bind**[23] the heart of the fathers to the children, and the heart of the children to their fathers, lest I come and smite the earth with a curse.

OLD TESTAMENT NOTES

1. Robert J. Matthews, *"A Plainer Translation:" Joseph Smith's Translation of the Bible, A History and Commentary* [1985], 154. Final revision by Joseph Smith.

2. Joseph Smith, *Teachings of the Prophet Joseph Smith*, comp. Joseph Fielding Smith [1938], 181.

3. *Teachings*, 181.

4. *Teachings*, 301.

5. *Plainer*, 147.

6. *Plainer*, 84. Manuscript OT 2.

7. *Plainer*, 436.

8. *Plainer*, 436.

9. *Plainer*, 436.

10. *Plainer*, 436.

11. *Plainer*, 438.

12. *Plainer*, 438.

13. *Plainer*, 159.

14. *Plainer*, 156.

15. *Plainer*, 157.

16. *Plainer*, 157.

17. *Plainer*, 158.

18. Joseph Smith, *The Words of Joseph Smith*, comp. Andrew F. Ehat and Lyndon W. Cook [1996], 247.

19. *Plainer*, 148.

20. *Plainer*, 149. Bernhisel rendition of correction.

21. *Plainer*, 186.

22. *Plainer*, 148. Manuscripts did not specify placing this verse in Isaiah 3; Book of Mormon (2 Nephi 14:1) retains King James Version placement in Isaiah 4.

23. *Teachings*, 330.

Selections from the

NEW TESTAMENT

OF OUR LORD AND SAVIOR

JESUS CHRIST

As translated by the
Prophet Joseph Smith

The Testimony of
SAINT MATTHEW

CHAPTER 1

1 The book of the generation of Jesus Christ, the son of David, the son of Abraham.

2 2–6 Abraham begat Isaac; and Isaac begat Jacob; and Jacob begat Judas and his brethren; and Judas begat Phares and Zara of Thamar; and Phares begat Esrom; and Esrom begat Aram; and Aram begat Aminadab; and Aminadab begat Naasson; and Naasson begat Salmon; and Salmon begat Booz of Rachab; and Booz begat Obed of Ruth; and Obed begat Jesse; and Jesse begat David the king;

3 6–11 And David the king begat Solomon of her ~~that had been the wife~~ **whom David had taken** of Urias; and Solomon begat Roboam; and Roboam begat Abia; and Abia begat Asa; and Asa begat Josaphat; and Josaphat begat Joram; and Joram begat Ozias; and Ozias begat Joatham; and Joatham begat Achaz; and Achaz begat Ezekias; and Ezekias begat Manasses; and Manasses begat Amon; and Amon begat Josias; and Josias begat Jechonias and his brethren, about the time they were carried away to Babylon.

4 12–16 And after they were brought to Babylon, Jechonias begat Salathiel; and Salathiel begat ~~Zorobabel~~ **Zorobable**; and ~~Zorobabel~~ **Zorobable** begat Abiud; and Abiud begat Eliakim; and Eliakim begat Azor; and Azor begat Sadoc; and Sadoc begat Achim; and Achim begat Eliud; and Eliud begat Eleazar; and Eleazar begat Matthan; and Matthan begat Jacob; and Jacob begat Joseph, the husband of Mary, of whom was born Jesus, **as the prophets have written**, who is called Christ.

5 17 So all the generations from Abraham to David, ~~are~~ **were** fourteen generations; and from David until the carrying away into Babylon, ~~are~~ **were** fourteen generations; and from the carrying away into Babylon ~~unto~~ **until** Christ, ~~are~~ **were** fourteen generations.

CHAPTER 2 1

1 18 Now, **as it is written,** the birth of Jesus Christ was on this wise. ~~When as~~ **After** his mother, Mary, was espoused to Joseph, before they came together, she was found with child of the Holy Ghost.

2 19 Then Joseph her husband, being a just *man*, and not willing to make her a publick example, was minded to put her away privily.

3 20 But while he thought on these things, behold, the angel of the Lord appeared unto him in a ~~dream~~ **vision**, saying, Joseph, thou son of David, fear not to take unto thee Mary thy wife; for that which is conceived in her, is of the Holy Ghost.

4 21 And she shall bring forth a son, and thou shalt call his name JESUS: for he shall save his people from their sins.

5 22 Now ~~all~~ this ~~was done~~ **took place**, that ~~it~~ **all things** might be fulfilled, which ~~was~~ **were** spoken of the Lord, by the ~~prophet~~ **prophets**, saying,

6 23 Behold, a virgin shall be with child, and shall bring forth a son, and they shall call his name Emmanuel, which being interpreted is, God with us.

7 24 Then Joseph ~~being raised from sleep~~, **awaking out of his vision,** did as the angel of the Lord had bidden him, and took unto him his wife;

8 25 And knew her not until she had brought forth her firstborn son; and ~~he~~ **they** called his name JESUS.

CHAPTER 3 2

1 Now when Jesus was born in Bethlehem of ~~Judaea~~ **Judea,** in the days of Herod the king, behold, there came wise men from the east to Jerusalem,

2 Saying, Where is ~~he~~ **the child** that is born ~~King~~, **the Messiah** of the Jews? for we have seen his star in the east, and ~~are~~ **have** come to worship him.

3 When Herod the king had heard ~~these things~~ **of the child**, he was troubled, and all Jerusalem with him.

4 And when he had gathered all the chief priests, and scribes* of the people together, he demanded of them, **saying,** Where **is the place that is written of by the prophets, in which** Christ should be born? **For he greatly feared, yet he believed not the prophets.**

5 And they said unto him, **It is written by the prophets, that he should be born** in Bethlehem of ~~Judaea~~ **Judea,** for thus ~~it is written by the prophet~~ **have they said,**

6 **The word of the Lord came unto us, saying,** And thou, Bethlehem, **which lieth*** *in* the land of ~~Juda~~ **Judea, in thee shall be born a prince, which** art not the least among the princes of ~~Juda~~ **Judea;** for out of thee shall come ~~a Governor~~ **the Messiah**, ~~that~~ **who** shall ~~rule~~ **save** my people Israel.

7 Then Herod, when he had ~~privily~~ called the wise men **privily**, inquired of them diligently **at** what time the star appeared.

8 And he sent them to Bethlehem, and said, Go and search diligently for the young child; and when ye have found ~~him~~ **the child**, bring me word again, that I may come and worship him also.

9 When they had heard the king, they departed; and lo, the star, which they saw in the east, went before them, till it came and stood over where the young child was.

10 When they saw the star, they rejoiced with exceeding great joy.

11 And when they were come into the house, they saw the young child with Mary his mother, and fell down, and worshipped him: and when they had opened their treasures, they presented unto him gifts; gold, and frankincense, and myrrh.

12 And being warned of God in a dream that they should not return to Herod, they departed into their own country another way.

13 And when they were departed, behold, the angel of the Lord, ~~appeareth~~ **appeared** to Joseph in a ~~dream~~ **vision**, saying, Arise and take the young child and his mother, and flee into Egypt, and ~~be~~ **tarry** thou there until I bring thee word; for Herod will seek the young child to destroy him.

14 ~~When~~ **And then** he arose, ~~he~~ **and** took the young child, and ~~his~~ **the child's** mother, by night, and departed into Egypt;

15 And was there until the death of Herod: that it might be fulfilled which was spoken of the Lord by the prophet, saying, Out of Egypt have I called my son.

16 Then Herod, when he saw that he was mocked of the wise men, was exceeding wroth; and sent forth and slew all the children ~~that~~ **which** were in Bethlehem, and ~~in~~ all the coasts thereof, from two years old and under,

according to the time which he had diligently inquired of the wise men.

17 Then was fulfilled that which was spoken by ~~Jeremy~~ **Jeremiah** the prophet, saying,

18 In ~~Rama was there~~ **Ramah there was** a voice heard, lamentation, and weeping, and great mourning; ~~Rachel~~ **Rachael** weeping *for* **the loss of** her children, and would not be comforted because they ~~are~~ **were** not.

19 But when Herod was dead, behold, an angel of the Lord ~~appeareth~~ **appeared** in a ~~dream~~ **vision** to Joseph in Egypt,

20 Saying, Arise, and take the young child and his mother, and go into the land of Israel; for they are dead ~~which~~ **who** sought the young child's life.

21 And he arose, and took the young child and his mother, and came into the land of Israel.

22 But when he heard that Archelaus did reign in ~~Judaea~~ **Judea,** in the ~~room~~ **stead** of his father Herod, he was afraid to go thither; **but,** notwithstanding, being warned of God in a ~~dream~~ **vision**, he ~~turned aside~~ **went** into the **eastern** ~~parts~~ **part** of Galilee;

23 And he came and dwelt in a city called Nazareth: that it might be fulfilled which was spoken by the prophets, He shall be called a Nazarene.

24 And it came to pass that Jesus grew up with his brethren, and waxed strong, and waited upon the Lord for the time of his ministry to come.

25 And he served under his father, and he spake not as other men, neither could he be taught; for he needed not that any man should teach him.

26 And after many years, the hour of his ministry drew nigh.

CHAPTER 3

27 1 **And** in those days came John the Baptist, preaching in the wilderness of ~~Judaea~~ **Judea,**

28 2 And saying, Repent ye: for the kingdom of heaven is at hand.

29 3 For ~~this is~~ **I am** he ~~that~~ **who** was spoken of by the prophet Esaias, saying, The voice of one crying in the wilderness, Prepare ye the way of the Lord **and** make his paths straight.

30 4 And the same John had his raiment of ~~camel's~~ **camels'** hair, and a leathern girdle about his loins; and his ~~meat~~ **food** was locusts and wild honey.

31 5 Then went out to him Jerusalem, and all Judaea, and all the region round about Jordan,

32 6 And **many** were baptized of him in Jordan, confessing their sins.

33 7 But when he saw many of the Pharisees and Sadducees come to his baptism, he said unto them, O generation of vipers, who hath warned you to flee from the wrath to come?

34 Why is it that ye receive not the preaching of him whom God hath sent? If ye receive not this in your hearts, ye receive not me; and if ye receive not me, ye receive not him of whom I am sent to bear record; and for your sins ye have no cloak.

35 8 **Repent, therefore, and** bring forth ~~therefore~~ fruits meet for repentance;

36 9 And think not to say within yourselves, We ~~have~~ **are the children of** Abraham, ~~to our father~~ **and we only have power to bring seed unto our father Abraham;** for I say unto you that God is able of these stones to raise up children unto Abraham.

37 10 And now, also, the axe is laid unto the root of the trees; therefore every tree which bringeth not forth

good fruit, is **shall be** hewn down, and cast into the fire.

38 11 I indeed baptize you with water, unto **upon your** repentance; but he that cometh after me **and when he of whom I bear record cometh, who** is mightier than I, whose shoes I am not worthy to bear, **(or whose place I am not able to fill,) as I said, I indeed baptize you before he cometh, that when he cometh** he shall **may** baptize you with the Holy Ghost and with fire.

39 12 **And it is he of whom I shall bear record,** whose fan is **shall be** in his hand, and he will throughly **thoroughly** purge his floor, and gather his wheat into the garner; but **in the fullness of his own time** he will burn up the chaff with unquenchable fire.

40 Thus came John, preaching and baptizing in the river of Jordan; bearing record, that he who was coming after him had power to baptize with the Holy Ghost and fire.

41 13 **And** then cometh Jesus from Galilee to Jordan, unto John, to be baptized of him;

42 14 But John forbad **refused** him, saying, I have need to be baptized of thee, and **why** comest thou to me?

43 15 And Jesus, answering, said unto him, Suffer it to be so now **me to be baptized of thee,** for thus it becometh us to fulfill all righteousness. Then he suffered him.

44 And John went down into the water and baptized him.

45 16 And Jesus when he was baptized, went up straightway out of the water; and **John saw, and** lo, the heavens were opened unto him, and he saw the Spirit of God descending like a dove and lighting upon him **Jesus**.

46 17 And lo, **he heard** a voice from heaven, saying, This is my beloved Son, in whom I am well pleased. **Hear ye him.**

CHAPTER 4

1 Then was Jesus **was** led up of the Spirit, into the wilderness, to be tempted of the devil **with God.**

2 And when he had fasted forty days and forty nights, **and had communed with God,** he was afterward **afterwards** an hungred **hungered, and was left to be tempted of the devil.**

3 And when the tempter came to him, he said, If thou be the Son of God, command that these stones be made bread.

4 But he **Jesus** answered and said, It is written, Man shall not live by bread alone, but by every word that proceedeth out of the mouth of God.

5 Then the devil taketh him **Jesus was taken** up into the holy city, and **the Spirit** setteth him on a **the** pinnacle of the temple,

6 And saith unto him **Then the devil came unto him and said,** If thou be the Son of God, cast thyself down, for it is written, He shall give his angels charge concerning thee, and in *their* hands they shall bear thee up, lest at any time thou dash thy foot against a stone.

7 Jesus said unto him, It is written again, Thou shalt not tempt the Lord thy God.

8 **And** again, the devil **Jesus was in the Spirit, and it** taketh him up into an exceeding high mountain, and showeth him all the kingdoms of the world and the glory of them.

9 And saith **the devil came** unto him **again, and said,** All these things will I give **unto** thee, if thou wilt fall down and worship me.

10 10–11 Then saith Jesus **said** unto him, Get thee hence, Satan; for it is written, Thou shalt worship the Lord thy God, and him only shalt thou serve. Then the devil leaveth him.

11 11–12 **And now Jesus knew that John was cast into prison, and he sent angels,** and, behold, ~~angels~~ **they** came and ministered unto him.

12 12–13 ~~Now~~ **And** ~~when~~ Jesus ~~had heard that John was cast into prison,~~ ~~he~~ departed into Galilee, and leaving Nazareth, **in Zebulon,** he came and dwelt in Capernaum, which is upon the sea coast, in the borders of ~~Zabulon and~~ Nephthalim,

13 14 That it might be fulfilled which was spoken by Esaias the prophet, saying,

14 15 The land of Zebulun, and the land of Nephthalim, ~~by~~ **in** the way of the sea, beyond Jordan, Galilee of the Gentiles;

15 16 The people which sat in darkness saw **a** great light, and ~~to~~ **unto** them ~~which~~ **that** sat in the region and shadow of death, light is sprung up.

16 17 From that time Jesus began to preach, and to say, Repent: for the kingdom of heaven is at hand.

17 18 And Jesus, walking by the sea of Galilee, saw two brethren, Simon called Peter, and Andrew his brother, casting a net into the sea: for they were fishers.

18 19 And he ~~saith~~ **said** unto them, **I am he of whom it is written by the prophets;** follow me, and I will make you fishers of men.

19 20 And they ~~straightway,~~ **believing on his words,** left *their* ~~nets~~ **net,** and **straightway** followed him.

20 21 And going on from thence, he saw ~~other~~ two **other** brethren, James ~~the son~~ of ~~Zebedee,~~ and John his brother, **the sons of Zebedee,** in a ship with Zebedee their father, mending their ~~nets~~ **net;** and he called them.

21 22 And they immediately left ~~the ship and~~ their father **in the ship,** and followed him.

22 23 And Jesus went about all Galilee teaching in their synagogues, and preaching the gospel of the kingdom; and healing all manner of sickness, and all manner of ~~disease~~ **diseases** among the people **which believed on his name**.

23 24 And his fame went throughout all Syria; and they brought unto him all sick people that were taken with divers diseases, and torments, and those ~~which~~ **who** were possessed with devils, and those ~~which~~ **who** were ~~lunatick~~ **lunatic,** and those that had the palsy; and he healed them.

24 25 And there followed him great multitudes of people from Galilee, and ~~from~~ Decapolis, and ~~from~~ Jerusalem, and ~~from~~ ~~Judaea~~ **Judea,** and ~~from~~ beyond Jordan.

CHAPTER 5

1 And **Jesus,** seeing the ~~multitudes~~ **multitude,** ~~he~~ went up into a mountain; and when he was set **down,** his disciples came unto him;

2 And he opened his mouth, and taught them, saying,

3 Blessed are they who shall believe on me; and again, more blessed are they who shall believe on your words, when ye shall testify that ye have seen me and that I am.

4 Yea, blessed are they who shall believe on your words, and come down into the depth of humility, and be baptized in my name; for they shall be visited with fire and the Holy Ghost, and shall receive a remission of their sins.

5 3 **Yea,** blessed *are* the poor in spirit, **who come unto me;** for theirs is the kingdom of heaven.

6 4 **And again,** blessed *are* they that mourn; for they shall be comforted.

7 5 **And** blessed *are* the meek; for they shall inherit the earth.

8 6 **And** blessed *are* **all** they ~~which~~ **that** do hunger and thirst after righteousness: for they shall be filled **with the Holy Ghost**.

9 7 **And** blessed *are* the merciful; for they shall obtain mercy.

10 8 **And** blessed *are* **all** the pure in heart; for they shall see God.

11 9 **And** blessed *are* **all** the peacemakers; for they shall be called the children of God.

12 10 Blessed are **all** they ~~which~~ **that** are persecuted for ~~righteousness'~~ **my name's** sake; for theirs is the kingdom of heaven.

13 11 **And** blessed are ye when *men* shall revile you, and persecute *you*, and shall say all manner of evil against you falsely, for my sake.

14 12 ~~Rejoice~~ **For ye shall have great joy**, and be exceeding glad; for great ~~is~~ **shall be** your reward in heaven; for so persecuted they the prophets which were before you.

15 13 ~~Ye are~~ **Verily, verily, I say unto you, I give unto you to be** the salt of earth; but if the salt ~~have lost his savour~~ **shall lose its savor**,* wherewith shall ~~it~~ **the earth** be salted? ~~it is the salt shall~~ thenceforth **be** good for nothing, but to be cast out, and to be trodden under foot of men.

16 14 ~~Ye are~~ **Verily, verily, I say unto you, I give unto you to be** the light of the world; a city that is set on a hill cannot be hid.

17 15 ~~Neither~~ **Behold**, do men light a candle and put it under a bushel? **Nay**, but on a candlestick; and it giveth light ~~unto~~ **to** all that are in the house.

18 16 **Therefore,** let your light so shine before ~~men~~ **this world**, that they may see your good works, and glorify your Father ~~which~~ **who** is in heaven.

19 17 **Think** not that I am come to destroy the law, or the prophets: I am not come to destroy, but to fulfil.

20 18 For verily I say unto you, ~~Till~~ Heaven and earth **must** pass **away, but** one jot or one tittle shall in no wise pass from the law, until all be fulfilled.

21 19 Whosoever, therefore, shall break one of these least commandments, and shall teach men so **to do**, he shall ~~be called the least~~ **in no wise be saved** in the kingdom of heaven; but whosoever shall do and teach ~~them~~ **these commandments of the law until it be fulfilled**, the same shall be called great, **and shall be saved** in the kingdom of heaven.

22 20 For I say unto you, ~~That~~ Except your righteousness shall exceed ~~the righteousness~~ **that** of the scribes* and Pharisees, ye shall in no case enter into the kingdom of heaven.

23 21 Ye have heard that it ~~was~~ **hath been** said by them of old time **that**, Thou shalt not kill; and whosoever shall kill, shall be in danger of the judgment **of God**.

24 22 But I say unto you, that whosoever is angry with his brother, ~~without a cause~~ shall be in danger of ~~the~~ **his** judgment; and whosoever shall say to his brother, Raca, **or Rabcah,** shall be in danger of the council; ~~but~~ **and** whosoever shall say **to his brother**, Thou fool, shall be in danger of hell fire.

25 23 Therefore, **if ye shall come unto me, or shall desire to come unto me, or** if thou bring thy gift to the altar, and there rememberest that thy brother hath ~~ought~~ **aught** against thee,

26 24 Leave ~~there~~ **thou** thy gift before the altar, and go thy way **unto thy brother, and** first be reconciled to thy brother, and then come and offer thy gift.

27 25 Agree with thine adversary quickly, ~~whiles~~ **while** thou art in the way with him; lest at any time ~~the~~ **thine** adversary deliver thee to the judge, and the judge deliver thee to the officer, and thou be cast into prison.

28 26 Verily I say unto thee, Thou shalt by no means come out thence, till thou hast paid the uttermost farthing.

29 27 ~~Ye have heard that it was said~~ **Behold, it is written** by them of old time, **that** thou shalt not commit adultery.

30 28 But I say unto you, That whosoever looketh on a woman to lust after her hath committed adultery with her ~~already~~ in his heart **already.**

31 Behold, I give unto you a commandment, that ye suffer none of these things to enter into your heart, for it is better that ye should deny yourselves of these things, wherein ye will take up your cross, than that ye should be cast into hell.

32 29 ~~And~~ **Therefore,** if thy right eye offend thee, pluck it out and cast *it* from thee; for it is profitable for thee that one of thy members should perish, and not *that* thy whole body should be cast into hell.

33 30 ~~And~~ **Or** if thy right hand offend thee, cut it off and cast *it* from thee; for it is profitable for thee that one of thy members should perish, and not *that* thy whole body should be cast into hell.

34 And now this I speak, a parable concerning your sins; wherefore, cast them from you, that ye may not be hewn down and cast into the fire.

35 31 It hath been ~~said~~ **written that,** Whosoever shall put away his wife, let him give her a writing of divorcement.

36 32 ~~But~~ **Verily, verily,** I say unto you, that whosoever shall put away his wife, saving for the cause of fornication, causeth her to commit adultery; and whosoever shall marry her that is divorced, committeth adultery.

37 33 Again, ~~ye have heard that~~ it hath been ~~said~~ **written** by them of old time, Thou shalt not forswear thyself, but shalt perform unto the Lord thine oaths.

38 34–36 But I say unto you, Swear not at all; neither by heaven; for it is God's throne: nor by the earth; for it is his footstool: neither by Jerusalem; for it is the city of the great King. Neither shalt thou swear by thy head, because thou canst not make one hair white or black.

39 37 But let your communication be, Yea, yea; Nay, nay: for whatsoever is more than these cometh of evil.

40 38 Ye have heard that it hath been said, An eye for an eye, and a tooth for a tooth:

41 39 But I say unto you, That ye resist not evil: but whosoever shall smite thee on thy right cheek, turn to him the other also.

42 40 And if any man will sue thee at the law, and take away thy coat, let him have **it; and if he sue thee again, let him have** *thy* ~~cloke~~ **cloak** also.

43 41 And whosoever shall compel thee to go a mile, go with him **a mile; and whosoever shall compel thee to go with him twain, thou shalt go with him** twain.

44 42 Give to him that asketh **of** thee; and from him that would borrow of thee, turn not thou away.

45 43 Ye have heard that it hath been said, Thou shalt love thy neighbour, and hate thine enemy.

46 44 But I say unto you, Love your enemies, bless them that curse you, do good to them that hate you, and pray for them which despitefully use you and persecute you;

47 45 That ye may be the children of your Father ~~which~~ **who** is in heaven; for he maketh his sun to rise on the evil and on the good, and sendeth rain on the just and on the unjust.

48 46 For if ye love **only** them which love you, what reward have ~~ye~~ **you**? Do not even the publicans the same?

49 47 And if ye salute your brethren only, what do ye more *than others*? Do not even the publicans ~~so~~ **the same**?

50 48 ~~Be~~ Ye **are** therefore **commanded to be** perfect, even as your Father ~~which~~ **who** is in heaven is perfect.

Chapter 6

1 **And it came to pass that, as Jesus taught his disciples, he said unto them,** Take heed that ye do not your alms before men, to be seen of them; otherwise ye have no reward of your Father ~~which~~ **who** is in heaven.

2 Therefore, when thou doest *thine* alms, do not sound a trumpet before thee, as the hypocrites do, in the synagogues and in the streets, that they may have glory of men. Verily I say unto you, They have their reward.

3 But when thou doest alms, let **it be unto thee as** ~~not~~ thy left hand ~~know~~ **not knowing** what thy right hand doeth;

4 That thine alms may be in secret; and thy Father ~~which~~ **who** seeth in secret, himself shall reward thee openly.

5 And when thou prayest, thou shalt not be as the hypocrites *are*; for they love to pray standing in the synagogues and in the corners of the streets, that they may be seen of men; **for,** verily, I say unto you, They have their reward.

6 But thou, when thou prayest, enter into thy closet, and when thou hast shut ~~thy~~ **the** door, pray to thy Father ~~which~~ **who** is in secret; and thy Father ~~which~~ **who** seeth in secret shall reward thee openly.

7 But when ye pray, use not vain repetitions, as the ~~heathen~~ **hypocrites** *do*; for they think that they shall be heard for their much speaking.

8 **Therefore** be ~~not~~ ye **not** ~~therefore~~ like unto them; for your Father knoweth what things ye have need of, before ye ask him.

9 **Therefore** after this manner ~~therefore pray~~ **shall** ye **pray, saying,**

10 9 Our Father ~~which~~ **who** art in heaven, Hallowed be thy name.

11 10 Thy kingdom come. Thy will be done ~~in~~ **on** earth, as *it is* **done** in heaven.

12 11 Give us this day, our daily bread.

13 12 And forgive us our ~~debts~~ **trespasses**, as we forgive ~~our debtors~~ **those who trespass against us**.

14 13 And ~~lead us not~~ **suffer us not to be led** into temptation, but deliver us from evil.

15 13 For thine is the kingdom, and the power, and the glory, forever **and ever,** Amen.

16 14–15 For if ye forgive men their trespasses, **who trespass against you,** your heavenly Father will also forgive you; but if ye forgive not men their trespasses, neither will your **heavenly** Father forgive **you** your trespasses.

17 16 Moreover when ye fast, be not, as the hypocrites, of a sad countenance: for they disfigure their faces, that they may appear unto men to fast. Verily I say unto you, They have their reward.

18 17–18 But thou, when thou fastest, anoint ~~thine~~ **thy** head and wash thy face**,** that thou appear not unto men to fast, but unto thy Father ~~which~~ **who** is in secret**;** and thy Father ~~which~~ **who** seeth in secret, shall reward thee openly.

19 Lay not up for yourselves treasures upon earth, where moth and rust doth corrupt, and where thieves break through and steal:

20 But lay up for yourselves treasures in heaven, where neither moth nor rust doth corrupt, and where thieves do not break through nor steal:

21 For where your treasure is, there will your heart be also.

22 The light of the body is the eye**;** if therefore thine eye be single **to the glory of God**, thy whole body shall be full of light.

23 But if thine eye be evil, thy whole body shall be full of darkness. If therefore the light ~~that~~ **which** is in thee be darkness, how great ~~is~~ **shall** that darkness **be.**

24 No man can serve two masters: for either he will hate the one, and love the other; or else he will hold to the one, and despise the other. Ye cannot serve God and mammon.

25 And, again, I say unto you, go ye into the world, and care not for the world; for the world will hate you, and will persecute you, and will turn you out of their synagogues.

26 Nevertheless, ye shall go forth from house to house, teaching the people; and I will go before you.

27 And your heavenly Father will provide for you, whatsoever things ye need for food, what you shall eat;

and for raiment, what ye shall wear or put on.

28 25 Therefore I say unto you, Take no thought for your life, what ye shall eat, or what ye shall drink; nor yet for your ~~body~~ **bodies**, what ye shall put on. Is not the life more than meat, and the body than raiment?

29 26 Behold the fowls of the air**,** for they sow not, neither do they reap, nor gather into barns; yet your heavenly Father feedeth them. Are ye not much better than they? **How much more will he not feed you?**

30 Wherefore take no thought for these things, but keep my commandments wherewith I have commanded you.

31 27 **For** which of you by taking thought can add one cubit unto his stature?

32 28 And why take ye thought for raiment? Consider the lilies of the field, how they grow; they toil not, neither do they spin:

33 29 And yet I say unto you, That even Solomon in all his glory was not arrayed like one of these.

34 30 ~~Wherefore~~ **Therefore**, if God so clothe the grass of the field, which today is, and tomorrow is cast into the oven, ~~shall he not~~ **how** much more ~~clothe~~ **will he not provide for** you, ~~O~~ **if** ye **are not** of little faith.

35 31 Therefore take no thought, saying, What shall we eat? or, What shall we drink? or, Wherewithal shall we be clothed?

36 32 **Why is it that ye murmur among yourselves, saying, We cannot obey thy word**˙ **because ye have not all these things, and seek to excuse yourselves, saying that,** ~~For~~ After all these things do the Gentiles seek.

37 32 ~~for~~ **Behold, I say unto you,**

that your heavenly Father knoweth that ye have need of all these things.

38 33 **Wherefore, seek not the things of this world;** but seek ye first **to build up** the kingdom of God, and **to establish** his righteousness, and all these things shall be added unto you.

39 34 Take, therefore, no thought for the morrow; for the morrow shall take thought for the things of itself. Sufficient unto the day ~~is~~ **shall be** the evil thereof.

Chapter 7

1 Now these are the words which Jesus taught his disciples that they should say unto the people.

2 1 Judge not **unrighteously**, that ye be not judged; **but judge righteous judgment.**

3 2 For with what judgment ye **shall** judge, ye shall be judged; and with what measure ye mete, it shall be measured to you again.

4 3 And **again, ye shall say unto them,** Why **is it that thou** beholdest ~~thou~~ the mote that is in thy brother's eye, but considerest not the beam that is in thine own eye?

5 4 Or how wilt thou say to thy brother, Let me pull out the mote out of thine eye; and **canst not** behold a beam ~~is~~ in thine own eye?

6 And Jesus said unto his disciples, Beholdest thou the scribes, and the **Pharisees, and the Priests, and the Levites?** They teach in their synagogues, but do not observe the law, nor the commandments; and all have gone out of the way, and are under sin.

7 Go thou and say unto them, Why teach ye men the law and the commandments, when ye yourselves are the children of corruption?

8 5 **Say unto them,** ~~Thou hypocrite~~ **Ye hypocrites,** first cast out the beam out of thine own ~~eye~~ **eyes;** and then shalt thou see clearly to cast out the mote out of thy brother's eye.

9 Go ye into the world, saying unto all, Repent, for the kingdom of heaven has come nigh unto you.

10 6 **And the mysteries of the kingdom ye shall keep within yourselves; for it is not meet to** give ~~not~~ that which is holy unto the dogs; neither cast ye your pearls ~~before~~ **unto** swine, lest they trample them under their feet.

11 6 **For the world cannot receive that which ye, yourselves, are not able to bear; wherefore ye shall not give your pearls unto them, lest they** ~~and~~ turn again and rend you.

12 7 **Say unto them, Ask of God;** ask, and it shall be given you; seek, and ye shall find; knock, and it shall be opened unto you.

13 8 For every one that asketh receiveth; and he that seeketh findeth; and to him that knocketh it shall be opened.

14 And then said his disciples unto him, They will say unto us, We ourselves are righteous, and need not that any man should teach us. God, we know, heard Moses and some of the prophets; but us he will not hear.

15 And they will say, We have the law for our salvation, and that is sufficient for us.

16 Then Jesus answered, and said unto his disciples, Thus shall ye say unto them,

17 What man among you, having a son, and he shall be standing out, and shall say, Father, open thy house that I may come in and sup with thee, will not say, Come in, my son; for mine is thine, and thine is mine?

18 9 Or what man is there ~~of~~ **among** you, ~~whom~~ **who**, if his son ask bread, will ~~he~~ give him a stone?

19 10 Or if he ask a fish, will he give him a serpent?

20 11 If ye then, being evil, know how to give good gifts unto your children, how much more shall your Father ~~which~~ **who** is in heaven give good things to them that ask him?

21 12 Therefore**,** all things whatsoever ye would that men should do ~~to~~ **unto** you, do ye even so to them**;** for this is the law and the prophets.

22 13 **Repent, therefore, and** enter ye in at the strait gate; for wide *is* the gate, and broad *is* the way that leadeth to ~~destruction~~ **death,**²⁴ and many there be ~~which~~ **who** go in thereat.

23 14 Because strait *is* the gate, and narrow *is* the way ~~which~~ **that** leadeth unto life, and few there be that find it.

24 15 **And, again,** beware of false prophets, ~~which~~ **who** come to you in sheep's clothing; but inwardly they are ravening wolves.

25 16 Ye shall know them by their fruits**;** **for** do men gather grapes of thorns, or figs of thistles?

26 17 Even so every good tree bringeth forth good fruit; but a corrupt tree bringeth forth evil fruit.

27 18 A good tree cannot bring forth evil fruit**;** neither ~~can~~ a corrupt tree bring forth good fruit.

28 19 Every tree that bringeth not forth good fruit is hewn down, and cast into the fire.

29 20 Wherefore by their fruits ye shall know them.

30 21 **Verily I say unto you, it is** not everyone that saith unto me, Lord, Lord, **that** shall enter into the kingdom of heaven; but he that doeth the will of my Father ~~which~~ **who** is in heaven.

31 **For the day soon cometh, that men shall come before me to judgment, to be judged according to their works.**

32 22 **And** many will say ~~to~~ **unto** me in that day, Lord, Lord, have we not prophesied in thy name**;** and in thy name ~~have~~ cast out devils**;** and in thy name done many wonderful works?

33 23 And then will I ~~profess~~ **say** ~~unto them,~~ **I Ye** never knew ~~you~~ **me;** depart from me ye that work iniquity.

34 24–25 Therefore**,** whosoever heareth these sayings of mine and doeth them, I will liken him unto a wise man, ~~which~~ **who** built his house upon a rock**,** and the ~~rain~~ **rains** descended, and the floods came, and the winds blew, and beat upon that house**,** and it fell not**;** for it was founded upon a rock.

35 26–27 And everyone that heareth these sayings of mine, and doeth them not, shall be likened unto a foolish man, ~~which~~ **who** built his house upon the sand**;** and the ~~rain~~ **rains** descended, and the floods came, and the winds blew, and beat upon that house**,** and it fell**;** and great was the fall of it.

36 28 And it came to pass when Jesus had ended these sayings **with his disciples**, the people were astonished at his doctrine**;**

37 29 For he taught them as *one* having authority **from God**, and not as **having authority from** the scribes.*

CHAPTER 8

1 **And** when ~~he~~ **Jesus** was come down from the mountain, great multitudes followed him.

2 And, behold, there came a leper ~~and worshipped~~ **worshiping** him, saying, Lord, if thou wilt, thou canst make me clean.

3 And Jesus put forth *his* hand, and touched him, saying, I will; be thou clean. And immediately his leprosy was cleansed.

4 And Jesus saith unto him, See thou tell no man; but go thy way **and** show thyself to the priest, and offer the gift that Moses commanded, for a testimony unto them.

5 5–6 And when Jesus was entered into Capernaum, there came unto him a centurion, beseeching him, and saying, Lord, my servant lieth at home sick of the palsy, grievously tormented.

6 7 And Jesus saith unto him, I will come and heal him.

7 8 The centurion answered and said, Lord, I am not worthy that thou shouldest come under my roof: but speak the word only, and my servant shall be healed.

8 9 For I am a man under authority, having soldiers under me: and I say to this *man*, Go, and he goeth; and to another, Come, and he cometh; and to my servant, Do this, and he doeth *it*.

9 10 **And when they that followed him, heard this, they marveled. And** when Jesus heard ~~it~~ **this**, he ~~marvelled, and~~ said ~~to~~ **unto** them that followed,

10 Verily I say unto you, I have not found so great faith, no, not in Israel.

11 And I say unto you, that many shall come from the east, and **the** west, and shall sit down with Abraham, and Isaac, and Jacob, in the kingdom of heaven.

12 But the children of the ~~kingdom~~ **wicked one** shall be cast out into outer darkness; there shall be weeping and gnashing of teeth.

13 And Jesus said unto the centurion, Go thy way; and as thou hast believed, *so* be it done unto thee. And his servant was healed in the selfsame hour.

14 And when Jesus was come into Peter's house, he saw his wife's mother laid, and sick of a fever.

15 And he touched her hand, and the fever left her: and she arose, and ministered unto them.

16 **Now** when the ~~even~~ **evening** was come, they brought unto him many that were possessed with devils; and he cast out the **evil** spirits with ~~his~~ **the** word, and healed all that were sick.

17 That it might be fulfilled which was spoken by Esaias the prophet, saying, Himself took our infirmities, and ~~bare~~ **bear** *our* sicknesses.

18 Now when Jesus saw great multitudes about him, he gave commandment to depart unto the other side **of the sea.**

19 And a certain scribe came ~~and said~~ unto him **and said**, Master, I will follow thee whithersoever thou goest.

20 And Jesus saith unto him, The foxes have holes, and the birds of the air *have* nests; but the Son of man hath not where to lay *his* head.

21 And another of his disciples said unto him, Lord, suffer me first to go and bury my father.

22 But Jesus said unto him, Follow me; and let the dead bury their dead.

23 And when he was entered into a ship, his disciples ~~followed~~ **came unto** him.

24 And, behold, there arose a great tempest in the sea, insomuch that the ship was covered with the waves: but he was asleep.

25 And his disciples came ~~to~~ **unto** *him*, and awoke him, saying, Lord, save us**, else** we perish.

26 And he saith unto them, Why are ye fearful, O ye of little faith?

27 26 Then he arose, and rebuked the winds and the sea; and there was a great calm.

28 27 But the men marvelled, saying, What manner of man is this, that even the winds and the sea obey him!

29 28 And when he was come to the other side, into the country of the Gergesenes, there met him ~~two~~ **a man** possessed ~~with~~ **of** devils, coming out of the tombs, exceeding fierce, so that no man ~~might~~ **could** pass ~~by~~ that way.

30 29 And, behold, ~~they~~ **he** cried out, saying, What have we to do with thee, Jesus, thou Son of God? Art thou come hither to torment us before the time?

31 30 And there was a good way off from them an herd of many swine feeding.

32 31 So the devils besought him, saying, If thou cast us out, suffer us to go ~~away~~ into the herd of swine.

33 32 And he said unto them, Go. And when they were come out, they went into the herd of swine: and, behold, the whole herd of swine ran violently down a steep place into the sea, and perished in the waters.

34 33 And they that kept them fled, and went their ~~ways~~ **way** into the city, and told everything **which took place,** and what was befallen ~~to~~ the possessed of the devils.

35 34 And, behold, the whole city came out to meet Jesus: and when they saw him, they besought *him* that he would depart out of their coasts.

CHAPTER 9

1 And ~~he~~ **Jesus** entered into a ship, and passed over, and came into his own city.

2 And, behold, they brought to him a man sick of the palsy, lying on a bed; and Jesus, ~~seeing~~ **knowing** their faith, said unto the sick of the palsy, Son, be of good cheer; thy sins be forgiven thee; **go thy way and sin no more.**

3 And, behold, certain of the scribes said within themselves, This *man* blasphemeth.

4 And Jesus, knowing their thoughts, said, Wherefore ~~think~~ **is it that** ye **think** evil in your hearts?

5 For ~~whether~~ is **it not** easier to say, *Thy* sins be forgiven thee, ~~or~~ **than** to say, Arise and walk.

6 But **I said this** that ye may know that the Son of Man hath power on earth to forgive sins.

7 6 Then ~~saith he~~ **Jesus said** ~~to~~ **unto** the sick of the palsy, Arise, take up thy bed, and go unto ~~thine~~ **thy** house.

8 7 And he **immediately** arose, and departed to his house.

9 8 But when the ~~multitudes~~ **multitude** saw *it*, they marveled and glorified God, ~~which~~ **who** had given such power unto men.

10 9 And as Jesus passed forth from thence, he saw a man named Matthew, sitting at the ~~receipt of custom~~ **place where they received tribute, as was customary in those days,** and he ~~saith~~ **said** unto him, Follow me. And he arose and followed him.

11 10 And it came to pass, as Jesus sat at meat in the house, behold, many publicans and sinners came and sat down with him, and **with** his disciples.

12 11 And when the Pharisees saw ~~it~~ **them,** they said unto his disciples, Why eateth your master with publicans and sinners?

13 12 But when Jesus heard ~~that~~ **them,** he said unto them, They that be whole need not a physician, but they that are sick.

14 13 But go ye and learn what ~~that~~ **this** meaneth, I will have mercy and not sacrifice; for I am not come to call

the righteous, but sinners to repentance.

15 14 **And while he was thus teaching,** ~~Then~~ **there** came to him the disciples of John, saying, Why do we and the Pharisees fast oft, but thy disciples fast not?

16 15 And Jesus said unto them, Can the children of the bridechamber mourn, as long as the bridegroom is with them?

17 15 But the days will come, when the bridegroom shall be taken from them, and then shall they fast.

18 Then said the Pharisees unto him, Why will ye not receive us with our baptism, seeing we keep the whole law?

19 But Jesus said unto them, Ye keep not the law. If ye had kept the law, ye would have received me, for I am he who gave the law.

20 I receive not you with your baptism, because it profiteth you nothing.

21 For when that which is new is come, the old is ready to be put away.

22 16 **For** no man putteth a piece of new cloth ~~unto~~ **on** an old garment; for that which is put in to fill it up, taketh from the garment, and the rent is made worse.

23 17 Neither do men put new wine into old bottles: else the bottles break, and the wine runneth out, and the bottles perish: but they put new wine into new bottles, and both are preserved.

24 18 While he spake these things unto them, behold, there came a certain ruler and worshiped him, saying, My daughter is even now ~~dead~~ **dying;** but come and lay thy hand upon her and she shall live.

25 19 And Jesus arose and followed him, and ~~so did~~ **also** his disciples,

and much people thronged him.

26 20 And, behold, a woman, which was diseased with an issue of blood twelve years, came behind *him*, and touched the hem of his garment:

27 21 For she said within herself, If I may but touch his garment, I shall be whole.

28 22 But Jesus turned him about, and when he saw her, he said, Daughter, be of good comfort; thy faith hath made thee whole. And the woman was made whole from that hour.

29 23 And when Jesus came into the ruler's house, and saw the minstrels and the people making a noise,

30 24 He said unto them, Give place: for the maid is not dead, but sleepeth. And they laughed him to scorn.

31 25 But when the people were put forth, he went in, and took her by the hand, and the maid arose.

32 26 And the fame ~~hereof~~ **of Jesus** went abroad into all that land.

33 27 And when Jesus departed thence, two blind men followed him, crying, and saying, **Jesus,** *thou* Son of David, have mercy on us.

34 28 And when he was come into the house, the blind men came to him: and Jesus saith unto them, Believe ye that I am able to do this? They said unto him, Yea, Lord.

35 29 Then touched he their eyes, saying, According to your faith be it unto you.

36 30 And their eyes were opened; and ~~Jesus~~ straitly **he** charged them, saying, **Keep my commandments, and** see **ye tell no man in this place,** *that* no man know *it*.

37 31 But they, when they were departed, spread abroad his fame in all that country.

38 32 **And** as they went out, behold,

they brought to him a dumb man possessed with a devil.

39 33 And when the devil was cast out, the dumb **man** spake. And the multitudes marveled, saying, It was never so seen in Israel.

40 34 But the Pharisees said, He casteth out **the** devils, through the prince of the devils.

41 35 And Jesus went about all the cities and villages, teaching in their synagogues, and preaching the gospel of the kingdom, and healing every sickness and ~~every~~ disease among the people.

42 36 But when he saw the multitudes, he was moved with compassion on them, because they fainted, and were scattered abroad, as sheep having no shepherd.

43 37 Then saith he unto his disciples, The harvest truly *is* plenteous, but the labourers *are* few.

44 38 Pray ye therefore the Lord of the harvest, that he will send forth labourers into his harvest.

CHAPTER 10

1 And when he had called unto *him* his twelve disciples, he gave them power ~~against~~ **over** unclean spirits, to cast them out, and to heal all manner of sickness and all manner of disease.

2 2–4 Now the names of the twelve apostles are these; the first Simon, who is called Peter, and Andrew his brother; James *the son* of Zebedee, and John his brother; Philip, and Bartholomew; Thomas, and Matthew the publican; James *the son* of ~~Alphaeus~~ **Alpheus**, and ~~Lebbaeus~~ **Lebbeus**, whose surname was ~~Thaddaeus~~ **Thaddeus**; Simon the Canaanite, and Judas Iscariot, who also betrayed him.

3 5 These twelve Jesus sent forth, and commanded them, saying,

4 5 Go not into the way of the Gentiles, and **enter ye not** into *any* city of the Samaritans ~~enter ye not.~~

5 6 But ~~go~~ rather **go** to the lost sheep of the house of Israel.

6 7 And as ye go, preach, saying, The kingdom of heaven is at hand.

7 8 Heal the sick, cleanse the lepers, raise the dead, cast out devils: freely ye have received, freely give.

8 9 Provide neither gold, nor silver, nor brass in your purses,

9 10 Nor scrip for *your* journey, neither two coats, neither shoes, nor yet staves: for the workman is worthy of his meat.

10 11 And into whatsoever ~~city or~~ town **or city** ye shall enter, inquire who in it is worthy, and there abide till ye go thence.

11 12–13 And when ye come into an house, salute it. And if the house be worthy, let your peace come upon it: but if it be not worthy, let your peace return to you.

12 14 And whosoever shall not receive you, nor hear your words, when ye depart out of that house, or city, shake off the dust of your feet **for a testimony against them**.

13 15 **And,** verily, I say unto you, It shall be more tolerable for the land of Sodom and Gomorrah in the day of judgment than for that city.

14 16 Behold, I send you forth as sheep in the midst of wolves; be ye therefore wise ~~as serpents~~ **servants**, and **as** harmless as doves.

15 17 But beware of men: for they will deliver you up to the councils, and they will scourge you in their synagogues;

16 18 And ye shall be brought before governors and kings for my sake, for a testimony against them and the Gentiles.

17 19–20 But when they deliver you up, take no thought how or what ye shall speak: for it shall be given you in that same hour what ye shall speak. For it is not ye that speak, but the Spirit of your Father which speaketh in you.

18 21 And the brother shall deliver up the brother to death, and the father the child: and the children shall rise up against *their* parents, and cause them to be put to death.

19 22 And ye shall be hated of all ~~men~~ **the world** for my name's sake; but he that endureth to the end shall be saved.

20 23 But when they persecute you in ~~this~~ **one** city, flee ye into another; for verily, I say unto you, Ye shall not have gone over the cities of Israel, till the Son of Man be come.

21 24–25 **Remember,** the disciple is not above *his* master; nor the servant above his lord. It is enough ~~for~~ **that** the disciple ~~that he~~ be as his master, and the servant as his lord.

22 25 If they have called the master of the house Beelzebub, how much more *shall they call* them of his household?

23 26 Fear them not therefore: for there is nothing covered, that shall not be revealed; and hid, that shall not be known.

24 27 What I tell you in darkness, ~~that speak~~ **preach** ye in light; and what ye hear in the ear, ~~that~~ preach ye upon the housetops.

25 28 And fear not them ~~which~~ **who are able to** kill the body, but are not able to kill the soul; but rather fear him ~~which~~ **who** is able to destroy both soul and body in hell.

26 29 Are not two sparrows sold for a farthing? And one of them shall not fall ~~on~~ **to** the ground without your Father **knoweth it.**

27 30–31 ~~But~~ **And** the very hairs of your head are all numbered. Fear ye not, therefore; ye are of more value than many sparrows.

28 32 Whosoever, therefore, shall confess me before men, him will I confess also before my Father ~~which~~ **who** is in heaven.

29 33 But whosoever shall deny me before men, him will I also deny before my Father ~~which~~ **who** is in heaven.

30 34 Think not that I am come to send peace on earth: I came not to send peace, but a sword.

31 35–36 For I am come to set a man at variance against his father, and the daughter against her mother, and the daughter in law against her mother in law. And a man's foes *shall be* they of his own household.

32 37 He ~~that~~ **who** loveth father ~~or~~ **and** mother more than me, is not worthy of me; and he ~~that~~ **who** loveth son or daughter more than me, is not worthy of me.

33 38 And he ~~that~~ **who** taketh not his cross and followeth after me, is not worthy of me.

34 39 He ~~that~~ **who** ~~findeth~~ **seeketh to save** his life shall lose it; and he ~~that~~ **who** loseth his life for my sake shall find it.

35 40 He ~~that~~ **who** receiveth you, receiveth me; and he ~~that~~ **who** receiveth me, receiveth him ~~that~~ **who** sent me.

36 41 He that receiveth a prophet in the name of a prophet shall receive a prophet's reward;

37 41 ~~and~~ He that receiveth a righteous man, in the name of a righteous man, shall receive a righteous man's reward.

38 42 And whosoever shall give to drink unto one of these little ones a cup of cold *water* only in the name of a disciple, verily I say unto you, he shall in no wise lose his reward.

CHAPTER 11

1 And it came to pass, when Jesus had made an end of commanding his twelve disciples, he departed thence to teach and to preach in their cities.

2 Now when John had heard in the prison the ~~works~~ **words** of Christ, he sent two of his disciples,

3 And **they** said unto him, Art thou he **of whom it is written in the prophets** that **he** should come, or do we look for another?

4 Jesus answered and said unto them, Go and ~~shew~~ **tell** John again **of** those things which ye do hear and see;

5 **How that** the blind receive their sight, and the lame walk, **and** the lepers are cleansed, and the deaf hear, **and** the dead are raised up, and the poor have the gospel preached ~~to~~ **unto** them.

6 And blessed is ~~he~~ **John, and** whosoever shall not be offended in me.

7 And as they departed, Jesus began to say unto the multitudes concerning John, What went ye out into the wilderness to see? **Was it** a reed shaken with the wind? **And they answered him, No.**

8 **And he said,** But what went ye out for to see? **Was it** a man clothed in soft raiment? Behold they that wear soft ~~clothing~~ **raiment** are in kings' houses.

9 But what went ye out for to see? A prophet? yea, I say unto you, and more than a prophet.

10 For this is ~~he~~ **the one** of whom it is written, Behold, I send my messenger before thy face, which shall prepare thy way before thee.

11 Verily I say unto you, Among them that are born of women there hath not risen a greater than John the Baptist: notwithstanding he that is least in the kingdom of heaven is greater than he.

12 And from the days of John the Baptist until now the kingdom of heaven suffereth violence, and the violent take it by force.

13 **But the day will come, when the violent shall have no power;** for all the prophets and the law prophesied **that it should be thus** until John.

14 **Yea, as many as have prophesied have foretold of these days.**

15 14 And if ye will receive *it*, **verily,** ~~this is~~ **he was the** Elias, ~~which~~ **who** was for to come **and prepare all things**.

16 15 He that hath ears to hear, let him hear.

17 16 But whereunto shall I liken this generation?

18 16–17 It is like unto children sitting in the markets, and calling unto their fellows, and saying, We have piped unto you, and ye have not danced; we have mourned ~~unto~~ **for** you, and ye have not lamented.

19 18 For John came neither eating nor drinking, and they say, He hath a devil.

20 19 The Son of Man came eating and drinking, and they say, Behold, a ~~man~~ gluttonous **man** and a wine bibber, a friend of publicans and sinners.

21 19 But ~~wisdom~~ **I say unto you, Wisdom** is justified of her children.

22 20 Then began he to upbraid the cities wherein most of his mighty works were done, because they repented not:

23 21 Woe unto thee, Chorazin! Woe unto thee, Bethsaida! For if the mighty works which were done in

you, had been done in Tyre and Sidon, they would have repented long ~~ago~~ **since** in sackcloth and ashes.

24 22 But I say unto you, It shall be more tolerable for Tyre and Sidon at the day of judgment, than for you.

25 23 And thou, Capernaum, which art exalted unto heaven, shalt be brought down to hell: for if the mighty works, which have been done in thee, had been done in Sodom, it would have remained until this day.

26 24 But I say unto you, ~~That~~ It shall be more tolerable for the land of Sodom in the day of judgment, than for thee.

27 25–26 **And** at that time**, there came a voice out of heaven, and** Jesus answered and said, I thank thee, O Father, Lord of heaven and earth, because thou hast hid these things from the wise and prudent, and hast revealed them unto babes. Even so, Father**,** for so it seemed good in thy sight**!**

28 27 All things are delivered unto me of my Father**;** and no man knoweth the Son, but the Father; neither knoweth any man the Father, save the Son, and ~~he~~ **they** to ~~whomsoever~~ **whom** the Son will reveal ~~him~~ **himself; they shall see the Father also.**

29 28 **Then spake Jesus, saying,** Come unto me, all *ye* that labor and are heavy laden, and I will give you rest.

30 29–30 Take my yoke upon you, and learn of me; for I am meek and lowly in heart: and ye shall find rest unto your souls. For my yoke *is* easy, and my burden is light.

CHAPTER 12

1 At that time Jesus went on the sabbath day through the corn; and his disciples were an hungred, and began to pluck the ears of corn, and to eat.

2 But when the Pharisees saw ~~it~~ **them**, they said unto him, Behold, thy disciples do that which is not lawful to do upon the Sabbath day.

3 3–4 But he said unto them, Have ye not read what David did, when he was an ~~hungred~~ **hungered**, and they that were with him? How he entered into the house of God, and did eat the shewbread, which was not lawful for him to eat, neither for them which were with him**;** but only for the priests?

4 5 Or have ye not read in the law, how that on the Sabbath ~~days~~ **day** the priests in the temple profane the Sabbath, and **ye say they** are blameless?

5 6 But I say unto you, That in this place is *one* greater than the temple.

6 7–8 But if ye had known what *this* meaneth, I will have mercy and not sacrifice, ye would not have condemned the guiltless. For the Son of Man is Lord even of the ~~sabbath day~~ **Sabbath**.

7 9 And when he was departed thence, he went into their ~~synagogue~~ **synagogues.**

8 10 And, behold, there was a man which had ~~his~~ **a** ~~hand~~ withered **hand**. And they asked him, saying, Is it lawful to heal on the Sabbath days? that they might accuse him.

9 11 And he said unto them, What man shall there be among you, that shall have one sheep, and if it fall into a pit on the sabbath day, will he not lay hold on it, and lift *it* out?

10 12 How much then is a man better than a sheep? Wherefore it is lawful to do well on the sabbath days.

11 13 Then ~~saith~~ **said** he to the man, Stretch forth ~~thine~~ **thy** hand**;** and he stretched *it* forth**,** and it was restored whole, like ~~as~~ **unto** the other.

12 14 Then the Pharisees went out, and held a council against him, how they might destroy him.

13 15–16 But ~~when~~ Jesus knew ~~it~~ **when they took counsel**, **and** he withdrew himself from thence; and great multitudes followed him, and he healed ~~them all~~ **their sick,** and charged them that they should not make him known;

14 17–18 That it might be fulfilled which was spoken by Esaias the prophet, saying, Behold my servant, whom I have chosen; my beloved, in whom my soul is well pleased:

15 18–19 I will put my spirit upon him, and he shall shew judgment to the Gentiles. He shall not strive, nor cry; neither shall any man hear his voice in the streets.

16 20 A bruised reed shall he not break, and smoking flax shall he not quench, till he send forth judgment unto victory.

17 21 And in his name shall the Gentiles trust.

18 22 Then was brought unto him one possessed with a devil, blind, and dumb: and he healed him, insomuch that the blind and dumb both spake and saw.

19 23 And all the people were amazed, and said, Is ~~not~~ this the Son of David?

20 24 But when the Pharisees heard ~~it~~ **that he had cast out the devil,** they said, This ~~fellow~~ **man** doth not cast out devils, but by Beelzebub the prince of devils.

21 25–26 And Jesus knew their thoughts, and said unto them, Every kingdom divided against itself is brought to desolation; and every city or house divided against itself, shall not stand. And if Satan cast out Satan, he is divided against himself; how

~~shall~~ then **shall** his kingdom stand?

22 27 And if I by Beelzebub cast out devils, by whom do your children cast ~~them~~ out **devils**? Therefore they shall be your judges.

23 28 But if I cast out devils by the Spirit of God, then the kingdom of God is come unto you. **For they also cast out devils by the Spirit of God, for unto them is given power over devils, that they may cast them out.**

24 29 Or else how can one enter into a strong man's house, and spoil his goods, except he first bind the strong man? and then he will spoil his house.

25 30 He that is not with me is against me; and he that gathereth not with me scattereth abroad.

26 31 Wherefore I say unto you, All manner of sin and blasphemy shall be forgiven unto men **who receive me and repent;** but the blasphemy *against* the *Holy* Ghost, **it** shall not be forgiven unto men.

27 32 And whosoever speaketh a word against the Son of man, it shall be forgiven him: but whosoever speaketh against the Holy Ghost, it shall not be forgiven him, neither in this world, neither in the *world* to come.

28 33 Either make the tree good and his fruit good; or else make the tree corrupt, and his fruit corrupt; for the tree is known by ~~his~~ **the** fruit.

29 34 **And Jesus said,** O **ye** generation of vipers! how can ye, being evil, speak good things? For out of the abundance of the heart the mouth speaketh.

30 35 A good man out of the good treasure of the heart bringeth forth good things: and an evil man out of the evil treasure bringeth forth evil things.

31 36 ~~But~~ **And again** I say unto you, That every idle word that men shall speak, they shall give account thereof in the day of judgment.

32 37 For by thy words thou shalt be justified, and by thy words thou shalt be condemned.

33 38–39 Then certain of the scribes and of the Pharisees answered, saying, Master, we would see a sign from thee. But he answered and said unto them,

34 39–40 An evil and adulterous generation seeketh after a sign; and there shall no sign be given to it, but the sign of the prophet Jonas: for as Jonas was three days and three nights in the whale's belly; so shall the Son of man be three days and three nights in the heart of the earth.

35 41 The men of Nineveh shall rise **up** in judgment with this generation, and shall condemn it, because they repented at the preaching of Jonas; and **ye**, behold, a greater than Jonas *is* here.

36 42 The queen of the south shall rise up in the **day of** judgment with this generation, and shall condemn it; for she came from the uttermost parts of the earth to hear the wisdom of Solomon; and **ye**, behold, a greater than Solomon *is* here.

37 Then came some of the scribes **and said unto him, Master, it is written that, Every sin shall be forgiven; but ye say, Whosoever speaketh against the Holy Ghost shall not be forgiven. And they asked him, saying, How can these things be?**

38 43–44 **And he said unto them,** When the unclean spirit is gone out of a man, he walketh through dry places, seeking rest and findeth none; **but when a man speaketh against the Holy Ghost,** then he saith, I will return into my house from whence I came out; and when he is come, he findeth ~~it~~ **him** empty, swept and

garnished; **for the good spirit leaveth him unto himself.**

39 45 Then goeth ~~he~~ the evil spirit, and taketh with ~~himself~~ **him** seven other spirits more wicked than himself; and they enter in and dwell there; and the last ~~state~~ **end** of that man is worse than the first. Even so shall it be also unto this wicked generation.

40 46 **And** while he yet talked to the people, behold, *his* mother and his brethren stood without, desiring to speak with him.

41 47 Then one said unto him, Behold, thy mother and thy brethren stand without, desiring to speak with thee.

42 48 But he answered and said unto ~~him~~ **the man** that told him, Who is my mother? and who are my brethren?

43 49 And he stretched forth his hand toward his disciples, and said, Behold my mother and my brethren!

44 50 **And he gave them charge concerning her, saying, I go my way, for my Father hath sent me.** ~~For~~ **And** whosoever shall do the will of my Father which is in heaven, the same is my brother, and sister, and mother.

CHAPTER 13

1 **And it came to pass** the same day ~~went,~~ Jesus **went** out of the house, and sat by the seaside.

2 And great multitudes were gathered together unto him, so that he went into a ship, and sat; and the whole multitude stood on the shore.

3 And he spake many things unto them in parables, saying, Behold, a sower went forth to sow;

4 And when he sowed, some *seeds* fell by the way side, and the fowls came and devoured them up:

5 5–6 Some fell upon stony places,

where they had not much earth; and forthwith they sprung up; ~~because they had no deepness of earth~~ and when the sun was up, they were scorched, **because they had no deepness of earth;** and because they had no root, they withered away.

6 7 And some fell among thorns, and ~~the~~ thorns, sprung up and choked them.

7 8–9 But ~~other~~ **others** fell into good ground, and brought forth fruit, some an hundredfold, some sixtyfold, some thirtyfold. Who hath ears to hear, let him hear.

8 10 ~~And~~ **Then** the disciples came and said unto him, Why speakest thou unto them in parables?

9 11 He answered and said unto them, Because it is given unto you to know the mysteries of the kingdom of heaven, but to them it is not given.

10 12 For whosoever ~~hath~~ **receiveth**, to him shall be given, and he shall have more abundance;

11 12 But whosoever ~~hath~~ **continueth** not **to receive**, from him shall be taken away even that he hath.

12 13 Therefore speak I to them in parables: because they seeing see not; and hearing they hear not, neither do they understand.

13 14 And in them is fulfilled the prophecy of Esaias **concerning them**, which saith, By hearing, ye shall hear and shall not understand; and seeing, ye shall see and shall not perceive.

14 15 For this people's heart is waxed gross, and *their* ears are dull of hearing, and their eyes they have closed, lest at any time they should see with *their* eyes and hear with *their* ears, and should understand with *their* ~~heart~~ **hearts**, and should be converted, and I should heal them.

15 16 But blessed *are* your eyes, for they see; and your ears, for they hear. **And blessed are you because these things are come unto you, that you might understand them.**

16 17 ~~For~~ **And** verily, I say unto you, ~~That~~ Many **righteous** prophets ~~and righteous men~~ have desired to see ~~those things~~ **these days** which ~~ye~~ **you** see, and have not seen *them*; and to hear ~~those things~~ **that** which ~~ye~~ **you** hear, and have not heard ~~them~~.

17 18 Hear ye therefore the parable of the sower.

18 19 When any one heareth the word of the kingdom, and understandeth ~~it~~ not, then cometh the wicked *one*, and ~~catcheth~~ **taketh** away that which was sown in his heart; this is he ~~which~~ **who** ~~received~~ **receiveth** seed by the wayside.

19 20–21 But he that received the seed into stony places, the same is he that heareth the word and ~~anon~~ **readily** with joy receiveth it, yet **he** hath ~~he~~ not root in himself, and ~~dureth~~ **endureth but** for a while; for when tribulation or persecution ariseth because of the word, by and by he is offended.

20 22 He also ~~that~~ **who** received seed among the thorns, is he that heareth the word; and the care of this world and the deceitfulness of riches, choke the word, and he becometh unfruitful.

21 23 But he ~~that~~ **who** received seed into the good ground, is he ~~that~~ **who** heareth the word and understandeth ~~it~~ **and endureth**; which also beareth fruit, and bringeth forth, some an hundredfold, some sixty, **and** some thirty.

22 24 Another parable put he forth unto them, saying, The kingdom of heaven is likened unto a man ~~which~~ **who** sowed good seed in his field;

23 25 But while ~~men~~ **he** slept, his enemy came and sowed tares among the wheat, and went his way.

24 26 But when the blade ~~was~~ sprung up, and brought forth fruit, then appeared the tares also.

25 27 So the servants of the householder came and said unto him, Sir, didst not thou sow good seed in thy field? ~~from~~ whence then hath it tares?

26 28 He said unto them, An enemy hath done this.

27 28 **And** the servants said unto him, Wilt thou then that we go and gather them up?

28 29 But he said, Nay; lest while ye gather up the tares, ye root up also the wheat with them.

29 30 Let both grow together until the harvest**,** and in the time of harvest**,** I will say to the reapers, Gather ye together first the ~~tares~~ **wheat into my barn;** and ~~bind them~~ **the tares are bound** in bundles to ~~burn them~~ **be burned** ~~but gather the wheat into my barn.~~

30 31 **And** another parable put he forth unto them, saying, The kingdom of heaven is like to a grain of mustard seed, which a man took and sowed in his field**;**

31 32 Which indeed is the least of all seeds: but when it is grown, it is the greatest among herbs, and becometh a tree, so that the birds of the air come and lodge in the branches thereof.

32 33 Another parable spake he unto them; The kingdom of heaven is like unto leaven, which a woman took, and hid in three measures of meal, till the whole was leavened.

33 34 All these things spake Jesus unto the ~~multitude~~ **multitudes** in parables; and without a parable spake he not unto them**.**

34 35 That it might be fulfilled which was spoken by the ~~prophet~~ **prophets**, saying, I will open my mouth in parables; I will utter things which have been kept secret from the foundation of the world.

35 36 Then Jesus sent the multitude away, and went into the house**.** And his disciples came unto him, saying, Declare unto us the parable of the tares of the field.

36 37 He answered and said unto them, He that soweth the good seed is the Son of man;

37 38 The field is the world; the good seed are the children of the kingdom; but the tares are the children of the wicked ~~one~~**.**

38 39 The enemy that sowed them is the devil;

39 The harvest is the end of the world**, or the destruction of the wicked** ~~and~~**.**

40 39 The reapers are the angels**, or the messengers sent of heaven.**

41 40 As**,** therefore**,** the tares are gathered and burned in the fire, so shall it be in the end of this world**, or the destruction of the wicked.**

42 41 **For in that day, before** the Son of Man **shall come, he** shall send forth his angels **and messengers of heaven.**

43 41–42 And they shall gather out of his kingdom all things that offend, and them which do iniquity, and shall cast them ~~into a furnace of fire~~ **out among the wicked; and** there shall be wailing and gnashing of teeth.

44 For the world shall be burned with fire.

45 43 Then shall the righteous shine forth as the sun in the kingdom of their Father. Who hath ears to hear, let him hear.

46 44 Again, the kingdom of heaven is like unto **a** treasure hid in a field.

And ~~the which~~ when a man hath found **a treasure which is hid**, he ~~hideth~~ **secureth it**, and, **straightway,** for joy thereof, goeth and selleth all that he hath, and buyeth that field.

47 45–46 **And** again, the kingdom of heaven is like unto a ~~merchant man~~ **merchantman**, seeking goodly pearls, who, when he had found one pearl of great price, **he** went and sold all that he had and bought it.

48 47–48 Again, the kingdom of heaven is like unto a net, that was cast into the sea, and gathered of every kind: which, when it was full, they drew to shore, and sat down, and gathered the good into vessels, but cast the bad away.

49 So shall it be at the end of the world:

50 **And the world is the children of the wicked.**

51 49–50 The angels shall come forth, and sever the wicked from among the just, and shall cast them **out** into the ~~furnace of fire~~ **world to be burned**. There shall be wailing and gnashing of teeth.

52 51 **Then** Jesus ~~saith~~ **said** unto them, Have ye understood all these things? They say unto him, Yea, Lord.

53 52 Then said he unto them, ~~Therefore~~ Every scribe ~~which is~~ **well** instructed ~~unto~~ **in the things of** the kingdom of heaven, is like unto a ~~man that is~~ an householder; **a man, therefore,** which bringeth forth out of his treasure ~~things~~ **that which is** new and old.

54 53 And it came to pass, ~~that~~ when Jesus had finished these parables, he departed thence.

55 54 And when he was come into his own country, he taught them in their ~~synagogue~~ **synagogues**, insomuch that they were astonished, and

said, Whence hath this ~~man~~ **Jesus** this wisdom and *these* mighty works?

56 55–56 Is not this the carpenter's son? is not his mother called Mary? and his brethren, James, and Joses, and Simon, and Judas? And his sisters, are they not all with us?

57 56–57 Whence then hath this *man* all these things? And they were offended ~~in~~ **at** him.

58 57 But Jesus said unto them, A prophet is not without honour, save in his own country, and in his own house.

59 58 And he did not many mighty works there because of their unbelief.

CHAPTER 14

1 1–2 At that time Herod the tetrarch heard of the fame of Jesus, and said unto his servants, This is John the Baptist; he is risen from the dead; and therefore mighty works do shew forth themselves in him.

2 3 For Herod had laid hold on John, and bound him, and put *him* in prison for Herodias' sake, his brother Philip's wife.

3 4 For John said unto him, It is not lawful for thee to have her.

4 5 And when he would have put him to death, he feared the multitude, because they counted him as a prophet.

5 6 But when Herod's birthday was kept, the daughter of Herodias danced before them and pleased Herod.

6 7 Whereupon he promised with an oath to give her ~~whatsoever~~ **whatever** she would ask.

7 8 And she, being before instructed of her mother, said, Give me here John Baptist's head in a charger.

8 9 And the king was sorry; nevertheless for the oath's sake, and them which sat with him at meat, he commanded *it* to be given ~~her~~.

9 10 And he sent, and beheaded John in the prison.

10 11 And his head was brought in a charger, and given to the damsel: and she brought *it* to her mother.

11 12 And his disciples came, and took up the body, and buried it, and went and told Jesus.

12 13 When Jesus heard ~~of it~~ **that John was beheaded**, he departed thence by ship into a desert place apart; and when the people had heard ~~thereof~~ **of him**, they followed him on foot out of the cities.

13 14 And Jesus went forth, and saw a great multitude, and was moved with compassion ~~toward~~ **towards** them, and he healed their sick.

14 15 And when it was evening, his disciples came to him, saying, This is a desert place, and the time is now past; send the multitude away, that they may go into the villages and buy themselves victuals.

15 16 But Jesus said unto them, They need not depart; give ye them to eat.

16 17–18 And they ~~say~~ **said** unto him, We have here but five loaves and two fishes. He said, Bring them hither to me.

17 19 And he commanded the multitude to sit down on the grass; and **he** took the five loaves and the two fishes, and looking up to heaven, he blessed and brake, and gave the loaves to ~~his~~ **the** disciples, and the disciples, to the multitude.

18 20–21 And they did all eat, and were filled. And they took up of the fragments that remained, twelve baskets full. And they that had eaten were about five thousand men, ~~beside~~ **besides** women and children.

19 22–23 And straightway Jesus constrained his disciples to get into a ship, and to go before him unto the other side, while he sent the multitudes away. And when he had sent the multitudes away, he went up into a mountain apart to pray:

20 23–24 And when the evening was come, he was there alone. But the ship was now in the midst of the sea, tossed with the waves: for the wind was contrary.

21 25 And in the fourth watch of the night Jesus went unto them, walking on the sea.

22 26 And when the disciples saw him walking on the sea, they were troubled, saying, It is a spirit; and they cried out for fear.

23 27 But straightway Jesus spake unto them, saying, Be of good cheer; it is I; be not afraid.

24 28–29 And Peter answered him and said, Lord, if it be thou, bid me come unto thee on the water. And he said, Come.

25 29–30 And when Peter was come down out of the ship, he walked on the water, to go to Jesus. But when he saw the wind boisterous, he was afraid; and beginning to sink, he cried, saying, Lord, save me.

26 31 And immediately Jesus stretched forth *his* hand, and caught him, and said unto him, O thou of little faith, wherefore didst thou doubt?

27 32 And when they were come into the ship, the wind ceased.

28 33 Then they that were in the ship came and worshipped him, saying, Of a truth thou art the Son of God.

29 34 And when they were gone over, they came into the land of Gennesaret.

30 35–36 And when the men of that place had knowledge of him, they sent out into all that country round about, and brought unto him all that were diseased; and besought him that they might only touch the hem of his garment: and as many as touched were made perfectly whole.

CHAPTER 15

1 Then came to Jesus scribes and Pharisees, which were of Jerusalem, saying,

2 Why do thy disciples transgress the tradition of the elders? for they wash not their hands when they eat bread.

3 But he answered and said unto them, Why do ye also transgress the commandment of God by your tradition?

4 For God commanded, saying, Honor thy father and mother; and, He that curseth father or mother, let him die the death **which Moses shall appoint.**

5 ~~5–6~~ But ye say, Whosoever shall say to ~~his~~ father or ~~his~~ mother, ~~It is a gift~~ By whatsoever thou mightest be profited by me**, it is a gift from me˙** and honor not his father or ~~his~~ mother, ~~he shall be free~~ **it is well.**

6 Thus have ye made the commandment of God of none effect by your ~~tradition~~ **traditions.**

7 ~~7–8~~ **O** *ye* hypocrites! well did Esaias prophesy of you, saying, This people ~~draweth~~ **draw** nigh unto me with their mouth, and honoreth me with *their* lips; but their heart is far from me.

8 ~~9~~ But in vain ~~they~~ do **they** worship me, teaching ~~for~~ **the** doctrines **and** ~~the~~ commandments of men.

9 10 And he called the multitude, and said unto them, Hear, and understand:

10 11 Not that which goeth into the mouth defileth a man; but that which

cometh out of the mouth, this defileth ~~a~~ **the** man.

11 12 Then came his disciples, and said unto him, Knowest thou that the Pharisees were offended, after they heard this saying?

12 13 But he answered and said, Every plant, which my heavenly Father hath not planted, shall be rooted up.

13 14 Let them alone: they be blind leaders of the blind. And if the blind lead the blind, both shall fall into the ditch.

14 15 Then answered Peter and said unto him, Declare unto us this parable.

15 16 And Jesus said, Are ye also yet without understanding?

16 17 Do ~~not~~ ye **not** yet understand, that whatsoever entereth in at the mouth goeth into the belly, and is cast ~~out~~ into the draught?

17 18 But those things which proceed out of the mouth come forth from the heart; and they defile the man.

18 19 For out of the heart proceed evil thoughts, murders, adulteries, fornications, thefts, false witness, blasphemies:

19 20 These are ~~the~~ *things* which defile a man. But to eat with unwashen hands defileth not a man.

20 21 Then Jesus went thence, and departed into the coasts of Tyre and Sidon.

21 22 And, behold, a woman of Canaan came out of the same coasts, and cried unto him, saying, Have mercy on me, O Lord, *thou* Son of David; my daughter is grievously vexed with a devil.

22 23 But he answered her not a word. And his disciples came and besought him, saying, Send her away; for she crieth after us.

23 24 ~~But~~ He answered ~~and said~~, I am not sent but unto the lost sheep of the house of Israel.

24 25 Then came she and worshipped him, saying, Lord, help me.

25 26 But he answered and said, It is not meet to take the children's bread, and to cast *it* to dogs.

26 27 And she said, Truth, Lord; yet the dogs eat the crumbs ~~which~~ **that** fall from ~~their~~ **the** ~~masters'~~ **master's** table.

27 28 Then Jesus answered and said unto her, O woman, great *is* thy faith: be it unto thee even as thou wilt. And her daughter was made whole from that very hour.

28 29 And Jesus departed from thence, and came nigh unto the sea of Galilee; and went up into a mountain, and sat down there.

29 30–31 And great multitudes came unto him, having with them ~~those that were~~ **some** lame, blind, dumb, maimed, and many others, and cast them down at Jesus' feet; and he healed them; insomuch that the multitude wondered, when they saw the dumb to speak, the maimed to be whole, the lame to walk, and the blind to see. And they glorified the God of Israel.

30 32 Then Jesus called his disciples ~~unto him~~ and said, I have compassion on the multitude, because they continue with me now three days, and have nothing to eat; and I will not send them away fasting, lest they faint in the way.

31 33 And his disciples say unto him, Whence should we have so much bread in the wilderness, **so** as to fill so great a multitude.

32 34 And Jesus saith unto them, How many loaves have ye? And they said, Seven, and a few little fishes.

33 35 And he commanded the multitude to sit down on the ground.

34 36 And he took the seven loaves and the fishes, and gave thanks, and brake ~~them~~ **the bread**, and gave to his disciples, and the disciples, to the multitude.

35 37 And they did all eat, and were filled. And they took up of the broken *meat* ~~that was left~~ seven baskets full.

36 38 And they that did eat were four thousand men, ~~beside~~ **besides** women and children.

37 39 And he sent away the multitude, and took ship, and came into the ~~coasts~~ **coast** of Magdala.

Chapter 16

1 The Pharisees also, with the Sadducees, came, and tempting **Jesus**, desired him that he would show them a sign from heaven.

2 2–3 **And** he answered and said unto them, When it is evening ye say, ~~It will be fair~~ **The** weather **is fair,** for the sky is red;* and in the morning **ye say,** ~~It will be foul~~ **The** weather **is foul** today; for the sky is red and ~~lowring~~ **lowering**.

3 O ~~ye~~ hypocrites! ye can discern the face of the sky; but ~~can~~ ye ~~not~~ **cannot** ~~discern~~ **tell** the signs of the times.

4 A wicked and adulterous generation seeketh after a sign; and there shall no sign be given unto it, but the sign of the prophet Jonas.

5 4 And he left them, and departed.

6 5 And when his disciples were come to the other side, they had forgotten to take bread.

7 6 Then Jesus said unto them, Take heed and beware of the leaven of the Pharisees and of the Sadducees.

8 7 And they reasoned among themselves, saying, ~~It is~~ **He said this** because we have taken no bread.

9 8 ~~Which~~ **And** when **they reasoned among themselves,** Jesus perceived **it; and** he said unto them, O ye of little faith! why reason ye among yourselves, because ye have brought no bread?

10 9 Do ye not yet understand, neither remember the five loaves of the five thousand, and how many baskets ye took up?

11 10 Neither the seven loaves of the four thousand, and how many baskets ye took up?

12 11 How is it that ye do not understand, that I spake ~~it~~ not ~~to~~ **unto** you concerning bread, that ye should beware of the leaven of the Pharisees and of the Sadducees?

13 12 Then understood they, how that he bade *them* not beware of the leaven of bread, but of the doctrine of the Pharisees and of ~~the~~ Sadducees.

14 13 **And** when Jesus came into the coasts of Caesarea Philippi, he asked his disciples, saying, Whom do men say that I, the Son of Man, am?

15 14 And they said, Some *say* ~~that thou art~~ John the Baptist; some Elias; and others Jeremias; or one of the prophets.

16 15 He saith unto them, But whom say ye that I am?

17 16 And Simon Peter answered and said, Thou art the Christ, the Son of the living God.

18 17 And Jesus answered and said unto him, Blessed art thou, Simon Bar-jona; for flesh and blood hath not revealed ~~it~~ **this** unto thee, but my Father ~~which~~ **who** is in heaven.

19 18 And I say also unto thee, That thou art Peter, and upon this rock I will build my church; and the gates of hell shall not prevail against it.

20 19 And I will give unto thee the keys of the kingdom of heaven: and whatsoever thou shalt bind on earth shall be bound in heaven: and whatsoever thou shalt loose on earth shall be loosed in heaven.

21 20 Then charged he his disciples that they should tell no man that he was Jesus the Christ.

22 21 From that time forth began Jesus to show unto his disciples, how that he must go ~~unto~~ **to** Jerusalem, and suffer many things of the elders, and chief priests, and scribes,* and be killed, and be raised again the third day.

23 22 Then Peter took him, and began to rebuke him, saying, Be it far from thee, Lord; this shall not be **done** unto thee.

24 23 But he turned, and said unto Peter, Get thee behind me, Satan: thou art an offence unto me; for thou savourest not the things ~~that~~ **which** be of God, but those that be of men.

25 24 Then said Jesus unto his disciples, If any *man* will come after me, let him deny himself, and take up his cross, and follow me.

26 And now for a man to take up his cross, is to deny himself all ungodliness, and every worldly lust, and keep my commandments.

27 25 **Break not my commandments for to save your lives;** for whosoever will save his life **in this world,** shall lose it **in the world to come.**

28 25 And whosoever will lose his life **in this world,** for my sake, shall find it **in the world to come**.

29 26 **Therefore, forsake the world, and save your souls;** for what is a man profited, if he shall gain the whole world, and lose his own soul? Or what shall a man give in exchange for his soul?

30 27 For the Son of man shall come in the glory of his Father with his angels; and then he shall reward every man according to his works.

31 28 Verily I say unto you, There be some standing here, which shall not taste of death, till they see the Son of man coming in his kingdom.

CHAPTER 17

1 1–2 And after six days Jesus taketh Peter, James, and John his brother, and bringeth them up into an high mountain apart, and was transfigured before them: and his face did shine as the sun, and his raiment was white as the light.

2 3 And, behold, there appeared unto them Moses and Elias talking with him.

3 4 Then answered Peter, and said unto Jesus, Lord, it is good for us to be here; if thou wilt, let us make here three tabernacles; one for thee, ~~and~~ one for Moses, and one for Elias.

4 5 While he yet spake, behold, a bright cloud overshadowed them: and behold a voice out of the cloud, which said, This is my beloved Son, in whom I am well pleased; hear ye him.

5 6 And when the disciples heard ~~it~~ **the voice**, they fell on their ~~face~~ **faces**, and were sore afraid.

6 7 And Jesus came and touched them, and said, Arise, ~~and~~ be not afraid.

7 8 And when they had lifted up their eyes, they saw no man, save Jesus only.

8 9 And as they came down from the mountain, Jesus charged them, saying, Tell the vision to no man, until the Son of man be risen again from the dead.

9 10 And his disciples asked him, saying, Why then say the scribes that Elias must first come?

10 11 And Jesus answered and said unto them, Elias truly shall first come, and restore all things, **as the prophets have written**.

11 12 ~~But~~ **And again** I say unto you that Elias ~~is~~ **has** come already, **concerning whom it is written, Behold, I will send my messenger, and he shall prepare the way before me;** and they knew him not, ~~but~~ **and** have done unto him, whatsoever they listed.

12 Likewise shall ~~also~~ the Son of Man suffer of them.

13 But I say unto you, Who is Elias? Behold, this is Elias, whom I sent to prepare the way before me.

14 13 Then the disciples understood that he spake unto them of John the Baptist, **and also of another who should come and restore all things, as it is written by the prophets.**

15 14–15 And when they were come to the multitude, there came to him a ~~certain~~ man kneeling down to him, and saying, Lord, have mercy on my son; for he is ~~lunatick~~ **lunatic**, and sore vexed; for ofttimes he falleth into the fire, and oft into the water.

16 And I brought him to thy disciples, and they could not cure him.

17 Then Jesus answered and said, O faithless and perverse generation, how long shall I be with you? how long shall I suffer you? bring him hither to me.

18 And Jesus rebuked the devil; and he departed out of him: and the child was cured from that very hour.

19 Then came the disciples to Jesus apart, and said, Why could not we cast him out?

20 And Jesus said unto them, Because of your unbelief; for, verily, I say unto you, If ye have faith as a grain of mustard seed, ye shall say unto this mountain, Remove ~~hence~~ to yonder

place, and it shall remove; and nothing shall be impossible unto you.

21 Howbeit this kind goeth not out but by prayer and fasting.

22 22–23 And while they abode in Galilee, Jesus said unto them, The Son of man shall be betrayed into the hands of men and they shall kill him, and the third day he shall be raised again. And they were exceeding sorry.

23 24–25 And when they were come to Capernaum, they that received tribute ~~money~~ came to Peter, and said, Doth not your master pay tribute? He ~~saith~~ **said,**˙ ~~Yes~~ **Yea.**

24 25 And when he was come into the house, Jesus ~~prevented~~ **rebuked** him, saying,

25 What thinkest thou, Simon? of whom do the kings of the earth take custom or tribute? of their own children, or of strangers?

26 26–27 Peter saith unto him, Of strangers. Jesus saith unto him, Then are the children free. Notwithstanding, lest we should offend them, go thou to the sea, and cast a hook, and take up the fish that first cometh up; and when thou hast opened his mouth, thou shalt find a piece of money: that take and give unto them for me and thee.

CHAPTER 18

1 At the same time came the disciples unto Jesus, saying, Who is the greatest in the kingdom of heaven?

2 2–3 And Jesus called a little child unto him, and set him in the midst of them, and said, Verily I say unto you, Except ye be converted, and become as little children, ye shall not enter into the kingdom of heaven.

3 4 Whosoever therefore shall humble himself as this little child, the same is greatest in the kingdom of heaven.

4 5 And whoso shall receive one such little child in my name receiveth me.

5 6 But whoso shall offend one of these little ones which believe in me, it were better for him that a millstone were hanged about his neck and ~~that~~ he were drowned in the depth of the sea.

6 7 Woe unto the world because of offences! for it must needs be that offences come; but woe to that man by whom the offence cometh!

7 8 Wherefore if thy hand or thy foot offend thee, cut ~~them~~ **it** off and cast ~~them~~ **it** from thee**; for** it is better for thee to enter into life halt or maimed, rather than having two hands or two feet to be cast into everlasting fire.

8 9 And if thine eye offend thee, pluck it out, and cast *it* from thee: it is better for thee to enter into life with one eye, rather than having two eyes to be cast into hell fire.

9 And a man's hand is his friend, and his foot, also; and a man's eye, are they of his own household.

10 Take heed that ye despise not one of these little ones; for I say unto you, that in heaven their angels do always behold the face of my Father ~~which~~ **who** is in heaven.

11 For the Son of Man is come to save that which was lost, **and to call sinners to repentance; but these little ones have no need of repentance, and I will save them.**

12 How think ye? if a man have an hundred sheep, and one of them be gone astray, doth he not leave the ninety and nine, and goeth into the mountains, and seeketh that which is gone astray?

13 And if **it** so be that he find it, verily, I say unto you, he rejoiceth more ~~of~~ **over** that ~~sheep~~ **which was lost,**

than ~~of~~ **over** the ninety and nine which went not astray.

14 Even so it is not the will of your Father which is in heaven, that one of these little ones should perish.

15 Moreover if thy brother shall trespass against thee, go and tell him his fault between thee and him alone: if he shall hear thee, thou hast gained thy brother.

16 But if he will not hear *thee, then* take with thee one or two more, that in the mouth of two or three witnesses every word may be established.

17 And if he shall neglect to hear them, tell *it* unto the church: but if he neglect to hear the church, let him be unto thee as an heathen man and a publican.

18 Verily I say unto you, Whatsoever ye shall bind on earth shall be bound in heaven: and whatsoever ye shall loose on earth shall be loosed in heaven.

19 Again**,** I say unto you, that if two of you shall agree on earth as touching anything that they shall ask, **that they may not ask amiss,** it shall be done for them of my Father ~~which~~ **who** is in heaven.

20 For where two or three are gathered together in my name, there am I in the midst of them.

21 Then came Peter to him, and said, Lord, how oft shall my brother sin against me, and I forgive him? till seven times?

22 Jesus saith unto him, I say not unto thee, Until seven times: but, Until seventy times seven.

23 Therefore is the kingdom of heaven likened unto a certain king, which would take account of his servants.

24 And when he had begun to reckon, one was brought unto him ~~which~~ **who** owed him ten thousand talents.

25 But forasmuch as he had not to pay, his lord commanded him to be sold, and his wife, and **his** children, and all that he had, and payment to be made.

26 **And** the servant ~~therefore fell down, and worshipped~~ **besought** him, saying, Lord, have patience with me, and I will pay thee all.

27 Then the lord of that servant was moved with compassion, and loosed him, and forgave him the debt. **The servant, therefore, fell down and worshiped him.**

28 But the same servant went out, and found one of his fellowservants, which owed him an hundred pence: and he laid hands on him, and took *him* by the throat, saying, Pay me that thou owest.

29 And his fellowservant fell down at his feet, and besought him, saying, Have patience with me, and I will pay thee all.

30 And he would not: but went and cast him into prison, till he should pay the debt.

31 So when his fellowservants saw what was done, they were very sorry, and came and told unto their lord all that was done.

32 32–33 Then his lord, after that he had called him, said unto him, O thou wicked servant, I forgave thee all that debt, because thou desiredst me: shouldest not thou also have had compassion on thy fellowservant, even as I had pity on thee?

33 34 And his lord was wroth, and delivered him to the tormentors, till he should pay all that was due unto him.

34 35 So likewise shall my heavenly Father do also unto you, if ye from your hearts forgive not every one his brother their trespasses.

CHAPTER 19

1 And it came to pass, ~~that~~ when Jesus had finished these sayings, he departed from Galilee, and came into the coasts of ~~Judaea~~ **Judea** beyond Jordan**.**

2 And great multitudes followed him; **and many believed on him,** and he healed them there.

3 The Pharisees ~~also~~ came **also** unto him, tempting him, and saying unto him, Is it lawful for a man to put away his wife for every cause?

4 And he answered and said unto them, Have ye not read, that he ~~which~~ **who** made ~~them~~ **man** at the beginning**,** made ~~them~~ **him,** male and female,

5 And said, For this cause shall a man leave father and mother, and shall cleave ~~to~~ **unto** his wife**;** and they twain shall be one flesh?

6 Wherefore they are no more twain, but one flesh. What therefore God hath joined together, let not man put asunder.

7 They say unto him, Why did Moses then command to give a writing of divorcement, and to put her away?

8 He saith unto them, Moses because of the hardness of your hearts suffered you to put away your wives: but from the beginning it was not so.

9 And I say unto you, Whosoever shall put away his wife, except ~~it be~~ for fornication, and shall marry another, committeth adultery; and whoso marrieth her ~~which~~ **that** is put away**,** doth commit adultery.

10 His disciples say unto him, If the case of the man be so with ~~his~~ **a**[*] wife, it is not good to marry.

11 But he said unto them, All ~~men~~ cannot receive this saying**; it is not for them** save ~~they~~ to whom it is given.

12 For there are some eunuchs, which were so born from *their* mother's womb**;** and there are some eunuchs which were made eunuchs of men**;** and there be eunuchs, which have made themselves eunuchs for the kingdom of heaven's sake. He that is able to receive *it*, let him receive *it* **my sayings**.

13 Then were there brought unto him little children, that he should put *his* hands on them and pray**.** And the disciples rebuked them**, saying, There is no need, for Jesus hath said, Such shall be saved.**

14 But Jesus said, Suffer little children **to come unto me**, and forbid them not, ~~to come unto me~~ for of such is the kingdom of heaven.

15 And he laid ~~his~~ hands on them, and departed thence.

16 And, behold, one came and said ~~unto him,~~ Good Master, what good thing shall I do, that I may have eternal life?

17 And he said unto him, Why callest thou me good? *there is* none good but one, *that is*, God: but if thou wilt enter into life, keep the commandments.

18 He saith unto him, Which? Jesus said, Thou shalt ~~do no murder~~ **not kill.** Thou shalt not commit adultery**.** Thou shalt not steal**.** Thou shalt not bear false witness.

19 Honor thy father and ~~thy~~ mother**.** And, Thou shalt love thy neighbor as thyself.

20 The young man saith unto him, All these things have I kept from my youth up: what lack I yet?

21 Jesus said unto him, If thou wilt be perfect, go**,** ~~and~~ sell that thou hast, and give to the poor, and thou shalt have treasure in heaven**,** and come *and* follow me.

22 But when the young man heard

that saying, he went away sorrowful: for he had great possessions.

23 Then said Jesus unto his disciples, Verily I say unto you, That a rich man shall hardly enter into the kingdom of heaven.

24 And again I say unto you, It is easier for a camel to go through the eye of a needle, than for a rich man to enter ~~into~~ the kingdom of God.

25 When his disciples heard ~~it~~ **this**, they were exceedingly amazed, saying, Who then can be saved?

26 But Jesus beheld ~~them~~ **their thoughts**, and said unto them, With men this is impossible; but **if they will forsake all things for my sake,** with God ~~all~~ **whatsoever** things **I speak** are possible.

27 Then answered Peter and said unto him, Behold, we have forsaken all, and followed thee; what shall we have therefore?

28 And Jesus said unto them, Verily I say unto you, that ye ~~which~~ **who** have followed me, **shall,** in the ~~regeneration~~ **resurrection,** when the Son of Man shall ~~sit in~~ **come sitting on** the throne of his glory, ye ~~also~~ shall **also** sit upon twelve thrones, judging the twelve tribes of Israel.

29 And everyone that hath forsaken houses, or brethren, or sisters, or father, or mother, or wife, or children, or lands, for my name's sake, shall receive an hundredfold, and shall inherit everlasting life.

30 But many ~~that are~~ **of the** first shall be last**,** and the last ~~shall be~~ first.

Chapter 20

1 For the kingdom of heaven is like unto a man, ~~that is~~ an householder, ~~which~~ **who** went out early in the morning to hire laborers into his vineyard.

2 And when he had agreed with the labourers for a penny a day, he sent them into his vineyard.

3 And he went out about the third hour, and ~~saw~~ **found** others standing idle in the marketplace**.**

4 And said unto them; Go ye also into the vineyard, and whatsoever is right I will give you. And they went their way.

5 Again he went out about the sixth and ninth hour, and did likewise.

6 And about the eleventh hour he went out, and found others standing idle, and saith unto them, Why stand ye here all the day idle?

7 They ~~say~~ **said** unto him, Because no man hath hired us.

8 7 He ~~saith~~ **said** unto them, Go ye also into the vineyard; and whatsoever is right ~~that shall~~ ye **shall** receive.

9 8 So when even was come, the lord of the vineyard saith unto his steward, Call the labourers and give them *their* hire, beginning from the last unto the first.

10 9 And when they came that ~~were hired~~ **began** about the eleventh hour, they received every man a penny.

11 10–12 But when the first came, they supposed that they should have received more; and they likewise received every man a penny. And when they had received ~~it~~ **a penny**, they murmured against the goodman of the house, saying, These last have wrought ~~but~~ one hour **only** and thou hast made them equal unto us, ~~which~~ **who** have borne the burden and heat of the day.

12 13 But he answered one of them, and said, Friend, I do thee no wrong: didst not thou agree with me for a penny?

13 14–15 Take ~~that~~ thine ~~is~~ and go thy way**;** I will give unto this last even

as unto thee. Is it not lawful for me to do what I will with mine own?

14 15 Is thine eye evil, because I am good?

15 16 So the last shall be first, and the first last; for many ~~be~~ **are** called, but few chosen.

16 17 And Jesus going up to Jerusalem took the twelve disciples apart in the way, and said unto them,

17 18–19 Behold, we go up to Jerusalem, and the Son of Man shall be betrayed unto the chief priests, and unto the scribes,* and they shall condemn him to death; and shall deliver him to the Gentiles to mock, and to scourge, and to crucify ~~him~~. And the third day he shall rise again.

18 20 Then came to him the mother of Zebedee's children with her sons, worshiping ~~him~~ **Jesus**, and desiring a certain thing of him.

19 21 And he said unto her, What wilt thou **that I should do**?

20 21 **And** she ~~saith~~ **said** unto him, Grant that these my two sons may sit, the one on thy right hand, and the other on thy left, in thy kingdom.

21 22 But Jesus answered and said, Ye know not what ye ask. Are ye able to drink of the cup that I shall drink of, and to be baptized with the baptism that I am baptized with?

22 They say unto him, We are able.

23 And he ~~saith~~ **said** unto them, Ye shall drink indeed of my cup, and be baptized with the baptism that I am baptized with; but to sit on my right hand, and on my left, is **for whom it is prepared of my Father**, **but** not mine to give ~~but it shall be given to them~~ ~~for whom it is prepared of my Father~~.

24 And when the ten heard ~~it~~ **this**, they were moved with indignation against the two brethren.

25 25–26 But Jesus called them ~~unto him~~, and said, Ye know that the princes of the Gentiles exercise dominion over them, and they that are great exercise authority upon them; but it shall not be so among you.

26 But whosoever will be great among you, let him be your minister;

27 And whosoever will be chief among you, let him be your servant:

28 Even as the Son of man came not to be ministered unto, but to minister, and to give his life a ransom for many.

29 And as they departed from Jericho, a great multitude followed him.

30 And, behold, two blind men sitting by the wayside, when they heard that Jesus passed by, cried out, saying, Have mercy on us, O Lord, ~~thou~~ Son of David.

31 And the multitude rebuked them, ~~because~~ **saying,** they should hold their peace; but they cried the more, saying, Have mercy on us, O Lord, ~~thou~~ Son of David.

32 And Jesus stood still, and called them, and said, What will ye that I shall do unto you?

33 They say unto him, Lord, that our eyes may be opened.

34 So Jesus had compassion ~~on them~~, and touched their eyes; and immediately their eyes received sight, and they followed him.

CHAPTER 21

1 And when ~~they~~ **Jesus** drew nigh unto Jerusalem, and **they** were come to Bethphage, ~~unto~~ **on** the mount of Olives, then sent Jesus two disciples,

2 2–3 Saying unto them, Go into the village over against you, and straightway ye shall find ~~an ass~~ **a colt** tied ~~and a colt with her~~; loose ~~them~~ **it**, and bring ~~them~~ **it** unto me; and if any man **shall** say ~~ought~~ **aught** unto you, ye shall say, The Lord hath need of ~~them~~ **it**; and straightway he will send ~~them~~ **it**.

3 4 All this was done, that it might be fulfilled which was spoken by the prophet, saying,

4 5 Tell ye the daughter of ~~Sion~~ **Zion**, Behold, thy king cometh unto thee, **and he is** meek, and **he is** sitting upon an ass, and a colt, the foal of an ass.

5 6–7 And the disciples went, and did as Jesus commanded them; and brought ~~the ass, and~~ the colt, and put on ~~them~~ **it** their clothes; and ~~they set him~~ **Jesus took the colt and sat** thereon; **and they followed him.**

6 8 And a very great multitude spread their garments in the way; others cut down branches from the trees, and ~~strawed~~ **strewed** ~~them~~ in the way.

7 9 And the multitudes that went before, and **also** that followed **after**, cried, saying, Hosanna to the Son of David; blessed *is* he ~~that~~ **who** cometh in the name of the Lord! Hosanna in the highest!

8 10 And when he was come into Jerusalem, all the city was moved, saying, Who is this?

9 11 And the multitude said, This is Jesus ~~the prophet~~ of Nazareth, **the prophet** of Galilee.

10 12–13 And Jesus went into the temple of God, and cast out all them that **bought and** sold ~~and bought~~ in the temple, and overthrew the tables of the moneychangers, and the seats of them that sold doves, and said unto them,

11 13 It is written, My house shall be called the house of prayer; but ye have made it a den of thieves.

12 14 And the blind and the lame came to him in the temple; and he healed them.

13 15–16 And when the chief priests and scribes* saw the wonderful things that he did, and the children **of the kingdom** crying in the temple, and saying, Hosanna to the Son of David! they were sore displeased, and said unto him, Hearest thou what these say?

14 16 And Jesus ~~saith~~ **said** unto them, Yea; have ye never read **the scriptures which saith**, Out of the ~~mouth~~ **mouths** of babes and sucklings, **O Lord**, thou hast perfected praise?

15 17 And he left them, and went out of the city into Bethany; and he lodged there.

16 18 Now in the morning as he returned into the city, he hungered.

17 19 And when he saw a fig tree in the way, he came to it, and ~~found nothing thereon~~ **there was not any fruit on it**, but leaves only. And **he** said unto it, Let no fruit grow on thee henceforward, forever. And presently the fig tree withered away.

18 20 And when the disciples saw ~~it~~ **this**, they marveled ~~saying~~ **and said**, How soon is the fig tree withered away!

19 21 Jesus answered and said unto them, Verily I say unto you, If ye have faith, and doubt not, ye shall not only do this ~~which is done~~ to the fig tree, but also, if ye shall say unto this mountain, Be thou removed, and be thou cast into the sea, it shall be done.

20 22 And all things, whatsoever ye shall ask in prayer, **in faith** believing, ye shall receive.

21 23 And when he was come into the temple, the chief priests and the elders of the people came unto him as he was teaching, and said, By what authority doest thou these things? and who gave thee this authority?

22 24 And Jesus answered and said unto them, I also will ask you one thing, which if ye tell me, I, ~~in like wise~~ **likewise**, will tell you by what authority I do these things.

23 25 The baptism of John, whence was it? from heaven, or of men?

24 25–27 And they reasoned with themselves, saying, If we shall say, From heaven; he will say unto us, Why did ye not then believe him? But if we shall say, Of men; we fear the people. For all **people** ~~hold~~ **held** John as a prophet. And they answered Jesus, and said, We cannot tell.

25 27 And he said ~~unto them~~, Neither tell I you by what authority I do these things.

26 28 But what think ye? A ~~certain~~ man had two sons; and he came to the first, ~~and said~~ **saying**, Son, go work today in my vineyard.

27 29 He answered and said, I will not: but ~~afterward~~ **afterwards** he repented, and went.

28 30 And he came to the second, and said likewise. And he answered and said, I ~~go, sir~~ **will serve;** and went not.

29 31 Whether of ~~them~~ **these** twain did the will of ~~his~~ **their** father?

30 31 They say unto him, The first.

31 Jesus ~~saith~~ **said** unto them, Verily I say unto you, That the publicans and the harlots **shall** go into the kingdom of God before you.

32 For John came unto you in the way of righteousness, **and bore*** **record of me,** and ye believed him not; but the publicans and the harlots believed him; and ye, **afterward,** when ye had seen ~~it~~ **me**, repented not ~~afterward,~~ that ye might believe him.

33 For he that believed not John concerning me, cannot believe me, except he first repent.

34 33 **And except ye repent, the preaching of John shall condemn you at*** **the day of judgment. And, again,** hear another parable;* **for unto you that believe not, I speak in parables; that your unrighteousness may be rewarded unto you.**

35 33 **Behold,** there was a certain householder, ~~which~~ **who** planted a vineyard, and hedged it round about, and digged a winepress in it; and built a tower, and let it out to husbandmen, and went into a far country.

36 34 And when the time of the fruit drew near, he sent his servants to the husbandmen, that they might receive the fruits of it.

37 35 And the husbandmen took his servants, and beat one, and killed another, and stoned another.

38 36 Again, he sent other servants more than the first: and they did unto them likewise.

39 37 But last of all he sent unto them his son, saying, They will reverence my son.

40 38 But when the husbandmen saw the son, they said among themselves, This is the heir; come, let us kill him, and let us seize on his inheritance.

41 39 And they caught him, and cast *him* out of the vineyard, and slew *him*.

42 40 **And Jesus said unto them,** When the lord therefore of the vineyard cometh, what will he do unto those husbandmen?

43 41 They say unto him, He will ~~miserably~~ destroy those **miserable,** wicked men, and will let out ~~his~~ **the** vineyard unto other husbandmen, ~~which~~ **who** shall render him the fruits in their seasons.

44 42 Jesus ~~saith~~ **said** unto them, Did ye never read in the scriptures,

The stone which the builders rejected, the same is become the head of the corner; this is the Lord's ~~doing~~ **doings**, and it is marvelous in our eyes.

45 43 Therefore say I unto you, The kingdom of God shall be taken from you, and given to a nation bringing forth the fruits thereof.

46 44 ~~And~~ **For** whosoever shall fall on this stone, shall be broken; but on whomsoever it shall fall, it will grind him to powder.

47 45 And when the chief priests and Pharisees had heard his parables, they perceived that he spake of them.

48 And they said among themselves, Shall this man think that he alone can spoil this great kingdom? And they were angry with him.

49 46 But when they sought to lay hands on him, they feared the multitude, because they **learned that the multitude** took him for a prophet.

50 And now his disciples came to him, and Jesus said unto them, Marvel ye at the words of the parable which I spake unto them?

51 Verily, I say unto you, I am the stone, and those wicked ones reject me.

52 I am the head of the corner. These Jews shall fall upon me, and shall be broken.

53 And the kingdom of God shall be taken from them, and shall be given to a nation bringing forth the fruits thereof; (meaning the Gentiles.)

54 Wherefore, on whomsoever this stone shall fall, it shall grind him to powder.

55 And when the Lord therefore of the vineyard cometh, he will destroy those miserable, wicked men, and will let again his vineyard unto other husbandmen, even in the last days, who shall render him the fruits in their seasons.

56 And then understood they the parable which he spake unto them, that the Gentiles should be destroyed also, when the Lord should descend out of heaven to reign in his vineyard, which is the earth and the inhabitants thereof.

Chapter 22

1 And Jesus answered **the people again,** and spake unto them ~~again by~~ **in** parables, and said,

2 The kingdom of heaven is like unto a certain king, ~~which~~ **who** made a marriage for his son.

3 And **when the marriage was ready, he** sent forth his servants to call them ~~that~~ **which** were bidden to the wedding; and they would not come.

4 Again he sent forth other servants, saying, Tell them ~~which~~ **that** are bidden, Behold, I have prepared ~~my dinner~~ my oxen, and *my* fatlings ~~are~~ **have been** killed, **and my dinner is ready,** and all things *are* ~~ready~~ **prepared;** **therefore** come unto the marriage.

5 But they made light of *it* **the servants**, and went their ways; one to his farm, another to his merchandise;

6 And the remnant took his servants, and entreated *them* spitefully, and slew *them*.

7 But when the king heard ~~thereof~~ **that his servants were dead**, he was wroth; and he sent forth his armies, and destroyed those murderers, and burned up their city.

8 Then said he to his servants, The wedding is ready; but they ~~which~~ **who** were bidden were not worthy.

9 Go ye therefore into the highways, and as many as ye shall find, bid to the marriage.

10 So those servants went out into

the highways, and gathered together all as many as they found, both bad and good: and the wedding was furnished with guests.

11 But when the king came in to see the guests, he saw there a man ~~which~~ **who** had not ~~on~~ a wedding garment.

12 And he saith unto him, Friend, how camest thou in hither not having a wedding garment? And he was speechless.

13 Then said the king ~~to~~ **unto** ~~the~~ **his** servants, Bind him hand and foot, and take **and cast** him away ~~and cast him~~ into outer darkness; there shall be weeping and gnashing of teeth.

14 For many are called, but few ~~are~~ chosen; **wherefore all do not have on the wedding garment.**

15 Then went the Pharisees and took counsel how they might entangle him in ~~his~~ talk.

16 And they sent out unto him their disciples with the Herodians, saying, Master, we know that thou art true, and teachest the way of God in truth, neither carest thou for any ~~man~~; for thou regardest not the person of men.

17 Tell us therefore, What thinkest thou? Is it lawful to give tribute unto Caesar, or not?

18 18–19 But Jesus perceived their wickedness, and said, **Ye hypocrites!** Why tempt ye me ~~ye hypocrites~~? Show me the tribute money.

19 And they brought unto him a penny.

20 ~~And~~ He ~~saith~~ **said** unto them, Whose ~~is this~~ image **is this,** and superscription?

21 They ~~say~~ **said** unto him, Caesar's. Then ~~saith~~ **said** he unto them, Render therefore unto Caesar, the things which are Caesar's; and unto God the things which are God's.

22 **And** when they had heard **him say** *these words*, they marveled, and left him, and went their way.

23 23–24 The same day came ~~to him~~ the Sadducees **to him**, ~~which~~ **who** say that there is no resurrection, and asked him, saying, Master, Moses said, If a man die, having no children, his brother shall marry his wife, and raise up seed unto his brother.

24 25 Now there were with us, seven brethren; and the first, when he had married a wife, deceased; and, having no issue, **he** left his wife unto his brother.

25 26 Likewise the second also, and the third, and **even** unto the seventh.

26 27 And last of all the woman died also.

27 28 Therefore in the resurrection whose wife shall she be of the seven? for they all had her.

28 29 Jesus answered and said unto them, Ye do err, not knowing the scriptures, nor the power of God.

29 30 For in the resurrection they neither marry, nor are given in marriage, but are as the angels of God in heaven.

30 31 But as touching the resurrection of the dead, have ye not read that which was spoken unto you ~~by~~ **of** God, saying,

31 32 I am the God of Abraham, and the God of Isaac, and the God of Jacob? God is not the God of the dead, but of the living.

32 33 And when the multitude heard ~~this~~ **him**, they were astonished at his doctrine.

33 34 But when the Pharisees ~~had~~ heard that he had put the Sadducees to silence, they were gathered together.

34 35 Then one of them, ~~which was~~ a lawyer, **tempting him,** asked ~~him a question,~~ ~~tempting him, and~~, saying,

35 36 Master, which *is* the great commandment in the law?

36 37 Jesus said unto him, Thou shalt love the Lord thy God with all thy heart, and with all thy soul, and with all thy mind.

37 38 This is the first and great commandment.

38 39 And the second *is* like unto it, Thou shalt love thy neighbour as thyself.

39 40 On these two commandments hang all the law and the prophets.

40 41–42 While the Pharisees were gathered together, Jesus asked them, saying, What think ye of Christ? whose son is he?

41 42 They say unto him, *The Son* of David.

42 43–44 He saith unto them, How then doth David in spirit call him Lord, saying, The Lᴏʀᴅ said unto my Lord, Sit thou on my right hand, till I make thine enemies thy footstool?

43 45 If David then ~~call~~ **called** him Lord, how is he his son?

44 46 And no man was able to answer him a word, neither durst any *man* from that day forth ask him any more *questions.*

Cʜᴀᴘᴛᴇʀ 23

1 1–2 Then spake Jesus to the multitude, and to his disciples, saying, The scribes and the Pharisees sit in Moses' seat:

2 3 All, therefore, whatsoever they bid you observe, ~~that~~ **they will make you** observe and do; **for they are ministers of the law, and they make themselves your judges.** But do not ye after their works; for they say, and do not.

3 4 For they bind heavy burdens ~~and grievous to be borne~~ and lay *them*

on men's shoulders, **and they are grievous to be borne**; but they ~~themselves~~ will not move them with one of their fingers.

4 5–7 ~~But~~ **And** all their works they do ~~for~~ to be seen of men. They make broad their phylacteries, and enlarge the borders of their garments, and love the uppermost rooms at feasts, and the chief seats in the synagogues, and greetings in the markets, and to be called of men, Rabbi, Rabbi, **(which is master.)**

5 8 But be not ye called Rabbi; for one is your Master, ~~even~~ **which is** Christ; and all ye are brethren.

6 9 And call no ~~man~~ **one** your ~~father~~ **creator** upon the earth, **or your heavenly Father;** for one is your **creator and heavenly** Father, **even he** ~~which~~ **who** is in heaven.

7 10 Neither be ye called ~~masters~~ **master;** for one is your Master, *even* **he whom your heavenly Father sent, which is** Christ; **for he hath sent him among you that ye might have life.**

8 11 But he that is greatest among you shall be your servant.

9 12 And whosoever shall exalt himself shall be abased **of him;** and he that shall humble himself shall be exalted **of him.**

10 13 But woe unto you, scribes and Pharisees, hypocrites! for ye shut up the kingdom of heaven against men: for ye neither go in *yourselves,* neither suffer ye them that are entering to go in.

11 14 Woe unto you, scribes* and Pharisees**! for ye are** hypocrites! ~~for~~ Ye devour widows' houses, and for a pretense make long ~~prayer~~ **prayers;** therefore ye shall receive the greater ~~damnation~~ **punishment.**

12 15 Woe unto you, scribes* and Pharisees, hypocrites! For ye compass sea and land to make one proselyte; and when he is made, ye make him twofold more the child of hell than **he was before, like unto** yourselves.

13 16 Woe unto you, ~~ye~~ blind guides, ~~which~~ **who** say, Whosoever shall swear by the temple, it is nothing; but whosoever shall swear by the gold of the temple, he **committeth sin, and** is a debtor.

14 17 ~~Ye~~ **You are** fools and blind; for ~~whether~~ **which** is **the** greater, the gold, or the temple that sanctifieth the gold?

15 18 And **ye say**, Whosoever ~~shall swear~~ **sweareth** by the altar, it is nothing; but whosoever sweareth by the gift that is upon it, he is guilty.

16 19 ~~Ye~~ **O** fools, and blind! ~~for whether~~ **For which** is **the** greater, the gift, or the altar that sanctifieth the gift?

17 20 **Verily I say unto you,** Whoso, therefore, ~~shall swear~~ **sweareth** by ~~the altar~~ **it**, sweareth by ~~it~~ **the altar**, and by all things thereon.

18 21 And whoso shall swear by the temple, sweareth by it, and by him ~~that~~ **who** dwelleth therein.

19 22 And he that shall swear by heaven, sweareth by the throne of God, and by him ~~that~~ **who** sitteth thereon.

20 23 Woe unto you, scribes* and Pharisees, hypocrites! For ~~ye~~ **you** pay tithe of mint, and anise, and cummin; and have omitted the weightier ~~matters~~ **things** of the law; judgment, mercy, and faith; these ought ye to have done, and not to leave the other undone.

21 24 ~~Ye~~ **You** blind guides, ~~which~~ **who** strain at a gnat, and swallow a camel; **who make yourselves appear unto men that ye would not commit the least sin, and yet you, yourselves, transgress the whole law.**

22 25 Woe unto you, scribes* and Pharisees, hypocrites! For ~~ye~~ **you** make clean the outside of the cup, and of the platter; but within they are full of extortion and excess.

23 26 ~~Thou~~ **Ye*** blind ~~Pharisee~~ **Pharisees!** Cleanse first ~~that which is within~~ the cup and platter **within**, that the outside of them may be clean also.

24 27 Woe unto you, scribes* and Pharisees, hypocrites! For ye are like unto whited sepulchres, which indeed appear beautiful ~~outward~~ **outwardly**, but are within full of ~~dead men's~~ **the** bones **of the dead**, and of all uncleanness.

25 28 Even so ~~ye~~ **you** also outwardly appear righteous unto men, but within ye are full of hypocrisy and iniquity.

26 29 Woe unto you, scribes* and Pharisees, hypocrites! Because ~~ye~~ **you** build the tombs of the prophets, and garnish the sepulchres of the righteous,

27 30 And say, If we had been in the days of our fathers, we would not have been partakers with them in the blood of the prophets.

28 31 Wherefore, ~~ye~~ **you** ~~be~~ **are** witnesses unto yourselves ~~that~~ **of your own wickedness; and** ye are the children of them ~~which~~ **who** killed the prophets;

29 32 **And will** fill ~~ye~~ up ~~then~~ the measure **then** of your fathers; **for ye,*** **yourselves, kill the prophets like unto your fathers.**

30 33 ~~Ye~~ **You** serpents, **and** ~~ye~~ generation of vipers! How can ye escape the damnation of hell?

31 34 Wherefore, behold, I send unto you prophets, and wise men, and scribes; and ~~some~~ of them ye shall kill and crucify; and ~~some~~ of them **ye*** ~~ye~~ scourge in your synagogues, and persecute ~~them~~ from city to city;

32 35 That upon you may come all the righteous blood shed upon the earth, from the blood of righteous Abel unto the blood of Zacharias son of Barachias, whom ye slew between the temple and the altar.

33 36 Verily I say unto you, All these things shall come upon this generation.

34 Ye* bear testimony against your fathers, when ye,* yourselves, are partakers of the same wickedness.

35 Behold your fathers did it through ignorance, but ye* do not; wherefore, their sins shall be upon your heads.

36 Then Jesus began to weep over Jerusalem, saying,

37 O Jerusalem! Jerusalem! thou Ye* that who killest will kill the prophets, and stonest will stone them which who are sent unto thee you; how often would I have gathered thy your children together, even as a hen gathereth gathers her chickens under her wings, and ye would not.

38 Behold, your house is left unto you desolate.

39 For I say unto you, that ye you shall not see me henceforth, and know that I am he of whom it is written by the prophets, till until ye shall say,

40 39 Blessed is he that who cometh in the name of the Lord, in the clouds of heaven, and all the holy angels with him.

41 Then understood his disciples that he should come again on the earth, after that he was glorified and crowned on the right hand of God.

CHAPTER 24

1 And Jesus went out, and departed from the temple; and his disciples came to him for to shew hear him,

saying, Master, show us concerning the buildings of the temple; as thou hast said; They shall be thrown down and left unto you desolate.

2 And Jesus said unto them, See ye not all these things? And do you not understand them? Verily I say unto you, There shall not be left here upon this temple, one stone upon another, that which shall not be thrown down.

3 And Jesus left them and went upon the mount of Olives.

4 3 And as he sat upon the mount of Olives, the disciples came unto him privately, saying, Tell us, when shall these things be which thou hast said concerning the destruction of the temple, and the Jews; and what shall be is the sign of thy coming; and of the end of the world? (or the destruction of the wicked, which is the end of the world.)

5 4 And Jesus answered and said unto them, Take heed that no man deceive you.

6 5 For many shall come in my name, saying, I am Christ; and shall deceive many.

7 9 Then shall they deliver you up to be afflicted, and shall kill you: and ye shall be hated of all nations for my name's sake.

8 10 And then shall many be offended, and shall betray one another, and shall hate one another.

9 11 And many false prophets shall rise, and shall deceive many.

10 12 And because iniquity shall abound, the love of many shall wax cold.

11 13 But he that shall endure unto the end remaineth steadfast, and is not overcome, the same shall be saved.

12 15 When ye you; therefore, shall see the abomination of desolation,

spoken of by Daniel the prophet, **concerning the destruction of Jerusalem, then you shall** stand in the holy place. (Whoso readeth let him understand.)

13 16 Then let them ~~which be~~ **who are** in ~~Judaea~~ **Judea,** flee into the mountains**.**

14 17 Let him ~~which~~ **who** is on the housetop**, flee, and** not ~~come down~~ **return** to take anything out of his house.

15 18 Neither let him ~~which~~ **who** is in the field**,** return back to take his clothes.

16 19 And woe unto them that are with child, and ~~to~~ **unto** them that give suck in those days!

17 20 ~~But~~ **Therefore,** pray ye **the Lord,** that your flight be not in the winter, neither on the Sabbath day**.**

18 21 For then**, in those days,** shall be great ~~tribulation~~ **tribulations on the Jews, and upon the inhabitants of Jerusalem;** such as was not **before sent upon Israel, of God,** since the beginning of ~~the world~~ **their kingdom** ~~to~~ **until** this time; no, nor ever shall be **sent again upon Israel.**

19 8,22 All ~~these~~ **things which have befallen them,** *are* **only** the beginning of **the** sorrows **which shall come upon them;** and except those days should be shortened, there should ~~no~~ **none of their** flesh be saved**.**

20 22 But for the elect's sake**, according to the covenant,** those days shall be shortened.

21 Behold these things I have spoken unto you concerning the Jews.

22 23 **And again, after the tribulation of those days which shall come upon Jerusalem,** ~~Then~~ if any man shall say unto you, Lo! here *is* Christ, or there; believe ~~it~~ **him** not.

23 24 For **in those days,** there shall **also** arise false Christs, and false prophets, and shall show great signs and wonders; insomuch that, if ~~it were~~ possible, they shall deceive the very elect, **who are the elect according to the covenant.**

24 Behold, I speak these things unto you for the elect's sake.

25 6 And ~~ye~~ **you** also shall hear of wars**,** and rumors of wars**;** see that ye be not troubled; for all ~~these things~~ **I have told you** must come to pass. But the end is not yet.

26 25–26 Behold, I have told you before. Wherefore if they shall say unto you, Behold, he is in the desert; go not forth: behold, *he is* in the secret chambers; believe *it* not.

27 For as the ~~lightning~~ **light of the morning** cometh out of the east, and shineth even unto the west**, and covereth the whole earth**; so shall also the coming of the Son of Man be.

28 And now I show unto you a parable. Behold, ~~For~~ wheresoever the ~~carcase~~ **carcass** is, there will the eagles be gathered together**; so likewise shall mine elect be gathered from the four quarters of the earth.**

29 And they shall hear of wars, and rumors of wars. Behold, I speak for mine elect's sake.

30 7 For nation shall rise against nation, and kingdom against kingdom**;** ~~and~~ there shall be ~~famines~~ **famine** and pestilences, and earthquakes in divers places.

31 And again, because iniquity shall abound, the love of men shall wax cold; but he that shall not be overcome, the same shall be saved.

32 14 And **again,** this gospel of the kingdom shall be preached in all the world**,** for a witness unto all nations, and then shall the end come, **or the destruction of the wicked.**

33 And again shall the abomination of desolation, spoken of by Daniel the prophet, be fulfilled.

34 29 **And** immediately after the tribulation of those days, ~~shall~~ the sun **shall** be darkened, and the moon shall not give her light, and the stars shall fall from heaven, and the powers of ~~the heavens~~ **heaven** shall be shaken.

35 34 Verily I say unto you, This generation, **in which these things shall be shown forth,** shall not pass away ~~till~~ **until** all ~~these things~~ **I have told you shall** be fulfilled.

36 35 **Although the days will come that** heaven and earth shall pass away, ~~but~~ **yet** my ~~words~~ **word** shall not pass away; **but all shall be fulfilled.**

37 30 And **as I said before, after the tribulation of those days, and the powers of the heavens shall be shaken,** then shall appear the sign of the Son of Man in heaven; and then shall all the tribes of the earth mourn.

38 30 And they shall see the Son of man coming in the clouds of heaven with power and great glory.

39 And whoso treasureth up my words, shall not be deceived.

40 31 **For the Son of Man shall come,** and he shall send his angels **before him** with ~~a~~ **the** great sound of a trumpet, and they shall gather together **the remainder of** his elect from the four winds; from one end of heaven to the other.

41 32 Now learn a parable of the fig tree, When ~~his~~ **its** ~~branch~~ **branches** ~~is~~ **are** yet tender, and ~~putteth~~ **it begins to put** forth leaves, ~~ye~~ **you** know that summer *is* nigh **at hand.**

42 33 So likewise ~~ye~~ **mine elect,** when ~~ye~~ **they** shall see all these things, **they shall** know that ~~it~~ **he** is near, *even* at the doors.

43 36 But of that day and hour **no** one knoweth ~~no man~~; no, not the angels of **God in** heaven, but my Father only.

44 37 But as **it was in** the days of ~~Noe were~~ **Noah**, so **it** shall **be** also **at** the coming of the Son of Man ~~be~~.

45 38–39 For **it shall be with them** as **it was** in the days ~~that~~ **which** were before the flood; **for until the day that Noah entered into the ark,** they were eating and drinking, marrying and giving in marriage, ~~until the day that Noe entered into the ark~~ and knew not until the flood came and took them all away; so shall also the coming of the Son of Man be.

46 Then shall be fulfilled that which is written, that, In the last days,

47 40 ~~Then~~ **Two** shall ~~two~~ be in the field; the one shall be taken and the other left.

48 41 Two ~~women~~ *shall be* grinding at the mill; the one ~~shall be~~ taken and the other left.

49 42 **And what I say unto one, I say unto all men;** Watch, therefore, for ~~ye~~ **you** know not **at** what hour your Lord doth come.

50 43 But know this, ~~that~~ if the goodman of the house had known in what watch the thief would come, he would have watched, and would not have suffered his house to ~~be~~ **have been** broken up; **but would have been ready.**

51 44 Therefore be ye also ready: for in such an hour as ye think not the Son of man cometh.

52 45 Who then is a faithful and wise servant, whom his lord hath made ruler over his household, to give them meat in due season?

53 46 Blessed *is* that servant, whom his lord when he cometh shall find so doing.

54 47 **And,** verily I say unto you, ~~That~~ He shall make him ruler over all his goods.

55 48–51 But ~~and~~ if that evil servant shall say in his heart, My Lord delayeth his coming; and shall begin to smite *his* fellow servants, and to eat and drink with the drunken; the Lord of that servant shall come in a day when he looketh not for *him*, and in an hour that he is not aware of, and shall cut him asunder, and **shall** appoint *him* his portion with the hypocrites; there shall be weeping and gnashing of teeth.

56 And thus cometh the end of the wicked according to the prophecy of Moses, saying, They should* be cut off from among the people. But the end of the earth is not yet; but bye and bye.

CHAPTER 25

1 ~~Then shall~~ **And then, at that day, before the Son of Man comes,** the kingdom of heaven **shall** be likened unto ten virgins, ~~which~~ **who** took their lamps, and went forth to meet the bridegroom.

2 And five of them were wise, and five **of them** *were* foolish.

3 3–4 They that *were* foolish took their lamps, and took no oil with them: but the wise took oil in their vessels with their lamps.

4 5 While the bridegroom tarried, they all slumbered and slept.

5 6 And at midnight there was a cry made, Behold, the bridegroom cometh; go ye out to meet him.

6 7 Then all those virgins arose, and trimmed their lamps.

7 8 And the foolish said unto the wise, Give us of your oil; for our lamps are gone out.

8 9 But the wise answered, saying, ~~Not so~~ Lest there be not enough for us and you, ~~but~~ go ~~ye~~ **you** rather to them that sell, and buy for yourselves.

9 10 And while they went to buy, the bridegroom came; and they that were ready went in with him to the marriage: and the door was shut.

10 11 Afterward came also the other virgins, saying, Lord, Lord, open ~~to~~ **unto** us.

11 12 But he answered and said, Verily I say unto you, ~~I~~ **Ye*** know ~~you~~ **me** not.

12 13 Watch therefore, for ~~ye~~ **you** know neither the day nor the hour wherein the Son of Man cometh.

13 Now I will liken these things unto a parable.

14 For ~~the kingdom of heaven~~ it *is* **like** as a man traveling into a far country, *who* called his own servants, and delivered unto them his goods.

15 And unto one he gave five talents, to another two, and to another one; to every man according to his several ability; and straightway ~~took~~ **went on** his journey.

16 Then he that had received the five talents, went and traded with the same; and ~~made them~~ **gained** other five talents.

17 And likewise he ~~that~~ **who** ~~had received~~ two **talents**, he also gained other two.

18 But he ~~that~~ **who** had received one, went and digged in the earth and hid his lord's money.

19 After a long time the lord of those servants cometh, and reckoneth with them.

20 And so he that had received **the** five talents came, and brought other five talents, saying, Lord, thou deliveredst unto me five talents; behold, I have gained ~~beside~~ **besides** them, five talents more.

21 His lord said unto him, Well done, ~~thou~~ good and faithful servant; thou hast been faithful over a few things, I will make thee ruler over many things; enter thou into the joy of thy lord.

22 He also that had received two talents came and said, Lord, thou deliveredst unto me two talents; behold, I have gained two ~~other~~ talents ~~beside~~ **besides** them.

23 His lord said unto him, Well done, good and faithful servant; thou hast been faithful over a few things, I will make thee ruler over many things: enter thou into the joy of thy lord.

24 Then he ~~which~~ **who** had received the one talent came, and said, Lord, I knew thee that thou art ~~an~~ **a** hard man, reaping where thou hast not sown, and gathering where thou hast not ~~strawed~~ **scattered.**

25 And I was afraid, and went and hid thy talent in the earth; **and** lo, ~~there~~ **here is thy talent; take it from me as** thou hast **from thine other servants, for it** ~~that~~ is thine.

26 His lord answered and said unto him, ~~Thou~~ **O** wicked and slothful servant! thou knewest that I reap where I sowed not, and gather where I have not ~~strawed~~ **scattered.**

27 **Having known this, therefore,** thou oughtest ~~therefore~~ to have put my money to the exchangers, and ~~then~~ at my coming I should have received mine own with usury.

28 **I will** take, therefore, the talent from ~~him~~ **you**, and give *it* unto him ~~which~~ **who** hath ten talents.

29 For unto everyone ~~that~~ **who** hath **obtained other talents,** shall be given, and he shall have **in** abundance.

30 29 But from him that hath not **obtained other talents,** shall be taken away even that which he hath **received.**

31 30 And **his lord shall say unto his servants,** Cast ye the unprofitable servant into outer darkness; there shall be weeping and gnashing of teeth.

32 31 When the Son of Man shall come in his glory, and all the holy angels with him, then **he** shall ~~he~~ sit upon the throne of his glory;

33 32–33 And before him shall be gathered all nations; and he shall separate them one from another, as a shepherd divideth ~~his~~ sheep from the goats; ~~And he shall set~~ the sheep on his right hand, but the goats on ~~the~~ **his**˙ left.

34 **And he shall sit upon his throne, and the twelve apostles with him.**

35 34 Then shall the King say unto them on his right hand, Come, ye blessed of my Father, inherit the kingdom prepared for you from the foundation of the world:

36 35–36 For I was an ~~hungred~~ **hungered**, and ye gave me meat; I was thirsty, and ye gave me drink; I was a stranger, and ye took me in; naked, and ye clothed me;

37 36 I was sick, and ye visited me: I was in prison, and ye came unto me.

38 37 Then shall the righteous answer him, saying, Lord, when saw we thee an ~~hungred~~ **hungered**, and fed *thee*; or thirsty, and gave *thee* drink?

39 38 When saw we thee a stranger, and took *thee* in? or naked, and clothed *thee?*

40 39 Or when saw we thee sick, or in prison, and came unto thee?

41 40 And the King shall answer and say unto them, Verily I say unto you, Inasmuch as ye have done *it* unto one of the least of these my brethren, ye have done *it* unto me.

42 41 Then shall he say also unto them on the left hand, Depart from

me, ye cursed, into everlasting fire, prepared for the devil and his angels:

43 42 For I was an ~~hungred~~ **hungered**, and ye gave me no meat; I was thirsty, and ye gave me no drink;

44 43 I was a stranger, and ye took me not in: naked, and ye clothed me not: sick, and in prison, and ye visited me not.

45 44 Then shall they also answer him, saying, Lord, when saw we thee an ~~hungred~~ **hungered**, or athirst, or a stranger, or naked, or sick, or in prison, and did not minister unto thee?

46 45 Then shall he answer them, saying, Verily I say unto you, Inasmuch as ye did *it* not to one of the least of these **my brethren**, ye did *it* not unto me.

47 46 And these shall go away into everlasting punishment: but the righteous into life eternal.

CHAPTER 26

1 And it came to pass, when Jesus had finished all these sayings, he said unto his disciples,

2 Ye know that after two days is ~~the feast of~~ the passover, and **then** the Son of Man is betrayed to be crucified.

3 3–4 Then assembled together the chief priests, and ~~the~~ scribes,* and the elders of the people, unto the palace of the high priest, who was called Caiaphas, and consulted that they might take Jesus by subtilty and kill *him*.

4 5 But they said, Not on the feast *day*, lest there be an uproar among the people.

5 6–7 Now when Jesus was in Bethany, in the house of Simon the leper, there came unto him a woman having an alabaster box of very precious ointment, and poured it on his head as he sat ~~at meat~~ **in the house.**

6 8–9 But when ~~his disciples~~ **some** saw ~~it~~ **this**, they had indignation, saying, ~~To~~ **Unto** what purpose *is* this waste? For this ointment might have been sold for much, and given to the poor.

7 10 When **they had said this,** Jesus understood ~~it~~ **them**, **and** he said unto them, Why trouble ye the woman [**and from whence is this evil in your hearts**]?[25] For [**verily I say unto you**][26] she hath wrought a good work upon me.

8 11 For ye have the poor always with you; but me ye have not always.

9 12 For ~~in that~~ she hath poured this ointment on my body, ~~she did it~~ for my burial.

`10 13 **And in this thing that she hath done, she shall be blessed; for** verily I say unto you, Wheresoever this gospel shall be preached in the whole world, ~~there shall also~~ this **thing** that this woman hath done, **shall also** be told for a memorial of her [**for in that she hath done for me she hath obtained a blessing of my Father**].[27]

11 14–15 Then one of the twelve, called Judas Iscariot, went unto the chief priests, and said ~~unto them~~, What will ye give me, and I will deliver him unto you? And they covenanted with him for thirty pieces of silver.

12 16 And from that time he sought opportunity to betray ~~him~~ **Jesus**.

13 17 Now **on** the first *day* of the ~~feast of~~ unleavened bread, the disciples came ~~to~~ **unto** Jesus, saying unto him, Where wilt thou that we prepare for thee to eat the passover?

14 18 And he said, Go into the city to such a man, and say unto him, The Master saith, My time is at hand; I will keep the passover at thy house with my disciples.

15 19 And the disciples did as Jesus

had appointed them; and they made ready the passover.

16 20 Now when the ~~even~~ **evening** was come, he sat down with the twelve.

17 21 And as they did eat, he said, Verily I say unto you, that one of you shall betray me.

18 22 And they were exceeding sorrowful, and began every one of them to say unto him, Lord, is it I?

19 23 And he answered and said, He that dippeth *his* hand with me in the dish, the same shall betray me.

20 24 **But** the Son of Man goeth as it is written of him; but woe unto that man by whom the Son of Man is betrayed! It had been good for that man if he had not been born.

21 25 Then Judas, ~~which~~ **who** betrayed him, answered and said, Master, is it I? He said unto him, Thou hast said.

22 26 And as they were eating, Jesus took bread and ~~blessed~~ **brake** *it*, and ~~brake~~ **blessed** *it*, and gave *it* to ~~the~~ **his** disciples, and said, Take, eat; this is **in remembrance of** my body **which I give a ransom for you.**

23 27 And he took the cup, and gave thanks, and gave *it* to them, saying, Drink ye all of it;

24 28 For this is **in remembrance of** my blood of the new testament, which is shed for **as** many **as shall believe on my name,** for the remission of **their** sins.

25 And I give unto you a commandment, that ye shall observe to do the things which ye have seen me do, and bear record of me even unto the end.

26 29 But I say unto you, I will not drink henceforth of this fruit of the vine, until that day when I **shall come and** drink it new with you in my Father's kingdom.

27 30 And when they had sung an hymn, they went out into the mount of Olives.

28 31 Then ~~saith~~ **said** Jesus unto them, All ye shall be offended because of me this night; for it is written, I will smite the ~~shepherd~~ **Shepherd**, and the sheep of the flock shall be scattered abroad.

29 32 But after I am risen again, I will go before you into Galilee.

30 33 Peter answered and said unto him, Though all *men* shall be offended because of thee, ~~yet will~~ I **will** never be offended.

31 34 Jesus said unto him, Verily I say unto thee, That this night, before the cock crow, thou shalt deny me thrice.

32 35 Peter said unto him, Though I should die with thee, yet will I not deny thee. Likewise also said all the disciples.

33 36 Then cometh Jesus with them unto a place called Gethsemane, and saith unto the disciples, Sit ye here, while I go and pray yonder.

34 37 And he took with him Peter and the two sons of Zebedee, and began to be sorrowful and very heavy.

35 38 Then saith he unto them, My soul is exceeding sorrowful, even unto death: tarry ye here, and watch with me.

36 39 And he went a little farther, and fell on his face, and prayed, saying, O my Father, if it be possible, let this cup pass from me: nevertheless not as I will, but as thou *wilt*.

37 40 And he cometh unto the disciples, and findeth them asleep, and saith unto Peter, What, could ye not watch with me one hour?

38 41 Watch and pray, that ye enter not into temptation: the spirit indeed *is* willing, but the flesh *is* weak.

39 42 He went away again the second time, and prayed, saying, O my Father, if this cup may not pass away from me, except I drink it, thy will be done.

40 43 And he came and found them asleep again: for their eyes were heavy.

41 44 And he left them, and went away again, and prayed the third time, saying the same words.

42 45 Then cometh he to his disciples, and saith unto them, Sleep on now and take ~~your~~ rest. Behold, the hour is at hand, and the Son of Man is betrayed into the hands of sinners.

43 46 **And after they had slept, he said unto them,** ~~Rise~~ **Arise**, **and** let us be going. Behold, he is at hand that doth betray me.

44 47 And while he yet spake, lo, Judas, one of the twelve, came, and with him a great multitude with swords and staves, from the chief priests and elders of the people.

45 48 Now he that betrayed him gave them a sign, saying, Whomsoever I shall kiss, that same is he: hold him fast.

46 49 And forthwith he came to Jesus, and said, Hail, Master! and kissed him.

47 50 And Jesus said unto him, ~~Friend~~ **Judas**, wherefore art thou come **to betray me with a kiss**?

48 50 Then came they, and laid hands on Jesus, and took him.

49 51 And, behold, one of them which were with Jesus, stretched out *his* hand and drew his sword, and struck a servant of the high ~~priest's~~ **priest**, and smote off his ear.

50 52 Then said Jesus unto him, Put up again thy sword into ~~his~~ **its** place; for all they that take the sword shall perish with the sword.

51 53 Thinkest thou that I cannot

now pray to my Father, and he shall presently give me more than twelve legions of angels?

52 54 But how then shall the scriptures be fulfilled, that thus it must be?

53 55 In that same hour said Jesus ~~to~~ **unto** the multitudes, Are ye come out as against a thief, with swords and staves, for to take me? I sat daily with you ~~teaching~~ in the temple, **teaching,** and ye laid no hold on me.

54 56 But all this was done, that the scriptures of the prophets might be fulfilled.

55 56 Then all the disciples forsook him, and fled.

56 57 And they that had laid hold on Jesus led *him* away to Caiaphas the high priest, where the scribes and the elders were assembled.

57 58 But Peter followed him afar off unto the high priest's palace, and went in, and sat with the servants, to see the end.

58 59–60 Now the chief priests, and elders, and all the council, sought false witness against Jesus, to put him to death; but found none:

59 60 Yea, though many false witnesses came, ~~yet found~~ they **found** none **that could accuse him**.

60 60–61 At the last came two false witnesses, and said, This ~~fellow~~ **man** said, I am able to destroy the temple of God, and to build it in three days.

61 62 And the high priest arose and said unto him, Answerest thou nothing? **Knowest thou** what ~~is it which~~ these witness against thee?

62 63 But Jesus held his peace.

63 And the high priest answered and said unto him,

64 63 I adjure thee by the living God, that thou tell us whether thou be the Christ, the Son of God.

65 64 Jesus saith unto him, Thou

hast said: nevertheless I say unto you, Hereafter shall ye see the Son of man sitting on the right hand of power, and coming in the clouds of heaven.

66 65–66 Then the high priest rent his clothes, saying, He hath spoken blasphemy; what further need have we of witnesses? behold, now ye have heard his blasphemy. What think ye?

67 66 They answered and said, He is guilty**, and worthy** of death.

68 67–68 Then did they spit in his face and ~~buffeted~~ **buffet** him; and others smote *him* with the palms of their hands, saying, Prophesy unto us, thou Christ, who is ~~he~~ **it** that smote thee?

69 Now Peter sat without in the palace: and a damsel came unto him, saying, Thou also wast with Jesus of Galilee.

70 But he denied before *them* all, saying, I know not what thou sayest.

71 And when he was gone out into the porch, another ~~maid~~ saw him, and said unto them that were there, This ~~fellow~~ **man** was also with Jesus of Nazareth.

72 And again he denied with an oath, **saying,** I do not know the man.

73 And after a while came ~~unto him~~ they that stood by, and said to Peter, Surely thou also art *one* of them; for thy speech ~~bewrayeth~~ **betrayeth** thee.

74 Then began he to curse and to swear, *saying,* I know not the man.

75 74 And immediately the cock crew.

76 75 And Peter remembered the ~~word~~ **words** of Jesus, which **he** said unto him, Before the cock crow, thou shalt deny me thrice. And he went out and wept bitterly.

CHAPTER 27

1 When the morning was come, all the chief priests and elders of the people took counsel against Jesus to put him to death:

2 And when they had bound him, they led *him* away, and delivered him to Pontius Pilate the governor.

3 Then Judas, ~~which~~ **who** had betrayed him, when he saw that he was condemned, repented himself, and brought again the thirty pieces of silver to the chief priests and elders,

4 Saying, I have sinned in that I have betrayed the innocent blood.

5 4 And they said **unto him**, What *is that* to us? See thou *to* ~~that~~ **it; thy sins be upon thee.**

6 5 And he cast down the pieces of silver in the temple, and departed, and went**,** and hanged himself **on a tree. And straightway he fell down, and his bowels gushed out, and he died**.

7 6 And the chief priests took the silver pieces, and said, It is not lawful for to put them ~~into~~ **in** the treasury, because it is the price of blood.

8 7–8 And they took counsel, and bought with them the potter's field, to bury strangers in. Wherefore that field was called, The field of blood, unto this day.

9 Then was fulfilled that which was spoken by Jeremy the prophet, saying, And they took the thirty pieces of silver, the price of him that was valued, whom they of the children of Israel did value;

10 **And therefore they took the pieces of silver,** and gave them for the potter's field, as the Lord appointed ~~me~~ **by the mouth of Jeremy.**

11 And Jesus stood before the governor: and the governor asked him, saying, Art thou the King of the Jews?

12 11 And Jesus said unto him, Thou sayest **truly; for thus it is written of me.**

13 12 And when he was accused of

the chief priests and elders, he answered nothing.

14 13 Then said Pilate unto him, Hearest thou not how many things they witness against thee?

15 14 And he answered him **not** to **his questions; yea,** never a word**,** insomuch that the governor marveled greatly.

16 15 Now at ~~that~~ **the** feast the governor was wont to release unto the people a prisoner, whom they would.

17 16 And they had then a notable prisoner, called Barabbas.

18 17 Therefore when they were gathered together, Pilate said unto them, Whom will ye that I release unto you? Barabbas, or Jesus which is called Christ?

19 18 For he knew that for envy they had delivered him.

20 19 When he was set down on the judgment seat, his wife sent unto him, saying, Have thou nothing to do with that just man**,** for I have suffered many things this day in a ~~dream~~ **vision** because of him.

21 20 But the chief priests and elders persuaded the multitude that they should ask Barabbas, and destroy Jesus.

22 21 **And** the governor ~~answered and~~ said unto them, Whether of the twain will ye that I release unto you? They said, Barabbas.

23 22 Pilate ~~saith~~ **said** unto them, What shall I do ~~then~~ with Jesus**,** which is called Christ?

24 22 ~~They~~ **And** all ~~say~~ **said** unto him, Let him be crucified.

25 23 And the governor said, Why, what evil hath he done? But they cried out the more, saying, Let him be crucified.

26 24 When Pilate saw that he could prevail nothing, but ~~that~~ rather **that**[*] a

tumult was made, he took water, and washed *his* hands before the multitude, saying, I am innocent of the blood of this just person**;** see ~~ye to it~~ **that ye do nothing unto him**.

27 25 Then answered all the people, and said, His blood ~~be on~~ **come upon** us and ~~on~~ our children.

28 26 Then released he Barabbas unto them: and when he had scourged Jesus, he delivered *him* to be crucified.

29 27 Then the soldiers of the governor took Jesus into the common hall, and gathered unto him the whole band ~~of soldiers~~.

30 28 And they stripped him, and put on him a ~~scarlet~~ **purple**[28] robe.

31 29 And when they had platted a crown of thorns, they put *it* upon his head, and a reed in his right hand: and they bowed the knee before him, and mocked him, saying, Hail, King of the Jews!

32 30 And they spit upon him, and took the reed, and smote him on the head.

33 31 And after that they had mocked him, they took the robe off from him, and put his own raiment on him, and led him away to crucify *him*.

34 32 And as they came out, they found a man of Cyrene, Simon by name: him they compelled to bear his cross.

35 33 And when they were come unto a place called Golgotha, (that is to say, a place of ~~a skull~~ **burial**,)

36 34 They gave him vinegar to drink mingled with gall**;** and when he had tasted ~~thereof~~ **the vinegar**, he would not drink.

37 35 And they crucified him, and parted his garments, casting lots**;** that it might be fulfilled which was spoken by the prophet, They parted my garments among them, and ~~upon~~ **for** my vesture **they** did ~~they~~ cast lots.

38 36 And sitting down they watched him there;

39 37 And ~~set up over his head his accusation written~~ **Pilate wrote a title, and put it on the cross, and the writing was,**

40 37 ~~This Is~~ JESUS OF NAZARETH, THE KING OF THE JEWS, **in letters of Greek, and Latin, and Hebrew**.

41 And the chief priests said unto Pilate, It should be written and set up over his head, his accusation, This is he that said he was Jesus, the King of the Jews.

42 But Pilate answered and said, What I have written, I have written; let it alone.

43 38 Then were there two thieves crucified with him, one on the right hand, and another on the left.

44 39–40 And they that passed by reviled him, wagging their heads, and saying, Thou that destroyest the temple, and buildest *it* **again** in three days, save thyself. If thou be the Son of God come down from the cross.

45 41–42 Likewise also the chief priests mocking ~~him~~ with the scribes* and **the** elders, said, He saved others, himself he cannot save. If he be the King of Israel, let him now come down from the cross, and we will believe him.

46 43 He trusted in God; let him deliver him now**;** if he will ~~have~~ **save** him**; let him save him;** for he said, I am the Son of God.

47 44 **One of** the thieves also, which were crucified with him, cast the same in his teeth. **But the other rebuked him, saying, Dost thou not fear God, seeing thou art under the same condemnation; and this man is just, and**

hath not sinned; and he cried unto the Lord that he would save him.

48 And the Lord said unto him, This day thou shalt be with me in Paradise.

49 45 Now from the sixth hour there was darkness over all the land unto the ninth hour.

50 46 And about the ninth hour Jesus cried with a loud voice, saying, Eli, Eli, lama sabachthani? that is to say, My God, my God, why hast thou forsaken me?

51 47 Some of them that stood there, when they heard ~~that~~ **him**, said, This *man* calleth for Elias.

52 48 And straightway one of them ran, and took a ~~spunge~~ **sponge**, and filled *it* with vinegar, and put *it* on a reed, and gave him to drink.

53 49 The rest said, Let **him** be, let us see whether Elias will come to save him.

54 50 Jesus when he had cried again with a loud voice, **saying, Father, it is finished, thy will is done,** yielded up the ghost.

55 51 And, behold, the veil of the temple was rent in twain from the top to the bottom; and the earth did quake, and the rocks rent;

56 52 And the graves were opened; and ~~many~~ **the** bodies of the saints which slept**,** arose, **who were many,***

57 53 And came out of the graves after his resurrection, ~~and~~ went into the holy city, and appeared unto many.

58 54 Now when the centurion, and they that were with him, watching Jesus, ~~saw~~ **heard** the earthquake, and **saw** those things ~~that~~ **which** were done, they feared greatly, saying, Truly this was the Son of God.

59 55–56 And many women were there beholding afar off, which followed Jesus from Galilee, ministering unto him **for his burial;** among ~~which~~ **whom** was Mary Magdalene, and Mary the mother of James and Joses, and the mother of Zebedee's children.

60 57–58 When the ~~even~~ **evening** was come, there came a rich man of Arimathea, named Joseph, who also himself was Jesus' disciple; he went to Pilate and begged the body of Jesus.

61 58 Then Pilate commanded the body to be delivered.

62 59–60 And when Joseph had taken the body, he wrapped it in a clean linen cloth, and laid it in his own new tomb, which he had hewn out in the rock: and he rolled a great stone to the door of the sepulchre, and departed.

63 61 And there was Mary Magdalene, and the other Mary, sitting over against the sepulchre.

64 62–63 Now the next day that followed the day of the preparation, the chief priests and Pharisees came together unto Pilate, saying, Sir, we remember that that deceiver said, while he was yet alive, After three days I will rise again.

65 64 Command therefore, that the sepulchre be made sure until the third day, lest his disciples come by night, and steal him away, and say unto the people, He is risen from the dead; so ~~the last error shall~~ **this last imposture will** be worse than the first.

66 65 Pilate said unto them, Ye have a watch: go your way, make *it* as sure as ~~ye~~ **you** can.

67 66 So they went, and made the sepulchre sure, sealing the stone, and setting a watch.

CHAPTER 28

1 In the end of the Sabbath **day**, as it began to dawn toward the first *day* of the week, **early in the morning,** came Mary Magdalene, and the other Mary to see the sepulchre.

2 And behold, there ~~was~~ **had been** a great earthquake; for ~~the angel~~ **two angels** of the Lord descended from heaven, and came and rolled back the stone from the door, and sat upon it.

3 3–4 ~~His~~ **And their** countenance was like lightning, and ~~his~~ **their** raiment white as snow; and for fear of ~~him~~ **them** the keepers did shake, and became as **though they were** dead ~~men~~.

4 5 And the ~~angel~~ **angels** answered and said unto the women, Fear not ye; for ~~I~~ **we** know that ye seek Jesus ~~which~~ **who** was crucified.

5 6–7 He is not here: for he is risen, as he said. Come, see the place where the Lord lay. And go quickly, and tell his disciples that he is risen from the dead; and, behold, he goeth before you into Galilee; there shall ye see him: lo, I have told you.

6 8 And they departed quickly from the sepulchre with fear and great joy; and did run to bring his disciples word.

7 9 And as they went to tell his disciples, behold, Jesus met them, saying, All hail.

8 9 And they came and held him by the feet, and worshipped him.

9 10 Then said Jesus unto them, Be not afraid: go tell my brethren that they go into Galilee, and there shall they see me.

10 11 Now when they were going, behold, some of the watch came into the city, and shewed unto the chief priests all the things that were done.

11 12 And when they were assembled with the elders, and had taken counsel, they gave large money unto the soldiers,

12 13 Saying, Say ye, His disciples

came by night, and stole him *away* while we slept.

13 14 And if this come to the governor's ears, we will persuade him, and secure you.

14 15 So they took the money, and did as they were taught: and this saying is commonly reported among the Jews until this day.

15 16 Then the eleven disciples went away into Galilee, into a mountain where Jesus had appointed them.

16 17 And when they saw him, they worshipped him: but some doubted.

17 18 And Jesus came and spake unto them, saying, All power is given unto me in heaven and in earth.

18 19 Go ye therefore, and teach all nations, baptizing them in the name of the Father, and of the Son, and of the Holy Ghost:

19 20 Teaching them to observe all things whatsoever I have commanded you; and, lo, I am with you alway **always**, *even* unto the end of the world. Amen.

The Testimony of

SAINT MARK

CHAPTER 1

1 1–2 The beginning of the gospel of Jesus Christ, the Son of God; as it is written in the prophets, Behold, I send my messenger before thy face, which shall prepare thy way before thee.

2 3 The voice of one crying in the wilderness, Prepare ye the way of the Lord, make his paths straight.

3 4 John did baptize in the wilderness, and preach the baptism of repentance for the remission of sins.

4 5 And there went out unto him all the land of Judaea **Judea**, and they of Jerusalem, and **many** were all baptized of him in the river of Jordan, confessing their sins.

5 6–7 And John was clothed with camel's **camels'** hair, and with a girdle of a skin about his loins; and he did eat locusts and wild honey; and preached, saying, There cometh one mightier than I after me, the latchet of whose shoes I am not worthy to stoop down and unloose.

6 8 I indeed have baptized you with water; but he shall **not only** baptize you with **water, but with fire, and** the Holy Ghost.

7 9 And it came to pass in those days, that Jesus came from Nazareth of Galilee, and was baptized of John in Jordan.

8 10 And straightway coming up out of the water, he saw the heavens opened, and the Spirit like a dove descending upon him:

9 11 And there came a voice from heaven, *saying*, Thou art my beloved Son, in whom I am well pleased. **And John bare record of it.**

10 12 And immediately the Spirit driveth **took** him into the wilderness.

11 13 And he was there in the wilderness forty days, tempted of Satan **seeking to tempt him**; and was with the wild beasts; and the angels ministered unto him.

12 14–15 Now after that John was put in prison, Jesus came into Galilee, preaching the gospel of the kingdom of God; and saying,

13 15 The time is fulfilled, and the kingdom of God is at hand: repent ye, and believe the gospel.

14 16 **And** now as he walked by the sea of Galilee, he saw Simon and Andrew his brother, casting a net into the sea; for they were fishers.

15 17 And Jesus said unto them, Come ye after me, and I will make you to become fishers of men.

16 18 And straightway they forsook their nets, and followed him.

17 19 And when he had gone a little farther thence, he saw James the *son* of Zebedee, and John his brother, who also were in the ship mending their nets.

18 20 And ~~straightway~~ he called them; and **straightway** they left their father Zebedee in the ship with the hired servants, and went after him.

19 21 And they went into Capernaum; and straightway on the sabbath day he entered into the synagogue, and taught.

20 22 And they were astonished at his doctrine: for he taught them as one that had authority, and not as the scribes.

21 23–24 And there was in their synagogue a man with an unclean spirit; and he cried out, saying, Let *us* alone; what have we to do with thee, thou Jesus of Nazareth? art thou come to destroy us? I know thee ~~who~~ **whom** thou art, the Holy One of God.

22 25 And Jesus rebuked him, saying, Hold thy peace, and come out of him.

23 26 And when the unclean spirit had torn him, and cried with a loud voice, he came out of him.

24 27 And they were all amazed, insomuch that they questioned among themselves, saying, What thing is this? what new doctrine *is* this? for with authority commandeth he even the unclean spirits, and they do obey him.

25 28 And immediately his fame spread abroad throughout all the region round about Galilee.

26 29 And forthwith, when they were come out of the synagogue, they entered into the house of Simon and Andrew, with James and John.

27 30 ~~But~~ **And** Simon's wife's mother lay sick of a fever; and ~~anon~~ they ~~tell~~ **besought** him ~~of~~ **for** her.

28 31 And he came and took her by the hand, and lifted her up; and immediately the fever left her, and she **came and** ministered unto them.

29 32–33 And at ~~even~~ **evening** ~~when the sun did set~~ **after sunset**, they brought unto him all that were diseased, and them that were possessed with devils; and all the city was gathered together at the door.

30 34 And he healed many that were sick of divers diseases, and cast out many devils; and suffered not the devils to speak, because they knew him.

31 35 And in the morning, rising up a great while before day, he went out, and departed into a solitary place, and there prayed.

32 36 And Simon and they that were with him followed after him.

33 37 And when they had found him, they said unto him, All *men* seek for thee.

34 38 And he said unto them, Let us go into the next towns, that I may preach there also: for therefore came I forth.

35 39 And he preached in their synagogues throughout all Galilee, and cast out devils.

36 40 And there came a leper to him, beseeching him, and kneeling down to him, ~~and saying~~ **said** ~~unto him,~~ If thou wilt, thou canst make me clean.

37 41 And Jesus, moved with compassion, put forth *his* hand, and touched him, and saith unto him, I will; be thou clean.

38 42 And as soon as he had spoken, immediately the leprosy departed from him, and he was cleansed.

39 43–44 And he straitly charged him, and forthwith sent him away; and saith unto him, See thou say nothing to any man: but go thy way, shew thyself to the ~~priest~~ **priests**, and offer for thy cleansing those things which Moses commanded, for a testimony unto them.

40 45 But he went out, and began to publish *it* much, and to blaze abroad the matter, insomuch that Jesus could no more openly enter into the city, but was without in ~~desert~~ **solitary** places; and they came to him from every quarter.

CHAPTER 2

1 And again, he entered into Capernaum after ~~some~~ **many** days; and it was noised **abroad** that he was in the house.

2 And straightway many were gathered together, insomuch that there was no room to receive ~~them~~ **the multitude**; no, not so much as about the door; and he preached the word unto them.

3 And they ~~come~~ **came** unto him, bringing one sick of the palsy, which was borne of four **persons**.

4 And when they could not come nigh unto him for the press, they uncovered the roof where he was: and when they had broken *it* up, they let down the bed wherein the sick of the palsy lay.

5 When Jesus saw their faith, he said unto the sick of the palsy, Son, thy sins be forgiven thee.

6 6–7 But there were certain of the scribes sitting there, and reasoning in their hearts, Why doth this *man* thus speak blasphemies? who can forgive sins but God only?

7 8–9 And immediately, when Jesus perceived in his spirit, that they so reasoned within themselves, he said unto them, Why reason ye these things in your hearts? ~~Whether~~ Is it **not** easier to say to the sick of the palsy, *Thy* sins be forgiven thee; ~~or~~ **than** to say, Arise, and take up thy bed and walk?

8 10–11 But that ye may know that the Son of Man ~~hath~~ **has** power on earth to forgive sins, (he ~~saith~~ **said** to the sick of the palsy,) I say unto thee, Arise, and take up thy bed, and go thy way into ~~thine~~ **thy** house.

9 12 And immediately he arose, took up the bed, and went forth before them all; insomuch that they were all amazed, and **many** glorified God, saying, We never saw ~~it on~~ **the power of God after** this ~~fashion~~ **manner**.

10 13 And ~~he~~ **Jesus** went forth again by the seaside; and all the multitude resorted unto him, and he taught them.

11 14 And as he passed by, he saw Levi the *son* of ~~Alphaeus~~ **Alpheus,** sitting at the ~~receipt of custom~~ **place where they receive tribute, as was customary in those days**, and **he** said unto him, Follow me; and he arose and followed him.

12 15 And it came to pass, that as Jesus sat at meat in his house, many publicans and sinners sat also together with ~~Jesus~~ **him** and his disciples; for there* were many, and they followed him.

13 16 And when the scribes and Pharisees saw him eat with publicans and sinners, they said unto his disciples, How is it that he eateth and drinketh with publicans and sinners?

14 17 When Jesus heard ~~it~~ **this**, he ~~saith~~ **said** unto them, They that are whole have no need of the physician, but they that are sick**.**

15 17 I came not to call the righteous, but sinners to repentance.

16 18 And **they came and said unto him,** The disciples of John and of the Pharisees used to fast**;** and ~~they come and say unto him~~, why do the disciples of John and of the Pharisees fast, but thy disciples fast not?

17 19 And Jesus said unto them, Can the children of the bridechamber fast, while the bridegroom is with them? as long as they have the bridegroom with them, they cannot fast.

18 20 But the days will come, when the bridegroom shall be taken away from them, and then shall they fast in those days.

19 21 No man also seweth a piece of new cloth on an old garment: else the new piece that filled it up taketh away from the old, and the rent is made worse.

20 22 And no man putteth new wine into old bottles: else the new wine doth burst the bottles, and the wine is spilled, and the bottles will be marred: but new wine must be put into new bottles.

21 23 And it came to pass, that he went through the corn fields on the sabbath day; and his disciples began, as they went, to pluck the ears of corn.

22 24 And the Pharisees said unto him, Behold, why do ~~they~~ **thy disciples** on the Sabbath day that which is not lawful?

23 25 And he said unto them, Have ye never read what David did, when he had need, and was an ~~hungred~~ **hungered**, he, and they that were with him?

24 26 How he went into the house of God in the days of Abiathar the high priest, and did eat the shewbread, which is not lawful to eat but for the priests, and gave also to them which were with him?

25 27 And he said unto them, The sabbath was made for man, and not man for the sabbath:

26 Wherefore the Sabbath was given unto man for a day of rest; and also that man should glorify God, and not that man should not eat;

27 28 **For the Son of Man made the Sabbath day,** therefore the Son of Man is Lord also of the Sabbath.

Chapter 3

1 And he entered again into the synagogue; and there was a man there which had a withered hand.

2 And they watched him **to see** whether he would heal him on the Sabbath day; that they might accuse him.

3 And he ~~saith~~ **said** unto the man which had the withered hand, Stand forth.

4 And he saith unto them, Is it lawful to do good on the sabbath days, or to do evil? To save life, or to kill? But they held their peace.

5 And when he had looked round about on them with anger, being grieved for the hardness of their hearts, he ~~saith~~ **said** unto the man, Stretch forth ~~thine~~ **thy** hand.

6 5 And he stretched ~~it~~ out **his hand;** and his hand was restored whole as the other.

7 6 And the Pharisees went forth, and straightway took counsel with the Herodians against him, how they might destroy him.

8 7–8 But Jesus withdrew himself, with his disciples, to the sea; and a great multitude from Galilee followed him, and from ~~Judaea~~ **Judea**, and from Jerusalem, and from ~~Idumaea~~ **Idumea** and *from* beyond Jordan; and they about Tyre and Sidon, a great multitude, when they ~~had~~ heard what great things he did, came unto him.

9 And he spake ~~to~~ **unto** his disciples, that a small ship should wait on him, because of the multitude, lest they should throng him.

10 10–11 For he had healed many; insomuch that they pressed upon him for to touch him, as many as had plagues. And unclean spirits, when they saw him, fell down before him, and cried, saying, Thou art the Son of God.

11 12 And he straitly charged them that they should not make him known.

12 13 And he goeth up into ~~a~~ **the** mountain, and calleth ~~unto him~~ whom he would; and they came unto him.

13 14–15 And he ordained twelve, that they should be with him, and that he might send them forth to preach, and to have power to heal sicknesses, and to cast out devils:

14 16–19 And Simon he surnamed Peter; and James the *son* of Zebedee, and John the brother of James; and he surnamed them Boanerges, which is, The sons of thunder: and Andrew, and Philip, and Bartholomew, and Matthew, and Thomas, and James the *son* of Alphaeus, and Thaddaeus, and Simon the Canaanite, and Judas Iscariot, which also betrayed him: and they went into an house.

15 20 And the multitude cometh together again, so that they could not so much as eat bread.

16 21 And when his friends heard *of*

~~it~~ **him speak**, they went out to lay hold on him; for they said, He is beside himself.

17 22 And the scribes which came down from Jerusalem said, He hath Beelzebub, and by the prince of the devils casteth he out devils.

18 23–24 **Now Jesus knew this,** and he called them ~~unto him~~, and said unto them in parables, How can Satan cast out Satan? And if a kingdom be divided against itself, **how can** that kingdom ~~cannot~~ stand?

19 25–26 And if a house be divided against itself, that house cannot stand. And if Satan rise up against himself and be divided, he cannot stand; but **speedily** hath an end.

20 27 No man can enter into a strong man's house, and spoil his goods, except he will first bind the strong man; and then he will spoil his house.

21 And then came certain men unto him, accusing him, saying, Why do ye receive sinners, seeing thou makest thyself the Son of God.

22 28 **But he answered them and said,** Verily I say unto you, All sins **which men have committed, when they repent,** shall be forgiven ~~unto the sons of men~~ **them; for I came to preach repentance unto the sons of men.**

23 28 And blasphemies, wherewithsoever they shall blaspheme, **shall be forgiven them that come unto me, and do the works which they see me do.**

24 29 But **there is a sin which shall not be forgiven.** He that shall blaspheme against the Holy Ghost, hath never forgiveness; but is in danger of **being cut down out of the world. And they shall inherit** eternal damnation.

25 30 **And this he said unto them** because they said, He hath an unclean spirit.

26 31 **While he was yet with them, and while he was yet speaking,** there came then **some of** his brethren, and his mother; and standing without, sent unto him, calling **unto** him.

27 32 And the multitude sat about him, and they said unto him, Behold, thy mother and thy brethren without seek for thee.

28 33 And he answered them, saying, Who is my mother, or **who are** my brethren?

29 34 And he looked round about on them which sat about him, and said, Behold my mother and my brethren!

30 35 For whosoever shall do the will of God, the same is my brother, and my sister, and mother.

CHAPTER 4

1 And he began again to teach by the sea side: and there was gathered unto him a great multitude, so that he entered into a ship, and sat in the sea; and the whole multitude was by the sea on the land.

2 And he taught them many things by parables,

3 2–3 And **he** said unto them in his doctrine, Hearken; Behold, there went out a sower to sow;

4 And it came to pass, as he sowed, some fell by the way side, and the fowls of the air came and devoured it up.

5 5–6 And some fell on stony ground, where it had not much earth; and immediately it sprang up, because it had no depth of earth: but when the sun was up, it was scorched; and because it had no root, it withered away.

6 7 And some fell among thorns, and the thorns grew up, and choked it, and it yielded no fruit.

7 8 And other **seed** fell on good ground, and did yield fruit, that sprang up and increased, and brought forth, some ~~thirty~~ **thirty-fold**, and some sixty, and some an hundred.

8 9 And he said unto them, He that hath ears to hear, let him hear.

9 10 And when he was alone **with the twelve, and they that believed on him**, they that were about him with the twelve, asked of him the parable.

10 11 And he said unto them, Unto you it is given to know the mystery of the kingdom of God: but unto them that are without, all *these* things are done in parables:

11 12 That seeing they may see, and not perceive; and hearing they may hear, and not understand; lest at any time they should be converted, and *their* sins should be forgiven them.

12 13 And he said unto them, Know ye not this parable? and how then will ye know all parables?

13 14 The sower soweth the word.

14 15 And these are they by the way side, where the word is sown; but when they have heard, Satan cometh immediately, and taketh away the word that was sown in their hearts.

15 16–17 And these are they likewise which ~~are sown~~ **receive the word** on stony ground; who, when they have heard the word, immediately receive it with gladness, and have no root in themselves, and so endure but for a time; **and** afterward, when affliction or persecution ariseth for the word's sake, immediately they are offended.

16 18–19 And these are they ~~which~~ **who** ~~are sown~~ **receive the word** among thorns; such as hear the word, and the cares of this world, and the deceitfulness of riches, and the ~~lusts~~ **lust** of other things entering in, choke the word, and it becometh unfruitful.

17 20 And these are they ~~which~~ **who** ~~are sown~~ **receive the word** on good ground; such as hear the word, and receive *it*, and bring forth fruit; some thirty-fold, some sixty and some an hundred.

18 21 And he said unto them, Is a candle brought to be put under a bushel, or under a bed, and not to be set on a candlestick? **I say unto you, Nay;**

19 22–23 For there is nothing hid which shall not be manifested; neither was anything kept secret, but that it should **in due time** come abroad. If any man have ears to hear, let him hear.

20 24–25 And he said unto them, Take heed what ~~ye~~ **you** hear; **for** with what measure ye mete, it shall be measured to you; and unto you that ~~hear~~ **continue to receive,** shall more be given; for he that ~~hath~~ **receiveth**, to him shall be given; ~~and~~ **but** he that ~~hath~~ **continueth** not **to receive**, from him shall be taken even that which he hath.

21 26–27 And he said, So is the kingdom of God, as if a man should cast seed into the ground; and should sleep, and rise night and day, and the seed should spring and grow up, he knoweth not how.

22 28 For the earth bringeth forth fruit of herself; first the blade, then the ear, after that the full corn in the ear.

23 29 But when the fruit is brought forth, immediately he putteth in the sickle, because the harvest is come.

24 30 And he said, Whereunto shall ~~we~~ **I** liken the kingdom of God? Or with what comparison shall we compare it?

25 31–32 *It is* like a grain of mustard seed, which, when it is sown in the earth, is less than all the seeds that be in the earth: But when it is sown, it groweth up, and becometh greater than all herbs, and shooteth out great branches; so that the fowls of the air may lodge under the shadow of it.

26 33–34 And with many such parables spake he the word unto them, as they were able to ~~hear it~~ **bear;** but without a parable spake he not unto them.

27 34 And when they were alone, he expounded all things to his disciples.

28 35 And the same day, when the even was come, he saith unto them, Let us pass over unto the other side.

29 36 And when they had sent away the multitude, they took him even as he was in the ship. And there were also with him other little ships.

30 37–38 And there arose a great storm of wind, and the waves beat **over** into the ship ~~so that it was now full~~; and he was in the hinder part of the ship asleep on a pillow; and they ~~awake~~ **awoke** him, and ~~say~~ **said** unto him, Master, carest thou not that we perish?

31 39 And he arose, and rebuked the wind, and said unto the sea, Peace, be still. And the wind ceased, and there was a great calm.

32 40 And he said unto them, Why are ye so fearful? how is it that ye have no faith?

33 41 And they feared exceedingly, and said one to another, What manner of man is this, that even the wind and the sea obey him?

CHAPTER 5

1 And they came over unto the other side of the sea, into the country of the Gadarenes.

2 2–3 And when he was come out of the ship, immediately there met him out of the tombs, a man with an unclean spirit, who had ~~his~~ **been** dwelling among the tombs.

3 3–4 And no man could bind him, no, not with chains: because that he had been often bound with fetters and chains, and the chains had been plucked asunder by him, and the fetters broken in pieces: neither could any *man* tame him.

4 5 And always, night and day, he was in the mountains, and in the tombs, crying, and cutting himself with stones.

5 6–8 But when he saw Jesus afar off, he ran and worshiped him, and cried with a loud voice and said, What have I to do with thee, Jesus, *thou* Son of the most high God? I adjure thee by God, that thou torment me not. For he said unto him, Come out of the man, ~~thou~~ unclean spirit.

6 9 And he ~~asked~~ **commanded** him **saying**, ~~What is~~ **Declare** thy name. And he answered, saying, My name *is* Legion; for we are many.

7 10 And he besought him much that he would not send them away out of the country.

8 11 Now there was there nigh unto the mountains a great herd of swine feeding.

9 12–13 And all the devils besought him, saying, Send us into the swine, that we may enter into them.

10 13 And forthwith Jesus gave them leave. And the unclean spirits went out, and entered into the swine: and the herd ran violently down a steep place into the sea, (they were about two thousand;) and were choked in the sea.

11 14 And they that fed the swine fled, and told ~~it~~ **the people** in the city, and in the country, **all that was done unto the swine**.

12 14–15 And they went out to see what it was that was done. And they come to Jesus, and see him that was possessed with the devil, and had the legion, sitting, and clothed, and in his right mind: and they were afraid.

13 16 And they that saw ~~it~~ **the miracle,** told them **that came out,** how it befell ~~to~~ him that was possessed with the devil, and ~~also~~ **how the devil was cast out, and** concerning the swine.

14 17 And they began **immediately** to pray him to depart out of their coasts.

15 18 And when he was come into the ship, he that had been possessed with the devil, **spoke to Jesus, and** prayed him that he might be with him.

16 19 Howbeit Jesus suffered him not, but saith unto him, Go home to thy friends, and tell them how great things the Lord hath done for thee, and hath had compassion on thee.

17 20 And he departed, and began to publish in Decapolis how great things Jesus had done for him: and all *men* did marvel.

18 21 And when Jesus ~~was~~ **had** passed over again by ship unto the other side, much people gathered unto him; and he was nigh unto the sea.

19 22–23 And behold there cometh one of the rulers of the synagogue, Jairus by name; and when he saw him he fell at his feet, and besought him greatly, saying, My little daughter lieth at the point of death; ~~I pray thee~~ come and lay thy hands on her that she may be healed; and she shall live.

20 24 And ~~Jesus~~ **he** went with him; and much people followed him and thronged him.

21 25–28 And a certain woman, which had an issue of blood twelve years, and had suffered many things of many physicians, and had spent all that she had, and was nothing bettered but rather grew worse; when she had heard of Jesus, **she** came in the press behind, and touched his garment; for she said, If I may touch but his clothes, I shall be whole.

22 29 And straightway the fountain of her blood was dried up; and she felt in *her* body that she was healed of that plague.

23 30 And Jesus, immediately knowing in himself that virtue had gone out of him, turned him about in the press, and said, Who touched my clothes?

24 31 And his disciples said unto him, Thou seest the multitude thronging thee, and sayest thou, Who touched me?

25 32–33 And he looked round about to see her that had done this thing. But the woman fearing and trembling, knowing what was done in her, came and fell down before him, and told him all the truth.

26 34 And he said unto her, Daughter, thy faith hath made thee whole; go in peace, and be whole of thy plague.

27 35 While he yet spake, there came from the ruler of the synagogue's *house* ~~certain~~, **a man** ~~which~~ **who** said, Thy daughter is dead; why troublest thou the Master any further?

28 36 As soon as **he spake,** Jesus heard the word that was spoken, ~~he saith~~ **and said** unto the ruler of the

synagogue, Be not afraid, only believe.

29 37 And he suffered no man to follow him, save Peter, and James, and John the brother of James.

30 38 And he cometh to the house of the ruler of the synagogue, and seeth the tumult, and them that wept and wailed greatly.

31 39–40 And when he was come in, he saith unto them, Why make ye this ado, and weep? the damsel is not dead, but sleepeth. And they laughed him to scorn.

32 40 But when he had put them all out, he taketh the father and the mother of the damsel, and them that were with him, and entereth in where the damsel was lying.

33 41 And he took the damsel by the hand, and said unto her, Talitha cumi; which is, being interpreted, Damsel, I say unto thee, arise.

34 42 And straightway the damsel arose and walked; for she was ~~of the age of~~ twelve years **old**. And they were astonished with a great astonishment.

35 43 And he charged them straitly that no man should know it; and commanded that something should be given her to eat.

CHAPTER 6

1 And he went out from thence, and came into his own country; and his disciples ~~follow~~ **followed** him.

2 And when the Sabbath day was come, he began to teach in the synagogue; and many hearing *him*, were astonished **at his words**, saying, From whence hath this *man* these things?

3 2 And what wisdom *is* this ~~which~~ **that** is given unto him, that even such mighty works are wrought by his hands?

4 3 Is not this the carpenter, the son

of Mary, the brother of James, and Joses, and of ~~Juda~~ **Judah** and Simon?

5 3 And are not his sisters here with us? And they were offended at him.

6 4 But Jesus said unto them, A prophet is not without honor, ~~but~~ **save** in his own country, and among his own kin, and in his own house.

7 5 And he could ~~there~~ do no mighty work **there**, save that he laid his hands upon a few sick ~~folk~~ **folks** and **they were** healed ~~them~~.

8 6 And he marvelled because of their unbelief. And he went round about the villages, teaching.

9 7–9 And he called ~~unto him~~ the twelve, and began to send them forth by two and two; and gave them power over unclean spirits; and commanded them that they should take nothing for *their* journey, save a staff only; no scrip, ~~no~~ **nor** bread, ~~no~~ **nor** money in *their* purse; but **should** *be* shod with sandals, and not ~~put on~~ **take** two coats.

10 And he said unto them, In ~~what~~ **whatsoever** place ~~soever~~ ye enter into ~~an~~ **a** house, there abide till ye depart from that place.

11 And whosoever shall not receive you, nor hear you; when ye depart thence shake off the dust ~~under~~ **of** your feet for a testimony against them.

12 11 Verily I say unto you, It shall be more tolerable for Sodom and Gomorrha in the day of judgment, than for that city.

13 12 And they went out, and preached that men should repent.

14 13 And they cast out many devils, and anointed with oil many that were sick, and **they were** healed ~~them~~.

15 14 And King Herod heard *of him* **Jesus**; for his name was spread abroad; and he said, That John the Baptist was risen from the dead, and therefore, mighty works do show forth themselves in him.

16 15 Others said, That it is Elias. And others said, That it is a prophet, or as one of the prophets.

17 16 But when Herod heard ~~thereof~~ **of him**, he said, It is John whom I beheaded; he is risen from the dead.

18 17 For Herod himself had sent forth and laid hold upon John, and bound him in prison for Herodias' sake, his brother Philip's wife: for he had married her.

19 18 For John had said unto Herod, It is not lawful for thee to have thy brother's wife.

20 19 Therefore Herodias had a quarrel against him, and would have killed him; but she could not:

21 20 For Herod feared John, knowing that he was a just man, and ~~an~~ **a** holy **man**, and **one who feared God and** observed **to worship** him; and when he heard him he did many things **for him**, and heard him gladly.

22 21 ~~And~~ **But** when ~~a convenient day~~ **Herod's birthday** was come, ~~that Herod on his birthday~~ **he** made a supper ~~to~~ **for** his lords, high captains, and **the** chief ~~estates~~ **priests** of Galilee.

23 22 And when the daughter of ~~the said~~ Herodias came in, and danced, and pleased Herod and them that sat with him, the king said unto the damsel, Ask of me whatsoever thou wilt, and I will give *it* thee.

24 23 And he sware unto her, Whatsoever thou shalt ask of me, I will give *it* thee, unto the half of my kingdom.

25 24 And she went forth, and said unto her mother, What shall I ask? And she said, The head of John the Baptist.

26 25 And she came in straightway with haste unto the king, and asked, saying, I will that thou give me by and by in a charger the head of John the Baptist.

27 26 And the king was exceeding sorry; ~~yet~~ **but** for his oath's sake, and for their sakes which sat with him, he would not reject her.

28 27 And immediately the king sent an executioner, and commanded his head to be brought: and he went and beheaded him in the prison,

29 28 And brought his head in a charger, and gave it to the damsel: and the damsel gave it to her mother.

30 29 And when ~~his~~ **John's** disciples heard *of it*, they came and took up his corpse and laid it in a tomb.

31 30 ~~And~~ **Now** the apostles gathered themselves together unto Jesus, and told him all things; both what they had done, and what they had taught.

32 31 And he said unto them, Come ye yourselves apart into a ~~desert~~ **solitary** place, and rest awhile; for there were many coming and going, and they had no leisure, **not** so much as to eat.

33 32 And they departed into a ~~desert~~ **solitary** place by ship, privately.

34 33 And the people saw them departing; and many knew ~~him~~ **Jesus**, and ran afoot thither out of all cities, and ~~outwent~~ **outran** them, and came together unto him.

35 34 And Jesus, when he came out, saw much people, and was moved with compassion ~~toward~~ **towards** them, because they were as sheep not having a shepherd; and he began to teach them many things.

36 35–36 And when the day was now far spent, his disciples came unto him and said, This is a ~~desert~~ **solitary** place, and now the time **for departure** *is* ~~far passed~~ **come,** send them away, that they may go into the country

round about, and into the villages, and buy themselves bread; for they have nothing to eat.

37 **And** he answered and said unto them, Give ye them to eat.

38 37 And they say unto him, Shall we go and buy two hundred pennyworth of bread, and give them to eat?

39 38 He saith unto them, How many loaves have ye? go and see.

40 38 And when they knew, they ~~say~~ **said**, Five, and two fishes.

41 39 And he commanded them to make all sit down by companies upon the green grass.

42 40 And they sat down in ranks, by hundreds, and by fifties.

43 41 And when he had taken the five loaves and ~~the~~ two fishes, he looked up to heaven, and blessed, and ~~brake~~ **break** the loaves, and gave ~~them~~ to his disciples to set before ~~them~~ **the multitude**; and the two fishes divided he among them all.

44 42 And they did all eat, and were filled.

45 43 And they took up twelve baskets full of the fragments, and of the fishes.

46 44 And they that did eat of the loaves were about five thousand men.

47 45 And straightway he constrained his disciples to get into the ship, and to go to the other side before **him,** unto Bethsaida, while he sent away the people.

48 46 And when he had sent them away, he departed into a mountain to pray.

49 47–48 And when even was come, the ship was in the midst of the sea, and he alone on the land. And he saw them toiling in rowing; for the wind was contrary unto them:

50 48 And about the fourth watch of the night he cometh unto them, walking upon the sea, ~~and~~ **as if he** would have passed by them.

51 49 ~~But~~ **And** when they saw him walking upon the sea, they supposed it had been a spirit, and cried out;

52 50 For they all saw him, and were troubled.

53 50 And immediately he talked with them, and saith unto them, Be of good cheer: it is I; be not afraid.

54 51 And he went up unto them into the ship; and the wind ceased: and they were sore amazed in themselves beyond measure, and wondered.

55 52 For they considered not ~~the miracle~~ of the loaves; for their ~~heart~~ **hearts** ~~was~~ **were** hardened.

56 53 And when they had passed over, they came into the land of Gennesaret, and drew to the shore.

57 54–55 And when they were come out of the ship, straightway ~~they~~ **the people** knew him, and ran through that whole region round about, and began to carry about in beds, those that were sick, where they heard he was.

58 56 And whithersoever he entered, into villages, or cities, or country, they laid the sick in the streets, and besought him that they might touch if it were but the border of his ~~garment~~ **garments;** and as many as touched him were made whole.

CHAPTER 7

1 Then came together unto him the Pharisees, and certain of the scribes, which came from Jerusalem.

2 And when they saw some of his disciples eat bread with defiled, that is to say, with unwashen, hands, they found fault.

3 For the Pharisees, and all the Jews, except they wash ~~their~~ hands

oft, eat not; holding the tradition of the elders.

4 And *when they come* from the market, except they wash **their bodies,** they eat not.

5 4 And many other things there be, which they have received to hold, *as* the washing of cups, and pots, brasen vessels, and of tables.

6 5 ~~Then~~ **And** the Pharisees and scribes asked him, Why walk not thy disciples according to the ~~tradition~~ **traditions** of the elders, but eat bread with unwashen hands?

7 6–7 He answered and said unto them, Well hath ~~Esaias~~ **Isaiah** prophesied of you hypocrites, as it is written, This people honoreth me with *their* lips, but their heart is far from me. Howbeit**,** in vain do they worship me, teaching ~~for~~ **the** doctrines ~~the~~ **and** commandments of men.

8 For laying aside the commandment of God, ye hold the tradition of men; ~~as~~ the washing of pots and **of** cups; and many other such like things ye do.

9 And he said unto them, ~~Full well~~ **Yea, altogether** ye reject the commandment of God, that ye may keep your own ~~tradition~~ **traditions**.

10 Full well is it written of you, by the prophets whom ye have rejected.

11 They testified these things of a truth, and their blood shall be upon you.

12 10 **Ye have kept not the ordinances of God;** for Moses said, Honor thy father and thy mother; and whoso curseth father or mother, let him die the death **of the transgressor, as it is written in your law; but ye keep not the law.**

13 11–13 ~~But~~ Ye say, If a man shall say to his father or mother, *It is*

Corban, that is to say, a gift, by whatsoever thou mightest be profited by me, ~~he shall be free~~ **is of age**. And ye suffer him no more to do ~~ought~~ **aught** for his father or his mother; making the word of God of none effect through your tradition, which ye have delivered; and many such like things do ye.

14 And when he had called all the people ~~unto him~~, he said unto them, Hearken unto me everyone ~~of you~~, and understand;

15 There is nothing from without ~~a man~~, that entering into ~~him~~ **a man**, can defile him**, which is food;** but the things which come out of him; those are they that defile the man**, that proceedeth forth out of the heart.**

16 If any man have ears to hear, let him hear.

17 And when he was entered into the house from **among** the people, his disciples asked him concerning the parable.

18 18–19 And he ~~saith~~ **said** unto them, Are ye ~~so~~ without understanding also? Do ye not perceive, that whatsoever thing from without entereth into the man, ~~it~~ cannot defile him; because it entereth not into his heart, but into the belly, and goeth out into the draught, purging all meats?

19 20 And he said, That which cometh out of ~~the~~ **a** man, ~~that~~ defileth the man.

20 21–22 For from within, out of the ~~heart~~ **hearts** of men, proceed evil thoughts, adulteries, fornications, murders, thefts, covetousness, wickedness, deceit, lasciviousness, an evil eye, blasphemy, pride, foolishness:

21 23 All these evil things come from within, and defile the man.

22 24 And from thence he arose, and went into the borders of Tyre and Sidon, and entered into ~~an~~ **a** house, and would ~~have~~ **that** no man ~~know it~~ **should come unto him**.

23 24 But he could not ~~be hid~~ **deny them; for he had compassion on all men.**

24 25 For a ~~certain~~ woman, whose young daughter had an unclean spirit, heard of him, and came and fell at his feet:

25 26 The woman was a Greek, a Syrophenician by nation; and she besought him that he would cast forth the devil out of her daughter.

26 27 But Jesus said unto her, Let the children **of the kingdom** first be filled; for it is not meet to take the children's bread, and to cast *it* unto the dogs.

27 28 And she answered and said unto him, Yes, Lord**; thou sayest truly,** yet the dogs under the table eat of the children's crumbs.

28 29 And he said unto her, For this saying go thy way; the devil is gone out of thy daughter.

29 30 And when she was come to her house, she found **that** the devil **had** gone out, and her daughter **was** laid upon the bed.

30 31 And again, departing from the coasts of Tyre and Sidon, he came unto the sea of Galilee, through the midst of the coasts of Decapolis.

31 32 And they ~~bring~~ **brought** unto him one that was deaf, and had an impediment in his speech; and they ~~beseech~~ **besought** him to put his hand upon him.

32 33 And he took him aside from the multitude, and put his fingers into his ears, and he spit, and touched his tongue;

33 34 And looking up to heaven, he sighed, and saith unto him, Ephphatha, that is, Be opened.

34 35 And straightway his ears were opened, and the string of his tongue was loosed, and he spake plain.

35 36 And he charged them that they should tell no man; but the more he charged them, so much the more a great deal they published ~~it~~ **him**;

36 37 And were beyond measure astonished, saying, He hath done all things well: he maketh both the deaf to hear, and the dumb to speak.

CHAPTER 8

1 In those days, the multitude being very great, and having nothing to eat, Jesus called his disciples ~~unto him~~, and ~~saith~~ **said** unto them,

2 2–3 I have compassion on the multitude, because they have now been with me three days, and have nothing to eat: and if I send them away fasting to their own houses, they will faint by the way: for divers of them came from far.

3 4 And his disciples answered him, From whence can a man satisfy these ~~men~~, **so great a multitude,** with bread here in the wilderness?

4 5 And he asked them, How many loaves have ye? And they said, Seven.

5 6 And he commanded the people to sit down on the ground; and he took the seven loaves, and gave thanks, and brake, and gave to his disciples to set before ~~them~~ **the people**; and they did set *them* before the people.

6 7 And they had a few small fishes; and he blessed **them**, and commanded to set them also before ~~them~~ **the people, that they should eat**.

7 8 So they did eat, and were filled, and they took up of the broken ~~meat~~ **bread** that was left, seven baskets.

8 9 And they that had eaten were about four thousand: and he sent them away.

9 10 And straightway he entered into a ship with his disciples, and came into the parts of Dalmanutha.

10 11 And the Pharisees came forth, and began to question with him, seeking of him a sign from heaven, tempting him.

11 12 And he sighed deeply in his spirit, and saith, Why doth this generation seek after a sign?

12 Verily I say unto you, There shall no sign be given unto this generation**, save the sign of the prophet Jonah; for as Jonah was three days and three nights in the whale's belly, so likewise shall the Son of Man be buried in the bowels of the earth**.

13 And he left them, and entering into the ship again departed to the other side.

14 Now *the* ~~disciples~~ **multitude** had forgotten to take bread; neither had they in the ship with them, more than one loaf.

15 And he charged them, saying, Take heed, **and** beware of the leaven of the Pharisees, and ~~of~~ the leaven of Herod.

16 And they reasoned among themselves, saying, ~~It is~~ **He hath said this,** because we have no bread.

17 And when **they said this among themselves,** Jesus knew *it*, **and** he ~~saith~~ **said** unto them,

18 17 Why reason ye because ye have no bread? Perceive ye not yet, neither understand **ye**? ~~have ye~~ **Are** your ~~heart~~ **hearts** yet hardened?

19 18 Having eyes, see ye not? and having ears, hear ye not? and do ye not remember?

20 19 When I brake the five loaves among **the** five thousand, how many baskets full of fragments took ye up? They say unto him, Twelve.

21 20 And when the seven among

the four thousand, how many baskets full of fragments took ye up? And they said, Seven.

22 21 And he said unto them, How is it that ye do not understand?

23 22 And he cometh to Bethsaida; and they bring a blind man unto him, and besought him to touch him.

24 23 And he took the blind man by the hand, and led him out of the town; and when he had spit ~~on~~ **upon** his eyes, and put his hands upon him, he asked him if he saw ~~ought~~ **aught**.

25 24 And he looked up, and said, I see men as trees, walking.

26 25 After that he put *his* hands again upon his eyes, and made him look up: and he was restored, and saw every man clearly.

27 26 And he sent him away to his house, saying, Neither go into the town, nor tell ~~it~~ **what is done,** to any in the town.

28 27 And Jesus went out, and his disciples, into the towns of Caesarea Philippi: and by the way he asked his disciples, saying unto them, Whom do men say that I am?

29 28 And they answered, John the Baptist: but some *say*, Elias; and others, One of the prophets.

30 29 And he saith unto them, But whom say ye that I am?

31 29 And Peter ~~answereth~~ **answered** and ~~saith~~ **said** unto him, Thou art the Christ, **the Son of the living God**.

32 30 And he charged them that they should tell no man of him.

33 31 And he began to teach them, that the Son of Man must suffer many things, and be rejected of the elders, and ~~of~~ the chief priests, and scribes, and be killed, and after three days rise again.

34 32 And he spake that saying

openly. And Peter took him, and began to rebuke him.

35 33 But when he had turned about and looked on his disciples, he rebuked Peter, saying, Get thee behind me, Satan: for thou savourest not the things that be of God, but the things that be of men.

36 34 And when he had called the people ~~unto him~~, with his disciples also, he said unto them, Whosoever will come after me, let him deny himself, and take up his cross, and follow me.

37 35 For whosoever will save his life, shall lose it; **or whosoever will save his life, shall be willing to lay it down for my sake; and if he is not willing to lay it down for my sake, he shall lose it.**

38 35 But whosoever shall **be willing to** lose his life for my sake, and the gospel's, the same shall save it.

39 36–37 For what shall it profit a man, if he shall gain the whole world, and lose his own soul? Or what shall a man give in exchange for his soul?

40 Therefore deny yourselves of these, and be not ashamed of me.

41 38 Whosoever ~~therefore~~ shall be ashamed of me, and of my words**,** in this adulterous and sinful generation**,** of him also shall the Son of Man be ashamed, when he cometh in the glory of his Father with the holy angels.

42 And they shall not have part in that resurrection when he cometh.

43 For verily I say unto you, That he shall come; and he that layeth down his life for my sake and the gospel's, shall come with him, and shall be clothed with his glory in the cloud, on the right hand of the Son of Man.

CHAPTER **8** 9

44 1 And he said unto them **again,** Verily I say unto you, That there be some of them that stand here, which shall not taste of death, till they have seen the kingdom of God come with power.

CHAPTER 9

1 2 And after six days Jesus taketh ~~with him~~ Peter, and James, and John, **who asked him many questions concerning his sayings;** and **Jesus** leadeth them up into ~~an~~ **a** high mountain apart by themselves. And he was transfigured before them.

2 3 And his raiment became shining, exceeding white**,** as snow; so **white** as no fuller on earth ~~can~~ **could** ~~white~~ **whiten** them.

3 4 And there appeared unto them Elias with Moses**, or in other words, John the Baptist and Moses;** and they were talking with Jesus.

4 5–6 And Peter answered and said to Jesus, Master, it is good for us to be here**,** and let us make three tabernacles; one for thee, and one for Moses, and one for Elias**;** for he ~~wist~~ **knew** not what to say; for they were sore afraid.

5 7 And there was a cloud that overshadowed them: and a voice came out of the cloud, saying, This is my beloved Son: hear him.

6 8 And suddenly, when they had looked round about **with great astonishment**, they saw no man anymore, save Jesus only**,** with themselves. **And immediately they departed.**

7 9 And as they came down from the mountain, he charged them that they should tell no man what things they had seen, till the Son of Man ~~were~~ **was** risen from the dead.

8 10 And they kept that saying with themselves, questioning one with another what the rising from the dead should mean.

9 11 And they asked him, saying,

Why say the scribes that Elias must first come?

10 12 And he answered and told them, **saying,** Elias verily cometh first, and ~~restoreth~~ **prepareth** all things; **and teacheth you of the prophets;** ~~and~~ how it is written of the Son of Man, that he must suffer many things, and be set at naught.

11 13 ~~But~~ **Again** I say unto you, That Elias is indeed come, ~~and~~ **but** they have done unto him whatsoever they listed**; and even** as it is written of him**; and he bore record of me, and they received him not. Verily this was Elias.**

12 14 And when he came to ~~his~~ **the** disciples, he saw a great multitude about them, and the scribes questioning with them.

13 15 And straightway all the people, when they beheld him, were greatly amazed, and running to *him* saluted him.

14 16 And ~~he~~ **Jesus** asked the scribes, What ~~question~~ **questioned** ye with them?

15 17–18 And one of the multitude answered**,** and said, Master, I have brought unto thee my son, ~~which~~ **who** hath a dumb spirit **that is a devil**; and ~~wheresoever~~ **when** he ~~taketh~~ **seizeth** him, he teareth him**;** and he foameth and gnasheth with his teeth, and pineth away**;** and I spake to thy disciples that they ~~should~~ **might** cast him out**,** and they could not.

16 19–20 ~~He answereth~~ **Jesus spake unto** him and ~~saith~~ **said**, O faithless generation! how long shall I be with you? How long shall I suffer you? Bring him unto me. And they brought him unto ~~him~~ **Jesus**.

17 20 And when ~~he~~ **the man** saw him, ~~straightway~~ **immediately he was torn by** the spirit ~~tare him~~; and he fell on the ground and wallowed, foaming.

18 21 And ~~he~~ **Jesus** asked his father, How long **a time** is it ~~ago~~ since this came unto him? And ~~he~~ **his father** said, ~~Of~~ **When** a child;

19 22 And ofttimes it hath cast him into the fire and into the waters, to destroy him, but if thou canst ~~do any thing,~~ **I ask thee to** have compassion on us, and help us.

20 23 Jesus said unto him, If thou ~~canst~~ **wilt** believe all things ~~are~~ **I shall say unto you, this is** possible to him that believeth.

21 24 And ~~straightway~~ **immediately** the father of the child cried out, and said, with tears, Lord, I believe; help thou mine unbelief.

22 25 When Jesus saw that the people came running together, he rebuked the foul spirit, saying unto him, ~~Thou dumb and deaf spirit~~ I charge thee **to** come out of him, and enter no more into him.

23 26 ~~And~~ **Now** *the* **dumb and deaf** *spirit* cried, and rent him sore, and came out of him; and he was as one dead, insomuch that many said, He is dead.

24 27 But Jesus took him by the hand, and lifted him up; and he arose.

25 28 ~~And~~ When ~~he~~ **Jesus** was come into the house, his disciples asked him privately, Why could not we cast him out?

26 29 And he said unto them, This kind can come forth by nothing, but by prayer and fasting.

27 30 And they departed thence, and passed through Galilee **privately**; ~~and~~ **for** he would not that any man should know *it.*

28 31 ~~For~~ **And** he taught his disciples, and said unto them, The Son of Man is delivered into the hands of men, and they shall kill him; and after that he is killed, he shall rise the third day.

29 32 But they understood not that saying, and were afraid to ask him.

30 33 And he came to Capernaum; and being in the house, he asked them, ~~What~~ **Why** was it that ye disputed among yourselves by the way?

31 34 But they held their peace, **being afraid,** for by the way they had disputed among themselves, who ~~should be~~ **was** the greatest **among them**.

32 35 ~~And he~~ **Now Jesus** sat down and called the twelve, and ~~saith~~ **said** unto them, If any man desire to be first, ~~the same~~ **he** shall be last of all, and servant of all.

33 36 And he took a child, and ~~set him~~ **sat** in the midst of them; and when he had taken ~~him~~ **the child** in his arms, he said unto them,

34 37 Whosoever shall ~~receive~~ **humble himself like** one of ~~such~~ **these** children ~~in my name,~~ **and** receiveth me, **ye shall receive in my name.**

35 37 And whosoever shall receive me, receiveth not me **only**, but him that sent me, **even the Father.**

36 38 And John ~~answered~~ **spake unto** him, saying, Master, we saw one casting out devils in thy name, and he ~~followeth~~ **followed** not us; and we forbade him, because he ~~followeth~~ **followed** not us.

37 39–40 But Jesus said, Forbid him not; for there is no man which shall do a miracle in my name, that can ~~lightly~~ speak evil of me. For he that is not against us is on our part.

38 41 ~~For~~ **And** whosoever shall give you a cup of water to drink, in my name, because ye belong to Christ, verily I say unto you, He shall not lose his reward.

39 42 And whosoever shall offend one of *these* little ones that believe in me, it is better for him that a millstone were hanged about his neck, and he were cast into the sea.

40 43 ~~And~~ **Therefore,** if thy hand offend thee, cut it off; **or if thy brother offend thee and confess not and forsake not, he shall be cut off.** It is better for thee to enter into life maimed, than having two hands, to go into hell.

41 43–44 **For it is better for thee to enter into life without thy brother, than for thee and thy brother to be cast into hell;** into the fire that never shall be quenched, where their worm dieth not, and the fire is not quenched.

42 45 And **again,** if thy foot offend thee, cut it off; **for he that is thy standard, by whom thou walkest, if he become a transgressor, he shall be cut off.**

43 45–46 It is better for thee to enter halt into life, than having two feet to be cast into hell, into the fire that never shall be quenched:

~~46 Where their worm dieth not, and the fire is not quenched.~~

44 Therefore, let every man stand or fall, by himself, and not for another; or not trusting another.

45 Seek unto my Father, and it shall be done in that very moment what ye shall ask, if ye ask in faith, believing that ye shall receive.

46 47 And if thine eye **which seeth for thee, him that is appointed to watch over thee to show thee light, become a transgressor and** offend thee, pluck ~~it~~ **him** out.

47 It is better for thee to enter into the kingdom of God, with one eye, than having two eyes to be cast into hell fire.

48 For it is better that thyself should be saved, than to be cast into hell with thy brother, where their worm dieth not, and **where** the fire is not quenched.

49 49–50 For everyone shall be salted with fire; and every sacrifice shall be salted with salt; **but the** salt ~~is~~ **must be** good.

50 ~~but~~ **For** if the salt have lost his saltness, wherewith will ye season it? **(the sacrifice;) therefore it must needs be that ye** have salt in yourselves, and have peace one with another.

Chapter 10

1 And he arose from thence and cometh into the coasts of ~~Judaea~~ **Judea** by the farther side of Jordan; and the people resort unto him again; and as he was ~~wont~~ **accustomed to teach,** he **also** taught them again.

2 And the Pharisees came to him and asked him, Is it lawful for a man to put away *his* wife? **This they said, thinking to** ~~tempting~~ **tempt** him.

3 And he answered and said unto them, What did Moses command you?

4 And they said, Moses suffered to write a bill of divorcement, and to put *her* away.

5 ~~And~~ Jesus answered and said unto them, For the hardness of your ~~heart~~ **hearts** he wrote you this precept;

6 But from the beginning of the creation God made them male and female.

7 7–9 For this cause shall a man leave his father and mother, and cleave to his wife; and they ~~twain~~ **two** shall be one flesh: so then they are no more ~~twain~~ **two,** but one flesh. What therefore God hath joined together, let not man put asunder.

8 10 And in the house his disciples

asked him again of the same *matter*.

9 11 And he saith unto them, Whosoever shall put away his wife, and marry another, committeth adultery against her.

10 12 And if a woman shall put away her husband, and be married to another, she committeth adultery.

11 13 And they brought young children to him, that he should touch them; and ~~his~~ **the** disciples rebuked those that brought *them*.

12 14 But when Jesus saw ~~it~~ **and heard them**, he was much displeased, and said unto them, Suffer the little children to come unto me, and forbid them not; for of such is the kingdom of God.

13 15 Verily I say unto you, Whosoever shall not receive the kingdom of God as a little child, he shall not enter therein.

14 16 And he took them up in his arms, put *his* hands upon them, and blessed them.

15 17 And when he was gone forth into the way, there came one running, and kneeled to him, and asked him, Good Master, what shall I do that I may inherit eternal life?

16 18 And Jesus said unto him, Why callest thou me good? ~~there is~~ None **is** good but one, *that is* God.

17 19 Thou knowest the commandments, Do not commit adultery, Do not kill, Do not steal, Do not bear false witness, Defraud not, Honour thy father and mother.

18 20 And ~~he~~ **the man** answered and said unto him, Master, all these have I observed from my youth.

19 21 Then Jesus beholding him loved him, and said unto him, One thing thou lackest:

20 21 Go thy way, sell whatsoever thou hast, and give to the poor, and thou shalt have treasure in heaven: and come, take up the cross, and follow me.

21 22 And ~~he~~ **the man** was sad at that saying, and went away grieved; for he had great possessions.

22 23 And Jesus looked round about, and ~~saith~~ **said** unto his disciples, How hardly shall they that have riches enter into the kingdom of ~~God~~ **my Father**!

23 24 And the disciples were astonished at his words. But Jesus ~~answereth~~ **spake** again, and ~~saith~~ **said** unto them, Children, how hard is it for them ~~that~~ **who** trust in riches to enter into the kingdom of God!

24 25 It is easier for a camel to go through the eye of a needle, than for a rich man to enter into the kingdom of God.

25 26 And they were astonished out of measure, saying among themselves, Who then can be saved?

26 27 And Jesus, looking upon them, ~~saith~~ **said**, With men **that trust in riches**, *it is* impossible; but not **impossible** with **men who trust in** God **and leave all for my sake,** for with ~~God~~ such all **these** things are possible.

27 28 Then Peter began to say unto him, Lo, we have left all, and have followed thee.

28 29 And Jesus answered and said, Verily I say unto you, There is no man that hath left house, or brethren, or sisters, or father, or mother, or wife, or children, or lands, for my sake, and the gospel's,

29 30 But he shall receive an hundredfold now in this time, houses, and brethren, and sisters, and mothers, and children, and lands, with persecutions; and in the world to come eternal life.

30 31 But **there are** many ~~that are~~ **who make themselves** first**, that** shall be last; and the last first.

31 32 **This he said, rebuking Peter;** and they were in the way going up to Jerusalem; and Jesus went before ~~them,~~ and they were amazed; and as they followed, they were afraid.

32 And he took again the twelve, and began to tell them what things should happen unto him,

33 ~~Saying~~ **And Jesus said,** Behold, we go up to Jerusalem; and the Son of Man shall be delivered unto the chief priests, and unto the scribes; and they shall condemn him to death; and shall deliver him to the Gentiles.

34 And they shall mock him, and shall scourge him, and shall spit upon him, and shall kill him: and the third day he shall rise again.

35 And James, and John, the sons of Zebedee, ~~come~~ **came** unto him, saying, Master, we would that thou shouldest do for us whatsoever we shall desire.

36 And he said unto them, What ~~would~~ **will** ye that I should do ~~for~~ **unto** you?

37 They said unto him, Grant unto us that we may sit, one on thy right hand, and the other on thy left hand, in thy glory.

38 But Jesus said unto them, Ye know not what ye ask: can ye drink of the cup that I drink of? and be baptized with the baptism that I am baptized with?

39 And they said unto him, We can.

40 39–40 And Jesus said unto them, Ye shall indeed drink of the cup that I drink of; and **be baptized** with the baptism that I am baptized ~~withal~~ **with** ~~shall ye be baptized~~; but to sit on my right hand, and on my left hand, is not mine to give; but ~~it shall be given~~ ~~to them~~ **they shall receive it** for whom it is prepared.

41 And when the ten heard ~~it~~, they began to be much displeased with James and John.

42 But Jesus called them ~~to him~~, and ~~saith~~ **said** unto them, Ye know that they ~~which~~ **who** are ~~accounted~~ **appointed** to rule over the Gentiles exercise lordship over them; and their great ones exercise authority upon them.

43 But ~~so~~ **it** shall ~~it~~ not be **so** among you; but whosoever will be great among you, shall be your minister.

44 And whosoever of you will be the chiefest, shall be servant of all.

45 For even the Son of man came not to be ministered unto, but to minister, and to give his life a ransom for many.

46 And they came to Jericho: and as he went out of Jericho with his disciples and a great number of people, blind Bartimaeus, the son of Timaeus, sat by the highway side begging.

47 And when he heard that it was Jesus of Nazareth, he began to cry out, and say, Jesus, ~~thou~~ Son of David, have mercy on me.

48 And many charged him that he should hold his peace; but he cried the more ~~a great deal~~ **exceedingly, saying,** ~~Thou~~ Son of David, have mercy on me.

49 And Jesus stood still, and commanded him to be called. And they ~~call~~ **called** the blind man, saying unto him, Be of good comfort; ~~rise~~ **arise,** he calleth thee.

50 And he, casting away his garment, ~~rose~~ **arose** and came to Jesus.

51 And Jesus ~~answered and~~ said unto him, What wilt thou that I should do unto thee?

52 51 **And** the blind man said unto

him, Lord, that I might receive my sight.

53 52 And Jesus said unto him, Go thy way; thy faith hath made thee whole.

54 52 And immediately he received his sight, and followed Jesus in the way.

CHAPTER 11

1 1–2 And when they came nigh to Jerusalem, unto Bethphage and Bethany, at the mount of Olives, he sendeth forth two of his disciples, and saith unto them,

2 Go your way into the village over against you; and as soon as ye ~~be~~ **have** entered into it, ye shall find a colt tied, whereon ~~never~~ **no** man **ever** sat; loose him and bring *him* **to me.**

3 And if any man say unto you, Why do ye this? say ye that the Lord hath need of him; and straightway he will send him hither.

4 And they went their way, and found the colt tied by the door without, in a place where two ways met; and they ~~loose~~ **loosed** him.

5 And certain of them ~~that~~ **who** stood ~~there~~ **by,** said unto ~~them~~ **the disciples,** ~~What~~ **Why** ~~do ye loosing~~ **loose ye** the colt?

6 And they said unto them even as Jesus had commanded: and they let them go.

7 And they brought the colt to Jesus, and cast their garments on ~~him~~ **it;** and ~~he~~ **Jesus** sat upon ~~him~~ **it.**

8 And many spread their garments in the way; and others cut down branches ~~off~~ **of** ~~the~~ trees, and ~~strawed~~ **strewed** *them* in the way.

9 And they that went before **him,** and they that followed **after,** cried, saying,

10 9 Hosanna! Blessed *is* he that cometh in the name of the Lord;

11 10 ~~Blessed be~~ **That bringeth** the kingdom of our father David;

12 10 **Blessed is he** that cometh in the name of the Lord; Hosanna in the highest.

13 11 And Jesus entered into Jerusalem, and into the temple. And when he had looked round about upon all things, and **blessed the disciples,** ~~now~~ the eventide was come; **and** he went out unto Bethany with the twelve.

14 12–13 And on the morrow, when they ~~were come~~ **came** from Bethany he was hungry; and seeing a fig tree afar off having leaves, he came **to it with his disciples; and as they supposed, he came to it to see** if ~~haply~~ he might find anything thereon.

15 13 And when he came to it, ~~he found~~ **there was** nothing but leaves; for ~~the time of~~ **as yet the** figs ~~was~~ **were** not **ripe** ~~yet.~~

16 14 And Jesus ~~answered~~ **spake** and said unto it, No man eat fruit of thee hereafter, forever. And his disciples heard ~~it~~ **him.**

17 15 And they ~~come~~ **came** to Jerusalem. And Jesus went into the temple, and began to cast out them that sold and bought in the temple, and overthrew the tables of the moneychangers, and the seats of them ~~that~~ **who** sold doves;

18 16 And would not suffer that any man should carry ~~any~~ **a** vessel through the temple.

19 17 And he taught, saying unto them, Is it not written, My house shall be called of all nations the house of prayer? but ye have made it a den of thieves.

20 18 And the scribes and chief priests heard ~~it~~ **him,** and sought how they might destroy him; for they feared him because all the people ~~was~~ **were** astonished at his doctrine.

21 19 And when even was come, he went out of the city.

22 20 And in the morning, as they passed by, they saw the fig tree dried up from the roots.

23 21 And Peter calling to remembrance saith unto him, Master, behold, the fig tree which thou cursedst is withered away.

24 22 And Jesus ~~answering~~ **spake and** ~~saith~~ **said** unto ~~them~~ **him**, Have faith in God.

25 23 For verily I say unto you, That whosoever shall say unto this mountain, Be thou removed, and be thou cast into the sea; and shall not doubt in his heart, but shall believe that those things which he saith shall come to pass; he shall have whatsoever he saith **fulfilled**.

26 24 Therefore I say unto you, ~~What~~ **Whatsoever** things ~~soever~~ ye desire, when ye pray, believe that ye receive ~~them~~, and ye shall have ~~them~~ **whatsoever ye ask**.

27 25 And when ye stand praying, forgive if ye have ~~ought~~ **aught** against any; that your Father also ~~which~~ **who** is in heaven, may forgive you your trespasses.

28 26 But if ~~ye~~ **you** do not forgive, neither will your Father ~~which~~ **who** is in heaven forgive your trespasses.

29 27–28 And they ~~come~~ **came** again to Jerusalem; and as he was walking in the temple, there ~~come~~ **came** to him the chief priests, and the scribes, and the elders, and ~~say~~ **said** unto him,

30 28 By what authority doest thou these things? and who gave thee this authority to do these things?

31 29 And Jesus answered and said unto them, I will also ask of you one question, ~~and~~ answer me, and **then** I will tell you by what authority I do these things.

32 30 **Was** the baptism of John ~~was it~~ from heaven, or of man? Answer me.

33 31 And they reasoned with themselves, saying, If we shall say, From heaven; he will say, Why then did ye not believe him?

34 32 But if we shall say, Of men; **we shall offend the people. Therefore** they feared the people; for all ~~men~~ **people** ~~counted~~ **believed** John, that he was a prophet indeed.

35 33 And they answered and said unto Jesus, We cannot tell.

36 33 And Jesus answering saith unto them, Neither do I tell you by what authority I do these things.

CHAPTER 12

1 And ~~he~~ **Jesus** began to speak unto them by parables, **saying,**

2 1–2 A ~~certain~~ man planted a vineyard, and set ~~an~~ **a** hedge about ~~it~~, and digged ~~a place for~~ the ~~winefat~~ **wine vat**, and built a tower, and let it out to husbandmen, and went into a far country.

3 2 And at the season he sent to the husbandmen a servant, that he might receive from the husbandmen of the fruit of the vineyard.

4 3 And they caught ~~him~~ **the servant**, and beat him, and sent *him* away empty.

5 4 And again he sent unto them another servant; and at him they cast stones, and wounded *him* in the head, and sent *him* away shamefully handled.

6 5 And again he sent another; and him they killed, and many others; beating some, and killing some.

7 6 Having yet therefore one son, his wellbeloved, he sent him also last unto them, saying, They will reverence my son.

8 7 But those husbandmen said among themselves, This is the heir;

come, let us kill him, and the inheritance shall be ours.

9 8 And they took him ~~and killed him~~ and cast *him* out of the vineyard**, and killed him**.

10 9 What shall therefore the lord of the vineyard do? **Lo,** he will come and destroy the husbandmen, and will give the vineyard unto others.

11 10–11 ~~And~~ **Again,** have ye not read this scripture; The stone which the builders rejected**,** is become the head of the corner**;** this was the Lord's doing, and it is marvelous in our eyes**.**

12 **And now they were angry when they heard these words;** and they sought to lay hold on him, but feared the people.

13 12 For they knew that he had spoken the parable against them: and they left him, and went their way.

14 13 And they send unto him certain of the Pharisees and of the Herodians, to catch him in *his* words.

15 14 And when they were come, they say unto him, Master, we know that thou art true, and carest for no man: for thou regardest not the person of men, but teachest the way of God in truth:

16 14–15 Is it lawful to give tribute to Caesar, or not? Shall we give, or shall we not give?

17 15 But he, knowing their hypocrisy, said unto them, Why tempt ye me? bring me a penny, that I may see *it*.

18 16 And they brought ~~it~~ **the penny;** and he ~~saith~~ **said** unto them; Whose ~~is this~~ image and superscription **is this?**

19 16 And they said unto him, Caesar's.

20 17 And Jesus answering said unto them, Render to Caesar the things

~~that~~ **which** are Caesar's**;** and to God the things that are God's.

21 17 And they marveled at ~~him~~ **it**.

22 18 Then ~~come~~ **came** unto him the Sadducees, ~~which~~ **who** say there is no resurrection; and they asked him, saying,

23 19 Master, Moses wrote unto us **in his law**, If a man's brother die, and leave ~~his~~ **a** wife *~~behind him~~*, and leave no children, that his brother should take his wife, and raise up seed unto his brother.

24 20 Now there were seven brethren: and the first took a wife, and dying left no seed.

25 21 And the second took her, and died, neither left he any seed: and the third likewise.

26 22 And the seven had her, and left no seed: last of all the woman died also.

27 23 In the resurrection therefore, when they shall rise, whose wife shall she be of them? for the seven had her to wife.

28 24 And Jesus answering said unto them, ~~Do~~ Ye ~~not therefore~~ **do** err **therefore**, because ye know not, **and understand not** the scriptures, neither the power of God.

29 25 For when they shall rise from the dead, they neither marry, nor are given in marriage; but are as the angels **of God** ~~which~~ **who** are in heaven.

30 26 And as touching the dead, that they rise: have ye not read in the book of Moses, how in the bush God spake unto him, saying,

31 26 I *am* the God of Abraham, and the God of Isaac, and the God of Jacob?

32 27 He is not **therefore** the God of the dead, but the God of the living; **for he raiseth them up out of their graves.** Ye therefore do greatly err.

33 28 And one of the scribes came, and having heard them reasoning together, and perceiving that he had answered them well, asked him, Which is the first commandment of all?

34 29 And Jesus answered him, The first of all the commandments *is*, **Hearken, and** hear, O Israel; The Lord our God is one Lord;

35 30 And thou shalt love the Lord thy God with all thy heart, and with all thy soul, and with all thy mind, and with all thy strength:

36 30–31 This is the first commandment. And the second *is* like ~~namely~~ this, Thou shalt love thy neighbor as thyself. There is none other commandment greater than these.

37 32 And the scribe said unto him, Well, Master, thou hast said the truth; for there is one God, and there is none other but ~~he~~ **him.**

38 33 And to love him with all the heart, and with all the understanding, and with all the soul, and with all the strength, and to love *his* neighbour as himself, is more than all whole burnt offerings and sacrifices.

39 34 And when Jesus saw that he answered discreetly, he said unto him, Thou art not far from the kingdom of God.

40 34 And no man after that durst ask him ~~any question~~, **saying, Who art thou?**

41 35 And Jesus ~~answered~~ **spake** and said, while he taught in the temple, How say the scribes that Christ is the Son of David?

42 36 For David himself said by the Holy Ghost, The Lord said to my Lord, Sit thou on my right hand, till I make thine enemies thy footstool.

43 37 David therefore himself calleth him Lord; and whence is he ~~then~~ his son?

44 37 And the common people heard him gladly; **but the high priest and the elders were offended at him.**

45 38–39 And he said unto them in his doctrine, Beware of the scribes which love to go in long clothing, and ~~love~~ **have** salutations in the marketplaces, and the chief seats in the synagogues, and the uppermost rooms at feasts;

46 40 ~~Which~~ **Who** devour widows' houses, and for a pretense make long prayers; these shall receive greater damnation.

47 41 And **after this,** Jesus sat over against the treasury, and beheld how the people cast money into the treasury; and many that were rich cast in much.

48 42 And there came a certain poor widow, and she ~~threw~~ **cast** in two mites, which make a farthing.

49 43 And ~~he~~ **Jesus** called ~~unto him~~ his disciples, and ~~saith~~ **said** unto them, Verily I say unto you, that this poor widow hath cast more in, than all they ~~which~~ **who** have cast into the treasury;

50 44 For all ~~they~~ **the rich** did cast in of their abundance; but she, ~~of~~ **notwithstanding** her want, did cast in all that she had; **yea,** *even* all her living.

CHAPTER 13

1 And as ~~he~~ **Jesus** went out of the temple, ~~one of~~ his disciples ~~saith~~ **came** ~~unto~~ **to** him **for to hear him, saying,** Master, ~~see what manner of stones and what~~ **show us concerning the** buildings ~~are here~~ **of the temple.**

2 And ~~Jesus~~ **he** ~~answering~~ said unto ~~him~~ **them,** ~~Seest thou~~ **Behold ye** these **stones of the temple, and all this** great **work, and** buildings **of the temple?**

3 **Verily I say unto you, they shall be thrown down and left unto the Jews desolate.**

4 **And Jesus said unto them, See ye not all these things, and do ye** not understand them?

5 2 **Verily I say unto you,** There shall not be left **here upon this temple,** one stone upon another, ~~that~~ **which** shall not be thrown down.

6 **And Jesus left them and went upon the mount of Olives.**

7 3 And as he sat upon the mount of Olives ~~over against the temple, Peter and James and John and Andrew~~ **the disciples** ~~asked~~ **came unto** him privately, **saying,**

8 4 Tell us, when shall these things be **which thou hast said, concerning the destruction of the temple, and the Jews?** ~~and what *shall be* the sign when all these things shall be fulfilled?~~

9 **And what is the sign of thy coming, and of the end of the world, (or the destruction of the wicked, which is the end of the world?)**

10 5–6 And Jesus ~~answering them began to say~~ **answered and said unto them,** Take heed ~~lest~~ **that** ~~any~~ **no** *man* deceive you; for many shall come in my name, saying, I am *Christ,* and shall deceive many.

11 13 ~~And ye~~ **Then** shall they deliver you up to be afflicted, and shall kill you, **and ye** shall be hated of all ~~men~~ **nations** for my name's sake.

12 ~~Now the brother shall betray the brother to death, and the father the son; and children shall rise up against *their* parents, and shall cause them to be put to death.~~ **And then shall many be offended, and shall betray one another; and many false prophets shall arise, and shall deceive many;**

13 **And because iniquity shall abound, the love of many shall wax**

cold; but he that shall endure unto the end, the same shall be saved.

14 ~~But~~ When ye **therefore** shall see the abomination of desolation, spoken of by Daniel the prophet **concerning the destruction of Jerusalem,** ~~standing where it ought not~~ **then ye** **shall stand in the holy place. (**~~let him that~~ **Whoso** readeth **let him** understand.**)**

15 14 Then let them ~~that~~ **who** be in ~~Judaea~~ **Judea** flee ~~to~~ **into** the mountains;

16 15 And let him ~~that~~ **who** is on the housetop ~~not go down into the house, neither enter *therein*~~ **flee, and not return** to take anything out of his house;

17 16 ~~And~~ **Neither** let him ~~that~~ **who** is in the field, ~~not turn~~ **return** back ~~again for~~ to take ~~up~~ his ~~garment~~ **clothes**.

18 17 ~~But~~ **And** woe ~~to~~ **unto** them that are with child, and ~~to~~ **unto** them ~~that~~ **who** give suck in those days**.**

19 18 ~~And~~ **Therefore** pray ye **the Lord,** that your flight be not in the winter**, neither on the Sabbath day**.

20 19 For **then,** *in* those days, shall be ~~affliction~~ **great tribulations on the Jews, and upon the inhabitants of Jerusalem;** such as was not **before** sent upon Israel, of God, ~~from~~ **since** the beginning of ~~the creation which God created unto~~ **their kingdom, (for it is written their enemies shall scatter them,) until** this time; ~~neither~~ **no, nor ever** shall be **sent again upon Israel**.

21 8 **All** these **things** *are* the beginnings of sorrows.

22 20 And except ~~that the Lord had shortened~~ those days **should be shortened, there should** no flesh ~~should~~ be saved; but for the elect's sake, ~~whom he hath chosen, he hath~~ **according to**

the covenant, those days shall be shortened ~~the days~~.

23 Behold these things I have spoken unto you concerning the Jews.

24 21 And then **immediately after the tribulation** of those days which shall come upon Jerusalem, if any man shall say ~~to~~ **unto** you, Lo, here *is* Christ; or ~~lo, *he is*~~ there; believe *him* not.

25 22 For **in those days there shall also arise** false Christs, and false prophets ~~shall rise~~, and shall show **great** signs and wonders; ~~to seduce~~ **insomuch, that** if ~~*it were*~~ possible, **they shall deceive** ~~even~~ the **very** elect, **who are the elect according to the covenant.**

26 23 ~~But take ye heed~~ Behold, I ~~have foretold~~ speak these things unto you ~~all things~~, **for the elect's sake.**

27 7 And ~~when ye~~ **you also** shall hear of wars, and rumors of wars; **see that ye** be ~~ye~~ not troubled; for ~~*such things*~~ **all I have told you** must ~~needs be~~ **come to pass,** but the end ~~*shall*~~ **is** not ~~*be*~~ yet.

28 Behold, I have told you before, wherefore if they shall say unto you, Behold, he is in the desert; go not forth; Behold, he is in the secret chambers; believe it not.

29 For as the light of the morning cometh out of the east, and shineth even unto the west, and covereth the whole earth, so shall also the coming of the Son of Man be.

30 And now I show unto you a parable. Behold, wheresoever the carcass is, there will the eagles be gathered together;

31 So likewise, shall mine elect be gathered from the four quarters of the earth.

32 And they shall hear of wars and rumors of wars. Behold, I speak

unto you for mine elect's sake.

33 8 For nation shall rise against nation, and kingdom against kingdom;

34 8 ~~and~~ There shall be ~~earthquakes in divers places, and there shall be~~ famines, and ~~troubles~~ **pestilences, and earthquakes in divers places.**

35 And again, because iniquity shall abound, the love of men shall wax cold; but he who shall not be overcome, the same shall be saved.

~~9 But take heed to yourselves: for they shall deliver you up to councils; and in the synagogues ye shall be beaten: and ye shall be brought before rulers and kings for my sake, for a testimony against them.~~

36 10 And ~~the~~ **again this** gospel **of the kingdom** ~~must first~~ **shall** be ~~published~~ **preached** ~~among~~ **in** all ~~nations~~ **the world, for a witness unto all nations, and then shall the end come, or the destruction of the wicked.**

~~11 But when they shall lead *you*, and deliver you up, take no thought beforehand what ye shall speak, neither do ye premeditate: but whatsoever shall be given you in that hour, that speak ye: for it is not ye that speak, but the Holy Ghost.~~

37 And again shall the abomination of desolation, spoken of by Daniel the prophet, be fulfilled.

38 24–25 ~~But in those days~~ **And immediately** after ~~that~~ **the** tribulation **of those days**, the sun shall be darkened, and the moon shall not give her light, and the stars ~~of heaven~~ shall fall **from heaven**, and the powers ~~that are in~~ **of** heaven shall be shaken.

39 30 Verily I say unto you, ~~that~~ This generation **in** which these **things shall be shown forth,** shall not pass **away** till all ~~these things~~ **I have told you shall** be **fulfilled** ~~done~~.

40 31 **Although the days will come that** heaven and earth shall pass away, ~~but~~ **yet** my words shall not pass away, **but all shall be fulfilled**.

41 And as I said before, After the tribulation of those days, and the powers of the heavens shall be shaken, then shall appear the sign of the Son of Man in heaven; and then shall all the tribes of the earth mourn;

42 26 And ~~then~~ **they** shall ~~they~~ see the Son of Man coming in the clouds **of heaven,** with ~~great~~ power and **great** glory.

43 And whoso treasureth up my words shall not be deceived.

44 27 ~~And then~~ **For the Son of Man shall come; and he** shall ~~he~~ send his angels **before him with the great sound of a trumpet,** and **they** shall gather together his elect from the four winds, from ~~the uttermost part of the earth to the uttermost part~~ **one end** of heaven **to the other**.

45 28 Now learn a parable of the fig tree. When ~~her~~ **his** ~~branch~~ **branches** ~~is~~ **are** yet tender, and putteth forth leaves, ye know that summer is ~~near~~ **nigh at hand**.

46 29 So ~~ye in like manner~~ **likewise, mine elect,** when ~~ye~~ **they** shall see **all** these things ~~come to pass,~~ **they shall** know that ~~it~~ **he** is ~~nigh~~ **near**, *even* at the doors.

47 32 But of that day and ~~that~~ hour **no one** knoweth ~~no man~~; no, not the angels ~~which are~~ **of God** in heaven, ~~neither the Son~~ but ~~the~~ **my** Father **only**.

~~33 Take ye heed, watch and pray: for ye know not when the time is.~~

~~34 *For the Son of man is* as a man taking a far journey, who left his house, and gave authority to his servants, and~~ ~~to every man his work, and commanded the porter to watch.~~

~~35 Watch ye therefore: for ye know not when the master of the house cometh, at even, or at midnight, or at the cockcrowing, or in the morning:~~

~~36 Lest coming suddenly he find you sleeping.~~

48 But as it was in the days of Noah, so it shall be also at the coming of the Son of Man; for it shall be with them as it was in the days which were before the flood.

49 Until the day that Noah entered into the ark, they were eating and drinking, marrying and giving in marriage, and knew not until the flood came and took them all away; so shall also the coming of the Son of Man be.

50 Then shall be fulfilled that which is written. That in the last days, two shall be in the field, one shall be taken and the other left.

51 Two shall be grinding at the mill; the one taken, and the other left.

52 37 And what I say unto ~~you~~ **one**, I say unto all **men**.

53 37 Watch **therefore, for ye know not at what hour your Lord doth come**.

54 But know this, if the goodman of the house had known in what watch the thief would come, he would have watched, and would not have suffered his house to have been broken up; but would have been ready.

55 Therefore, be ye also ready, for in such an hour as ye think not, the Son of Man cometh.

56 Who then is a faithful and wise servant, whom his lord hath made ruler over his household, to give them meat in due season?

57 Blessed is that servant whom his lord, when he cometh, shall find so doing.

58 And verily I say unto you, he shall make him ruler over all his goods.

59 But if that evil servant shall say in his heart, My lord delayeth his coming; and shall begin to smite his fellow servants, and to eat and drink with the drunken;

60 The lord of that servant shall come in a day when he looketh not for him, and in an hour that he is not aware of, and shall cut him asunder, and shall appoint him his portion with the hypocrites.

61 There shall be weeping and gnashing of teeth; and thus cometh the end.

CHAPTER 14

1 After two days was ~~the feast of~~ the passover, and **the feast** of unleavened bread.

2 1 And the chief priests, and the scribes, sought how they might take ~~him~~ **Jesus** by craft, and put *him* to death.

3 2 But they said **among themselves**, **Let us** not **take him** on the feast *day*, lest there be an uproar ~~of~~ **among** the people.

4 3 And **Jesus** being in Bethany, in the house of Simon the leper, as he sat at meat, there came a woman having an alabaster box of ointment of spikenard, very precious, and she brake the box, and poured ~~it~~ **the ointment** on his head.

5 4–5 And there were some **among the disciples** ~~that~~ **who** had indignation within themselves, and said, Why was this waste of the ointment made? for it might have been sold for more than three hundred pence, and have been given to the poor. And they murmured against her.

6 And Jesus said **unto them**, Let her alone; why trouble ye her? **For** she hath wrought a good work on me.

7 ~~For~~ Ye have the poor with you always, and whensoever ye will, ye may do them good; but me ye have not always.

8 She ~~hath~~ **has** done what she could, **and this which she has done unto me, shall be had in remembrance in generations to come, wheresoever my gospel shall be preached; for verily** she ~~is~~ **has** come ~~aforehand~~ **beforehand** to anoint my body to the burying.

9 Verily I say unto you, Wheresoever this gospel shall be preached throughout the whole world, ~~this also that~~ **what** she hath done shall be spoken of **also** for a memorial of her.

10 12 And **now** the first day of unleavened bread, when they killed the passover, his disciples said unto him, Where wilt thou that we go and prepare, that thou mayest eat the passover?

11 13 And he sendeth forth two of his disciples, and saith unto them, Go ye into the city, and there shall meet you a man bearing a pitcher of water: follow him.

12 14 And wheresoever he shall go in, say ye to the goodman of the house, The Master saith, Where is the guestchamber, where I shall eat the passover with my disciples?

13 15 And he will shew you a large upper room furnished *and* prepared: there make ready for us.

14 16 And his disciples went forth and came into the city, and found as he had said unto them: and they made ready the passover.

15 17 And in the evening he cometh with the twelve.

16 18 And as they sat and did eat, Jesus said, Verily I say unto you, One of you ~~which~~ **who** eateth with me shall betray me.

17 19 And they all began to be **very** sorrowful, and **began** to say unto him one by one, *Is* it I? and another *said, Is* it I?

18 20 And he answered and said unto them, *It is* one of the twelve ~~that~~ **who** dippeth with me in the dish.

19 21 The Son of man indeed goeth, as it is written of him: but woe to that man by whom the Son of man is betrayed! good were it for that man if he had never been born.

20 22 And as they did eat, Jesus took bread and blessed **it**, and brake ~~it~~, and gave to them, and said, Take **it, and** eat ~~this is my body~~.

21 Behold, this is for you to do in remembrance of my body; for as oft as ye do this ye will remember this hour that I was with you.

22 23 And he took the cup, and when he had given thanks, he gave *it* to them: and they all drank of it.

23 24 And he said unto them, This is **in remembrance of** my blood ~~of the new testament~~ which is shed for many**, and the new testament which I give unto you; for of me, ye shall bear record unto all the world.**

24 And as oft as ye do this ordinance, ye will remember me in this hour that I was with you and drank with you of this cup, even the last time in my ministry.

25 Verily I say unto you, **Of this ye shall bear record; for** I will **no more** drink ~~no more~~ of the fruit of the vine **with you**, until that day that I drink it new in the kingdom of God.

26 And now they were grieved, and wept over him.

27 26 And when they had sung an hymn, they went out into the mount of Olives.

28 27 And Jesus saith unto them, All ye shall be offended because of me this night: for it is written, I will smite the shepherd, and the sheep shall be scattered.

29 28 But after that I am risen, I will go before you ~~into~~ **unto** Galilee.

30 And he said unto Judas Iscariot, What thou doest, do quickly; but beware of innocent blood.

31 10 ~~And~~ **Nevertheless,** Judas Iscariot, **even** one of the twelve, went unto the chief priests to betray ~~him~~ **Jesus** unto them**; for he turned away from him, and was offended because of his words**.

32 11 And when ~~they~~ **the chief priests** heard ~~it~~ **of him** they were glad, and promised to give him money**;** and he sought how he might conveniently betray ~~him~~ **Jesus**.

33 29 But Peter said unto ~~him~~ **Jesus**, Although all **men** shall be offended **with thee**, yet I *will* ~~not I~~ **never be offended**.

34 30 And Jesus saith unto him, Verily I say unto thee, That this day, *even* in this night, before the cock crow twice, thou shalt deny me thrice.

35 31 But he spake the more vehemently, If I should die with thee, ~~I~~ **yet** will **I** not deny thee in any wise. Likewise also said they all.

36 32–33 And they came to a place which was named Gethsemane, **which was a garden; and the disciples** began to be sore amazed, and to be very heavy, **and to complain in their hearts, wondering if this be the Messiah.**

37 32 And ~~he~~ **Jesus knowing their hearts,** ~~saith~~ **said** to his disciples, Sit ye here, while I shall pray.

38 33–34 And he taketh with him, Peter, and James, and John, **and**

rebuked them, and ~~saith~~ said unto them, My soul is exceeding sorrowful, **even** unto death; tarry ye here and watch.

39 35 And he went forward a little, and fell on the ground, and prayed that, if it were possible, the hour might pass from him.

40 36 And he said, Abba, Father, all things *are* possible unto thee; take away this cup from me; nevertheless, not ~~what I~~ **my** will, but ~~what thou wilt~~ **thine** be done.

41 37 And he cometh, and findeth them sleeping, and saith unto Peter, Simon, sleepest thou? couldest not thou watch one hour?

42 38 Watch ye and pray, lest ye enter into temptation.

43 38 **And they said unto him,** The spirit truly *is* ready, but the flesh *is* weak.

44 39 And again he went away, and prayed, and spake the same words.

45 40 And when he returned, he found them asleep again, for their eyes were heavy; neither ~~wist~~ **knew** they what to answer him.

46 41 And he cometh **to them** the third time, and ~~saith~~ **said** unto them, Sleep on now and take ~~your~~ rest; it is enough, the hour is come; behold, the Son of Man is betrayed into the hands of sinners.

47 42 **And after they had finished their sleep, he said,** Rise up, let us go; lo, he ~~that~~ **who** betrayeth me is at hand.

48 43 And immediately, while he yet spake, cometh Judas, one of the twelve, and with him a great multitude with swords and staves, from the chief priests and the scribes and the elders.

49 44 And he ~~that~~ **who** betrayed him, had given them a token, saying,

Whomsoever I shall kiss, that same is he; take him, and lead *him* away safely.

50 45 And as soon as he was come, he goeth straightway to him, and saith, Master, master; and kissed him.

51 46 And they laid their hands on him, and took him.

52 47 And one of them, ~~that~~ **who** stood by, drew ~~a~~ **his** sword, and smote a servant of the high priest, and cut off his ear.

53 But Jesus commanded him to return his sword, saying, He who taketh the sword shall perish with the sword. And he put forth his finger and healed the servant of the high priest.

54 48 And Jesus answered and said unto them, Are ye come out as against a thief, with swords and ~~with~~ staves to take me?

55 49 I was daily with you in the temple teaching, and ye took me not: but the scriptures must be fulfilled.

56 50 And ~~they~~ **the disciples, when they heard this saying,** all forsook him and fled.

57 51–52 And there followed him a certain young man, **a disciple,** having a linen cloth cast about *his* naked *body*; and the young men laid hold on him, and he left the linen cloth and fled from them naked, **and saved himself out of their hands**.

58 53 And they led Jesus away to the high priest: and with him were assembled all the chief priests and the elders and the scribes.

59 54 And Peter followed him afar off, even ~~into~~ **unto** the palace of the high priest; and he sat with the servants, and warmed himself at the fire.

60 55 And the chief priests and all the council sought for witness against

Jesus, to put him to death, ~~and~~ **but** found none;

61 56 ~~For~~ **Though** many bare false witness against him, ~~but~~ **yet** their witness agreed not together.

62 57–58 And there arose certain **men** and bare false witness against him, saying, We heard him say, I will destroy this temple that is made with hands, and within three days I will build another made without hands;

63 59 But neither ~~so~~ did their witness agree together.

64 60 And the high priest stood up in the midst, and asked Jesus, saying,

65 60 Answerest thou nothing? **Knowest thou not** what ~~is it which~~ these witness against thee?

66 61 But he held his peace, and answered nothing.

67 61 Again the high priest asked him, and said unto him, Art thou the Christ, the Son of the Blessed?

68 62 And Jesus said, I am: and ye shall see the Son of man sitting on the right hand of power, and coming in the clouds of heaven.

69 63–64 Then the high priest rent his clothes and ~~saith~~ **said**, What need we any further witnesses? Ye have heard the blasphemy; what think ye?

70 64 And they all condemned him to be guilty of death.

71 65 And some began to spit on him, and to cover his face, and to buffet him, and to say unto him, Prophesy:

72 65 And the servants did strike him with the palms of their hands.

73 66 And as Peter was beneath in the palace, there cometh one of the maids of the high priest:

74 67 And when she saw Peter warming himself, she looked upon him and said, ~~And~~ Thou also wast with Jesus of Nazareth.

75 68 But he denied, saying, I know not, neither understand I what thou sayest.

76 68 And he went out into the porch; and the cock crew.

77 69 And a maid saw him again, and began to say to them ~~that~~ **who** stood by, This is *one* of them.

78 70 And he denied it again.

79 70–71 And a little after, they ~~that~~ **who** stood by, said again to Peter, Surely thou art *one* of them; for thou art a Galilean, ~~and~~ thy speech agreeth *thereto*. But he began to curse and to swear, *saying*, I know not this man of whom ye speak.

80 72 And the second time the cock crew.

81 72 And Peter called to mind the ~~word~~ **words** ~~that~~ **which** Jesus said unto him, Before the cock crow twice, thou shalt deny me thrice.

82 72 And ~~when~~ he ~~thought thereon~~ **went out, and fell upon his face, and** ~~he~~ wept **bitterly**.

CHAPTER 15

1 And straightway in the morning the chief priests held a consultation with the elders and scribes;

2 1 And the whole council **condemned him**, and bound ~~Jesus~~ **him**, and carried *him* away, and delivered *him* to Pilate.

3 2 And Pilate asked him, Art thou the King of the Jews?

4 2 And ~~he~~ **Jesus** answering, said unto him, **I am, even as** thou sayest ~~it~~.

5 3 And the chief priests accused him of many things: but he answered nothing.

6 4 And Pilate asked him again, saying, Answerest thou nothing? behold how many things they witness against thee.

7 5 But Jesus yet answered nothing; so that Pilate marvelled.

8 6 Now **it was common** at ~~that~~ the feast**, for** ~~he~~ **Pilate to** ~~released~~ **release** unto them one prisoner, whomsoever they desired.

9 7 And there was ~~one~~ **a man** named Barabbas, ~~which lay~~ **bound** with them ~~that~~ **who** had made insurrection with him, who had committed murder in the insurrection.

10 8 And the multitude**,** crying aloud**,** began to desire *him to* ~~do as he had ever done~~ **deliver Jesus** unto them.

11 9 But Pilate answered **unto** them, saying, Will ye that I release unto you the King of the Jews?

12 10 For he knew that the chief priests had delivered him for envy.

13 11 But the chief priests moved the people that he should rather release Barabbas unto them**, as he had before done unto them**.

14 12 And Pilate ~~answered~~ **spake again** and said ~~again~~ unto them, What will ye then that I shall do ~~unto~~ **with** *him* whom ye call the King of the Jews?

15 13 And they cried out again, **Deliver him unto us to be crucified. Away with him.** Crucify him.

16 14 Then Pilate said unto them, Why, what evil hath he done?

17 14 ~~And~~ **But** they cried out the more exceedingly, Crucify him.

18 15 And ~~so~~ **now** Pilate, willing to content the people, released Barabbas unto them, and delivered Jesus, when he had scourged *him*, to be crucified.

19 16 And the soldiers led him away into the hall, called Praetorium; and they call together the whole band.

20 17 And they clothed him with purple, and platted a crown of thorns, and put it about his *head*,

21 18 And began to salute him, **Saying,** Hail, King of the Jews**.**

22 19 And they smote him on the head with a reed, and did spit upon him, and bowing *their* knees worshipped him.

23 20 And when they had mocked him, they took off the purple from him, and put his own clothes on him, and led him out to crucify him.

24 21 And they ~~compel~~ **compelled** one Simon**,** a Cyrenian, who passed by, coming out of the country, the father of Alexander and Rufus, to bear his cross.

25 22 And they bring him unto the place **called** Golgotha, which is, (being interpreted,) The place of a ~~skull~~ **burial**.

26 23 And they gave him to drink**,** ~~wine~~ **vinegar** mingled with ~~myrrh~~ **gall;** ~~but~~ **and when he had tasted the vinegar,** he ~~received~~ *~~it~~* **would** not **drink**.

27 24 And when they had crucified him, they parted his garments, casting lots upon them, what every man should take.

28 25 And it was the third hour, ~~and~~ **when** they crucified him.

29 26 And **Pilate wrote** ~~the superscription of~~ his accusation ~~was written over~~ **and put it upon the cross**, THE KING OF THE JEWS.

30 There were certain of the chief priests who stood by, and˙ said unto Pilate, Write, that he said, I am the King of the Jews.

31 But Pilate said unto them, What I have written, I have written.

32 27 And with him they ~~crucify~~ **crucified** two thieves**,** the one on his right hand, and the other on his left.

33 28 And the scripture was fulfilled, which saith, And he was numbered with the transgressors.

34 29–30 And they ~~that~~ **who** passed by railed on him, wagging their heads, and saying, Ah, thou ~~that~~ **who** destroyest the temple and buildest *it* in three days, save thyself, and come down from the cross.

35 31 Likewise also the chief priests mocking said among themselves with the scribes, He saved others; himself he cannot save.

36 32 Let Christ the King of Israel descend now from the cross, that we may see and believe.

37 32 And ~~they~~ **one of them** ~~that~~ **who** ~~were~~ **was** crucified with him, reviled him **also, saying, If thou art the Christ, save thyself and us.**

38 33 And when the sixth hour was come, there was darkness over the whole land until the ninth hour.

39 34 And at the ninth hour Jesus cried with a loud voice, saying, Eloi, Eloi, lama sabachthani? which is, being interpreted, My God, my God, why hast thou forsaken me?

40 35 And some of them ~~that~~ **who** stood by, when they heard ~~it~~ **him**, said, Behold, he calleth Elias.

41 36 And one ran and filled a ~~spunge~~ **sponge** full of vinegar, and put *it* on a reed and gave him to drink; **others spake,** saying, Let **him** alone; let us see whether Elias will come to take him down.

42 37 And Jesus cried with a loud voice, and gave up the ghost.

43 38 And the veil of the temple was rent in twain from the top to the bottom.

44 39 And when the centurion ~~which~~ **who** stood over against him, saw that he so cried out and gave up the ghost, he said, Truly, this man ~~was~~ **is** the Son of God.

45 40–41 There were also women looking on afar off, among whom was Mary Magdalene, and Mary the ~~less~~ **younger,** and of Joses, and Salome; who also when he was in Galilee, followed him and ministered unto him; and many other women ~~which~~ **who** came ~~up~~ with him unto Jerusalem.

46 42 And now, when the even was come; because it was the preparation **day**, that is the day before the Sabbath,

47 43–44 Joseph of ~~Arimathaea~~ **Arimathea**, an honorable counsellor, ~~which~~ **who** also waited for the kingdom of God, came and went in boldly unto Pilate, and craved the body of Jesus. And Pilate marveled, **and asked** if he were already dead.

48 44 And calling ~~unto him~~ the centurion, he asked him, ~~whether~~ **if** he had been any while dead?

49 45 And when he knew *it* of the centurion, he gave the body to Joseph.

50 46 And ~~he~~ **Joseph** bought fine linen, and took him down, and wrapped him in the linen, and laid him in a sepulchre which was hewn out of a rock, and rolled a stone unto the door of the sepulchre.

51 47 And Mary Magdalene and Mary *the mother* of Joses beheld where he was laid.

CHAPTER 16

1 And when the Sabbath was past, Mary Magdalene, and Mary the *mother* of James and Salome, ~~had~~ bought sweet spices, that they might come and anoint him.

2 2–3 And very early in the morning the first *day* of the week, they came unto the sepulchre at the rising of the sun. And they said among themselves, Who shall roll us away the stone from the door of the sepulchre?

3 4–5 ~~And~~ **But** when they looked,

they saw that the stone was rolled away, (for it was very great,) ~~And entering into the sepulchre, they saw a young man~~ **and two angels** sitting ~~on the right side~~ **thereon**, clothed in ~~a~~ long white ~~garment~~ **garments**; and they were affrighted.

4 6 ~~And~~ **But** ~~he~~ **the angels** ~~saith~~ **said** unto them, Be not affrighted; ye seek Jesus of Nazareth, ~~which~~ **who** was crucified; he is risen; he is not here; behold the place where they laid him;

5 7 ~~But~~ **And** go your way, tell his disciples and Peter, that he goeth before you into Galilee; there shall ye see him as he said unto you.

6 And they, entering into the sepulchre, saw the place where they laid Jesus.

7 8 And they went out quickly, and fled from the sepulchre; for they trembled and were amazed: neither said they any thing to any *man*; for they were afraid.

8 9 Now when *Jesus* was risen, early **on** the first *day* of the week, he appeared first to Mary Magdalene, out of whom he had cast seven devils;

9 10 *And* she went and told them ~~that~~ **who** had been with him, as they mourned and wept.

10 11 And they, when they had heard that he was alive, and had been seen of her, believed not.

11 12 After that he appeared in another form unto two of them, as they walked, and went into the country.

12 13 And they went and told *it* unto the residue: neither believed they them.

13 14 Afterward he appeared unto the eleven as they sat at meat, and upbraided them with their unbelief and hardness of heart, because they believed not them which had seen him after he was risen.

14 15 And he said unto them, Go ye into all the world, and preach the gospel to every creature.

15 16 He that believeth and is baptized shall be saved; but he that believeth not shall be damned.

16 17 And these signs shall follow them that believe;

17 In my name shall they cast out devils; they shall speak with new tongues;

18 They shall take up serpents; and if they drink any deadly thing, it shall not hurt them;

19 18 They shall lay hands on the sick, and they shall recover.

20 19 So then after the Lord had spoken unto them, he was received up into heaven, and sat on the right hand of God.

21 20 And they went forth, and preached every where, the Lord working with *them*, and confirming the word with signs following. Amen.

The Testimony of
SAINT LUKE

CHAPTER 1

1 ~~Forasmuch~~ As **I am a messenger of Jesus Christ, and knowing that** many have taken in hand to set forth in order a declaration of those things which are most surely believed among us;

2 Even as they delivered them unto us, ~~which~~ **who** from the beginning were eyewitnesses and ministers of the word;

3 It seemed good to me also, having had perfect understanding of all things from the very first, to write unto thee in order, most excellent Theophilus,

4 That thou mightest know the certainty of those things, wherein thou hast been instructed.

5 There was in the days of Herod, the king of ~~Judaea~~ **Judea**, a certain priest named Zacharias, of the course of Abia; and his wife *was* **being** of the daughters of Aaron, and her name *was* ~~Elisabeth~~ **Elizabeth**,

6 ~~And they~~ Were both righteous before God, walking in all the commandments and ordinances of the Lord blameless;

7 And they had no child. ~~because that Elisabeth~~ **Elizabeth** was barren, and they ~~both~~ were *now* **both** well stricken in years.

8 And ~~it came to pass, that~~ while he executed the priest's office before God, in the order of his ~~course~~ **priesthood**,

9 According to the ~~custom of the priest's office~~ **law**, (his lot was to burn incense when he went into the temple of the Lord,)

10 ~~And~~ The whole multitude of the people were praying without at the time of incense.

11 And there appeared unto him an angel of the Lord standing on the right side of the altar of incense.

12 And when Zacharias saw ~~him~~ **the angel**, he was troubled and fear fell upon him.

13 But the angel said unto him, Fear not, Zacharias: for thy prayer is heard; and thy wife Elisabeth shall bear thee a son, and thou shalt call his name John.

14 ~~And~~ Thou shalt have joy and gladness, and many shall rejoice at his birth;

15 For he shall be great in the sight of the Lord, and shall drink neither wine nor strong drink; and he shall be filled with the Holy Ghost, even from his mother's womb.

16 And many of the children of Israel shall he turn to the Lord their God.

17 And he shall go before ~~him~~ **the Lord** in the spirit and power of Elias, to turn the hearts of the fathers to the children, and the disobedient to the wisdom of the just, to make ready a people prepared for the Lord.

18 And Zacharias said unto the angel, Whereby shall I know this? for I am an old man, and my wife **is** well stricken in years.

19 And the angel answering, said unto him, I am Gabriel, ~~that~~ **who** stand in the presence of God, and am sent to speak unto thee, and to show thee these glad tidings.

20 And, behold, thou shalt be dumb, and not able to speak, until the day

that these things shall be performed, because thou believest not my words, which shall be fulfilled in their season.

21 And the people waited for Zacharias, and marvelled that he tarried so long in the temple.

22 And when he came out, he could not speak unto them: and they perceived that he had seen a vision in the temple: for he beckoned unto them, and remained speechless.

23 And ~~it came to pass, that~~ as soon as the days of his ministration were accomplished, he departed to his own house.

24 And after those days his wife Elisabeth conceived, and hid herself five months, saying,

25 Thus hath the Lord dealt with me in the days wherein he looked on *me*, to take away my reproach **from** among men.

26 And in the sixth month the angel Gabriel was sent from God unto a city of Galilee, named Nazareth,

27 To a virgin espoused to a man whose name was Joseph, of the house of David; and the virgin's name *was* Mary.

28 And the angel came in unto her**,** and said, Hail, *thou ~~that~~* **virgin, who** *art* highly favored **of the Lord.** The Lord *is* with thee**,** ~~blessed *art*~~ **for** thou **art chosen and blessed** among women.

29 And when she saw ~~*him*~~ **the angel**, she was troubled at his saying, and ~~cast~~ **pondered** in her mind what manner of salutation this should be.

30 And the angel said unto her, Fear not, Mary: for thou hast found favour with God.

31 And behold, thou shalt conceive ~~in thy womb~~, and bring forth a son, and ~~shalt~~ **shall** call his name JESUS.

32 He shall be great, and shall be called the Son of the Highest: and the Lord God shall give unto him the throne of his father David:

33 And he shall reign over the house of Jacob for ever; and of his kingdom there shall be no end.

34 Then said Mary unto the angel**;** How ~~shall~~ **can** this be ~~seeing I know not a man~~?

35 And the angel answered and said unto her, **Of** the Holy Ghost ~~shall come upon thee~~, and the power of the Highest ~~shall overshadow thee.~~ Therefore also, that holy ~~thing which~~ **child that** shall be born of thee shall be called the Son of God.

36 And behold, thy cousin ~~Elisabeth~~ **Elizabeth**, she hath also conceived a son**,** in her old age**;** and this is the sixth month with her who ~~was~~ **is** called barren.

37 For with God nothing ~~shall~~ **can** be impossible.

38 And Mary said, Behold the handmaid of the Lord; be it unto me according to thy word. And the angel departed from her.

39 And ~~Mary arose~~ in those days, ~~and~~ **Mary** went into the hill country with haste, into a city of ~~Juda~~ **Judea,**

40 And entered into the house of Zacharias, and saluted Elisabeth.

41 And it came to pass, that, when Elisabeth heard the salutation of Mary, the babe leaped in her womb;

42 41–42 And Elisabeth was filled with the Holy Ghost: and she spake out with a loud voice, and said, Blessed *art* thou among women, and blessed *is* the fruit of thy womb.

43 43–44 And ~~whence~~ **why** *is* **it, that** this ~~to~~ **blessing is upon** me, that the mother of my Lord should come to me? For lo, as soon as the voice of thy salutation sounded in mine ears, the babe leaped in my womb for joy.

44 45 And blessed ~~is she that~~ **art thou who** believed**,** for ~~there shall be a performance of~~ those things which were told ~~her~~ **thee** ~~from~~ **by the angel of** the Lord**, shall be fulfilled**.

45 46 And Mary said, My soul doth magnify the Lord,

46 47 And my spirit ~~hath rejoiced~~ **rejoiceth** in God my Savior.

47 48 For he hath regarded the low estate of his handmaiden: for, behold, from henceforth all generations shall call me blessed.

48 49 For he ~~that~~ **who** is mighty hath done to me great things; and ~~holy is~~ **I will magnify** his **holy** name,

49 50 ~~And~~ **For** his mercy ~~is~~ on ~~them~~ **those** ~~that~~ **who** fear him from generation to generation.

50 51 He hath shewed strength with his arm; he hath scattered the proud in the imagination of their hearts.

51 52 He hath put down the mighty from *their* **high** seats**;** and exalted them of low degree.

52 53 He hath filled the hungry with good things; ~~and~~ **but** the rich he hath sent empty away.

53 54 He hath ~~holpen~~ **helped** his servant Israel in remembrance of ~~his~~ mercy,

54 55 As he spake to our fathers, to Abraham, and to his seed for ever.

55 56 And Mary abode with ~~her~~ **Elizabeth** about three months, and returned to her own house.

56 57 **And** now ~~Elisabeth's~~ **Elizabeth's** full time came that she should be delivered; and she brought forth a son.

57 58 And her neighbours and her cousins heard how the Lord had shewed great mercy upon her; and they rejoiced with her.

58 59 And it came to pass, that on the eighth day they came to circumcise the child; and they called him Zacharias, after the name of his father.

59 60 And his mother answered and said, Not *so*; but he shall be called John.

60 61 And they said unto her, There is none of thy kindred that is called by this name.

61 62 And they made signs to his father, **and asked him** how he would have him called.

62 63 And he asked for a writing table, and wrote, saying, His name is John**,** and they **all** marveled ~~all~~.

63 64 And his mouth was opened immediately, and ~~his tongue loosed, and~~ he spake **with his tongue**, and praised God.

64 65 And fear came on all ~~that~~ **who** dwelt round about them**.** And all these sayings were noised abroad throughout all the hill country of ~~Judaea~~ **Judea**.

65 66 And all they that heard *them* laid *them* up in their hearts, saying, What manner of child shall this be! And the hand of the Lord was with him.

66 67 And his father Zacharias was filled with the Holy Ghost, and prophesied, saying,

67 68 Blessed *be* the Lord God of Israel; for he hath visited and redeemed his people,

68 69 And hath raised up an horn of salvation for us in the house of his servant David;

69 70 As he spake by the mouth of his holy prophets, ~~which have been~~ **ever** since the world began**,**

70 71 That we should be saved from our enemies, and from the hand of all ~~that~~ **those˚ who** hate us;

71 72 To perform the mercy *promised*

to our fathers, and to remember his holy covenant;

72 73 The oath which he sware to our father Abraham,

73 74 That he would grant unto us, that we being delivered out of the hand of our enemies might serve him without fear,

74 75 In holiness and righteousness before him, all the days of our ~~life~~ **lives**.

75 76 And thou, child, shalt be called the prophet of the Highest: for thou shalt go before the face of the Lord to prepare his ways;

76 77 To give knowledge of salvation unto his people, by **baptism for** the remission of their sins,

77 78 Through the tender mercy of our God; whereby the dayspring from on high hath visited us,

78 79 To give light to them ~~that~~ **who** sit in darkness and ~~in~~ the shadow of death; to guide our feet into the way of peace.

79 80 And the child grew, and waxed strong in spirit, and was in the deserts till the day of his shewing unto Israel.

CHAPTER 2

1 And it came to pass in those days, that there went out a decree from Caesar Augustus, that all ~~the world~~ **his empire** should be taxed.

2 ~~And~~ This **same** taxing was ~~first made~~ when Cyrenius was governor of Syria.

3 And all went to be taxed, everyone ~~into~~ **in** his own city.

4 And Joseph also went up from Galilee, out of the city of Nazareth, into Judaea, unto the city of David, which is called Bethlehem; (because he was of the house and lineage of David:)

5 To be taxed, with Mary his es-poused wife, **she** being great with child.

6 And so it was, that, while they were there, the days were accomplished that she should be delivered.

7 And she brought forth her first-born son, and wrapped him in swaddling clothes, and laid him in a manger, because there was ~~no~~ **none to give** room for them in the ~~inn~~ **inns**.

8 And there were in the same country, shepherds abiding in the field, keeping watch over their ~~flock~~ **flocks** by night.

9 And lo, ~~the~~ **an** angel of the Lord ~~came upon~~ **appeared unto** them, and the glory of the Lord shone round about them; and they were sore afraid.

10 ~~And~~ **But** the angel said unto them, Fear not, for behold, I bring you good tidings of great joy, which shall be to all people.

11 For unto you is born this day, in the city of David, a Savior, ~~which~~ **who** is Christ the Lord.

12 And this ~~shall be a sign unto you~~ **is the way** ~~Ye~~ **you** shall find the babe, **he is** wrapped in swaddling clothes, **and is** lying in a manger.

13 And suddenly there was with the angel a multitude of the heavenly host praising God, and saying,

14 Glory to God in the highest; and on earth, peace; goodwill ~~toward~~ **to** men.

15 And it came to pass, ~~as~~ **when** the angels were gone away from them into heaven, the shepherds said one to another, Let us now go, even unto Bethlehem, and see this thing which is come to pass, which the Lord ~~hath~~ **has** made known unto us.

16 And they came with haste, and found Mary, and Joseph, and the babe lying in a manger.

17 And when they had seen ~~it~~, they made known abroad the saying which was told them concerning this child.

18 ~~And~~ All they ~~that~~ **who** heard *it*, wondered at those things which were told them by the shepherds;

19 But Mary kept all these things, and pondered *them* in her heart.

20 And the shepherds returned, glorifying and praising God for all the things ~~that~~ **which** they had heard and seen, as ~~it was told~~ **they were manifested** unto them.

21 And when eight days were accomplished for the circumcising of the child, his name was called Jesus; which was so named of the angel, before he was conceived ~~in the womb~~.

22 And when the days of her purification according to the law of Moses were accomplished, they brought him to Jerusalem, to present *him* to the Lord;

23 As it is written in the law of the Lord, Every male ~~that~~ **which** openeth the womb shall be called holy to the Lord;

24 And to offer a sacrifice according to that which is ~~said~~ **written** in the law of the Lord, A pair of turtledoves, or two young pigeons.

25 And behold, there was a man ~~in~~ **at** Jerusalem, whose name *was* Simeon; and the same man *was* just and devout, waiting for the consolation of Israel; and the Holy Ghost was upon him.

26 And it was revealed unto him by the Holy Ghost, that he should not see death, before he had seen the Lord's Christ.

27 And he came by the Spirit into the temple; and when the parents brought in the child, **even** Jesus, to do for him after the custom of the law,

28 Then took he him up in his arms, and blessed God, and said,

29 Lord, now lettest ~~thou~~ thy servant depart in peace, according to thy word;

30 For mine eyes have seen thy salvation,

31 Which thou hast prepared before the face of all people;

32 A light to lighten the Gentiles, and the glory of thy people Israel.

33 And Joseph, and ~~his mother~~ **Mary**, marveled at those things which were spoken of ~~him~~ **the child**.

34 And Simeon blessed them, and said unto Mary ~~his mother~~, Behold, this *child* is set for the fall and rising again of many in Israel; and for a sign which shall be spoken against;

35 Yea, a ~~sword~~ **spear** shall pierce through ~~thy~~ **him to the wounding of thine** own soul also; that the thoughts of many hearts may be revealed.

36 And there was one Anna, a prophetess, the daughter of Phanuel, of the tribe of ~~Aser~~ **Asher.** She was of ~~a~~ great age, and had lived with ~~an~~ **a** husband **only** seven years ~~from her virginity~~, **whom she married in her youth,**

37 And she ~~was~~ **lived** a widow ~~of~~ about fourscore and four years, ~~which~~ **who** departed not from the temple, but served *God* with fastings and prayers, night and day.

38 And she, coming in that instant, gave thanks likewise unto the Lord, and spake of him, to all ~~them~~ **those** ~~that~~ **who** looked for redemption in Jerusalem.

39 And when they had performed all things according to the law of the Lord, they returned into Galilee, to their own city Nazareth.

40 And the child grew, and waxed strong in spirit, **being** filled with wisdom, and the grace of God was upon him.

41 Now his parents went to Jerusalem every year at the feast of the passover.

42 And when he was twelve years old, they went up to Jerusalem, after the custom, ~~of~~ **to** the feast.

43 And when they had fulfilled the days, as they returned, the child Jesus tarried behind, in Jerusalem; and Joseph and his mother knew not ~~of it~~ **that he tarried**;

44 But they, supposing him to have been in the company, went a day's journey; and they sought him among ~~their kinsfolk~~ **his kindred** and acquaintance.

45 And when they found him not, they turned back again to Jerusalem, seeking him.

46 And it came to pass, ~~that~~ after three days they found him in the temple, sitting in the midst of the doctors, ~~both~~ **and they were** hearing ~~them~~ **him**, and asking ~~them~~ **him** questions.

47 And all ~~that~~ **who** heard him were astonished at his understanding, and answers.

48 And when ~~they~~ **his parents** saw him, they were amazed; and his mother said unto him, Son, why hast thou thus dealt with us? Behold, thy father and I have sought thee sorrowing.

49 And he said unto them, ~~How~~ **Why** is it that ye sought me? ~~wist~~ **Know** ye not that I must be about my Father's business?

50 And they understood not the saying which he spake unto them.

51 And he went down with them, and came to Nazareth, and was subject unto them. ~~but~~ **And** his mother kept all these sayings in her heart.

52 And Jesus increased in wisdom and stature, and in favour with God and man.

CHAPTER 3

1 1–2 Now in the fifteenth year of the reign of Tiberius Caesar, Pontius Pilate being governor of Judaea, and Herod being tetrarch of Galilee, and his brother Philip tetrarch of Ituraea and of the region of Trachonitis, and Lysanias the tetrarch of Abilene, Annas and Caiaphas being the high priests,

2 **Now in this same year,** the word of God came unto John, the son of Zacharias, in the wilderness.

3 And he came into all the country about Jordan, preaching the baptism of repentance for the remission of sins;

4 As it is written in the book of the ~~words of~~ **prophet** Esaias ~~the prophet~~; **and these are the words,** saying, The voice of one crying in the wilderness, Prepare ye the way of the Lord, and make his paths straight.

5 For behold, and lo, he shall come, as it is written in the book of the prophets, to take away the sins of the world, and to bring salvation unto the heathen nations, to gather together those who are lost, who are of the sheepfold of Israel;

6 Yea, even the dispersed and afflicted; and also to prepare the way, and make possible the preaching of the gospel unto the Gentiles;

7 And to be a light unto all who sit in darkness, unto the uttermost parts of the earth; to bring to pass the resurrection from the dead, and to ascend up on high, to dwell on the right hand of the Father,

8 Until the fullness of time, and the law and the testimony shall be sealed, and the keys of the kingdom shall be delivered up again unto the Father;

9 To administer justice unto all; to come down in judgment upon all, and to convince all the ungodly of their ungodly deeds, which they have committed; and all this in the day that he shall come;

10 5 **For it is a day of power;** yea, every valley shall be filled, and every mountain and hill shall be brought low; ~~and~~ the crooked shall be made straight, and the rough ways ~~shall be~~ made smooth;

11 6 And all flesh shall see the salvation of God.

12 7 Then said ~~he~~ **John** to the multitude that came forth to be baptized of him, **crying against them with a loud voice, saying,** O generation of vipers, who hath warned you to flee from the wrath to come?

13 8 Bring forth therefore fruits worthy of repentance, and begin not to say within yourselves, ~~We have~~ Abraham ~~to~~ *is* our father; **we have kept the commandments of God, and none can inherit the promises but the children of Abraham;** for I say unto you, That God is able of these stones to raise up children unto Abraham.

14 9 And now also, the axe is laid unto the root of the trees; every tree therefore which bringeth not forth good fruit, ~~is~~ **shall be** hewn down, and cast into the fire.

15 10 And the people asked him, saying, What shall we do then?

16 11 He ~~answereth~~ **answered** and ~~saith~~ **said** unto them, He ~~that~~ **who** hath two coats, let him impart to him that hath none; and he that hath meat, let him do likewise.

17 12 Then came also publicans to be baptized, and said unto him, Master, what shall we do?

18 13 And he said unto them, Exact no more than that which is appointed unto you.

19 For it is well known unto you, Theophilus, that after the manner of the Jews, and according to the custom of their law in receiving money into the treasury, that out of the abundance which was received, was appointed unto the poor, every man his portion;

20 And after this manner did the publicans also, wherefore John said unto them, Exact no more than that which is appointed you.

21 14 And the soldiers likewise demanded of him, saying, And what shall we do? And he said unto them, Do violence to no man, neither accuse *any* falsely; and be content with your wages.

22 15 And as the people were in expectation, and all men mused in their hearts of John, whether he were the Christ, or not;

23 16 John answered, saying unto ~~them~~ all, I indeed baptize you with water, but ~~one mightier than I~~ **there** cometh **one mightier than I**, the latchet of whose shoes I am not worthy to unloose, he shall baptize you with the Holy Ghost, and with fire;

24 17 Whose fan *is* in his hand, and he will ~~throughly~~ **thoroughly** purge his floor, and will gather the wheat into his garner; but the chaff he will burn with fire unquenchable.

25 18 And many other things in his exhortation preached he unto the people.

26 19 But Herod, the tetrarch, being reproved ~~by~~ **of** him for Herodias, his brother Philip's wife, and for all the evils which Herod had done;

27 20 Added yet this above all, that he shut up John in prison.

28 21 Now when all the people were

baptized, it came to pass that Jesus also **came unto John; and** being baptized **of him**, and praying, the heaven was opened;

29 22 And the Holy Ghost descended, in ~~a~~ bodily shape like a dove, upon him; and a voice came from heaven, which said, Thou art my beloved Son, in thee I am well pleased.

30 23 And Jesus himself began to be about thirty years of age, **having lived with his father,** being, as was supposed **of the world,** the son of Joseph, ~~which~~ **who** was **from** *the son* **loins** of Heli,

31 24 ~~Which~~ **Who** was **from** *the son* **loins** of Matthat, ~~which~~ **who** was *the son* of Levi, ~~which~~ **who** was ~~*the son*~~ **a descendant** of Melchi, **and** ~~which was the son~~ of Janna, ~~which was the son~~ **and** of Joseph,

32 25 ~~Which was the son~~ **And** of Mattathias, ~~which was the son~~ **and** of Amos, ~~which was the son~~ **and** of Naum, ~~which was the son~~ **and** of Esli, ~~which was the son~~ **and** of Nagge,

33 26 ~~Which was the son~~ **And** of Maath ~~which was the son~~ **and** of Mattathias, ~~which was the son~~ **and** of Semei, ~~which was the son~~ **and** of Joseph, ~~which was the son~~ **and** of Juda,

34 27 ~~Which was the son~~ **And** of Joanna, ~~which was the son~~ **and** of ~~Rhesa~~ **Resa**, ~~which was the son~~ **and** of Zorobabel, ~~which was the son~~ **and** of Salathiel, ~~which~~ **who** was *the son* of Neri,

35 28 ~~Which~~ **Who** was ~~*the son*~~ **a descendant** of Melchi, ~~which was the son~~ **and** of Addi, ~~which was the son~~ **and** of Cosam, ~~which was the son~~ **and** of Elmodam, ~~which was the son~~ **and** of Er,

36 29 ~~Which was the son~~ **And** of Jose, ~~which was the son~~ **and** of Eliezer, ~~which was the son~~ **and** of ~~Jorim~~ **Joram**,

~~which was the son~~ **and** of Matthat, ~~which was the son~~ **and** of Levi,

37 30 ~~Which was the son~~ **And** of Simeon, ~~which was the son~~ **and** of Juda, ~~which was the son~~ **and** of Joseph, ~~which was the son~~ **and** of Jonan, ~~which was the son~~ **and** of Eliakim,

38 31 ~~Which was the son~~ **And** of Melea, ~~which was the son~~ **and** of Menan, ~~which was the son~~ **and** of Mattatha, ~~which was the son~~ **and** of Nathan, ~~which was the son~~ **and** of David,

39 32 ~~Which was the son~~ **And** of Jesse, ~~which was the son~~ **and** of Obed, ~~which was the son~~ **and** of Booz, ~~which was the son~~ **and** of Salmon, ~~which was the son~~ **and** of Naasson,

40 33 ~~Which was the son~~ **And** of Aminadab, ~~which was the son~~ **and** of Aram, ~~which was the son~~ **and** of Esrom, ~~which was the son~~ **and** of Phares, ~~which was the son~~ **and** of Juda,

41 34 ~~Which was the son~~ **And** of Jacob, ~~which was the son~~ **and** of Isaac, ~~which was the son~~ **and** of Abraham, ~~which was the son~~ **and** of Thara, ~~which was the son~~ **and** of Nachor,

42 35 ~~Which was the son~~ **And** of Saruch, ~~which was the son~~ **and** of Ragau, ~~which was the son~~ **and** of Phalec, ~~which was the son~~ **and** of Heber, ~~which was the son~~ **and** of Sala,

43 36 ~~Which was the son~~ **And** of Cainan, ~~which was the son~~ **and** of Arphaxad, ~~which was the son~~ **and** of ~~Sem~~ **Shem**, ~~which was the son~~ **and** of ~~Noe~~ **Noah**, ~~which was the son~~ **and** of Lamech,

44 37 ~~Which was the son~~ **And** of Mathusala, ~~which was the son~~ **and** of Enoch, ~~which was the son~~ **and** of Jared, ~~which was the son~~ **and** of Maleleel, ~~which was the son~~ **and** of Cainan,

45 38 ~~Which was the son~~ **And** of Enos, ~~which was the son~~ **and** of Seth,

~~which was the son~~ **and** of Adam, ~~which~~ **who** was ~~the son~~ **formed** of God, **and the first man upon the earth.**

CHAPTER 4

1 And Jesus being full of the Holy Ghost returned from Jordan, and was led by the Spirit into the wilderness,

2 ~~Being~~ **And after** forty days, ~~tempted of~~ the devil **came unto him, to tempt him**. And in those days, he did eat nothing; and when they were ended, he ~~afterward~~ **afterwards** hungered.

3 And the devil said unto him, If thou be the Son of God, command this stone that it be made bread.

4 And Jesus answered him, saying, It is written, That man shall not live by bread alone, but by every word of God.

5 And the ~~devil, taking~~ **Spirit taketh** him up into ~~an~~ **a** high mountain, ~~shewed unto him~~ **and he beheld** all the kingdoms of the world, in a moment of time.

6 And the devil ~~said~~ **came** unto him, **and said unto him,** All this power will I give **unto** thee, and the glory of them; for ~~that is~~ **they are** delivered unto me, and to whomsoever I will, I give ~~it~~ **them**.

7 If thou therefore wilt worship me, all shall be thine.

8 ~~And~~ Jesus answered and said unto him, Get thee behind me, Satan; for it is written, Thou shalt worship the Lord thy God, and him only shalt thou serve.

9 And ~~he~~ **the Spirit** brought him to Jerusalem, and set him on a pinnacle of the temple. **And the devil came unto him,** and said unto him, If thou be the Son of God, cast thyself down from hence;

10 10–11 For it is written, He shall give his angels charge over thee, to keep thee; and in ~~their~~ **his** hands they shall bear thee up, lest at any time thou dash thy foot against a stone.

11 12 And Jesus answering, said unto him, It is ~~said~~ **written**, Thou shalt not tempt the Lord thy God.

12 13 And when the devil had ended all the temptation, he departed from him for a season.

13 14 And Jesus returned in the power of the Spirit into Galilee:

14 And there went out a fame of him through all the region round about.

15 And he taught in their synagogues, being glorified of all **who believed on his name**.

16 And he came to Nazareth, where he had been brought up; and as his custom was he went into the synagogue on the Sabbath day, and stood up ~~for~~ to read.

17 And there was delivered unto him the book of the prophet Esaias. And when he had opened the book, he found the place where it was written,

18 The Spirit of the Lord *is* upon me, because he hath anointed me to preach the gospel to the poor; he hath sent me to heal the brokenhearted, to preach deliverance to the captives, and **the** recovering of sight to the blind; to set at liberty them that are bruised;

19 To preach the acceptable year of the Lord.

20 And he closed the book, and he gave *it* again to the minister, and **he** sat down.

21 20–21 And the eyes of all ~~them~~ **those** ~~that~~ **who** were in the synagogue, were fastened on him, And he began to say unto them, This day is this scripture fulfilled in your ears.

22 And all bare him witness, and wondered at the gracious words which

proceeded out of his mouth. And they said, Is not this Joseph's son?

23 And he said unto them, Ye will surely say unto me this proverb, Physician, heal thyself. Whatsoever we have heard **was** done in Capernaum, do also here in thy country.

24 And he said, Verily I say unto you, No prophet is accepted in his own country.

25 But I tell you ~~of a~~ **the** truth, many widows were in Israel in the days of Elias, when the heaven was shut up three years and six months, ~~when~~ **and** great famine was throughout all the land;

26 But unto none of them was Elias sent, save unto Sarepta, ~~a city~~ of Sidon, unto a woman ~~that~~ **who** *was* a widow.

27 And many lepers were in Israel, in the time of Eliseus the prophet; and none of them ~~was~~ **were** cleansed, ~~saving~~ **save** Naaman the Syrian.

28 And all they in the synagogue, when they heard these things, were filled with wrath,

29 And rose up, and thrust him out of the city, and led him unto the brow of the hill, whereon ~~their~~ **the** city was built, that they might cast him down headlong.

30 But he passing through the midst of them went his way,

31 And came down to Capernaum, a city of Galilee, and taught them on the sabbath ~~days~~ **day**.

32 And they were astonished at his doctrine; for his ~~word~~ **words** ~~was~~ **were** with power.

33 And in the synagogue there was a man which had a spirit of an unclean devil, and **he** cried out with a loud voice,

34 Saying, Let *us* alone; what have we to do with thee, ~~thou~~ Jesus of Nazareth? Art thou come to destroy us? I know thee, who thou art, The Holy One of God.

35 ~~And~~ Jesus rebuked him, saying, Hold thy peace, and come out of him. And when the devil had thrown him in the midst, he came out of him, and hurt him not.

36 And they were all amazed, and spake among themselves, saying, What a word *is* this! for with authority and power he commandeth the unclean spirits, and they come out.

37 And the fame of him went out ~~into~~ **in** every place ~~of the country~~ round about.

38 And he arose, **and went** out of the synagogue, and entered into Simon's house. And Simon's wife's mother was taken with a great fever; and they besought him for her, **to heal her**.

39 And he stood over her, and rebuked the fever; and it left her: and immediately she arose and ministered unto them.

40 Now, when the sun was setting, all they ~~that~~ **who** had any sick, with divers diseases, brought them unto him, and he laid his hands on everyone of them, and healed them.

41 And devils also came out of many, crying out, and saying, Thou art Christ the Son of God. And he rebuking *them* suffered them not to speak: for they knew that he was Christ.

42 And when it was day, he departed and went into a ~~desert~~ **solitary** place; and the people sought him, and came unto him, and ~~stayed~~ **desired** him that he should not depart from them.

43 **But** ~~And~~ he said unto them, I must preach the kingdom of God to other cities also, for therefore am I sent.

44 And he preached in the synagogues of Galilee.

Chapter 5

1 And it came to pass, ~~that~~ as the people pressed upon him, to hear the word of God, he stood by the lake of Gennesaret,

2 And saw two ships standing ~~by~~ **on** the lake; but the fishermen were gone out of them, and were ~~washing~~ **wetting** *their* nets.

3 And he entered into one of the ships, which was Simon's, and prayed him that he would thrust out a little from the land. And he sat down, and taught the people out of the ship.

4 Now, when he had ~~left~~ **done** speaking, he said ~~unto~~ **to** Simon, Launch out into the deep, and let down your ~~nets~~ **net** for a draught.

5 And Simon answering said unto him, Master, we have toiled all the night, and have taken nothing: nevertheless at thy word I will let down the net.

6 And when they had this done, they inclosed a great multitude of fishes: and their net brake.

7 And they beckoned unto *their* partners, ~~which~~ **who** were in the other ship, that they should come and help them. And they came and filled both the ships, so that they began to sink.

8 When Simon Peter saw ~~it~~ **the multitude of fishes**, he fell down at Jesus' knees, saying, Depart from me; for I am a sinful man, O Lord.

9 For he was astonished, and all ~~that~~ **who** were with him, at the draught of the fishes which they had taken.

10 And so ~~was~~ **were** also James, and John, the sons of Zebedee, ~~which~~ **who** were partners with Simon. And Jesus said unto Simon, Fear not from henceforth, **for** thou shalt catch men.

11 And when they had brought their ships to land, they forsook all, and followed him.

12 And it came to pass, when he was in a certain city, behold a man full of leprosy: who seeing Jesus fell on *his* face, and besought him, saying, Lord, if thou wilt, thou canst make me clean.

13 And he put forth *his* hand, and touched him, saying, I will: be thou clean. And immediately the leprosy departed from him.

14 And he charged him to tell no man; but **said unto him,** Go and show thyself to the ~~priest~~ **priests**, and offer for thy cleansing, according as Moses commanded, for a testimony unto them.

15 But so much the more went there a fame abroad of him: and great multitudes came together to hear, and to be healed by him of their infirmities.

16 And he withdrew himself into the wilderness, and prayed.

17 And it came to pass on a certain day, as he was teaching, that there were Pharisees and doctors of the law sitting by, ~~which~~ **who** were come out of every town of Galilee, and ~~Judaea~~ **Judea**, and Jerusalem. And the power of the Lord was *present* to heal them.

18 And behold, men brought in a bed, a man ~~which~~ **who** was taken with a palsy; and they sought ~~means~~ to bring him in, and to lay *him* before ~~him~~ **Jesus**.

19 And when they **found that they** could not ~~find by what *way* they might~~ bring him in ~~because of~~ **for** the multitude, they went upon the housetop, and let him down through the tiling, with *his* couch, into the midst, before Jesus.

20 ~~And when~~ **Now** he saw their faith, **and** ~~he~~ said unto ~~him~~ **the man,** Thy sins are forgiven thee.

21 And the scribes and ~~the~~ Pharisees began to reason, saying, Who is this ~~which~~ **that** speaketh blasphemies? Who can forgive sins but God alone?

22 But ~~when~~ Jesus perceived their thoughts, **and** he ~~answering~~ said unto them, What reason ye in your hearts?

23 ~~Whether is easier~~ **Does it require more power** to ~~say, Thy~~ **forgive** sins ~~be forgiven thee; or to say~~ **than to make the sick** rise up and walk?

24 But, that ye may know that the Son of Man hath power upon earth to forgive sins, **I said it. And** he said unto the sick of the palsy, I say unto thee, Arise, and take up thy couch, and go ~~into~~ **unto** ~~thine~~ **thy** house.

25 And immediately he rose up before them, and took up that whereon he lay, and departed to his own house, glorifying God.

26 And they were all amazed, and they glorified God, and were filled with fear, saying, We have seen strange things to day.

27 And after these things he went forth, and saw a publican, named Levi, sitting at the ~~receipt of~~ **place where they received** custom; and he said unto him, Follow me.

28 And he left all, rose up, and followed him.

29 And Levi made him a great feast in his own house: and there was a great company of publicans and of others that sat down with them.

30 But ~~their~~ **the** scribes and Pharisees murmured against his disciples, saying, Why do ye eat and drink with publicans and sinners?

31 ~~And~~ Jesus answering**,** said unto them, They that are whole need not a physician; but they that are sick.

32 I came not to call the righteous, but sinners to repentance.

33 And they said unto him, Why do the disciples of John fast often, and make prayers, and likewise *the disciples* of the Pharisees; but thine eat and drink?

34 And he said unto them, Can ye make the children of the bridechamber fast, while the bridegroom is with them?

35 But the days will come, when the bridegroom shall be taken away from them, and then shall they fast in those days.

36 And he spake also a parable unto them**, saying,** No man putteth a piece of ~~a~~ new ~~garment~~ **cloth** upon an old **garment**; if ~~otherwise~~ **so**, then ~~both~~ the new maketh a rent, and ~~the piece that was *taken* out of the new~~ agreeth not with the old.

37 And no man putteth new wine into old bottles; else the new wine will burst the bottles, and be spilled, and the bottles shall perish.

38 But new wine must be put into new bottles; and both are preserved.

39 No man also, having drunk old *wine* ~~straightway~~, desireth new**;** for he saith, The old is better.

CHAPTER 6

1 And it came to pass on the second Sabbath after ~~the first~~ **this**, that he went through the cornfields;* and his disciples plucked the ears of corn, and did eat, rubbing *them* in *their* hands.

2 And certain of the Pharisees said unto them, Why do ye that which is not lawful to do on the sabbath days?

3 ~~And~~ Jesus answering them**,** said, Have ye not read so much as this, what David did, when **he** himself was an ~~hungred~~ **hungered**, and they ~~which~~ **who** were with him;

4 How he went into the house of God, and did take and eat the shewbread, and gave also to them ~~that~~ **who**

were with him, which it is not lawful to eat, but for the priests alone?

5 And he said unto them, That the Son of man is Lord also of the sabbath.

6 And it came to pass also on another sabbath, that he entered into the synagogue and taught: and there was a man whose right hand was withered.

7 And the scribes and Pharisees watched him, whether he would heal on the sabbath day; that they might find an accusation against him.

8 But he knew their thoughts, and said to the man ~~which~~ **who** had the withered hand, Rise up, and stand forth in the midst. And he arose and stood forth.

9 Then said Jesus unto them, I will ask you one thing; Is it lawful on the Sabbath days to do good, or to do evil? To save life, or to destroy ~~it~~?

10 And looking round about upon them all, he said unto the man, Stretch forth thy hand. And he did so: and his hand was restored whole as the other.

11 And they were filled with madness; and communed one with another what they might do to Jesus.

12 And it came to pass in those days, that he went out into a mountain to pray, and continued all night in prayer to God.

13 And when it was day, he called ~~unto him~~ his disciples; and of them he chose twelve, whom also he named apostles.

14 Simon, (whom he also named Peter,) and Andrew his brother, James and John, Philip and Bartholomew,

15 Matthew and Thomas, James the *son* of Alphaeus, and Simon called Zelotes,

16 And Judas *the brother* of James, and Judas Iscariot, ~~which~~ **who** also was the traitor.

17 And he came down with them and stood in the plain, and the company of his disciples, and a great multitude of people out of all ~~Judaea~~ **Judea** and Jerusalem, and from the ~~sea coast~~ **seacoasts** of Tyre and Sidon, ~~which~~ **who** came to hear him, and to be healed of their diseases;

18 And they ~~that~~ **who** were vexed with unclean spirits; and they were healed.

19 And the whole multitude sought to touch him: for there went virtue out of him, and healed *them* all.

20 And he lifted up his eyes on his disciples, and said, Blessed ~~be ye~~ **are the** poor; for ~~yours~~ **theirs** is the kingdom of God.

21 Blessed *are ~~ye~~* **they** ~~that~~ **who** hunger now; for ~~ye~~ **they** shall be filled. Blessed *are ~~ye~~* **they** ~~that~~ **who** weep now; for ~~ye~~ **they** shall laugh.

22 Blessed are ye when men shall hate you, and when they shall separate you *~~from~~ ~~their company~~* **among them**, and shall reproach *you*, and cast out your name as evil, for the Son of Man's sake.

23 Rejoice ye in that day, and leap for joy; for behold your reward ~~*is*~~ **shall be** great in heaven; for in the like manner did their fathers unto the prophets.

24 But woe unto you that are rich! for ye have received your consolation.

25 Woe unto you ~~that~~ **who** are full! For ye shall hunger. Woe unto you ~~that~~ **who** laugh now! For ye shall mourn and weep.

26 Woe unto you, when all men shall speak well of you! for so did their fathers to the false prophets.

27 But I say unto you ~~which~~ **who** hear **my words**, Love your enemies, do good to them ~~which~~ **who** hate you.

28 Bless them ~~that~~ **who** curse you, and pray for them ~~which~~ **who** despitefully use you **and persecute you**.

29 And unto him ~~that~~ **who** smiteth thee on the ~~one~~ cheek, offer also the other; **or, in other words, it is better to offer the other, than to revile again.** And him ~~that~~ **who** taketh away thy ~~cloke~~ **cloak,** forbid not *to take thy* coat also.

30 For it is better that thou suffer thine enemy to take these things, than to contend with him. Verily I say unto you, Your heavenly Father who seeth in secret, shall bring that wicked one into judgment.

31 30 **Therefore** give to every man ~~that~~ **who** asketh of thee; and of him ~~that~~ **who** taketh away thy goods**,** ask *them* not again.

32 31 And as ye would that men should do to you, do ye also to them likewise.

33 32–33 For if ye love them **only** ~~which~~ **who** love you, what ~~thank~~ **reward** have ~~ye~~ **you**? [for sinners also love those that love them. And if ye do good to them which do good to you, what thank have ye?][29] For sinners also do even the same.

34 And if ye lend *to them* of whom ye hope to receive, what ~~thank~~ **reward** have ~~ye~~ **you**? for sinners also lend to sinners, to receive as much again.

35 But love ye your enemies, and do good, and lend, hoping for nothing again; and your reward shall be great, and ye shall be the children of the Highest: for he is kind unto the unthankful and *to* the evil.

36 Be ye therefore merciful, as your Father also is merciful.

37 Judge not, and ye shall not be judged: condemn not, and ye shall not be condemned: forgive, and ye shall be forgiven:

38 Give, and it shall be given unto you; good measure, pressed down, and shaken together, and running over, shall men give into your bosom. For with the same measure that ye mete withal it shall be measured to you again.

39 And he spake a parable unto them, Can the blind lead the blind? shall they not both fall into the ditch?

40 ~~The~~ **A** disciple is not above his master; but everyone that is perfect shall be as his master.

41 And why beholdest thou the mote ~~that~~ **which** is in thy brother's eye, but perceivest not the beam ~~that~~ **which** is in thine own eye?

42 ~~Either~~ **Again,** how canst thou say to thy brother, ~~Brother~~ Let me pull out the mote that is in thine eye, when thou thyself beholdest not the beam ~~that~~ **which** is in thine own eye? Thou hypocrite, cast out first the beam out of thine own eye, and then shalt thou see clearly to pull out the mote ~~that~~ **which** is in thy brother's eye.

43 For a good tree bringeth not forth corrupt fruit; neither doth a corrupt tree bring forth good fruit.

44 For every tree is known by ~~his~~ **its** own fruit. For of thorns men do not gather figs, nor of a bramble bush gather they grapes.

45 A good man out of the good treasure of his heart bringeth forth that which is good; and an evil man out of the evil treasure of his heart bringeth forth that which is evil: for of the abundance of the heart his mouth speaketh.

46 And why call ye me, Lord, Lord, and do not the things which I say?

47 Whosoever cometh to me, and heareth my sayings, and doeth them, I will shew you to whom he is like:

48 He is like a man ~~which~~ **who** built

~~an~~ **a** house, and digged deep, and laid the foundation on a rock, and when the flood arose, the stream beat vehemently upon that house, and could not shake it; for it was founded upon a rock.

49 But he that heareth, and doeth not, is like a man that without a foundation built an house upon the earth; against which the stream did beat vehemently, and immediately it fell; and the ruin of that house was great.

CHAPTER 7

1 Now when he had ended all ~~his~~ **these** sayings in the audience of the people, he entered into Capernaum.

2 And a certain centurion's servant, who was dear unto him, was sick, and ready to die.

3 And when he heard of Jesus, he sent unto him the elders of the Jews, beseeching him that he would come and heal his servant.

4 And when they came to Jesus, they besought him instantly, saying, That he was worthy for whom he should do this:

5 For he loveth our nation, and he hath built us a synagogue.

6 Then Jesus went with them. And when he was now not far from the house, the centurion sent friends to him, saying unto him, Lord, trouble not thyself: for I am not worthy that thou shouldest enter under my roof:

7 Wherefore neither thought I myself worthy to come unto thee: but say ~~in a~~ **the** word, and my servant shall be healed.

8 For I also am a man set under authority, having under me soldiers, and I say unto one, Go, and he goeth; and to another, Come, and he cometh; and to my servant, Do this, and he doeth *it*.

9 When Jesus heard these things, he marveled at him, and turned him about, and said unto the people ~~that~~ **who** followed him, I say unto you, I have not found so great faith, no, not in Israel.

10 And they ~~that~~ **who** were sent, returning to the house, found the servant whole ~~that~~ **who** had been sick.

11 And it came to pass the day after, that he went into a city called Nain; and many of his disciples went with him, and much people.

12 Now, when he came nigh to the gate of the city, behold, there was a dead man carried out, the only son of his mother, and she was a widow; and ~~much~~ **many** people of the city ~~was~~ **were** with her.

13 And ~~when~~ **now** the Lord saw her, ~~he~~ **and** had compassion on her, and **he** said unto her, Weep not.

14 And he came and touched the bier; and they that bare ~~him~~ **it** stood still, and he said, Young man, I say unto thee, Arise.

15 And he ~~that~~ **who** was dead, sat up, and began to speak; and he delivered him to his mother.

16 And there came a fear on all: and they glorified God, saying, That a great prophet is risen up among us; and, That God hath visited his people.

17 And this rumour of him went forth throughout all Judaea, and throughout all the region round about.

18 And the disciples of John shewed him of all these things.

19 And John calling ~~unto him~~ two of his disciples, sent *them* to Jesus, saying, Art thou he that should come, or look we for another?

20 When the men were come unto

him, they said, John Baptist hath sent us unto thee, saying, Art thou he ~~that~~ **who** should come, or look we for another?

21 And in ~~that~~ **the** same hour he cured many of ~~their~~ infirmities, and plagues, and of evil spirits, and unto many ~~that were~~ blind he gave sight.

22 Then Jesus, answering, said unto them, Go your way, and tell John what things ye have seen and heard; how that the blind see, the lame walk, the lepers are cleansed, the deaf hear, the dead are raised, **and** to the poor the gospel is preached.

23 And blessed ~~is he, whosoever~~ **are they who** shall not be offended in me.

24 24–25 And when the messengers of John were departed, he began to speak unto the people concerning John; What went ye out into the wilderness ~~for~~ to see? A reed shaken with the wind? ~~But what went ye out for to see?~~ **Or** a man clothed in soft raiment?

25 Behold, they ~~which~~ **who** are gorgeously apparelled, and live delicately, are in kings' courts.

26 But what went ye out for to see? A prophet? Yea, I say unto you, and much more than a prophet.

27 This is ~~he~~ **the one** of whom it is written, Behold I send my messenger before thy face, ~~which~~ **who** shall prepare thy way before thee.

28 For I say unto you, Among those ~~that~~ **who** are born of women, there is not a greater prophet than John the Baptist; but he ~~that~~ **who** is least in the kingdom of God is greater than he.

29 And all the people ~~that~~ **who** heard *him*, and the publicans, justified God, being baptized with the baptism of John.

30 But the Pharisees and lawyers rejected the counsel of God against

themselves, **not** being ~~not~~ baptized of him.

31 And the Lord said, Whereunto then shall I liken the men of this generation? and to what are they like?

32 They are like unto children sitting in the marketplace, and calling one to another, and saying, We have piped ~~unto~~ **for** you, and ye have not danced; we have mourned ~~to~~ **for** you, and ye have not wept.

33 For John the Baptist came neither eating bread nor drinking wine; and ye say, He hath a devil.

34 The Son of man is come eating and drinking; and ye say, Behold a gluttonous man, and a winebibber, a friend of publicans and sinners!

35 But wisdom is justified of all her children.

36 And one of the Pharisees desired him that he would eat with him. And he went into the Pharisee's house, and sat down to meat.

37 And behold, a woman in the city, ~~which~~ **who** was a sinner, when she knew that *Jesus* sat at meat in the Pharisee's house, brought an alabaster box of ointment.

38 And stood at his feet ~~behind him~~ weeping, and began to wash his feet with tears, and did wipe *them* with the hairs of her head, and kissed his feet, and anointed *them* with the ointment.

39 Now when the Pharisee ~~which~~ **who** had bidden him saw ~~it~~ **this**, he spake within himself, saying, This man, if he were a prophet, would have known who ~~and~~**, or** what manner of woman *this is* ~~that~~ **who** toucheth him; for she is a sinner.

40 And Jesus answering said unto him, Simon, I have somewhat to say unto thee. And he saith, Master, say on.

41 **And Jesus said,** There was a certain creditor ~~which~~**, who** had two debtors; the one owed **him** five hundred pence, and the other fifty.

42 And when **he found** they had nothing to pay, he frankly forgave them both. Tell me therefore, which of them will love him most?

43 Simon answered and said, I suppose ~~that~~ **the** *he* **man** to whom he forgave most. And he said unto him, Thou hast rightly judged.

44 And he turned to the woman, and said unto Simon, Seest thou this woman? I entered into ~~thine~~ **thy** house, thou gavest me no water for my feet; but she hath washed my feet with tears, and wiped *them* with the hairs of her head.

45 Thou gavest me no kiss: but this woman since the time I came in hath not ceased to kiss my feet.

46 My head with oil thou didst not anoint: but this woman hath anointed my feet with ointment.

47 Wherefore I say unto thee, Her sins, which are many, are forgiven; for she loved much: but to whom little is forgiven, *the same* loveth little.

48 And he said unto her, Thy sins are forgiven.

49 And they that sat at meat with him began to say within themselves, Who is this that forgiveth sins also?

50 And he said to the woman, Thy faith hath saved thee; go in peace.

CHAPTER 8

1 And it came to pass afterward, that he went throughout every city and village, preaching and showing the glad tidings of the kingdom of God; and the twelve **who were ordained of him,** *were* with him,

2 And certain women ~~which~~ **who** had been healed of evil spirits and infirmities, Mary called Magdalene, out of whom went seven devils;

3 And Joanna the wife of Chuza, Herod's steward, and Susanna, and many others, ~~which~~ **who** ministered unto him ~~of~~ **with** their substance.

4 And when much people were gathered together, and were come to him out of every city, he spake by a parable**, saying,**

5 A sower went out to sow his seed: and as he sowed, some fell by the way side; and it was trodden down, and the fowls of the air devoured it.

6 And some fell upon a rock; and as soon as it was sprung up, it withered away, because it lacked moisture.

7 And some fell among thorns; and the thorns sprang up with it, and choked it.

8 And ~~other~~ **others** fell on good ground, and sprang up, and ~~bare~~ **bear** fruit an hundredfold.

9 8–9 And when he had said these things, he cried, He ~~that~~ **who** hath ears to hear, let him hear. And his disciples asked him, saying, What might this parable be?

10 And he said, Unto you it is given to know the mysteries of the kingdom of God: but to others in parables; that seeing they might not see, and hearing they might not understand.

11 Now the parable is this: The seed is the word of God.

12 ~~Those~~ **That which fell** by the wayside are they ~~that~~ **who** hear; ~~then cometh~~ **and** the devil **cometh** and taketh away the word out of their hearts, lest they should believe and be saved.

13 ~~They~~ **That which fell** on the rock *are they*, ~~which~~ **who**, when they hear, receive the word with joy; and ~~these~~ **they** have no root, ~~which~~ **but** for a while believe, and in **a** time of temptation fall away.

14 And that which fell among **the** thorns are they, ~~which~~ **who**, when they have heard, go forth and are choked with cares, and riches, and pleasures of ~~this~~ life, and bring no fruit to perfection.

15 But that **which fell** on the good ground are they, ~~which~~ **who receive the word** in an honest and good heart, having heard the word, keep ~~it~~ **what they hear**, and bring forth fruit with patience.

16 **For** no man, when he hath lighted a candle, covereth it with a vessel, or putteth *it* under a bed; but setteth *it* on a candlestick, that they ~~which~~ **who** enter in may see the light.

17 For nothing is secret, ~~that~~ **which** shall not be made manifest; neither ~~any thing~~ hid, ~~that~~ **which** shall not be **made** known, and ~~come~~ **go** abroad.

18 Take heed therefore how ye hear; for whosoever ~~hath~~ **receiveth**, to him shall be given; and whosoever ~~hath~~ **receiveth** not, from him shall be taken even that which he seemeth to have.

19 Then came to him *his* mother and his brethren, and could not ~~come~~ **speak** ~~at~~ **to** him for the ~~press~~ **multitude**.

20 And ~~it was told him by certain which~~ **some who stood by,** said **unto him**, Thy mother and thy brethren stand without, desiring to see thee.

21 And he answered and said unto them, My mother and my brethren are ~~these~~ **those** ~~which~~ **who** hear the word of God, and do it.

22 Now it came to pass on a certain day, that he went into a ship with his disciples: and he said unto them, Let us go over unto the other side of the lake. And they launched forth.

23 But as they sailed he fell asleep; and there came down a storm of wind on the lake; and they were filled *with* ~~water~~ **fear**, and were in ~~jeopardy~~ **danger**.

24 And they came to him and awoke him, saying, Master, Master, we perish. Then he arose, and rebuked the wind and the raging of the ~~water~~ **waters,** and they ceased; and there was a calm.

25 And he said unto them, Where is your faith? And they being afraid, wondered, saying one to another, What manner of man is this? For he commandeth even the winds and ~~water~~ **waters**, and they obey him.

26 And they arrived at the country of the Gadarenes, which is over against Galilee.

27 And when he went forth to land, there met him out of the city a certain man, ~~which~~ **who** had devils **for a** long time, and ~~ware~~ **he would wear** no clothes, neither abode in ~~any~~ **a** house, but in the tombs.

28 When he saw Jesus, he cried out, and fell down before him, and with a loud voice said, What have I to do with thee, Jesus, *thou* Son of God most high? I beseech thee, torment me not.

29 (For he had commanded the unclean spirit to come out of the man. For oftentimes it had caught him: and he was kept bound with chains and in fetters; and he brake the bands, and was driven of the devil into the wilderness.)

30 And Jesus asked him, saying, What is thy name? And he said, Legion: because many devils were entered into him.

31 32 And there was there ~~an~~ **a** herd of many swine, feeding on the mountain.

32 And they besought him that he would suffer them to enter into the ~~them~~ **swine,** and he suffered them.

33 31 And they besought him **also,** that he would not command them to go out into the deep. **And he said unto them, Come out of the man.**

34 33 Then went the devils out of the man, and entered into the swine: and the herd ran violently down a steep place into the lake, and were choked.

35 34 When they ~~that~~ **who** fed ~~them~~ **the swine** saw what was done, they fled, and went and told ~~it~~ **the people** in the city and in the country.

36 35 Then they went out to see what was done; and came to Jesus, and found the man, out of whom the devils were departed, sitting at the feet of Jesus, clothed, and in his right mind: and they were afraid.

37 36 They also ~~which~~ **who** saw ~~it~~ **the miracle**, told them by what means he ~~that~~ **who** was possessed of the devils was healed.

38 37 Then the whole multitude of the country of the Gadarenes round about, besought ~~him~~ **Jesus** to depart from them; for they were taken with great fear. And ~~he~~ **Jesus** went up into the ship, and returned back again.

39 38 Now the man out of whom the devils were departed besought him that he might be with him: but Jesus sent him away, saying,

40 39 Return to thine own house, and shew how great things God hath done unto thee. And he went his way, and published throughout the whole city how great things Jesus had done unto him.

41 40 And it came to pass, that, when Jesus was returned, the people ~~gladly~~ received him; for they were all waiting for him.

42 41 And, behold, there came a man named Jairus, and he was a ruler of the synagogue: and he fell down at Jesus' feet, and besought him that he would come into his house:

43 42 For he had ~~one~~ **an** only daughter, about twelve years of age, and she lay a-dying. But as he went, the people thronged him.

44 43 And a woman, having an issue of blood twelve years, ~~which~~ **who** had spent all her living upon physicians, neither could be healed of any,

45 44 Came behind ~~him~~ **Jesus**, and touched the border of his garment; and immediately her issue of blood ~~stanched~~ **staunched**.

46 45 And Jesus said, Who touched me? When all denied, Peter and they that were with him, said, Master, the multitude throng thee, and press **upon** *thee*, and sayest thou, Who touched me?

47 46 And Jesus said, ~~Somebody~~ **Someone** hath touched me; for I perceive that virtue is gone out of me.

48 47 And when the woman ~~saw~~ **found** that she was not hid, she came trembling, and falling down before him, she declared unto him before all the people for what cause she had touched him, and how she was healed immediately.

49 48 And he said unto her, Daughter, be of good comfort: thy faith hath made thee whole; go in peace.

50 49 While he yet spake, there cometh one from the ruler of the synagogue's *house*, saying to him, Thy daughter is dead; trouble not the Master.

51 50–51 But ~~when~~ Jesus heard ~~it~~ **him, and** he ~~answered him, saying~~ **said unto the ruler of the synagogue**, Fear not; believe only, and she shall be made whole. And when he came into the house, he suffered no man to go in, save Peter, and James, and John, and the father and the mother of the maiden.

52 52–53 And all wept, and bewailed her: but he said, Weep not; she is not dead, but sleepeth. And they laughed him to scorn, knowing that she was dead.

53 54 And he put them all out, and took her by the hand, and he called, saying, Maid, arise.

54 55 And her spirit came again, and she arose straightway: and he commanded to give her meat.

55 56 And her parents were astonished: but he charged them that they should tell no man what was done.

CHAPTER 9

1 Then he called his twelve disciples together, and **he** gave them power and authority over all devils, and to cure diseases.

2 And he sent them to preach the kingdom of God, and to heal the sick.

3 And he said unto them, Take nothing for *your* journey, neither staves, nor scrip, neither bread, neither money; neither have two coats apiece.

4 And **into** whatsoever house ye enter into, there abide and thence **until ye** depart **thence.**

5 And whosoever will not receive you, when ye go out of that city, shake off the very dust from your feet for a testimony against them.

6 And they departed, and went through the towns, preaching the gospel, and healing every where.

7 Now Herod the tetrarch heard of all that was done by him **Jesus;** and he was perplexed, because that it was said of some, that John was risen from the dead;

8 And of some, that Elias had appeared; and of others, that one of the old prophets was risen again.

9 And Herod said, John have I beheaded: but who is this, of whom I hear such things? And he desired to see him.

10 And the apostles, when they were returned, told him **Jesus** all that they had done. And he took them, and went aside privately into a desert **solitary** place belonging to the city called Bethsaida.

11 And the people, when they knew *it,* followed him; and he received them, and spake unto them of the kingdom of God, and healed them that **who** had need of healing.

12 And when the day began to wear away, then came the twelve, and said unto him, Send the multitude away, that they may go into the towns and country round about, and lodge, and get victuals; for we are here in a desert **solitary** place.

13 But he said unto them, Give ye them to eat. And they said, We have no more but five loaves and two fishes; **and** except we should go and buy meat**, we can provide no more food** for all this people **multitude.**

14 For they were **in number** about five thousand men. And he **Jesus** said to **unto** his disciples, Make them sit down by fifties in a company.

15 And they did so, and made them all sit down.

16 Then he took the five loaves and the two fishes, and looking up to heaven, he blessed them, and brake, and gave to the disciples to set before the multitude.

17 And they did eat, and were all filled**.** And there was taken up of **the** fragments that **which** remained**,** twelve baskets.

18 And it came to pass, as he was **went** alone praying **with** his disciples were with him **to pray,** and he asked them, saying, Whom **Who** say the people that I am?

19 They answering said, **Some say,** John the Baptist; but ~~some~~ **others** *say*, Elias; and others ~~say~~, that one of the old prophets is risen again.

20 He said unto them, But ~~whom~~ **who**[*] say ye that I am? Peter answering said, The Christ, **the Son** of God.

21 And he straitly charged them, and commanded *them* to tell no man ~~that thing~~ **of him,**

22 Saying, The Son of man must suffer many things, and be rejected of the elders and chief priests and scribes, and be slain, and be raised the third day.

23 And he said ~~to~~ **unto** *them* all, If any *man* will come after me, let him deny himself, and take up his cross daily, and follow me.

24 For whosoever will save his life ~~shall,~~ **must be willing to** lose it **for my sake;** ~~but~~ **and** whosoever will **be willing to** lose his life for my sake, the same shall save it.

25 For what ~~is a man advantaged~~ **doth it profit a man** if he gain the whole world, **and yet he receive him not whom God hath ordained,** and **he** lose **his own soul, and he** himself ~~or~~ be **a** castaway?

26 For whosoever shall be ashamed of me, and of my words, of him shall the Son of Man be ashamed, when he shall come in his own ~~glory and *in his* Father's, and of~~ **kingdom, clothed in the glory of his Father, with** the holy angels.

27 ~~But~~ **Verily,** I tell you of a truth, there ~~be~~ **are** some standing here ~~which~~ **who** shall not taste of death, until they see the kingdom of God **coming in power**.

28 And it came to pass, ~~about an~~ eight days after these sayings, **that** he took Peter and John and James, and went up into a mountain to pray.

29 And as he prayed, the fashion of his countenance was ~~altered~~ **changed**, and his raiment ~~was~~ **became** white *and* ~~glistering~~ **glittering**.

30 And behold, there **came and** talked with him two men, ~~which were~~ **even** Moses and Elias,

31 Who appeared in glory, and spake of his ~~decease~~ **death, and also his resurrection,** which he should accomplish at Jerusalem.

32 But Peter and they ~~that~~ **who** were with him were heavy with sleep; and when they were awake they saw his glory, and the two men ~~that~~ **who** stood with him.

33 And ~~it came to pass~~ **after the two men** ~~as they~~ departed from him, Peter said unto Jesus, Master, it is good for us to be here; and let us make three tabernacles; one for thee, and one for Moses, and one for Elias; not knowing what he said.

34 While he thus spake, there came a cloud, and overshadowed them **all;** and they feared as they entered into the cloud.

35 And there came a voice out of the cloud, saying, This is my beloved Son: hear him.

36 And when the voice was past, Jesus was found alone. And **these things** they kept ~~it~~ close, and **they** told no man, in those days, any of ~~those~~ **the** things which they had seen.

37 And it came to pass, that on the next day, when they were come down from the hill, much people met him.

38 And, behold, a man of the company cried out, saying, Master, I beseech thee, look upon my son: for he is mine only child.

39 And, lo, a spirit taketh him, and he suddenly crieth out; and it teareth him, that he foameth ~~again,~~ and bruising him hardly, departeth from him.

40 And I besought thy disciples to cast him out; and they could not.

41 And Jesus answering said, O faithless and perverse generation, how long shall I be with you, and suffer you? Bring thy son hither.

42 And as he was ~~yet a~~ coming, the devil threw him down, and ~~tare~~ **tore** *him* **again**. And Jesus rebuked the unclean spirit, and healed the child, and delivered him again to his father.

43 And they were all amazed at the mighty power of God. But while they wondered every one at all things which Jesus did, he said unto his disciples,

44 Let these sayings sink down into your ~~ears~~ **hearts;** for the Son of Man shall be delivered into the hands of men.

45 But they understood not this saying, and it was hid from them, that they perceived it not: and they feared to ask him of that saying.

46 Then there arose a reasoning among them, ~~which~~ **who** of them should be greatest.

47 And Jesus perceiving the ~~thought~~ **thoughts** of their ~~heart~~ **hearts**, took a child, and set him ~~by him~~ **in the midst;**

48 And said unto them, Whosoever shall receive this child in my name**,** receiveth me**;** and whosoever shall receive me**,** receiveth him ~~that~~ **who** sent me**;** for he ~~that~~ **who** is least among you all, the same shall be great.

49 And John ~~answered~~ **spake** and said, Master, we saw one casting out devils in thy name; and we ~~forbad~~ **forbade** him, because he followeth not with us.

50 And Jesus said unto him, Forbid *him* not **any;** for he ~~that~~ **who** is not against us is for us.

51 And it came to pass, when the time was come that he should be received up, he stedfastly set his face to go to Jerusalem,

52 And sent messengers before his face: and they went, and entered into a village of the Samaritans, to make ready for him.

53 And ~~they did~~ **the Samaritans would** not receive him, because his face was **turned** as though he would go to Jerusalem.

54 And when his disciples**,** James and John, saw ~~this~~ **that they would not receive him**, they said, Lord, wilt thou that we command fire to come down from heaven and consume them, even as Elias did?

55 But he turned, and rebuked them, and said, Ye know not what manner of spirit ye are of.

56 For the Son of man is not come to destroy men's lives, but to save *them*. And they went to another village.

57 And it came to pass, ~~that~~ as they went in the way, a certain *man* said unto him, Lord, I will follow thee whithersoever thou goest.

58 And Jesus said unto him, Foxes have holes, and birds of the air *have* nests; but the Son of man hath not where to lay *his* head.

59 And he said unto another, Follow me. But he said, Lord, suffer me first to go and bury my father.

60 Jesus said unto him, Let the dead bury their dead: but go thou and preach the kingdom of God.

61 And another also said, Lord, I will follow thee; but let me first go **and** bid them farewell ~~which~~ **who** are at ~~home at~~ my house.

62 And Jesus said unto him, No man, having put his hand to the plough, and looking back, is fit for the kingdom of God.

CHAPTER 10

1 After these things the Lord appointed other seventy also, and sent them two and two before his face, into every city and place ~~whither~~ **where** he himself would come.

2 ~~Therefore~~ **And he** said ~~he~~ unto them, The harvest truly *is* great, but the laborers ~~are~~ few; pray ye therefore the Lord of the harvest, that he would send forth laborers into his harvest.

3 Go your ways: behold, I send you forth as lambs among wolves.

4 Carry neither purse, nor scrip, nor shoes; ~~and~~ **nor** salute ~~no~~ **any** man by the way.

5 And into whatsoever house ye enter, first say, Peace ~~be~~ to this house.

6 And if the son of peace be there, your peace shall rest upon it: if not, it shall turn to you again.

7 And ~~in the same~~ **into whatsoever** house **they receive you**, remain, eating and drinking such things as they give; for the laborer is worthy of his hire. Go not from house to house.

8 And into whatsoever city ye enter, and they receive you, eat such things as are set before you:

9 And heal the sick that are therein, and say ~~unto them~~, The kingdom of God is come nigh unto you.

10 But into whatsoever city ye enter, and they receive you not, go your ways out into the streets of the same, and say,

11 Even the very dust of your city which cleaveth on us, we do wipe off against you; notwithstanding, be ~~ye~~ sure of this, that the kingdom of God is ~~come~~ nigh unto you.

12 But I say unto you, that it shall be more tolerable in ~~that~~ **the** day **of judgment** for Sodom, than for that city.

13 Then began he to upbraid the people in every city wherein his mighty works were done, who received him not, saying,

14 13 Woe unto thee, Chorazin! Woe unto thee, Bethsaida! For if the mighty works had been done in Tyre and Sidon, which have been done in you, they ~~had a great while ago~~ **would have** repented, sitting in sackcloth and ashes.

15 14 But it shall be more tolerable for Tyre and Sidon at the **day of** judgment, than for you.

16 15 And thou, Capernaum, which art exalted to heaven, ~~shalt~~ **shall** be ~~thrust~~ **cast** down to hell.

17 16 **And he said unto his disciples,** He that heareth you, heareth me; and he that despiseth you, despiseth me; and he that despiseth me, despiseth him ~~that~~ **who** sent me.

18 17 And the seventy returned again with joy, saying, Lord, even the devils are subject ~~unto~~ **to** us through thy name.

19 18 And he said unto them, ~~I beheld Satan~~ As lightning ~~fall~~ **falleth** from heaven, **I beheld Satan also falling**.

20 19 Behold, I **will** give unto you power ~~to tread on~~ **over** serpents and scorpions, and over all the power of the enemy; and nothing shall by any means hurt you.

21 20 Notwithstanding in this rejoice not, that the spirits are subject unto you; but rather rejoice, because your names are written in heaven.

22 21 In that hour Jesus rejoiced in spirit, and said, I thank thee, O Father, Lord of heaven and earth, that thou hast hid these things from ~~the~~ **them who think they are** wise and prudent, and hast revealed them unto babes; even so, Father; for so it seemed good in thy sight.

23 22 All things are delivered to me of my Father; and no man knoweth ~~who~~ **that** the Son is ~~but~~ the Father, and ~~who~~ the Father is ~~but~~ the Son, ~~and he~~ **but him** to whom the Son will reveal ~~him~~ **it**.

24 23 And he turned him unto ~~his~~ **the** disciples, and said privately, Blessed *are* the eyes which see the things that ye see.

25 24 For I tell you, that many prophets and kings have desired to see those things which ye see, and have not seen *them*; and to hear those things which ye hear, and have not heard *them*.

26 25 And, behold, a certain lawyer stood up, and tempted him, saying, Master, what shall I do to inherit eternal life?

27 26 He said unto him, What is written in the law? how readest thou?

28 27 And he answering said, Thou shalt love the Lord thy God with all thy heart, and with all thy soul, and with all thy strength, and with all thy mind; and thy neighbour as thyself.

29 28 And he said unto him, Thou hast answered right: this do, and thou shalt live.

30 29 But he, willing to justify himself, said unto Jesus, And who is my neighbour?

31 30 And Jesus answering said, A certain *man* went down from Jerusalem to Jericho, and fell among thieves, which stripped him of his raiment, and wounded *him*, and departed, leaving *him* half dead.

32 31 And by chance, there came down a certain priest that way; and when he saw him, he passed by on the other side **of the way**.

33 32 And likewise a Levite, when he was at the place, came and looked ~~on~~ **upon** *him*, and passed by on the

other side **of the way; for they desired in their hearts that it might not be known that they had seen him.**

33 But a certain Samaritan, as he journeyed, came where he was: and when he saw him, he had compassion *on him*,

34 And went to *him*, and bound up his wounds, pouring in oil and wine, and set him on his own beast, and brought him to an inn, and took care of him.

36 35 And on the morrow, when he departed, he took ~~out two pence~~ **money**, and gave ~~them~~ to the host, and said unto him, Take care of him, and whatsoever thou spendest more, when I come again, I will repay thee.

37 36 ~~Which~~ **Who** now of these three, thinkest thou, was neighbor unto him that fell among the thieves?

38 37 And he said, He ~~that~~ **who** showed mercy on him. Then said Jesus unto him, Go, and do ~~thou~~ likewise.

39 38 Now it came to pass, as they went, ~~that he~~ **they** entered into a certain village; and a certain woman named Martha received him into her house.

40 39 And she had a sister, called Mary, ~~which~~ **who** also sat at Jesus' feet, and heard his ~~word~~ **words**.

41 40 But Martha was cumbered about much serving, and came to him, and said, Lord, dost thou not care that my sister hath left me to serve alone? bid her therefore that she help me.

42 41 And Jesus answered and said unto her, Martha, Martha, thou art careful and troubled about many things:

43 42 But one thing is needful: and Mary hath chosen that good part, which shall not be taken away from her.

CHAPTER 11

1 And it came to pass, ~~that~~ as ~~he~~ **Jesus** was praying in a certain place, when he ceased, one of his disciples said unto him, Lord, teach us to pray, as John also taught his disciples.

2 And he said unto them, When ye pray, say, Our Father ~~which~~ **who** art in heaven, hallowed be thy name. Thy kingdom come. Thy will be done as in heaven, so in earth.

3 Give us day by day our daily bread.

4 And forgive us our sins; for we also forgive everyone ~~that~~ **who** is indebted to us. And ~~lead~~ **let** us not **be led** into temptation; but deliver us from evil; **for thine is the kingdom and power. Amen.**

5 And he said unto them, **Your heavenly Father will not fail to give unto you whatsoever ye ask of him. And he spake a parable, saying,**

6 5 Which of you shall have a friend, and shall go unto him at midnight, and say unto him, Friend, lend me three loaves;

7 6 For a friend of mine ~~in his journey is~~ **has** come to me **in his journey**, and I have nothing to set before him;

8 7 And he from within shall answer and say, Trouble me not: the door is now shut, and my children are with me in bed; I cannot rise and give thee.

9 8 I say unto you, Though he will not rise and give him, because he is his friend, yet because of his importunity he will rise and give him as many as he needeth.

10 9 And I say unto you, Ask, and it shall be given you; seek, and ye shall find; knock, and it shall be opened unto you.

11 10 For everyone ~~that~~ **who** asketh, receiveth; and he that seeketh, findeth;

and to him ~~that~~ **who** knocketh, it shall be opened.

12 11 If a son shall ask bread of any of you ~~that~~ **who** is a father, will he give him a stone? or, if ~~he ask~~ a fish, will he for a fish give him a serpent?

13 12 Or if he shall ask an egg, will he offer him a scorpion?

14 13 If ye then, being evil, know how to give good gifts unto your children, how much more shall *your* heavenly Father give **good gifts, through** the Holy Spirit, to them ~~that~~ **who** ask him.

15 14 And he was casting ~~out~~ a devil **out of a man**, and ~~it~~ **he** was dumb. And it came to pass, when the devil was gone out, the dumb spake; and the people wondered.

16 15 But some of them said, He casteth out devils through Beelzebub the chief of the devils.

17 16 And others tempting *him*, sought of him a sign from heaven.

18 17 But he, knowing their thoughts, said unto them, Every kingdom divided against itself is brought to desolation; and a house *divided* ~~against a house~~ **cannot stand, but** falleth.

19 18 If Satan also be divided against himself, how ~~shall~~ **can** his kingdom stand? **I say this,** because ~~ye~~ **you** say ~~that~~ I cast out devils through Beelzebub.

20 19 And if I, by Beelzebub, cast out devils, by whom do your sons cast ~~them~~ out **devils**? Therefore shall they be your judges.

21 20 But if I, with the finger of God cast out devils, no doubt the kingdom of God ~~is~~ **has** come upon you.

22 21 When a strong man armed keepeth his palace, his goods are in peace:

23 22 But when a stronger than he

shall come upon him, and overcome him, he taketh from him all his armor wherein he trusted and divideth his ~~spoils~~ **goods**.

24 23 He that is not with me, is against me: and he that gathereth not with me scattereth.

25 24 When the unclean spirit is gone out of a man, ~~he~~ **it** walketh through dry places, seeking rest; and finding none, ~~he~~ **it** saith, I will return unto my house whence I came out.

26 25 And when ~~he~~ **it** cometh, ~~he~~ **it** findeth ~~it~~ **the house** swept and garnished.

27 26 Then goeth ~~he~~ **the evil spirit**, and taketh ~~to him~~ seven other spirits more wicked than himself, and they enter in, and dwell there; and the last ~~state~~ **end** of that man is worse than the first.

28 27 And it came to pass, as he spake these things, a certain woman of the company, lifted up her voice, and said unto him, Blessed *is* the womb ~~that~~ **which** bare thee, and the paps which thou hast sucked.

29 28 ~~But~~ **And** he said, Yea ~~rather,~~ **and** blessed *are* **all** they ~~that~~ **who** hear the word of God, and keep it.

30 29 ~~And~~ When the people were gathered thick together, he began to say, This is an evil generation; they seek a sign, and there shall no sign be given ~~it~~ **them**, but the sign of Jonas the prophet.

31 30 For as Jonas was a sign unto the Ninevites, so ~~shall~~ also **shall** the Son of Man be to this generation.

32 31 The queen of the south shall rise up in the **day of** judgment with the men of this generation, and condemn them; for she came from the utmost parts of the earth, to hear the wisdom of Solomon; and, behold, a greater than Solomon *is* here.

33 32 The men of ~~Nineve~~ **Nineveh** shall rise up in the **day of** judgment with this generation; and shall condemn it; for they repented at the preaching of Jonas; and, behold, a greater than Jonas *is* here.

34 33 No man when he hath lighted a candle, putteth *it* in a secret place, neither under a bushel, but on a candlestick, that they ~~which~~ **who** come in may see the light.

35 34 The light of the body is the eye: therefore when thine eye is single, thy whole body also is full of light; but when *thine eye* is evil, thy body also *is* full of darkness.

36 35 Take heed therefore that the light which is in thee be not darkness.

37 36 If thy whole body therefore ~~be~~ **is** full of light, having no part dark, the whole shall be full of light, as when the bright shining of a candle **lighteneth a room and** doth give ~~thee~~ **the** light **in all the room**.

38 37 And as he spake, a certain Pharisee besought him to dine with him: and he went in, and sat down to meat.

39 38 And when the Pharisee saw ~~it~~ **him**, he marveled that he had not first washed before dinner.

40 39 And the Lord said unto him; Now do ~~ye~~ **you** Pharisees make clean the outside of the cup and the platter; but your inward ~~part~~ **parts** ~~is~~ **are** full of ravening and wickedness.

41 40 ~~Ye~~ **O** fools, did not he ~~that~~ **who** made that which is without, make that which is within also?

42 41 But **if ye would** rather give alms of such things as ye have; and ~~behold~~ **observe to do** all things **which I have commanded you, then would your inward parts** ~~are~~ **be** clean ~~unto you~~ **also**.

43 42 But **I say unto you,** Woe **be** unto you, Pharisees! For ye tithe mint, and rue, and all manner of herbs, and pass over judgment, and the love of God; these ought ye to have done, and not to leave the other undone.

44 43 Woe unto you, Pharisees! for ~~ye~~ **you** love the uppermost seats in the ~~synagogues~~ **synagogue**, and greetings in the markets.

45 44 Woe unto you, scribes and Pharisees, hypocrites! For ye are as graves which appear not, and the men ~~that~~ **who** walk over ~~them~~ are not aware *of them*.

46 45 Then answered one of the lawyers, and said unto him, Master, thus saying thou reproachest us also.

47 46 And he said, Woe unto you ~~also, ye,~~ lawyers**, also**! For ye lade men with burdens grievous to be borne, and ye yourselves touch not the burdens with one of your fingers.

48 47 Woe unto you! For ~~ye~~ **you** build the sepulchres of the prophets, and your fathers killed them.

49 48 Truly ye bear witness that ye allow the deeds of your fathers: for they indeed killed them, and ye build their sepulchres.

50 49 Therefore also said the wisdom of God, I will send them prophets and apostles, and *some* of them they shall slay and persecute:

51 50–51 That the blood of all the prophets, which was shed from the foundation of the world, may be required of this generation; from the blood of Abel unto the blood of Zacharias, ~~which~~ **who** perished between the altar and the temple.

52 51 Verily I say unto you, It shall be required of this generation.

53 52 Woe unto you, lawyers! For ye have taken away the key of knowledge**, the fullness of the scriptures;**

ye entered not in yourselves **into the kingdom;** and ~~them~~ **those** ~~that~~ **who** were entering in, ye hindered.

54 53 And as he said these things unto them, the scribes and ~~the~~ Pharisees began **to be angry, and** to urge ~~him~~ vehemently, ~~and~~ **endeavoring** to provoke him to speak of many things;

55 54 Laying wait for him, and seeking to catch something out of his mouth, that they might accuse him.

<h2 style="text-align:center">CHAPTER 12</h2>

1 In the mean time, when there were gathered together an innumerable multitude of people, insomuch that they trode one upon another, he began to say unto his disciples first of all, Beware ye of the leaven of the Pharisees, which is hypocrisy.

2 For there is nothing covered ~~that~~ **which** shall not be revealed; neither hid ~~that~~ **which** shall not be known.

3 Therefore whatsoever ye have spoken in darkness shall be heard in the light; and that which ye have spoken in the ear in closets shall be proclaimed upon the housetops.

4 And I say unto you my friends, Be not afraid of them ~~that~~ **who** kill the body, and after that have no more that they can do;

5 But I will forewarn you whom ye shall fear; fear him, ~~which~~ **who** after he hath killed, hath power to cast into hell; yea, I say unto you, Fear him.

6 Are not five sparrows sold for two farthings, and not one of them is forgotten before God?

7 But even the very hairs of your head are all numbered. Fear not therefore: ye are of more value than many sparrows.

8 Also I say unto you, Whosoever shall confess me before men, him shall

the Son of man also confess before the angels of God:

9 But he ~~that~~ **who** denieth me before men**,** shall be denied before the angels of God.

10 Now his disciples knew that he said this, because they had spoken evil against him before the people; for they were afraid to confess him before men.

11 And they reasoned among themselves, saying, He knoweth our hearts, and he speaketh to our condemnation, and we shall not be forgiven. But he answered them, and said unto them,

12 10 ~~And~~ Whosoever shall speak a word against the Son of Man, **and repenteth,** it shall be forgiven him**;** but unto him ~~that~~ **who** blasphemeth against the Holy Ghost**,** it shall not be forgiven.

13 11 And **again I say unto you,** ~~when~~ They **shall** bring you unto the synagogues, and ~~unto~~ **before** magistrates, and powers. **When they do this,** take ye no thought how, or what thing ye shall answer, or what ye shall say**;**

14 12 For the Holy Ghost shall teach you in the same hour what ye ought to say.

15 13 And one of the company said unto him, Master, speak to my brother, that he divide the inheritance with me.

16 14 And he said unto him, Man, who made me a judge or a divider over you?

17 15 And he said unto them, Take heed, and beware of covetousness: for a man's life consisteth not in the abundance of the things which he possesseth.

18 16 And he spake a parable unto them, saying, The ground of a certain rich man brought forth plentifully:

19 17 And he thought within himself, saying, What shall I do, because I have no room where to bestow my fruits?

20 18 And he said, This will I do: I will pull down my barns, and build greater; and there will I bestow all my fruits and my goods.

21 19 And I will say to my soul, Soul, thou hast much goods laid up for many years; take thine ease, eat, drink, *and* be merry.

22 20 But God said unto him, *Thou fool, this night thy soul shall be required of thee: then whose shall those things be, which thou hast provided?*

23 21 So ~~is~~ **shall it be with** ~~he~~ **him** ~~that~~ **who** layeth up treasure for himself, and is not rich toward God.

24 22 And he said unto his disciples, Therefore I say unto you, Take no thought for your life, what ye shall eat; neither for the body, what ye shall put on.

25 23 **For** the life is more than meat, and the body ~~is more~~ than raiment.

26 24 Consider the ravens**;** for they neither sow nor reap; which neither have storehouse nor barn; ~~and~~ **nevertheless** God feedeth them**.** ~~how much more~~ Are ye **not** better than the fowls?

27 25 And ~~which~~ **who** of you ~~with~~ **by** taking thought**,** can add to his stature one cubit?

28 26 If ye then be not able to do that ~~thing~~ which is least, why take ye thought for the rest?

29 27 Consider the lilies how they grow: they toil not, they spin not; and yet I say unto you, that Solomon in all his glory was not arrayed like one of these.

30 28 If then God so clothe the grass, which is today in the field, and tomorrow is cast into the oven; how much more *will he* ~~clothe~~ **provide for** you, ~~O~~ **if** ye **are not** of little faith?

31 29 ~~And~~ **Therefore,** seek not ~~ye~~ what ye shall eat, or what ye shall drink, neither be ye of doubtful mind;

32 30 For all these things do the nations of the world seek after; and your Father **who is in heaven,** knoweth that ye have need of these things.

33 And ye are sent unto them to be their ministers, and the laborer is worthy of his hire; for the law saith, That a man shall not muzzle the ox that treadeth out the corn.

34 31 ~~But rather~~ **Therefore** seek ye **to bring forth** the kingdom of God, and all these things shall be added unto you.

35 32 Fear not, little flock; for it is your Father's good pleasure to give you the kingdom.

36 33 **This he spake unto his disciples, saying,** Sell that ye have and give alms; provide **not for** yourselves bags which wax ~~not~~ old, **but rather provide** a treasure in the heavens, that faileth not; where no thief approacheth, neither moth corrupteth.

37 34 For where your treasure is, there will your heart be also.

38 35 Let your loins be girded about and **have** *your* lights burning;

39 36 ~~And~~ **That** ye yourselves **may be** like unto men ~~that~~ **who** wait for their lord, when he will return from the wedding; that**,** when he cometh and knocketh, they may open unto him immediately.

40 37 **Verily I say unto you,** Blessed *are* those servants, whom the Lord when he cometh shall find watching; ~~verily I say unto you that~~ **for** he shall gird himself, and make them ~~to~~ sit down to meat, and will come forth and serve them.

41 For, behold, he cometh in the first watch of the night, and he shall also come in the second watch, and again he shall come in the third watch.

42 38 **And verily I say unto you, He hath already come, as it is written of him;** and ~~if~~ **again when** he shall come in the second watch, or come in the third watch, ~~and find them so~~ blessed are those servants **when he cometh, that he shall find so doing;**

43 For the Lord of those servants shall gird himself, and make them to sit down to meat, and will come forth and serve them.

44 And now, verily I say these things unto you, that ye may know this, that the coming of the Lord is as a thief in the night.

45 And it is like unto a man who is an householder, who, if he watcheth not his goods, the thief cometh in an hour of which he is not aware, and taketh his goods, and divideth them among his fellows.

46 39 And ~~this know~~ they said **among themselves**, ~~that~~ if the goodman of the house had known what hour the thief would come, he would have watched, and not have suffered his house to be broken through **and the loss of his goods**.

47 40 **And he said unto them, Verily I say unto you,** be ye therefore ready also; for the Son of Man cometh at an hour when ye think not.

48 41 Then Peter said unto him, Lord, speakest thou this parable unto us, or ~~even to~~ **unto** all?

49 42 And the Lord said, ~~Who then is that faithful and wise steward~~ **I speak unto those** whom *~~his~~* **the** Lord shall make ~~ruler~~ **rulers** over his household, to give *~~them~~* **his children** *their* portion of meat in due season.

50 And they said, Who then is that faithful and wise servant?

51 And the Lord said unto them, It is that servant who watcheth, to impart his portion of meat in due season.

52 43 Blessed *is* **be** that servant whom his Lord **shall find,** when he cometh, shall find so doing.

53 44 Of a truth I say unto you, that he will make him ruler over all that he hath.

54 45 But **the evil servant is he who is not found watching.** And if that servant **is not found watching, he will** say in his heart, My Lord delayeth his coming; and shall begin to beat the menservants and **the** maidens, and to eat and drink, and to be drunken.

55 46 The Lord of that servant will come in a day when he looketh not for *him*, and at an hour when he is not aware, and will cut him in sunder **down**, and will appoint him his portion with the unbelievers.

56 47 And that servant which **who** knew his Lord's will, and prepared not *himself* **for his Lord's coming,** neither did according to his will, shall be beaten with many *stripes*.

57 48 But he that knew not **his Lord's will**, and did commit things worthy of stripes, shall be beaten with few *stripes*. For unto whomsoever much is given, of him shall be much **be** required; and to whom men have **the Lord has** committed much, of him they will **men** ask the more.

58 49 **For they are not well pleased with the Lord's doings; therefore** I am come to send fire on the earth; and what will I **is it to you**, if **I will that** it be already kindled?

59 50 But I have a baptism to be baptized with; and how am I straitened

straitened till **until** it be accomplished!

60 51 Suppose ye that I am come to give peace on earth? I tell you, Nay; but rather division:

61 52 For from henceforth there shall be five in one house divided, three against two, and two against three.

62 53 The father shall be divided against the son, and the son against the father; the mother against the daughter, and the daughter against the mother; the mother in law against her daughter in law, and the daughter in law against her mother in law.

63 54 And he said also to **unto** the people, When ye **you** see a cloud rise out of the west, **ye say** straightway ye say, There cometh a shower; and so it is.

64 55 And when ye see the south wind blow **blows**, ye say, There will be heat; and it cometh to pass.

65 56 Ye **O** hypocrites! Ye can discern the face of the sky, and of the earth; but how is it that ye do not discern this time?

66 57 Yea, and why even of yourselves judge ye not what is right?

67 58 When **Why** thou goest **thou** with **to** thine adversary to the **for a** magistrate, when *as thou art* in the way **with thine enemy? Why not** give diligence that thou mayest be delivered from him, lest he hale thee to the judge, and the judge deliver thee to the officer, and the officer cast thee into prison?

68 59 I tell thee, thou shalt not depart thence, till thou hast paid the very last mite.

CHAPTER 13

1 **And** there were present at that season **time**, some that **who** told **spake unto** him of the Galilaeans **Galileans**,

whose blood Pilate had mingled with their sacrifices.

2 And Jesus ~~answering~~ said unto them, Suppose ye that these ~~Galilaeans~~ **Galileans** were sinners above all the ~~Galilaeans~~ **Galileans**, because they suffered such things?

3 I tell you, Nay: but except ye repent, ye shall all likewise perish.

4 Or those eighteen, ~~upon~~ **on** whom the tower in Siloam fell, and slew them; think ye that they were sinners above all men that dwelt in Jerusalem?

5 I tell you, Nay: but, except ye repent, ye shall all likewise perish.

6 He spake also this parable**,** A certain ~~man~~ **husbandman** had a fig tree planted in his vineyard**.** ~~and~~ He came and sought fruit thereon and found none.

7 Then said he unto the dresser of his vineyard, Behold, these three years I come seeking fruit on this fig tree, and find none: cut it down; why cumbereth it the ground?

8 And he answering said unto him, Lord, let it alone this year also, till I shall dig about it, and dung *it*:

9 And if it bear fruit, ~~well~~ **the tree is saved,** and if not, ~~then~~ after that thou shalt cut it down. **And many other parables spake he unto the people.**

10 And **after this, as** he was teaching in one of the synagogues on the Sabbath;

11 ~~And~~ Behold, there was a woman ~~which~~ **who** had a spirit of infirmity eighteen years, and was bowed together, and could in no wise ~~lift~~ **straighten** up ~~herself~~.

12 And when Jesus saw her, he called ~~her to him~~ and said unto her, Woman, thou art loosed from thine ~~infirmity~~ **infirmities**.

13 And he laid ~~his~~ hands on her; and immediately she was made straight, and glorified God.

14 And the ruler of the synagogue ~~answered~~ **was filled** with indignation, because that Jesus had healed on the Sabbath day, and said unto the people, There are six days in which men ought to work; in them therefore come and be healed, and not on the Sabbath day.

15 The Lord then ~~answered~~ **said unto** him, ~~and said Thou~~ **O** hypocrite! Doth not each one of you on the Sabbath loose ~~his~~ **an** ox or ~~his~~ **an** ass from the stall, and lead *him* away to watering?

16 And ought not this woman, being a daughter of Abraham, whom Satan hath bound, lo, these eighteen years, be loosed from this bond on the sabbath day?

17 And when he had said these things, all his adversaries were ashamed; and all ~~the people~~ **his disciples** rejoiced for all the glorious things ~~that~~ **which** were done by him.

18 Then said he, Unto what is the kingdom of God like? and whereunto shall I resemble it?

19 It is like a grain of mustard ~~seed~~, which a man took, and cast into his garden; and it grew, and waxed a great tree; and the fowls of the air lodged in the branches of it.

20 And again he said, Whereunto shall I liken the kingdom of God?

21 It is like leaven, which a woman took and hid in three measures of meal, till the whole was leavened.

22 And he went through the cities and villages, teaching, and journeying toward Jerusalem.

23 ~~Then~~ **And there** said one unto him, Lord, are there few **only** that be saved? And he ~~said unto~~ **answered** ~~them~~ **him, and said,**

24 Strive to enter in at the strait gate; for ~~many~~ I say unto you, **Many ~~will~~ shall** seek to enter in, and shall not be able; **for the Lord shall not always strive with man.**

25 **Therefore,** when once the ~~master~~ **Lord** of the ~~house~~ **kingdom** is risen up, and hath shut ~~to~~ the door **of the kingdom,** ~~and~~ **then** ye ~~begin to~~ **shall** stand without, and ~~to~~ knock at the door, saying, Lord, Lord, open unto us. ~~and he~~ **But the Lord** shall answer and say unto you, **I will not receive you, for** ~~I~~ **ye** know ~~you~~ not **from** whence ye are.

26 Then shall ye begin to say, We have eaten and drunk in thy presence, and thou hast taught in our streets.

27 But he shall say, I tell you, ~~I~~ **ye** know ~~you~~ not **from** whence ye are; depart from me, all ~~ye~~ workers of iniquity.

28 There shall be weeping and gnashing of teeth **among you**, when ye shall see Abraham, and Isaac, and Jacob, and all the prophets, in the kingdom of God, and you ~~yourselves~~ **are** thrust out.

29 And **verily I say unto you,** They shall come from the east, and ~~from~~ the west; and from the north, and ~~from~~ the south, and shall sit down in the kingdom of God;

30 And, behold, there are last which shall be first, and there are first which shall be last, **and shall be saved therein.**

31 ~~The same day~~ **And as he was thus teaching,** there came **to him** certain of the Pharisees, saying unto him, Get thee out, and depart hence; for Herod will kill thee.

32 And he said unto them, Go ye and tell ~~that fox~~ **Herod**, Behold, I cast out devils, and ~~I~~ do cures today and tomorrow, and the third *day* I shall be perfected.

33 Nevertheless, I must walk today and tomorrow, and the **third** *day* ~~following~~; for it cannot be that a prophet perish out of Jerusalem.

34 **This he spake, signifying of his death. And in this very hour he began to weep over Jerusalem.**

35 34 **Saying,** O Jerusalem, Jerusalem, **thou** ~~which~~ **who** killest the prophets, and stonest them ~~that~~ **who** are sent unto thee; how often would I have gathered thy children together, as a hen ~~doth gather~~ her brood under *her* wings, and ye would not.

36 35 Behold, your house is left unto you desolate. And verily I say unto you, Ye shall not ~~see~~ **know** me, **until ye have received from the hand of the Lord a just recompense for all your sins;** until *the time* come when ye shall say, Blessed *is* he that cometh in the name of the Lord.

CHAPTER 14

1 And it came to pass, as he went into the house of one of the chief Pharisees to eat bread on the sabbath day, that they watched him.

2 And, behold, there was a certain man before him, ~~which~~ **who** had the dropsy.

3 And Jesus ~~answering~~ spake unto the lawyers, and Pharisees, saying, Is it lawful to heal on the Sabbath day?

4 And they held their peace. And he took ~~him~~ **the man**, and healed him, and let him go;

5 And ~~answered~~ **spake unto** them **again**, saying, Which of you shall have an ass or an ox fallen into a pit and will not straightway pull him out on the Sabbath day?

6 And they could not answer him ~~again~~ to these things.

7 And he put forth a parable ~~to~~ **unto them concerning** those ~~which~~ **who**

were bidden ~~when he marked~~ **to a wedding; for he knew** how they chose out the chief rooms, **and exalted themselves one above another; wherefore he spake unto them,** saying ~~unto them,~~

8 When thou art bidden of any *man* to a wedding, sit not down in the highest room; lest a more honourable man than thou be bidden of him;

9 And he ~~that~~ **who** bade thee, **and with** him **who is more honorable,** come, and say to thee, Give this man place; and thou begin with shame to take the lowest room.

10 But when thou art bidden, go and sit down in the lowest room; that when he ~~that~~ **who** bade thee, cometh, he may say unto thee, Friend, go up higher; then shalt thou have ~~worship~~ **honor of God,** in the presence of them ~~that~~ **who** sit at meat with thee.

11 For whosoever exalteth himself shall be abased; and he ~~that~~ **who** humbleth himself shall be exalted.

12 Then said he also ~~to~~ **concerning** him ~~that~~ **who** bade ~~him~~ **to the wedding,** When thou makest a dinner, or a supper, call not thy friends, nor thy brethren, neither thy kinsmen, nor ~~thy~~ rich neighbors; lest they also bid thee again, and a recompense be made thee.

13 But when thou makest a feast, call the poor, the maimed, the lame, the blind:

14 And thou shalt be blessed; for they cannot recompense thee: for thou shalt be recompensed at the resurrection of the just.

15 And when one of them ~~that~~ **who** sat at meat with him, heard these things, he said unto him, Blessed *is* he ~~that~~ **who** shall eat bread in the kingdom of God.

16 Then said he unto him, A certain man made a great supper, and bade many:

17 And sent his ~~servant~~ **servants** at supper time, to say to them ~~that~~ **who** were bidden, Come, for all things are now ready.

18 And they all with one *consent* began to make excuse. The first said unto him, I have bought a piece of ground, and I must needs go and see it: I pray thee have me excused.

19 And another said, I have bought five yoke of oxen, and I go to prove them: I pray thee have me excused.

20 And another said, I have married a wife, ~~and~~ therefore I cannot come.

21 So that servant came and showed his lord these things. Then the master of the house, being angry, said to his ~~servant~~ **servants,** Go out quickly into the streets and lanes of the city, and bring hither the poor, and the maimed, ~~and~~ the halt and the blind.

22 And the servant said, Lord, it is done as thou hast commanded, and yet there is room.

23 ~~And~~ The lord said unto ~~the~~ **his** servant, Go out into the highways, and hedges, and compel ~~them~~ **men** to come in, that my house may be filled;

24 For I say unto you, That none of those men ~~which~~ **who** were bidden, shall taste of my supper.

25 **And when he had finished these sayings, he departed thence,** and there went great multitudes with him, and he turned and said unto them,

26 If any *man* come to me, and hate not his father, and mother, and wife, and children, and brethren, and sisters, **or husband,** yea and his own life also; **or in other words, is afraid to lay down their life for my sake,** he cannot be my disciple.

27 And whosoever doth not bear his

cross, and come after me, cannot be my disciple.

28 Wherefore, settle this in your hearts, that ye will do the things which I shall teach, and command you.

29 28 For which of you intending to build a tower, sitteth not down first, and counteth the cost, whether he have ~~sufficient~~ **money** to finish ~~it~~ **his work**?

30 29 Lest, ~~haply~~ **unhappily**, after he ~~hath~~ **has** laid the foundation and is not able to finish ~~it~~ **his work**, all ~~that~~ **who** behold ~~it,~~ begin to mock him,

31 30 Saying, This man began to build, and was not able to finish. **And this he said, signifying there should not any man follow him, unless he was able to continue; saying,**

32 31 Or what king, going to make war against another king, sitteth not down first, and consulteth whether he be able with ten thousand**,** to meet him ~~that~~ **who** cometh against him with twenty thousand**.**

33 32 Or else, while the other is yet a great way off, he sendeth an ~~ambassage~~ **embassage**, and desireth conditions of peace.

34 33 So likewise, whosoever ~~he be~~ of you ~~that~~ forsaketh not all that he hath he cannot be my disciple.

35 Then certain of them came to him, saying, Good Master, we have Moses and the prophets, and whosoever shall live by them, shall he not have life?

36 34 **And Jesus answered, saying, Ye know not Moses, neither the prophets; for if ye had known them, ye would have believed on me; for to this intent they were written. For I am sent that ye might have life. Therefore I will liken it unto** salt **which** *is* good;

37 34 But if the salt ~~have~~ **has** lost ~~his~~ **its** savor, wherewith shall it be seasoned?

38 35 It is neither fit for the land, nor yet for the dunghill; ~~but~~ men cast it out. He ~~that~~ **who** hath ears to hear, let him hear. **These things he said, signifying that which was written, verily must all be fulfilled.**

CHAPTER 15

1 Then drew near unto him**,** ~~all~~ **many of** the publicans**,** and sinners ~~for,~~ to hear him.

2 And the Pharisees and scribes murmured, saying, This man receiveth sinners, and eateth with them.

3 And he spake this parable unto them, saying,

4 What man of you having ~~an~~ **a** hundred sheep, if he lose one of them, doth not leave the ninety and nine**,** **and go** ~~in~~ **into** the wilderness ~~and go~~ after that which is lost, until he find it?

5 And when he hath found *it*, he layeth *it* on his shoulders, rejoicing.

6 And when he cometh home, he calleth together *his* friends and neighbors, ~~saying~~ **and saith** unto them, Rejoice with me; for I have found my sheep which was lost.

7 I say unto you, that likewise joy shall be in heaven over one sinner that repenteth, more than over ninety and nine just persons, ~~which~~ **who** need no repentance.

8 Either what woman having ten pieces of silver, if she lose one piece, doth not light a candle, and sweep the house, and seek diligently till she find *it*?

9 And when she hath found *it*, she calleth *her* friends and *her* neighbors together, saying, Rejoice with me; for I have found the piece which I had lost.

10 Likewise I say unto you, there is joy in the presence of the angels of God over one sinner ~~that~~ **who** repenteth.

11 And he said, A certain man had two sons:

12 And the younger of them said to *his* father, Father, give me the portion of goods ~~that~~ **which** falleth *to me*. And he divided unto them *his* living.

13 And not many days after the younger son gathered all together, and took his journey into a far country, and there wasted his substance with riotous living.

14 And when he had spent all, there arose a mighty famine in that land; and he began to be in want.

15 And he went and joined himself to a citizen of that country; and he sent him into his fields to feed swine.

16 And he would fain have filled his belly with the husks ~~that~~ **which** the swine did eat; and no man gave unto him.

17 And when he came to himself, he said, How many hired servants of my father's have bread enough and to spare, and I perish with hunger!

18 I will arise and go to my father, and will say unto him, Father, I have sinned against heaven, and before thee,

19 And am no more worthy to be called thy son: make me as one of thy hired servants.

20 And he arose, and came to his father. But when he was yet a great way off, his father saw him, and had compassion, and ran, and fell on his neck, and kissed him.

21 And the son said unto him, Father, I have sinned against heaven, and in thy sight, and am no more worthy to be called thy son.

22 But the father said ~~to~~ **unto** ~~his~~ **the** servants, Bring forth the best robe,

and put *it* on him; and put a ring on his ~~hand~~ **finger**, and shoes on *his* feet;

23 And bring hither the fatted calf, and kill *it*; and let us eat, and be merry:

24 For this my son was dead, and is alive again; he was lost, and is found. And they began to be merry.

25 Now his elder son was in the field: and as he came and drew nigh to the house, he heard musick and dancing.

26 And he called one of the servants, and asked what these things meant.

27 And he said unto him, Thy brother is come; and thy father hath killed the fatted calf, because he hath received him safe and sound.

28 And he was angry, and would not go in: therefore came his father out, and intreated him.

29 And he answering, said to *his* father, Lo, these many years do I serve thee, neither transgressed I at any time thy commandment; and ~~yet~~ thou never gavest me a kid, that I might make merry with my friends;

30 But as soon as this thy son was come, ~~which~~ **who** hath devoured thy living with harlots, thou hast killed for him the fatted calf.

31 And he said unto him, Son, thou art ever with me, and all that I have is thine.

32 It was meet that we should make merry, and be glad; for this thy brother was dead, and is alive again; ~~and~~ was lost, and is found.

CHAPTER 16

1 And he said also unto his disciples, There was a certain rich man ~~which~~ **who** had a steward; and the same was accused unto him, that he had wasted his goods.

2 And he called him, and said unto

him, How is it that I hear this of thee? give an account of thy stewardship; for thou mayest be no longer steward.

3 Then the steward said within himself, What shall I do? for my lord taketh away from me the stewardship: I cannot dig; to beg I am ashamed.

4 I am resolved what to do, that, when I am put out of the stewardship, they may receive me into their houses.

5 So he called everyone of his lord's debtors ~~unto him~~, and said unto the first, How much owest thou unto my lord?

6 And he said, An hundred measures of oil. And he said unto him, Take thy bill, and sit down quickly, and write fifty.

7 Then said he to another, And how much owest thou? And he said, An hundred measures of wheat. And he said unto him, Take thy bill, and write fourscore.

8 And the lord commended the unjust steward, because he had done wisely; for the children of this world are **wiser** in their generation, ~~wiser~~ than the children of light.

9 And I say unto you, Make to yourselves friends of the mammon of unrighteousness; that, when ye fail, they may receive you into everlasting habitations.

10 He ~~that~~ **who** is faithful in that which is least, is faithful also in much; and he ~~that~~ **who** is unjust in the least, is ~~unjust~~ also **unjust** in much.

11 If therefore ye have not been faithful in the unrighteous mammon, who will commit to your trust the true *riches*?

12 And if ye have not been faithful in that which is another man's, who shall give **unto** you that which is your own?

13 No servant can serve two masters:

for either he will hate the one, and love the other; or else he will hold to the one, and despise the other. Ye cannot serve God and mammon.

14 And the Pharisees also, who were covetous, heard all these things: and they derided him.

15 And he said unto them, Ye are they ~~which~~ **who** justify yourselves before men; but God knoweth your hearts; for that which is highly esteemed among men, is **an** abomination in the sight of God.

16 And they said unto him, We have the law, and the prophets; but as for this man we will not receive him to be our ruler; for he maketh himself to be a judge over us.

17 16 **Then said Jesus unto them,** The law and the prophets ~~were~~ **testify of me; yea, and all the prophets who have written, even** ~~until~~ **unto** John, **have foretold of these days.**

18 16 Since that time, the kingdom of God is preached, and every man **who seeketh truth** presseth into it.

19 17 And it is easier for heaven and earth to pass, than **for** one tittle of the law to fail.

20 And why teach ye the law, and deny that which is written; and condemn him whom the Father hath sent to fulfill the law, that ye might all be redeemed?

21 O fools! for you have said in your hearts, There is no God. And you pervert the right way; and the kingdom of heaven suffereth violence of you; and you persecute the meek; and in your violence you seek to destroy the kingdom; and ye take the children of the kingdom by force. Woe unto you, ye adulterers!

22 And they reviled him again, being angry for the saying, that they were adulterers.

23 18 **But he continued, saying,** Whosoever putteth away his wife, and marrieth another, committeth adultery; and whosoever marrieth her ~~that~~ **who** is put away from *her* husband, committeth adultery. **Verily I say unto you, I will liken you unto the rich man.**

24 19 **For** there was a certain rich man, ~~which~~ **who** was clothed in purple, and fine linen, and fared sumptuously every day.

25 20 And there was a certain beggar named Lazarus, ~~which~~ **who** was laid at his gate, full of sores,

26 21 And desiring to be fed with the crumbs which fell from the rich man's table: moreover the dogs came and licked his sores.

27 22 And it came to pass, that the beggar died, and was carried ~~by~~ **of** the angels into Abraham's bosom. The rich man also died, and was buried.

28 23 And in hell he ~~lift~~ **lifted** up his eyes, being in torments, and ~~seeth~~ **saw** Abraham afar off, and Lazarus in his bosom.

29 24 And he cried and said, Father Abraham, have mercy on me, and send Lazarus, that he may dip the tip of his finger in water, and cool my tongue; for I am tormented in this flame.

30 25 But Abraham said, Son, remember that thou in thy lifetime receivedst thy good things, and likewise Lazarus evil things: but now he is comforted, and thou art tormented.

31 26 And beside all this, between us and you, there is a great gulf fixed; so that they ~~which~~ **who** would pass from hence to you, cannot; neither can they pass to us that *would come* from thence.

32 27 Then he said, I pray thee therefore, father, that thou wouldest send him to my father's house:

33 28 For I have five brethren; that he may testify unto them, lest they also come into this place of torment.

34 29 Abraham saith unto him, They have Moses and the prophets; let them hear them.

35 30 And he said, Nay, father Abraham: but if one went unto them from the dead, they will repent.

36 31 And he said unto him, If they hear not Moses and the prophets, neither will they be persuaded, though one ~~rose~~ **should rise** from the dead.

CHAPTER 17

1 Then said he unto the disciples, It is impossible but that offenses will come; but woe ~~unto~~ **to** *him* through whom they come.

2 It were better for him that a millstone were hanged about his neck, and he cast into the sea, than that he should offend one of these little ones.

3 Take heed to yourselves. If ~~thy~~ **your** brother trespass against ~~thee~~ **you**, rebuke him; and if he repent, forgive him.

4 And if he trespass against ~~thee~~ **you** seven times in a day, and seven times in a day turn ~~again~~ to ~~thee~~ **you again**, saying, I repent; ~~thou~~ **you** ~~shalt~~ **shall** forgive him.

5 And the apostles said unto ~~the Lord~~ **him, Lord**, increase our faith.

6 And the Lord said, If ~~ye~~ **you** had faith as a grain of mustard seed, ~~ye~~ **you** might say unto this ~~sycamine~~ **sycamore** tree, Be thou plucked up by the ~~root~~ **roots**, and be thou planted in the sea; and it should obey you.

7 But ~~which~~ **who** of you, having a servant plowing, or feeding cattle, will say unto him ~~by and by~~ when he is come from the field, Go and sit down to meat?

8 ~~And~~ Will **he** not rather say unto him, Make ready wherewith I may sup, and gird ~~thyself~~ **yourself** and serve me till I have eaten and drunken; and afterward**, by and by,** ~~thou~~ **you** shalt eat and drink?

9 Doth he thank that servant because he ~~did~~ **doeth** the things ~~that~~ **which** were commanded him? I ~~trow not~~ **say unto you, Nay**.

10 So likewise ye, when ye shall have done all those things which are commanded you, say, We are unprofitable servants**.** We have done that which was **no more than** our duty to do.

11 And it came to pass, as he went to Jerusalem, that he passed through the midst of ~~Samaria~~ **Galilee** and ~~Galilee~~ **Samaria**.

12 And as he entered into a certain village, there met him ten men ~~that~~ **who** were lepers, ~~which~~ **who** stood afar off**;**

13 And they lifted up *their* voices, and said, Jesus, Master, have mercy on us.

14 And ~~when he saw *them*~~ he said unto them, Go show yourselves unto the priests. And it came to pass, ~~that~~ as they went, they were cleansed.

15 ~~And~~ One of them, when he saw ~~that~~ he was healed, turned back, and with a loud voice glorified God,

16 And fell down on *his* face at ~~his~~ **Jesus'** feet, giving him thanks**;** and he was a Samaritan.

17 And Jesus answering said, Were there not ten cleansed? but where *are* the nine?

18 There are not found that returned to give glory to God, save this stranger.

19 And he said unto him, Arise, go thy way: thy faith hath made thee whole.

20 And when he was demanded of the Pharisees, when the kingdom of God should come, he answered them and said, The kingdom of God cometh not with observation:

21 Neither shall they say, Lo**,** here! or, Lo**,** there! For, behold, the kingdom of God ~~is within~~ **has already come unto** you.

22 And he said unto the disciples, The days will come, when ~~ye~~ **they** ~~shall~~ **will** desire to see one of the days of the Son of Man, and ~~ye~~ **they** shall not see *it*.

23 And **if** they shall say to you, See here! or, See there! Go not after *them*, nor follow *them*.

24 For as the ~~lightning~~ **light of the morning**, that ~~lighteneth~~ **shineth** out of the one *part* under heaven, **and** ~~shineth~~ **lighteneth** ~~unto~~ **to** the other *part* under heaven; so shall also the Son of Man be in his day.

25 But first **he** must ~~he~~ suffer many things, and be rejected of this generation.

26 And as it was in the days of Noe, so shall it be also in the days of the Son of man.

27 They did eat, they drank, they married wives, they were given in marriage, until the day that Noe entered into the ark, and the flood came, and destroyed them all.

28 Likewise also as it was in the days of Lot; they did eat, they drank, they bought, they sold, they planted, they builded;

29 But the same day that Lot went out of Sodom it rained fire and brimstone from heaven, and destroyed *them* all.

30 Even thus shall it be in the day when the Son of man is revealed.

31 In that day, ~~he~~ **the disciple** ~~which~~ **who** shall be ~~upon~~ **on** the housetop, and his stuff in the house, let him not come down to take it away**;** and he

~~that~~ **who** is in the field, let him likewise not return back.

32 Remember Lot's wife.

33 Whosoever shall seek to save his
life shall lose it; and whosoever shall
lose his life shall preserve it.

34 34–35 I tell you, in that night
there shall be two ~~men~~ in one bed; the
one shall be taken, and the other shall
be left. Two ~~women~~ shall be grinding
together; the one shall be taken, and
the other left.

35 36 Two ~~men~~ shall be in the field;
the one shall be taken, and the other
left.

36 37 And they answered and said
unto him, Where, Lord, **shall they be
taken.**

37 And he said unto them, Wheresoever the body *is* **gathered; or, in
other words, whithersoever the
saints are gathered;** thither will the
eagles be gathered together**; or, thither will the remainder be gathered
together.**

**38 This he spake, signifying the
gathering of his saints; and of angels
descending and gathering the remainder unto them; the one from
the bed, the other from the grinding, and the other from the field,
whithersoever he listeth.**

**39 For verily there shall be new
heavens, and a new earth, wherein
dwelleth righteousness.**

**40 And there shall be no unclean
thing; for the earth becoming old,
even as a garment, having waxed in
corruption, wherefore it vanisheth
away, and the footstool remaineth
sanctified, cleansed from all sin.**

CHAPTER 18

1 And he spake a parable unto them
~~to this end~~, **saying,** that men ought always to pray and not ~~to~~ faint.

2 Saying, There was in a city a judge,
~~which~~ **who** feared not God, ~~neither~~
nor regarded man**.**

3 And there was a widow in that
city; and she came unto him, saying,
Avenge me of mine adversary.

4 And he would not for a while: but
afterward he said within himself,
Though I fear not God, nor regard
man;

5 Yet because this widow troubleth
me, I will avenge her, lest by her continual coming she weary me.

6 And the Lord said, Hear what the
unjust judge saith.

7 And shall not God avenge his own
elect, ~~which~~ **who** cry day and night
unto him, though he bear long with
~~them~~ **men**?

8 I tell you that he will **come, and
when he does come, he will** avenge
~~them~~ **his saints** speedily. Nevertheless**,** when the Son of Man cometh,
shall he find faith on the earth?

9 ~~And~~ He spake this parable unto
certain **men**, ~~which~~ **who** trusted in
themselves that they were righteous,
and despised others**.**

10 Two men went up into the temple
to pray; the one a Pharisee, and the
other a publican.

11 The Pharisee stood and prayed
thus with himself, God, I thank thee,
that I am not as other men *are*, extor-
tioners, unjust, adulterers, or even as
this publican.

12 I fast twice in the week, I give
tithes of all that I possess.

13 ~~And~~ **But** the publican, standing
afar off, would not lift up so much as
his eyes unto heaven, but smote upon
his breast, saying, God be merciful to
me a sinner.

14 I tell you, this man went down to
his house justified, *rather* than the
other**;** for everyone ~~that~~ **who** exalteth

himself, shall be abased; and he ~~that~~ **who** humbleth himself, shall be exalted.

15 And they brought unto him also, infants, that he ~~would~~ **might** touch them; but when *his* disciples saw *it*, they rebuked them.

16 But Jesus called them ~~unto him~~, and said, Suffer little children to come unto me, and forbid them not; for of such is the kingdom of God.

17 Verily I say unto you, Whosoever ~~shall~~ **will** not receive the kingdom of God as a little child, shall in no wise enter therein.

18 And a certain ruler asked him, saying, Good Master, what shall I do to inherit eternal life?

19 And Jesus said unto him, Why callest thou me good? none *is* good, save one, *that is*, God.

20 Thou knowest the commandments, Do not commit adultery, Do not kill, Do not steal, Do not bear false witness, Honour thy father and thy mother.

21 And he said, All these have I kept from my youth up.

22 Now when Jesus heard these things, he said unto him, Yet **thou** lackest ~~thou~~ one thing; sell all that thou hast, and distribute unto the poor, and thou shalt have treasure in heaven, and come, follow me.

23 And when he heard this, he was very sorrowful: for he was very rich.

24 And when Jesus saw that he was very sorrowful, he said, How hardly shall they ~~that~~ **who** have riches enter into the kingdom of God!

25 For it is easier for a camel to go through a needle's eye, than for a rich man to enter into the kingdom of God.

26 And they that heard *it* said **unto him**, Who then can be saved?

27 And he said **unto them, It is** ~~The things which are~~ impossible ~~with men are~~ **for them who trust in riches, to enter into the kingdom of God; but he who forsaketh the things which are of this world, it is** possible with God**, that he should enter in.**

28 Then Peter said, Lo, we have left all, and followed thee.

29 And he said unto them, Verily I say unto you, There is no man ~~that~~ **who** has left house, or parents, or brethren, or wife, or children, for the kingdom of God's sake,

30 Who shall not receive manifold more in this present time, and in the world to come life everlasting.

31 Then he took ~~unto him~~ the twelve, and said unto them, Behold, we go up to Jerusalem, and all things ~~that~~ **which** are written by the prophets concerning the Son of Man, shall be accomplished.

32 For he shall be delivered unto the Gentiles, and shall be mocked, and spitefully entreated, and spitted on:

33 And they shall scourge ~~him~~ and put him to death; and the third day he shall rise again.

34 And they understood none of these things; and this saying was hid from them; neither ~~knew~~ **remembered** they the things which were spoken.

35 And it came to pass, ~~that~~ as he was come nigh unto Jericho, a certain blind man sat by the wayside begging.

36 And hearing the multitude pass by, he asked what it meant.

37 And they told him that Jesus of Nazareth passeth by.

38 And he cried, saying, Jesus, ~~thou~~ Son of David, have mercy on me.

39 And they ~~which~~ **who** went before, rebuked him, **telling him** that he should hold his peace; but he cried

so much the more, **saying,** ~~Thou~~ Son
of David, have mercy on me.

40 And Jesus stood, and commanded him to be brought unto him: and
when he was come near, he asked
him,

41 Saying, What wilt thou that I
shall do unto thee? And he said, Lord,
that I may receive my sight.

42 And Jesus said unto him, Receive
thy sight: thy faith hath saved thee.

43 And immediately he received his
sight; and **he** followed him, glorifying
God. And all the ~~people~~ **disciples**
when they saw ~~it~~ **this**, gave praise unto
God.

Chapter 19

1 And *Jesus* entered and passed
through Jericho.

2 And behold, *there was* a man
named Zacchaeus, ~~which~~ **who** was
~~the~~ chief among the publicans; and he
was rich.

3 And he sought to see Jesus who he
was; and could not for the press, because he was little of stature.

4 And he ran before, and climbed
up into a sycomore tree to see him: for
he was to pass that *way*.

5 And when Jesus came to the place,
he looked up, and saw him, and said
unto him, Zacchaeus, make haste,
and come down; for to day I must
abide at thy house.

6 And he made haste, and came
down, and received him joyfully.

7 And when ~~they~~ **the disciples** saw
it, they all murmured, saying, That he
was gone to be guest with a man ~~that~~
who is a sinner.

8 And Zacchaeus stood, and said
unto the Lord, Behold, Lord, the half
of my goods I give to the poor; and if
I have taken anything from any man
by ~~false accusation~~ **unjust means**, I
restore ~~him~~ fourfold.

9 And Jesus said unto him, This day
is salvation come to this house, ~~forso-
much~~ **forasmuch** as he also is a son of
Abraham**.**

10 For the Son of man is come to
seek and to save that which was lost.

11 And as they heard these things,
he added and spake a parable, because
he was nigh to Jerusalem, and because
~~they~~ **the Jews** ~~thought~~ **taught** that the
kingdom of God should immediately
appear.

12 He said therefore, A certain nobleman went into a far country to receive for himself a kingdom, and to
return.

13 And he called his ten servants,
and delivered them ten pounds, and
said unto them, Occupy till I come.

14 But his citizens hated him, and
sent a ~~message~~ **messenger** after him,
saying, We will not have this *man* to
reign over us.

15 And it came to pass, that when
he was returned, having received the
kingdom, then he commanded these
servants to be called unto him, to
whom he had given the money, that
he might know how much every man
had gained by trading.

16 Then came the first, saying, Lord,
thy pound hath gained ten pounds.

17 And he said unto him, Well
done, thou good servant; because
thou hast been faithful in a very little,
have thou authority over ten cities.

18 And the second came, saying,
Lord, thy pound hath gained five
pounds.

19 And he said likewise to him, Be
thou also over five cities.

20 And another came, saying, Lord,
behold ~~here is~~ thy pound which I have
kept laid up in a napkin;

21 For I feared thee, because thou
art an austere man; thou takest up

that thou layedst not down, and reapest that **which** thou didst not sow.

22 And he ~~saith~~ **said** unto him, Out of thine own mouth will I judge thee, ~~thou~~ **O** wicked servant. Thou knewest that I was an austere man, taking up that I laid not down, and reaping that I did not sow.

23 Wherefore then, gavest not thou my money into the bank, that at my coming I might have ~~required~~ **received** mine own with usury?

24 And he said unto them ~~that~~ **who** stood by, Take from him the pound, and give *it* to him ~~that~~ **who** hath ten pounds.

~~25 (And they said unto him, Lord, he hath ten pounds.)~~

25 26 For I say unto you, That unto everyone ~~which~~ **who** ~~hath~~ **occupieth**, shall be given; and from him ~~that~~ **who** ~~hath~~ **occupieth** not, even that he hath **received** shall be taken away from him.

26 27 But those mine enemies, ~~which~~ **who** would not that I should reign over them, bring **them** hither, and slay *them* before me.

27 28 And when he had thus spoken, he went before, ascending up to Jerusalem.

28 29 And it came to pass, when he was come nigh to Bethphage and Bethany, at the mount called *the mount* of Olives, he sent two of his disciples,

29 30 Saying, Go ye into the village over against *you*, in the which at your entering ye shall find a colt tied, whereon yet never man sat; loose him, and bring *him* ~~hither~~ **to me**.

30 31 And if any man ask you, Why do ye loose ~~him~~ **the colt**? Thus shall ye say unto him, Because the Lord hath need of him.

31 32 And they ~~that~~ **who** were sent,

went their way, and found even as he had said unto them.

32 33 And as they were loosing the colt, the owners thereof said unto them, Why loose ye the colt?

33 34 And they said, The Lord hath need of him.

34 35 And they brought him to Jesus: and they cast their garments upon the colt, and they set Jesus thereon.

35 36 And as he went, they spread their clothes in the way.

36 37 And when he was come nigh, even now at the descent of the mount of Olives, the whole multitude of the disciples began to rejoice and praise God with a loud voice for all the mighty works that they had seen;

37 38 Saying, Blessed ~~be~~ **is** the King that cometh in the name of the Lord, peace in heaven, and glory in the highest!

38 39 And some of the Pharisees from among the multitude said unto him, Master, rebuke thy disciples.

39 40 And he answered and said unto them, ~~I tell you that~~ If these should hold their peace, the stones would immediately cry out.

40 41 And when he was come near, he beheld the city, and wept over it,

41 42 Saying, If thou hadst known, even thou, at least in this thy day, the things *which belong* unto thy peace! but now they are hid from thine eyes.

42 43 For the days shall come upon thee, that thine enemies shall cast a trench about thee, and compass thee round, and keep thee in on every side,

43 44 And shall lay thee even with the ground, and thy children within thee; and they shall not leave in thee one stone upon another; because thou knewest not the time of thy visitation.

44 45 And he went into the temple, and began to cast out them that sold therein, and them ~~that~~ **who** bought,

45 46 Saying unto them, It is written, My house is ~~the~~ **a** house of prayer; but ye have made it a den of thieves.

46 47 And he taught daily in the temple. But the chief priests and the scribes and the chief of the people sought to destroy him,

47 48 And could not find what they might do: for all the people were very attentive to hear him.

CHAPTER 20

1 And it came to pass, *that* on one of those days, as he taught the people in the temple, and preached the gospel, the chief priests and the scribes came upon *him* with the elders,

2 And spake unto him, saying, Tell us, by what authority doest thou these things? Or, who is he ~~that~~ **who** gave thee this authority?

3 And he answered, and said unto them, I will also ask you one thing; ~~and~~ answer me:

4 The baptism of John, was it from heaven, or of men?

5 And they reasoned with themselves, saying, If we shall say, From heaven; he will say, Why then believed ye him not?

6 ~~But~~ **And** if we say, Of men, all the people will stone us; for they ~~be~~ **are** persuaded that John was a prophet.

7 And they answered, that they could not tell whence *it was*.

8 ~~And~~ Jesus said unto them, Neither tell I you, by what authority I do these things.

9 Then began he to speak to the people, this parable. A certain man planted a vineyard, and let it ~~forth~~ **out** to husbandmen, and went into a far

country for a long time.

10 And at the season **of the harvest,** he sent ~~a~~ **his** servant to the husbandmen, that they should give him of the fruit of the vineyard; but the husbandmen beat him, and sent *him* away empty.

11 And again he sent another servant: and they beat him also, and entreated *him* shamefully, and sent *him* away empty.

12 And again he sent a third: and they wounded him also, and cast *him* out.

13 Then said the lord of the vineyard, What shall I do? I will send my beloved son: it may be they will reverence *him* when they see him.

14 But when the husbandmen saw him, they reasoned among themselves, saying, This is the heir: come, let us kill him, that the inheritance may be ours.

15 So they cast him out of the vineyard, and killed *him*. What therefore shall the lord of the vineyard do unto them?

16 He shall come and destroy these husbandmen, and shall give the vineyard to others. And when they heard ~~it~~ **this**, they said, God forbid!

17 And he beheld them, and said, What is this then ~~that~~ **which** is written, The stone which the builders rejected, the same is become the head of the corner?

18 Whosoever shall fall upon that stone, shall be broken; but on whomsoever it shall fall, it ~~will~~ **shall** grind him to powder.

19 And the chief priests, and the scribes, the same hour, sought to lay hands on him; ~~and~~ **but** they feared the people; for they perceived that he had spoken this parable against them.

20 And they watched *him*, and sent

forth spies, ~~which~~ **who** should feign themselves just men, that they might take hold of his words, that so **doing**, they might deliver him unto the power and authority of the governor.

21 And they asked him, saying, Master, we know that thou sayest and teachest rightly; neither ~~acceptest~~ **regardest** thou the person *of any*, but teachest the way of God truly.

22 Is it lawful for us to give tribute unto Caesar, or no?

23 But he perceived their craftiness, and said unto them, Why tempt ye me?

24 Shew me a penny. Whose image and superscription hath it? They answered and said, Caesar's.

25 And he said unto them, Render therefore unto Caesar the things which be Caesar's, and unto God the things which be God's.

26 And they could not take hold of his words before the people: and they marvelled at his answer, and held their peace.

27 Then came to *him* certain of the Sadducees, ~~which~~ **who** deny ~~that~~ there is any resurrection; and they asked him,

28 Saying, Master, Moses wrote unto us, **saying,** If any man's brother die, having a wife, and he die without children, that his brother should take his wife, and raise up seed unto his brother.

29 There were therefore seven brethren: and the first took a wife, and died without children.

30 And the second took her to wife, and ~~he~~ died childless.

31 And the third took her; and in like manner the seven also: and they left no children, and died.

32 **And** last of all, the woman died also.

33 Therefore in the resurrection whose wife of them is she? for seven had her to wife.

34 And Jesus answering said unto them, The children of this world marry, and are given in marriage:

35 But they ~~which~~ **who** shall be accounted worthy to obtain that world, ~~and the~~ **through** resurrection from the dead, neither marry nor are given in marriage.

36 Neither can they die any more: for they are equal unto the angels; and are the children of God, being the children of the resurrection.

37 Now that the dead are raised, even Moses shewed at the bush, when he calleth the Lord the God of Abraham, and the God of Isaac, and the God of Jacob.

38 For he is not a God of the dead, but of the living: for all live unto him.

39 Then certain of the scribes answering said, Master, thou hast well said.

40 And after that they durst not ask him any *question at all.*

41 And he said unto them, How say they that Christ is David's son?

42 And David himself saith in the book of Psalms, The Lord said unto my Lord, Sit thou on my right hand,

43 Till I make thine enemies thy footstool.

44 David therefore calleth him Lord, how is he then his son?

45 Then in the audience of all the people he said unto his disciples,

46 Beware of the scribes, ~~which~~ **who** desire to walk in long robes, and love greetings in the markets, and the highest seats in the synagogues, and the chief rooms at feasts;

47 ~~Which~~ **Who** devour widows' houses, and for a show, make long

prayers; the same shall receive greater damnation.

Chapter 21

1 And he looked up, and saw the rich men casting **in** their gifts into the treasury;

2 And ~~he~~ saw also**,** a certain poor widow casting in thither two mites.

3 And he said, Of a truth I say unto you, that this poor widow hath cast in more than they all:

4 For all these have of their abundance cast in unto the offerings of God: but she of her penury hath cast in all the living that she had.

5 And as some spake of the temple, how it was adorned with goodly stones and gifts, he said,

6 ~~As for~~ These things which ye behold, the days will come, in the which there shall not be left one stone upon another, ~~that~~ **which** shall not be thrown down.

7 And ~~they~~ **the disciples** asked him, saying, Master, ~~but~~ when shall these things be? And what sign ~~will there be~~ **wilt thou show,** when these things shall come to pass?

8 And he said, **The time draweth near, and therefore** take heed that ye be not deceived; for many shall come in my name, saying, I am *Christ*; ~~and the time draweth near~~ go ye not therefore after them.

9 ~~But~~ **And** when ye shall hear of wars and commotions, be not terrified; for these things must first come to pass; but ~~the end~~ **this** *is* not ~~by and by~~ **the end.**

10 10–11 Then said he unto them, Nation shall rise against nation, and kingdom against kingdom: and great earthquakes shall be in divers places, and famines, and pestilences; and fearful sights and great signs shall there be from heaven.

11 12 But before all these **things shall come**, they shall lay their hands on you, and persecute *you*; delivering *you* up to the synagogues, and into prisons; being brought before kings and rulers for my name's sake.

12 14 Settle ~~it~~ **this** therefore in your hearts, not to meditate before what ye shall answer;

13 15 For I will give you a mouth and wisdom, which all your adversaries shall not be able to gainsay nor resist.

14 13 And it shall turn to you for a testimony.

15 16 And ye shall be betrayed both by parents, and brethren, and kinsfolks, and friends; and *some* of you shall they cause to be put to death.

16 17 And ye shall be hated of all ~~men~~ **the world** for my name's sake.

17 18 But there shall not an hair of your head perish.

18 19 In your patience possess ye your souls.

19 20 And when ye shall see Jerusalem compassed with armies, then know that the desolation thereof is nigh.

20 21 Then let them ~~which~~ **who** are in ~~Judaea~~ **Judea** flee to the mountains; and let them ~~which~~ **who** are in the midst of it, depart out; and let not them ~~that~~ **who** are in the countries**,** **return to** enter ~~thereinto~~ **into the city.**

21 22 For these be the days of vengeance, that all things which are written may be fulfilled.

22 23 But woe unto them ~~that~~ **who** are with child, and to them ~~that~~ **who** give suck, in those days! For there shall be great distress in the land, and wrath upon this people.

23 24 And they shall fall by the edge of the sword, and shall be led away

captive into all nations: and Jerusalem shall be trodden down of the Gentiles, until the times of the Gentiles be fulfilled.

24 Now these things he spake unto them, concerning the destruction of Jerusalem. And then his disciples asked him, saying, Master, tell us concerning thy coming?

25 And **he answered them, and said, In the generation in which the times of the Gentiles shall be fulfilled,** there shall be signs in the sun, and in the moon, and in the stars; and upon the earth distress of nations with perplexity, **like** the sea and the waves roaring. **The earth also shall be troubled, and the waters of the great deep;**

26 Men's hearts failing them for fear, and for looking after those things which are coming on the earth: for the powers of heaven shall be shaken.

27 28 And when these things begin to come to pass, then look up and lift up your heads, for **the day of** your redemption draweth nigh.

28 27 And then shall they see the Son of Man coming in a cloud, with power and great glory.

29 And he spake to them a parable, **saying,** Behold the fig tree, and all the trees.

30 When they now shoot forth, ye see and know of your own selves that summer is now nigh at hand.

31 So likewise ye, when ye see these things come to pass, know ye that the kingdom of God is nigh at hand.

32 Verily I say unto you, This generation, **the generation when the times of the Gentiles be fulfilled,** shall not pass away till all be fulfilled.

33 Heaven and earth shall pass away: but my words shall not pass away.

34 ~~And~~ **Let my disciples therefore** take heed to ~~yourselves~~ **themselves,** lest at any time ~~your~~ **their** hearts be overcharged with surfeiting, and drunkenness, and cares of this life, and ~~so~~ that day come upon ~~you~~ **them** unawares.

35 For as a snare shall it come on all them ~~that~~ **who** dwell on the face of the whole earth.

36 **And what I say unto one, I say unto all,** Watch ye therefore, and pray always, **and keep my commandments,** that ye may be ~~accounted~~ **counted** worthy to escape all these things ~~that~~ **which**˙ shall come to pass, and to stand before the Son of Man **when he shall come clothed in the glory of his Father**.

37 And in the day time, he was teaching in the temple; and at night, he went out and abode in the mount that is called ~~the mount~~ Olives.

38 And the people came early in the morning to him in the temple, ~~for~~ to hear him.

Chapter 22

1 Now the feast of unleavened bread drew nigh, which is called the Passover.

2 And the chief priests, and **the** scribes, sought how they might kill him; ~~for~~ **but** they feared the people.

3 Then entered Satan into Judas surnamed Iscariot, being of the number of the twelve.

4 And he went his way, and communed with the chief priests and captains, how he might betray him unto them.

5 And they were glad, and covenanted to give him money.

6 And he promised **them**, and sought opportunity to betray him unto them in the absence of the multitude.

7 Then came the day of unleavened

bread, when the passover must be killed.

8 And he sent Peter and John, saying, Go and prepare us the passover, that we may eat.

9 And they said unto him, Where wilt thou that we prepare?

10 And he said unto them, Behold, when ye ~~are~~ **have** entered into the city, there shall a man meet you, bearing a pitcher of water; follow him into the house where he entereth in.

11 And ye shall say unto the goodman of the house, The Master saith unto ~~thee~~ **you**, Where is the guestchamber, where I shall eat the passover with my disciples?

12 And he shall shew you a large upper room furnished: there make ready.

13 And they went, and found as he had said unto them: and they made ready the passover.

14 And when the hour was come, he sat down, and the twelve apostles with him.

15 And he said unto them, With desire I have desired to eat this passover with you before I suffer:

16 For I say unto you, I will not anymore eat thereof, until it be fulfilled **which is written in the prophets concerning me. Then I will partake with you,** in the kingdom of God.

17 And he took the cup, and gave thanks, and said, Take this and divide ~~it~~ among yourselves;

18 For I say unto you, **That** I will not drink of the fruit of the vine, until the kingdom of God shall come.

19 And he took bread, and gave thanks, and brake ~~it~~, and gave unto them, saying, This is my body which is given for you; this do in remembrance of me.

20 Likewise also the cup after supper, saying, This cup *is* the new testament in my blood, which is shed for you.

21 But, behold, the hand of him ~~that~~ **who** betrayeth me *is* with me on the table.

22 And truly the Son of man goeth, as it was determined: but woe unto that man by whom he is betrayed!

23 And they began to enquire among themselves, which of them it was that should do this thing.

24 ~~And~~ There was also a strife among them, ~~which~~ **who** of them should be accounted the greatest.

25 And he said unto them, The kings of the Gentiles exercise lordship over them**,** and they ~~that~~ **who** exercise authority upon them**,** are called benefactors.

26 But ~~ye shall~~ **it ought** not **to** *be* so **with you;** but he ~~that~~ **who** is greatest among you, let him be as the younger; and he ~~that~~ **who** is chief, as he ~~that~~ **who** doth serve.

27 For whether *is* **he** greater, ~~he that~~ **who** sitteth at meat, or he ~~that~~ **who** serveth? ~~is~~ **I am** not **as** he ~~that~~ **who** sitteth at meat**,** but I am among you as he ~~that~~ **who** serveth.

28 Ye are they ~~which~~ **who** have continued with me in my temptations.

29 And I appoint unto you a kingdom, as my Father hath appointed unto me;

30 That ~~ye~~ **you** may eat and drink at my table in my kingdom; and sit on **twelve** thrones, judging the twelve tribes of Israel.

31 And the Lord said, Simon, Simon, behold Satan hath desired ~~to have~~ you, that he may sift ~~you~~ **the children of the kingdom** as wheat.

32 But I have prayed for ~~thee~~ **you**, that ~~thy~~ **your** faith fail not; and when ~~thou~~ **you** ~~art~~ **are** converted strengthen ~~thy~~ **your** brethren.

33 And he said unto him, **being aggrieved,** Lord, I am ready to go with ~~thee~~ **you**, both into prison, and ~~to~~ **unto** death.

34 And ~~he~~ **the Lord** said, I tell ~~thee~~ **you**, Peter, **that** the cock shall not crow this day, before that ~~thou~~ **you** ~~shalt~~ **will** thrice deny that ~~thou~~ **you** ~~knowest~~ **know** me.

35 And he said unto them, When I sent you without purse, and scrip, and shoes, lacked ye any thing? And they said, Nothing.

36 Then said he unto them, ~~But now~~ **I say unto you again**, He ~~that~~ **who** hath a purse, let him take *it*, and likewise *his* scrip; and he ~~that~~ **who** hath no sword, let him sell his garment and buy one.

37 For I say unto you, ~~that~~ This that is written must ~~yet~~ be accomplished in me, And he was reckoned among the transgressors; for the things concerning me have an end.

38 And they said, Lord, behold, here *are* two swords. And he said unto them, It is enough.

39 And he came out, and went, as he was ~~wont~~ **accustomed**, to the mount of Olives; and his disciples ~~also~~ followed him.

40 And when he was at the place, he said unto them, Pray that ye enter not into temptation.

41 And he was withdrawn from them about a stone's cast, and kneeled down, and prayed,

42 Saying, Father, if thou be willing, remove this cup from me: nevertheless not my will, but thine, be done.

43 And there appeared an angel unto him from heaven, strengthening him.

44 And being in an agony, he prayed more earnestly; and ~~his~~ **he** sweat ~~was~~ as it were great drops of blood falling down to the ground.

45 And when he rose up from prayer, and was come to his disciples, he found them sleeping; for **they were filled with** sorrow;

46 And **he** said unto them, Why sleep ye? rise and pray, lest ye enter into temptation.

47 And while he yet spake, behold, a multitude, and he ~~that~~ **who** was called Judas, one of the twelve, went before them, and drew near unto Jesus to kiss him.

48 But Jesus said unto him, Judas, betrayest thou the Son of man with a kiss?

49 When they ~~which~~ **who** were about him, saw what would follow, they said unto him, Lord, shall we smite with ~~the~~ **a** sword?

50 And one of them smote the servant of the high priest, and cut off his right ear.

51 And Jesus answered and said, Suffer ye thus far. And he touched his ear, and healed him.

52 Then Jesus said unto the chief priests, and captains of the temple, and the elders, ~~which~~ **who** were come to him, ~~Be~~ **Are** ye come out as against a thief, with swords and staves?

53 When I was daily with you in the temple, ye stretched forth no hands against me: but this is your hour, and the power of darkness.

54 Then took they him, and led *him*, and brought him into the high priest's house. And Peter followed afar off.

55 And when they had kindled a fire in the midst of the hall, and were set down together, Peter sat down among them.

56 But a certain maid beheld him as he sat by the fire, and earnestly looked upon him, and said, This man was also with him.

57 And he denied him, saying, Woman, I know him not.

58 And after a little while another saw him, and said, Thou art also of them. And Peter said, Man, I am not.

59 And about the space of one hour ~~after,~~ another confidently affirmed, saying, Of a truth, this ~~fellow~~ **man was** also ~~was~~ with him; for he is a ~~Galilaean~~ **Galilean**.

60 And Peter said, Man, I know not what thou sayest. And immediately, while he yet spake, the cock crew.

61 And the Lord turned, and looked upon Peter. And Peter remembered the word of the Lord, how he had said unto him, Before the cock crow, thou shalt deny me thrice.

62 And Peter went out, and wept bitterly.

63 And the men ~~that~~ **who** held Jesus, mocked him, and smote *him*.

64 And when they had blindfolded him, they struck him on the face, and asked him, saying, Prophesy, who is it ~~that~~ **who** smote thee?

65 And many other things blasphemously spake they against him.

66 And as soon as it was day, the elders of the people and the chief priests and the scribes came together, and led him into their council, saying,

67 Art thou the Christ? tell us. And he said unto them, If I tell you, ye will not believe.

68 And if I also ask *you*, ye will not answer me, nor let *me* go.

69 Hereafter shall the Son of man sit on the right hand of the power of God.

70 Then said they all, Art thou then the Son of God? And he said unto them, Ye say that I am.

71 And they said, What need ~~we~~ **ye** any further witness? For we ourselves have heard of his own mouth.

CHAPTER 23

1 And the whole multitude of them arose, and led him unto Pilate.

2 And they began to accuse him, saying, We found this ~~fellow~~ **man** perverting the nation, and forbidding to give tribute to Caesar, saying, that he himself is Christ, a king.

3 And Pilate asked him, saying, Art thou the King of the Jews? And he answered him, and said, **Yea,** thou sayest *it.*

4 Then said Pilate to the chief priests and ~~to~~ the people, I find no fault in this man.

5 And they were the more fierce, saying, He stirreth up the people, teaching throughout all Jewry, beginning from Galilee to this place.

6 When Pilate heard of Galilee, he asked whether the man were a Galilaean.

7 And as soon as he knew that he belonged unto Herod's jurisdiction, he sent him to Herod, who himself also was at Jerusalem at that time.

8 And when Herod saw Jesus, he was exceeding glad; for he was desirous to see him, of a long ~~season~~ **time**, because he had heard many things of him; and ~~he~~ hoped to have seen some miracle done by him.

9 Then he questioned with him in many words; but he answered him nothing.

10 And the chief priests and scribes stood and vehemently accused him.

11 And Herod with his men of war set him at ~~nought~~ **naught**, and mocked *him*, and arrayed him in a gorgeous robe, and sent him again to Pilate.

12 And the same day Pilate and Herod were made friends together; for before **this** they were at enmity between themselves.

13 And Pilate, when he had called together the chief priests and the rulers and the people,

14 Said unto them, ~~Ye~~ **You** have brought this man unto me, as one ~~that~~ **who** perverteth the people; and behold, I, having examined *him* before you, have found no fault in this man, touching those things whereof ye accuse him.

15 No, nor yet Herod: for I sent you to him; and, lo, nothing worthy of death is done unto him.

16 I will therefore chastise him, and release *him*.

17 (For of necessity he must release one unto them at the feast.)

18 ~~And~~ **But** they cried out all at once, saying, Away with this *man*, and release unto us Barabbas;

19 (Who for a certain sedition made in the city, and for murder, was cast into prison.)

20 Pilate therefore, willing to release Jesus, spake again to them.

21 But they cried, saying, Crucify *him*, crucify him.

22 And he said unto them the third time, Why, what evil hath he done? I have found no cause of death in him: I will therefore chastise him, and let *him* go.

23 And they were instant ~~with~~ **in** loud voices, requiring that he might be crucified; and the voices of them, and of the chief priests, prevailed.

24 And Pilate gave sentence that it should be as they required.

25 And he released unto them him ~~that~~ **who** for sedition and murder was cast into prison, whom they had desired; ~~but~~ **and** ~~he~~ delivered Jesus to their will.

26 And as they led him away, they laid hold upon one Simon, a Cyrenian, coming out of the country, and on

him they laid the cross, that he might bear *it* after Jesus.

27 And there followed him a great company of people, and of women, which also bewailed and lamented him.

28 But Jesus ~~turning~~ **turned** unto them **and** said, Daughters of Jerusalem, weep not for me, but weep for yourselves, and for your children.

29 For behold, the days are coming, in the which they shall say, Blessed *are* the barren, and the wombs ~~that~~ **which** never bare, and the paps which never gave suck.

30 Then shall they begin to say to the mountains, Fall on us; and to the hills, Cover us.

31 ~~For~~ **And** if ~~they do~~ these things **are done** in ~~a~~ **the** green tree, what shall be done in the dry **tree**?

32 This he spake, signifying the scattering of Israel, and the desolation of the heathen, or in other words, the Gentiles.

33 32 And there were also two ~~other~~ **others**, malefactors, led with him to be put to death.

34 33 And when they were come to the place, which is called Calvary, there they crucified him, and the malefactors, one on the right hand, and the other on the left.

35 34 Then said Jesus, Father, forgive them; for they know not what they do. **(Meaning the soldiers who crucified him,)** and they parted his raiment, and cast lots.

36 35 And the people stood, beholding, and the rulers also with them, derided *him*, saying, He saved others; let him save himself, if he be the Christ, the chosen of God.

37 36 And the soldiers also mocked him, coming to him, and offering him vinegar,

38 37 And saying, If thou be the king of the Jews, save thyself.

39 38 And a superscription also was written over him in letters of Greek, and Latin, and Hebrew, THIS IS THE KING OF THE JEWS.

40 39 And one of the malefactors ~~which~~ **who** ~~were hanged~~ **was crucified with him**, railed on him, saying, If thou be **the** Christ, save thyself and us.

41 40 But the other answering**,** rebuked him, saying, Dost ~~not~~ thou **not** fear God, seeing thou art in the same condemnation?

42 41 And we indeed justly; for we receive the due reward of our deeds: but this man hath done nothing amiss.

43 42 And he said ~~unto~~ **to** Jesus, Lord, remember me when thou comest into thy kingdom.

44 43 And Jesus said unto him, Verily I say unto thee, Today shalt thou be with me in ~~paradise~~ **the world of spirits**.[30]

45 44 And it was about the sixth hour, and there was ~~a~~ darkness over all the earth until the ninth hour.

46 45 And the sun was darkened, and the veil of the temple was rent in the midst.

47 46 And when Jesus had cried with a loud voice, he said, Father, into thy hands I commend my spirit: and having said thus, he gave up the ghost.

48 47 Now when the centurion saw what was done, he glorified God, saying, Certainly this was a righteous man.

49 And all the people ~~that~~ **who** came together to that sight, beholding the things which were done, smote their breasts, and returned.

50 49 And all his acquaintance, and ~~the~~ women ~~that~~ **who** followed him from Galilee, stood afar off, beholding these things.

51 50 And, behold, ~~there was~~ a man named Joseph, a counselor; ~~and he was~~ a good man and a just **one;**

52 51 The same **day** had not consented to the counsel and deed of them**;** ~~he was~~ **a man** of ~~Arimathaea~~ **Arimathea**, a city of the Jews**;** who also himself waited for the kingdom of God.

53 52 ~~This man~~ **He** went unto Pilate, and begged the body of Jesus.

54 53 And he took it down and wrapped it in linen, and laid it in a sepulchre, ~~that~~ **which** was hewn in **a** stone, wherein never man before was laid.

55 54 And that day was the preparation, and the sabbath drew on.

56 55 And the women also, ~~which~~ **who** came with him from Galilee, followed after, and beheld the sepulchre, and how his body was laid.

57 56 And they returned, and prepared spices and ointments; and rested the sabbath day according to the commandment.

CHAPTER 24

1 Now upon the first *day* of the week, very early in the morning, ~~they~~ **the women** came unto the sepulchre, bringing the spices which they had prepared, and certain *others* with them.

2 And they found the stone rolled away from the sepulchre, **and two angels standing by it in shining garments.**

3 3–4 And they entered ~~in~~ **into the sepulchre,** and ~~found~~ not **finding** the body of the Lord Jesus, ~~And it came to pass, as~~ they were much perplexed thereabout**;** ~~behold, two men stood by them in shining garments~~

4 5 And ~~as they~~ were ~~afraid~~ **affrighted**, and bowed down *their* faces to the

earth. ~~they~~ **But behold the angels** said unto them, Why seek ye the living among the dead?

5 6 He is not here, but is risen: remember how he spake unto you when he was yet in Galilee,

6 7 Saying, The Son of man must be delivered into the hands of sinful men, and be crucified, and the third day rise again.

7 8 And they remembered his words,

8 9 And returned from the sepulchre, and told all these things unto the eleven, and to all the rest.

9 10 It was Mary Magdalene, and Joanna, and Mary *the mother* of James, and other *women* ~~that~~ **who** *were* with them, ~~which~~ **who** told these things unto the apostles.

10 11 And their words seemed to them as idle tales, and they believed them not.

11 12 Then arose Peter, and ran unto the sepulchre and ~~stooping down~~ **went in**, **and** he beheld the linen clothes laid by themselves; and departed, wondering in himself at that which was come to pass.

12 13 And behold, two of them went that same day to a village called Emmaus, which was from Jerusalem ~~about~~ threescore furlongs.

13 14 And they talked together of all these things which had happened.

14 15 And it came to pass, that, while they communed *together* and reasoned, Jesus himself drew near, and went with them.

15 16 But their eyes were holden, **or covered,** that they ~~should~~ **could** not know him.

16 17 And he said unto them, What manner of communications *are* these ~~that~~ **which** ~~ye~~ **you** have one ~~to~~ **with** another, as ye walk and are sad?

17 18 And ~~the~~ one of them, whose name was Cleopas, answering, said unto him, Art thou ~~only~~ a stranger in Jerusalem, and hast not known the things which are come to pass there in these days?

18 19 And he said unto them, What things? And they said unto him, Concerning Jesus of Nazareth, ~~which~~ **who** was a prophet mighty in deed and word before God and all the people;

19 20 And how the chief priests and our rulers delivered him to be condemned to death, and have crucified him.

20 21 But we trusted that it had been he ~~which~~ **who** should have redeemed Israel. And ~~beside~~ **besides** all this, today is the third day since these things were done;

21 22 Yea, and certain women also of our company made us astonished, ~~which~~ **who** were early at the sepulchre;

22 23 And when they found not his body, they came, saying, that they had also seen a vision of angels, ~~which~~ **who** said that he was alive.

23 24 And certain of them ~~which~~ **who** were with us, went to the sepulchre, and found *it* even so as the women had said; but him they saw not.

24 25 Then he said unto them, O fools, and slow of heart to believe all that the prophets have spoken:

25 26 Ought not Christ to have suffered these things, and to enter into his glory?

26 27 And beginning at Moses and all the prophets, he expounded unto them in all the scriptures the things concerning himself.

27 28 And they drew nigh unto the village whither they went; and he made as though he would have gone ~~further~~ **farther**.

28 29 But they constrained him, saying, Abide with us: for it is toward evening, and the day is far spent. And he went in to tarry with them.

29 30 And it came to pass, as he sat at meat with them, he took bread, and blessed ~~it~~, and brake, and gave to them.

30 31 And their eyes were opened, and they knew him; and he ~~vanished~~ **was taken up** out of their sight.

31 32 And they said one to another, Did not our ~~heart~~ **hearts** burn within us, while he talked with us by the way, and while he opened to us the scriptures?

32 33 And they rose up the same hour and returned to Jerusalem, and found the eleven gathered together, and ~~them~~ **those** ~~that~~ **who** were with them,

33 34 Saying, The Lord is risen indeed, and hath appeared to Simon.

34 35 And they told what things ~~were done~~ **they saw and heard** in the way, and how he was known ~~of~~ **to** them, in breaking of bread.

35 36 And as they thus spake, Jesus himself stood in the midst of them, and saith unto them, Peace *be* unto you.

36 37 But they were terrified and affrighted, and supposed that they had seen a spirit.

37 38 And he said unto them, Why are ~~ye~~ **you** troubled? and why do thoughts arise in your hearts?

38 39 Behold my hands and my feet, that it is I: myself, handle me, and see; for a spirit hath not flesh and bones, as ye see me have.

39 40 ~~And~~ When he had thus spoken, he showed them *his* hands and *his* feet.

40 41 And while they yet **wondered and** believed not for joy, ~~and wondered~~ he said unto them, Have ye here any meat?

41 42 And they gave him a piece of a broiled fish, and ~~of an~~ **a** honey comb.

42 43 And he took *it*, and did eat before them.

43 44 And he said unto them, These *are* the words which I spake unto you, while I was yet with you, that all things must be fulfilled, which were written in the law of Moses, and *in* the prophets, and *in* the psalms, concerning me.

44 45 Then opened he their understanding, that they might understand the scriptures,

45 46 And said unto them, Thus it is written, and thus it behoved Christ to suffer, and to rise from the dead the third day:

46 47 And that repentance and remission of sins should be preached in his name among all nations, beginning at Jerusalem.

47 48 And ye are witnesses of these things.

48 49 And, behold, I send the promise of my Father upon you: but tarry ye in the city of Jerusalem, until ye be endued with power from on high.

49 50 And he led them out as far as ~~to~~ Bethany, and he lifted up his hands and blessed them.

50 51 And it came to pass, while he blessed them, he was ~~parted~~ **taken** from them, and carried up into heaven.

51 52 And they worshipped him, and returned to Jerusalem with great joy:

52 53 And were continually in the temple, praising and blessing God. Amen.

The Testimony of
SAINT JOHN

CHAPTER 1

1 In the beginning was the ~~Word~~ **gospel preached through the Son. And the gospel was the word,** and the word was with ~~God~~ **the Son**, **and the Son was with God,** and the ~~Word~~ **Son** was **of** God.

2 The same was in the beginning with God.

3 All things were made by him; and without him was not anything made ~~that~~ **which** was made.

4 In him was ~~life~~ **the gospel,** and the ~~life~~ **gospel was the life, and the life** was the light of men;

5 And the light shineth in ~~darkness~~ **the world,** and the ~~darkness~~ **world** ~~comprehended~~ **perceiveth** it not.

6 ~~There~~ **Then** was a man sent from God, whose name *was* John.

7 The same came **into the world** for a witness, to bear witness of the Light, **to bear record of the gospel through the Son, unto all,** that ~~all men~~ through him **men** might believe.

8 He was not that Light, but ~~was sent~~ **came** to bear witness of that Light.

9 ~~That~~ **Which** was the true Light, which lighteth every man ~~that~~ **who** cometh into the world;

10 **Even the Son of God. He who** was in the world, and the world was made by him, and the world knew him not.

11 He came unto his own, and his own received him not.

12 But as many as received him, to them gave he power to become the sons of God; ~~even~~ **only** to them ~~that~~ **who** believe on his name.

13 ~~Which were~~ **He was** born, not of blood, nor of the will of the flesh, nor of the will of man, but of God.

14 And the **same** Word was made flesh, and dwelt among us, and we beheld his glory, the glory as of the Only Begotten of the Father, full of grace and truth.

15 John ~~bare~~ **bear** witness of him, and cried, saying, This was he of whom I spake; He ~~that~~ **who** cometh after me, is preferred before me; for he was before me.

16 **For in the beginning was the Word, even the Son, who is made flesh, and sent unto us by the will of the Father. And as many as believe on his name shall receive of his fullness.** And of his fullness have all we received, ~~and grace for~~ **even immortality and eternal life, through his** grace.

17 For the law was given ~~by~~ **through** Moses, *but* ~~grace~~ **life** and truth came ~~by~~ **through** Jesus Christ.

18 **For the law was after a carnal commandment, to the administration of death; but the gospel was after the power of an endless life, through Jesus Christ, the Only Begotten Son, who is in the bosom of the Father.**

19 18 **And** no man hath seen God at any time, **except he hath borne record of** the ~~only begotten~~ Son; ~~which is in the bosom of the Father, he hath declared him~~ **for except it is through him no man can be saved.**

20 19 And this is the record of John, when the Jews sent priests and Levites from Jerusalem to ask him, Who art thou?

21 20 And he confessed, and denied not **that he was Elias**; but confessed, **saying;** I am not the Christ.

22 21 And they asked him, ~~What then~~ **saying; How** art thou **then** Elias? And he ~~saith~~ **said**, I am not **that Elias who was to restore all things. And they asked him, saying,** Art thou that prophet? And he answered, No.

23 22 Then said they unto him, Who art thou? that we may give an answer to them that sent us. What sayest thou of thyself?

24 23 He said, I *am* the voice of one crying in the wilderness, Make straight the way of the Lord, as said the prophet Esaias.

25 24 And they ~~which~~ **who** were sent were of the Pharisees.

26 25 And they asked him, and said unto him, Why baptizest thou then, if thou be not ~~that~~ **the** Christ, nor Elias **who was to restore all things**, neither that prophet?

27 26 John answered them, saying, I baptize with water: but there standeth one among you, whom ye know not;

28 27 He it is **of whom I bear record. He is the prophet, even Elias,** who, coming after me, is preferred before me, whose shoe's latchet I am not worthy to unloose, **or whose place I am not able to fill; for he shall baptize, not only with water, but with fire, and with the Holy Ghost.**

29 The next day John seeth Jesus coming unto him, and ~~saith~~ **said;** Behold the Lamb of God, ~~which~~ **who** taketh away the sin of the world!

30 30–31 **And John bare record of him unto the people, saying,** This is he of whom I said; After me cometh a man ~~which~~ **who** is preferred before me; for he was before me, and I knew

him ~~not~~, ~~but~~ **and** that he should be made manifest to Israel; therefore am I come baptizing with water.

31 32 And John bare record, saying; **When he was baptized of me,** I saw the Spirit descending from heaven like a dove, and it abode upon him.

32 33 And I knew him ~~not~~; ~~but~~ **for** he ~~that~~ **who** sent me to baptize with water, the same said unto me; Upon whom thou shalt see the Spirit descending, and remaining on him, the same is he ~~which~~ **who** baptizeth with the Holy Ghost.

33 34 And I saw, and bare record that this is the Son of God.

34 28 These things were done in Bethabara, beyond Jordan, where John was baptizing.

35 Again the next day after John stood, and two of his disciples;

36 And looking upon Jesus as he walked, he ~~saith~~ **said;** Behold the Lamb of God!

37 And the two disciples heard him speak, and they followed Jesus.

38 Then Jesus turned, and saw them following **him**, and ~~saith~~ **said** unto them, What seek ye? They ~~said~~ **say** unto him, Rabbi, (which is to say, being interpreted, Master;) where dwellest thou?

39 **And** he ~~saith~~ **said** unto them; Come and see. **And** they came and saw where he dwelt, and abode with him that day; for it was about the tenth hour.

40 One of the two ~~which~~ **who** heard John ~~speak~~, and followed ~~him~~ **Jesus**, was Andrew, Simon Peter's brother.

41 He first findeth his own brother Simon, and saith unto him, We have found the Messias, which is, being interpreted, the Christ.

42 And he brought him to Jesus. And when Jesus beheld him, he said,

Thou art Simon, the son of Jona; thou shalt be called Cephas, which is, by interpretation, a **seer, or a** stone. **And they were fishermen. And they straightway left all, and followed Jesus.**

43 The day following Jesus would go forth into Galilee, and findeth Philip, and saith unto him, Follow me.

44 Now Philip was ~~of~~ **at** Bethsaida, the city of Andrew and Peter.

45 Philip findeth Nathanael, and saith unto him, We have found him, of whom Moses in the law, and the prophets, did write, Jesus of Nazareth, the son of Joseph.

46 And Nathanael said unto him, Can there any good thing come out of Nazareth? Philip saith unto him, Come and see.

47 Jesus saw Nathanael coming ~~to~~ **unto** him, and ~~saith~~ **said** of him, Behold an Israelite indeed, in whom is no guile!

48 Nathanael ~~saith~~ **said** unto him, Whence knowest thou me? Jesus ~~answered~~ **answering** ~~and~~ said unto him, Before ~~that~~ Philip called thee, when thou wast under the fig tree, I saw thee.

49 Nathanael answered and saith unto him, Rabbi, thou art the Son of God; thou art the King of Israel.

50 Jesus answered and said unto him, Because I said unto thee, I saw thee under the fig tree, believest thou? thou shalt see greater things than these.

51 And he ~~saith~~ **said** unto him, Verily, verily, I say unto you, Hereafter ye shall see heaven open, and the angels of God ascending and descending upon the Son of Man.

CHAPTER 2

1 And on the third day **of the week,** there was a marriage in Cana of Galilee; and the mother of Jesus was there.

2 And ~~both~~ Jesus was called, and his disciples, to the marriage.

3 And when they wanted wine, ~~the~~ **his** mother ~~of Jesus saith~~ **said** unto him, They have no wine.

4 Jesus ~~saith~~ **said** unto her, Woman, what **wilt thou** have ~~I~~ **me** ~~to~~ do ~~with~~ **for** thee? **that will I do; for** mine hour is not yet come.

5 His mother ~~saith~~ **said** unto the servants, Whatsoever he saith unto you, **see that ye** do *it.*

6 ~~And~~ There were set there six waterpots of stone, after the manner of the purifying of the Jews, containing two or three firkins apiece.

7 Jesus saith unto them, Fill the waterpots with water. And they filled them up to the brim.

8 And he ~~saith~~ **said** ~~unto them,~~ Draw out now, and bear unto the governor of the feast. And they bare ~~it~~ **unto him**.

9 When the ~~ruler~~ **governor** of the feast had tasted the water ~~that~~ **which** was made wine, (and **he** knew not whence it was, but the servants ~~which~~ **who** drew the water knew,) the governor of the feast called the bridegroom,

10 And saith unto him, Every man at the beginning doth set forth good wine; and when men have well drunk, then that which is worse: *but* thou hast kept the good wine until now.

11 This beginning of miracles did Jesus in Cana of Galilee, and manifested forth his glory; and **the faith of** his disciples ~~believed on~~ **was strengthened in** him.

12 After this he went down to Capernaum, he, and his mother, and his brethren, and his disciples: and they continued there not many days.

13 And the Jews' passover was at hand, and Jesus went up to Jerusalem,

14 And found in the temple those ~~that~~ **who** sold oxen**,** and sheep**,** and doves, and the changers of money sitting**.**

15 And when he had made a scourge of small cords, he drove them all out of the temple, and the sheep, and the oxen; and poured out the changers' money, and overthrew the tables;

16 And said unto them ~~that~~ **who** sold doves, Take these things hence; make not my Father's house ~~an~~ **a˙** house of merchandise.

17 And his disciples remembered that it was written, The zeal of ~~thine~~ **thy** house hath eaten me up.

18 Then ~~answered~~ **spake** the Jews and said unto him, What sign showest thou unto us, seeing ~~that~~ thou doest these things?

19 Jesus answered and said unto them, Destroy this temple, and in three days I will raise it up.

20 Then said the Jews, Forty and six years was this temple in building, and wilt thou rear it up in three days?

21 But he spake of the temple of his body.

22 When therefore he was risen from the dead, his disciples remembered that he had said this unto them**,** and they ~~believed~~ **remembered** the scripture, and the word which Jesus had said **unto them.**

23 Now when he was in Jerusalem, at the passover, ~~in~~ **on** the feast *day*, many believed ~~in~~ **on** his name, when they saw the miracles which he did.

24 But Jesus did not commit himself unto them, because he knew all ~~men~~ **things**,

25 And needed not that any should testify of man: for he knew what was in man.

CHAPTER 3

1 There was a man of the Pharisees, named Nicodemus, a ruler of the Jews:

2 The same came to Jesus by night, and said unto him, Rabbi, we know that thou art a teacher come from God**;** for no man can do these miracles ~~that~~ **which** thou doest, except God be with him.

3 Jesus answered and said unto him, Verily, verily, I say unto thee, Except a man be born again, he cannot see the kingdom of God.

4 Nicodemus saith unto him, How can a man be born when he is old? can he enter the second time into his mother's womb, and be born?

5 Jesus answered, Verily, verily, I say unto thee, Except a man be born of water**,** and ~~of~~ the Spirit, he cannot enter into the kingdom of God.

6 That which is born of the flesh is flesh; and that which is born of the Spirit is spirit.

7 Marvel not that I said unto thee, Ye must be born again.

8 The wind bloweth where it listeth, and thou hearest the sound thereof, but canst not tell whence it cometh, and whither it goeth**;** so is everyone ~~that~~ **who** is born of the Spirit.

9 Nicodemus answered and said unto him, How can these things be?

10 Jesus answered and said ~~unto him~~, Art thou a master of Israel, and knowest not these things?

11 Verily, verily, I say unto thee, We speak that we do know, and testify that we have seen; and ye receive not our witness.

12 If I have told you earthly things, and ye believe not, how shall ye believe if I tell you ~~of~~ heavenly things?

13 **I tell you,** ~~And~~ No man hath ascended up to heaven, but he ~~that~~ **who**

came down from heaven, *even* the Son of Man ~~which~~ **who** is in heaven.

14 And as Moses lifted up the serpent in the wilderness, even so must the Son of man be lifted up:

15 That whosoever believeth ~~in~~ **on** him should not perish, but have eternal life.

16 For God so loved the world, that he gave his Only Begotten Son, that whosoever believeth ~~in~~ **on** him should not perish; but have everlasting life.

17 For God sent not his Son into the world to condemn the world; but that the world through him might be saved.

18 He ~~that~~ **who** believeth on him is not condemned; but he ~~that~~ **who** believeth not is condemned already, because he hath not believed ~~in~~ **on** the name of the Only Begotten Son of God**, which before was preached by the mouth of the holy prophets; for they testified of me.**

19 And this is the condemnation, that light is come into the world, and men ~~loved~~ **love** darkness rather than light, because their deeds ~~were~~ **are** evil.

20 For everyone ~~that~~ **who** doeth evil hateth the light, neither cometh to the light, lest his deeds should be reproved.

21 But he ~~that~~ **who** ~~doeth~~ **loveth** truth, cometh to the light, that his deeds may be made manifest.

22 21 **And he who obeyeth the truth, the works which he doeth** ~~that~~ they are ~~wrought in~~ **of** God.

23 22 After these things came Jesus and his disciples into the land of Judaea; and there he tarried with them, and baptized.

24 23 And John also was baptizing in Ænon near to Salim, because there was much water there: and they came, and were baptized.

25 24 For John was not yet cast into prison.

26 25 Then there arose a question between *some* of John's disciples and the Jews about purifying.

27 26 And they came unto John, and said unto him, Rabbi, he ~~that~~ **who** was with thee beyond Jordan, to whom thou barest witness, behold, the same baptizeth, and **he receiveth of** all ~~men~~ **people who** come ~~to~~ **unto** him.

28 27 John answered and said, A man can receive nothing, except it be given him from heaven.

29 28 Ye yourselves bear me witness, that I said, I am not the Christ, but that I am sent before him.

30 29 He ~~that~~ **who** hath the bride**,** is the bridegroom; but the friend of the bridegroom, ~~which~~ **who** standeth and heareth him, rejoiceth greatly because of the bridegroom's voice; this my joy therefore is fulfilled.

31 30 He must increase, but I *must* decrease.

32 31–32 He ~~that~~ **who** cometh from above is above all; he ~~that~~ **who** is of the earth is earthly, and speaketh of the earth; he ~~that~~ **who** cometh from heaven is above all. And what he hath seen and heard, that he testifieth; and **but** ~~no~~ **few** ~~man~~ **men** ~~receiveth~~ **receive** his testimony.

33 He ~~that~~ **who** hath received his testimony, hath set to his seal that God is true.

34 For he whom God hath sent, speaketh the words of God; for God giveth **him** not the Spirit by measure ~~unto him~~**, for he dwelleth in him, even the fullness.**

35 The Father loveth the Son, and hath given all things into his ~~hand~~ **hands** .

36 **And** he ~~that~~ **who** believeth on

the Son hath everlasting life; **and shall
receive of his fullness.** ~~and~~ **But** he
~~that~~ **who** believeth not the Son, shall
not ~~see life~~ **receive of his fullness**; ~~but~~
for the wrath of God ~~abideth~~ **is** ~~on~~
upon him.

CHAPTER 4

1 When therefore ~~the Lord knew
how~~ the Pharisees had heard that Jesus
made and baptized more disciples
than John,

**2 They sought more diligently
some means that they might put
him to death; for many received
John as a prophet, but they believed
not on Jesus.**

3 2 **Now the Lord knew this,**
though ~~Jesus~~ **he** himself baptized not
~~but~~ **so many as** his disciples;

**4 For he suffered them for an ex-
ample, preferring one another.**

5 3 **And** he left ~~Judaea~~ **Judea**, and
departed again into Galilee,

6 4 And ~~he~~ **said unto his disciples,**
I must needs go through Samaria.

7 5 Then **he** cometh ~~he~~ to ~~a~~ **the** city
of Samaria which is called Sychar, near
to the parcel of ground ~~that~~ **which** Jacob gave to his son Joseph; **the place
where Jacob's well was.**

8 6 Now ~~Jacob's well was there~~ Jesus
~~therefore~~ being ~~wearied~~ **weary** with
~~his~~ **the** journey, **it being about the
sixth hour,** sat ~~thus~~ **down** on the well
~~and it was about the sixth hour;~~

9 7 **And** there ~~cometh~~ **came** a
woman of Samaria to draw water;
Jesus ~~saith~~ **said** unto her, Give me to
drink.

10 8 ~~For~~ **Now** his disciples were
gone away ~~unto~~ **into** the city to buy
meat.

11 9 ~~Then~~ **Wherefore he being
alone, the woman of Samaria** ~~saith~~
said ~~the woman of Samaria~~ unto him,
How is it that thou being a Jew, askest

drink of me, ~~which~~ **who** am a woman
of Samaria? ~~for~~ The Jews have no
dealings with the Samaritans.

12 10 Jesus answered and said unto
her, If thou knewest the gift of God,
and who it is that saith to thee, Give
me to drink; thou wouldest have asked
of him, and he would have given thee
living water.

13 11 The woman saith unto him,
Sir, thou hast nothing to draw with,
and the well is deep: from whence
then hast thou that living water?

14 12 Art thou greater than our father Jacob, ~~which~~ **who** gave us the
well, and drank thereof himself, and
his children, and his cattle?

15 13 Jesus answered and said unto
her, Whosoever ~~drinketh~~ **shall drink**
of this ~~water~~ **well,** shall thirst again;

16 14 But whosoever drinketh of
the water ~~that~~ **which** I shall give him
shall never thirst; but the water that I
shall give him shall be in him a well of
water springing up into everlasting
life.

17 15 The woman ~~saith~~ **said** unto
him, Sir, give me **of** this water that I
thirst not, neither come hither to
draw.

18 16 Jesus saith unto her, Go, call
thy husband, and come hither.

19 17 The woman answered and
said, I have no husband. Jesus said
unto her, Thou hast well said, I have
no husband:

20 18 For thou hast had five husbands; and he whom thou now hast is
not thy husband: in that saidst thou
truly.

21 19 The woman saith unto him,
Sir, I perceive that thou art a prophet.

22 20 Our fathers worshipped in
this mountain; and ye say, that in Jerusalem is the place where men ought
to worship.

23 21 Jesus saith unto her, Woman, believe me, the hour cometh, when ye shall neither in this mountain, nor yet at Jerusalem, worship the Father.

24 22 Ye worship ye know not what; we know what we worship; ~~for~~ **and** salvation is of the Jews.

25 23 ~~But~~ **And** the hour cometh, and now is, when the true worshipers shall worship the Father in spirit and in truth; for the Father seeketh such to worship him.

26 24 **For unto such hath** God ~~is a~~ **promised his** Spirit. And they ~~that~~ **who** worship him, must worship ~~him~~ in spirit and in truth.

27 25 The woman ~~saith~~ **said** unto him, I know that Messias cometh, ~~which~~ **who** is called Christ; when he is come, he will tell us all things.

28 26 Jesus ~~saith~~ **said** unto her, I ~~that~~ **who** speak unto thee am ~~he~~ **the Messias.**

29 27 And upon this came his disciples, and marvelled that he talked with the woman: yet no man said, What seekest thou? or, Why talkest thou with her?

30 28 The woman then left her waterpot, and went her way into the city, and saith to the men,

31 29 Come see a man ~~which~~ **who** told me all things that ~~ever~~ I ~~did~~ **have ever done.** Is not this the Christ?

32 30 Then they went out of the city, and came unto him.

33 31 In the ~~mean while~~ **meantime** his disciples prayed him, saying, Master, eat.

34 32 But he said unto them, I have meat to eat that ye know not of.

35 33 Therefore said the disciples one to another, Hath any man brought him ~~ought~~ **meat** to eat?

36 34 Jesus ~~saith~~ **said** unto them, My meat is to do the will of him ~~that~~

who sent me, and to finish his work.

37 35 Say not ye, There are yet four months, and *then* cometh harvest? behold, I say unto you, Lift up your eyes, and look on the fields; for they are white already to harvest.

38 36 And he ~~that~~ **who** reapeth, receiveth wages, and gathereth fruit unto life eternal; that both he ~~that~~ **who** soweth, and he ~~that~~ **who** reapeth, may rejoice together.

39 37 And herein is that saying true, One soweth, and another reapeth.

40 38 I **have** sent you to reap that whereon ye bestowed no labor; ~~other men~~ **the prophets have** labored, and ye ~~are~~ **have** entered into their labors.

41 39 And many of the Samaritans of that city believed on him for the saying of the woman, ~~which~~ **who** testified, **saying,** He told me all **things** ~~that~~ I **have** ever ~~I did~~ **done**.

42 40 So when the Samaritans were come unto him, they besought him that he would tarry with them: and he abode there two days.

43 41 And many more believed because of his own word;

44 42 And said unto the woman, Now we believe, not because of thy saying; ~~for~~ we have heard ~~him~~ **for** ourselves, and know that this is indeed the Christ, the Savior of the world.

45 43 Now after two days he departed thence, and went into Galilee.

46 44 For Jesus himself testified, that a prophet hath no honour in his own country.

47 45 Then when he was come into Galilee, the Galilaeans received him, having seen all the things that he did at Jerusalem at the feast: for they also went unto the feast.

48 46 So Jesus came again into Cana of Galilee, where he made the water wine. And there was a certain nobleman, whose son was sick at Capernaum.

49 47 When he heard that Jesus was come out of Judaea into Galilee, he went unto him, and besought him that he would come down, and heal his son: for he was at the point of death.

50 48 Then said Jesus unto him, Except ye see signs and wonders, ye will not believe.

51 49 The nobleman ~~saith~~ **said** unto him, Sir, come down ~~ere~~ **before** my child die.

52 50 Jesus ~~saith~~ **said** unto him, Go thy way, thy son liveth. And the man believed the word ~~that~~ **which** Jesus had spoken unto him, and he went his way.

53 51 And as he was ~~now~~ going down **to his house**, his servants met him, and ~~told him~~ **spake**, saying, Thy son liveth.

54 52 Then inquired he of them the hour when he began to ~~amend~~ **mend**. And they said unto him, Yesterday at the seventh hour the fever left him.

55 53 So the father knew that ~~it~~ **his son** *was* **healed** ~~at~~ **in** the same hour in the which Jesus said unto him, Thy son liveth; and himself believed, and his whole house;

56 54 This ~~is again~~ **being** the second miracle ~~that~~ **which** Jesus ~~did~~ **had done** when he ~~was~~ **had** come out of ~~Judaea~~ **Judea** into Galilee.

CHAPTER 5

1 After this there was a feast of the Jews; and Jesus went up to Jerusalem.

2 Now there is at Jerusalem by the sheep *market* a pool, which is called in the Hebrew tongue Bethesda, having five porches.

3 In these **porches** lay a great ~~multitude of~~ **many** impotent folk, of blind,

halt, withered, waiting for the moving of the water.

4 For an angel went down at a certain season into the pool, and troubled the water: whosoever then first after the troubling of the water stepped in was made whole of whatsoever disease he had.

5 And a certain man was there, ~~which~~ **who** had an infirmity thirty and eight years.

6 And Jesus saw him lie, and knew that he had been now a long time ~~in that case~~ **afflicted; and** he ~~saith~~ **said** unto him, Wilt thou be made whole?

7 The impotent man answered him, Sir, I have no man, when the water is troubled, to put me into the pool: but while I am coming, another steppeth down before me.

8 Jesus saith unto him, Rise, take up thy bed, and walk.

9 And immediately the man was made whole, and took up his bed, and walked; and **it was** on ~~the same day was~~ the Sabbath **day**.

10 The Jews therefore said unto him ~~that~~ **who** was cured, It is the Sabbath day; it is not lawful for thee to carry *thy* bed.

11 He answered them, He ~~that~~ **who** made me whole, ~~the same~~ said unto me, Take up thy bed and walk.

12 Then ~~asked~~ **answered** they him, **saying,** What man is ~~that~~ **he** ~~which~~ **who** said unto thee, Take up thy bed and walk?

13 And he ~~that~~ **who** was healed ~~wist~~ **knew** not who it was; for Jesus had conveyed himself away, a multitude being in *that* place.

14 Afterward Jesus findeth him in the temple, and said unto him, Behold, thou art made whole: sin no more, lest a worse thing come unto thee.

15 The man departed, and told the

Jews that it was Jesus ~~which~~ **who** had made him whole;

16 And therefore did the Jews persecute Jesus, and sought to slay him, because he had done these things on the sabbath day.

17 But Jesus answered them, My Father worketh hitherto, and I work.

18 Therefore the Jews sought the more to kill him, because he not only had broken the sabbath, but said also that God was his Father, making himself equal with God.

19 Then answered Jesus and said unto them, Verily, verily, I say unto you, The Son can do nothing of himself, but what he seeth the Father do: for what things soever he doeth, these also doeth the Son likewise.

20 For the Father loveth the Son, and sheweth him all things that himself doeth: and he will shew him greater works than these, that ye may marvel.

21 For as the Father raiseth up the dead, and quickeneth *them*; even so the Son quickeneth whom he will.

22 For the Father judgeth no man, but hath committed all judgment unto the Son:

23 That all ~~men~~ should honor the Son, even as they honor the Father. He ~~that~~ **who** honoreth not the Son, honoreth not the Father ~~which~~ **who** hath sent him.

24 Verily, verily, I say unto you, He ~~that~~ **who** heareth my word, and believeth on him ~~that~~ **who** sent me, hath everlasting life, and shall not come into condemnation; but is passed from death ~~unto~~ **into** life.

25 Verily, verily, I say unto you, The hour is coming, and now is, when the dead shall hear the voice of the Son of God; and they ~~that~~ **who** hear shall live.

26 For as the Father hath life in himself; so hath he given to the Son to have life in himself;

27 And hath given him authority to execute judgment also, because he is the Son of man.

28 Marvel not at this; for the hour is coming, in the which all ~~that~~ **who** are in ~~the~~ **their** graves shall hear his voice,

29 And shall come forth; they ~~that~~ **who** have done good, ~~unto~~ **in** the resurrection of ~~life~~ **the just**; and they ~~that~~ **who** have done evil, ~~unto~~ **in** the resurrection of ~~damnation~~ **the unjust**.

30 ~~I can of mine own self do nothing~~ **And shall all be judged of the Son of Man. For** as I hear, I judge, and my judgment is just;

31 30 **For I can of mine own self do nothing;** because I seek not mine own will, but the will of the Father ~~which~~ **who** hath sent me.

32 31 **Therefore** if I bear witness of myself, **yet** my witness is ~~not~~ true.

33 32 **For I am not alone,** there is another ~~that~~ **who** beareth witness of me, and I know that the ~~witness~~ **testimony** which he ~~witnesseth~~ **giveth** of me is true.

34 33 Ye sent unto John, and he bare witness **also** unto the truth.

35 34 ~~But I~~ **And he** ~~receive~~ **received** not **his** testimony ~~from~~ **of** man, but **of God, and ye yourselves say that he is a prophet, therefore ye ought to receive his testimony.** These things I say that ye might be saved.

36 35 He was a burning and a shining light: and ye were willing for a season to rejoice in his light.

37 36 But I have **a** greater witness than ~~that~~ **the testimony** of John; for the works which the Father hath given me to finish, the same works that I do, bear witness of me, that the Father hath sent me.

38 37 And the Father himself ~~which~~ **who** hath sent me, hath borne witness of me. **And verily I testify unto you, that** ye have ~~neither~~ **never** heard his voice at any time, nor seen his shape;

39 38 ~~And~~ **For** ye have not his word abiding in you; ~~for~~ **and him** whom he hath sent, ~~him~~ ye believe not.

40 39 Search the scriptures; for in them ye think ye have eternal life: and they are they which testify of me.

41 40 And ye will not come to me that ye might have life, **lest ye should honor me**.

42 41 I receive not honour from men.

43 42 But I know you, that ye have not the love of God in you.

44 43 I am come in my Father's name, and ye receive me not: if another shall come in his own name, him ye will receive.

45 44 How can ye believe, ~~which~~ **who** ~~receive~~ **seek** honor one of another, and seek not the honor ~~that~~ **which** *cometh* from God only?

46 45 Do not think that I will accuse you to the Father; there is ~~one~~ **Moses** ~~that~~ **who** accuseth you, ~~even Moses~~ in whom ye trust.

47 46 For had ye believed Moses, ye would have believed me: for he wrote of me.

48 47 But if ye believe not his writings, how shall ye believe my words?

Chapter 6

1 After these things Jesus went over the sea of Galilee, which is *the sea* of Tiberias.

2 And a great multitude followed him, because they saw his miracles which he did on them that were diseased.

3 And Jesus went up into a mountain, and there he sat with his disciples.

4 And the passover, a feast of the Jews, was nigh.

5 When Jesus then lifted up *his* eyes, and saw a great company come unto him, he saith unto Philip, Whence shall we buy bread, that these may eat?

6 And this he said to prove him: for he himself knew what he would do.

7 Philip answered him, Two hundred pennyworth of bread is not sufficient for them, that every one of them may take a little.

8 One of his disciples, Andrew, Simon Peter's brother, saith unto him,

9 There is a lad here, which hath five barley loaves, and two small fishes: but what are they among so many?

10 And Jesus said, Make the men sit down. Now there was much grass in the place. So the men sat down, in number about five thousand.

11 And Jesus took the loaves; and when he had given thanks, he distributed to the disciples, and the disciples to them that were set down; and likewise of the fishes as much as they would.

12 When they **had eaten and** were ~~filled~~ **satisfied**, he said unto his disciples, Gather up the fragments that remain, that nothing be lost.

13 Therefore they gathered *them* together, and filled twelve baskets with the fragments of the five barley loaves, which remained over and above unto them that had eaten.

14 Then those men, when they had seen the miracle that Jesus did, said, This is of a truth that prophet that should come into the world.

15 When Jesus therefore perceived that they would come and take him

by force, to make him a king, he departed again into a mountain himself alone.

16 And when even was *now* come, his disciples went down unto the sea,

17 And entered into a ship, and went over the sea toward Capernaum. And it was now dark, and Jesus ~~was~~ **had** not come to them.

18 And the sea arose by reason of a great wind that blew.

19 So when they had rowed about five and twenty or thirty furlongs, they ~~see~~ **saw** Jesus walking on the sea, and drawing nigh unto the ship; and they were afraid.

20 But he saith unto them, It is I; be not afraid.

21 Then they willingly received him into the ship: and immediately the ship was at the land whither they went.

22 The day following, when the people which stood on the other side of the sea saw that there was none other boat there, save that one whereinto his disciples were entered, and that Jesus went not with his disciples into the boat, but *that* his disciples were gone away alone;

23 (Howbeit there came other boats from Tiberias nigh unto the place where they did eat bread, after that the Lord had given thanks:)

24 When the people therefore saw that Jesus was not there, neither his disciples, they also took shipping, and came to Capernaum, seeking for Jesus.

25 And when they had found him on the other side of the sea, they said unto him, Rabbi, ~~when~~ **how** camest thou hither?

26 Jesus answered them and said, Verily, verily, I say unto you, Ye seek me, not because **ye desire to keep my sayings, neither because** ye saw the miracles, but because ye did eat of the loaves and were filled.

27 Labor not for the meat which perisheth, but for that meat which endureth unto everlasting life, which the Son of Man ~~shall~~ **hath power to** give unto you; for him hath God the Father sealed.

28 Then said they unto him, What shall we do, that we might work the works of God?

29 Jesus answered and said unto them, This is the work of God, that ye believe on him whom he hath sent.

30 They said therefore unto him, What sign shewest thou then, that we may see, and believe thee? what dost thou work?

31 Our fathers did eat manna in the desert; as it is written, He gave them bread from heaven to eat.

32 Then Jesus said unto them, Verily, verily, I say unto you, Moses gave you not that bread from heaven; but my Father giveth you the true bread from heaven.

33 For the bread of God is he which cometh down from heaven, and giveth life unto the world.

34 Then said they unto him, Lord, evermore give us this bread.

35 And Jesus said unto them, I am the bread of life: he that cometh to me shall never hunger; and he that believeth on me shall never thirst.

36 But I said unto you, That ye also have seen me, and believe not.

37 All that the Father giveth me shall come to me; and him that cometh to me I will in no wise cast out.

38 For I came down from heaven, not to do mine own will, but the will of him that sent me.

39 And this is the Father's will which hath sent me, that of all which he

hath given me I should lose nothing, but should raise it up again at the last day.

40 And this is the will of him that sent me, that everyone which seeth the Son, and believeth on him, may have everlasting life; and I will raise him up **in the resurrection of the just** at the last day.

41 The Jews then murmured at him, because he said, I am the bread which came down from heaven.

42 And they said, Is not this Jesus, the son of Joseph, whose father and mother we know? how is it then that he saith, I came down from heaven?

43 Jesus therefore answered and said unto them, Murmur not among yourselves.

44 No man can come to me, except ~~the~~ **he doeth the will of my** Father ~~which~~ **who** hath sent me. ~~draw him~~ **And this is the will of him who hath sent me, that ye receive the Son; for the Father beareth record of him; and he who receiveth the testimony, and doeth the will of him who sent me,** ~~and~~ I will raise ~~him~~ up ~~at the last day~~ **in the resurrection of the just.**

45 **For** it is written in the prophets, And ~~they~~ **these** shall ~~be~~ all **be** taught of God. Every man therefore that hath heard, and hath learned of the Father, cometh unto me.

46 Not that any man hath seen the Father, save he which is of God, he hath seen the Father.

47 Verily, verily, I say unto you, He that believeth on me hath everlasting life.

48 I am that bread of life.

49 50 This is the bread which cometh down from heaven, that a man may eat thereof, and not die.

50 49 Your fathers did eat manna in the wilderness, and are dead.

51 **But** I am the living bread which came down from heaven; if any man eat of this bread, he shall live forever; and the bread that I will give is my flesh, which I will give for the life of the world.

52 The Jews therefore strove among themselves, saying, How can this man give us *his* flesh to eat?

53 Then Jesus said unto them, Verily, verily, I say unto you, Except ye eat the flesh of the Son of man, and drink his blood, ye have no life in you.

54 Whoso eateth my flesh, and drinketh my blood, hath eternal life; and I will raise him up **in the resurrection of the just** at the last day;

55 For my flesh is meat indeed, and my blood is drink indeed.

56 He that eateth my flesh, and drinketh my blood, dwelleth in me, and I in him.

57 As the living Father hath sent me, and I live by the Father: so he that eateth me, even he shall live by me.

58 This is that bread which came down from heaven: not as your fathers did eat manna, and are dead: he that eateth of this bread shall live for ever.

59 These things said he in the synagogue, as he taught in Capernaum.

60 Many therefore of his disciples, when they had heard *this*, said, This is an hard saying; who can hear it?

61 When Jesus knew in himself that his disciples murmured at it, he said unto them, Doth this offend you?

62 *What* and if ye shall see the Son of man ascend up where he was before?

63 It is the spirit that quickeneth; the flesh profiteth nothing: the words that I speak unto you, *they* are spirit, and *they* are life.

64 But there are some of you that

believe not. For Jesus knew from the beginning who they were that believed not, and who should betray him.

65 And he said, Therefore said I unto you, that no man can come unto me, except ~~it were given unto him~~ **he doeth the will** of my Father **who hath sent me**.

66 From that *time* many of his disciples went back, and walked no more with him.

67 Then said Jesus unto the twelve, Will ye also go away?

68 Then Simon Peter answered him, Lord, to whom shall we go? thou hast the words of eternal life.

69 And we believe and are sure that thou art that Christ, the Son of the living God.

70 Jesus answered them, Have not I chosen you twelve, and one of you is a devil?

71 He spake of Judas Iscariot *the son* of Simon: for he it was that should betray him, being one of the twelve.

CHAPTER 7

1 After these things Jesus walked in Galilee: for he would not walk in Jewry, because the Jews sought to kill him.

2 Now the Jews' feast of tabernacles was at hand.

3 His brethren therefore said unto him, Depart hence, and go into ~~Judaea~~ **Judea**, that thy disciples **there** also may see the works that thou doest.

4 For *there is* no man *that* doeth anything in secret, and he himself seeketh to be known openly. If thou do these things, show thyself to the world.

5 For neither did his brethren believe in him.

6 Then Jesus said unto them, My time is not yet come: but your time is alway ready.

7 The world cannot hate you; but me it hateth, because I testify of it, that the works thereof are evil.

8 Go ye up unto this feast: I go not up yet unto this feast; for my time is not yet full come.

9 When he had said these words unto them, he ~~abode~~ **continued** *still* in Galilee.

10 But ~~when~~ **after** his brethren were gone up, then went he also up unto the feast, not openly, but as it were in secret.

11 Then the Jews sought him at the feast, and said, Where is he?

12 And there was much murmuring among the people concerning him: for some said, He is a good man: others said, Nay; but he deceiveth the people.

13 Howbeit no man spake openly of him for fear of the Jews.

14 Now about the midst of the feast Jesus went up into the temple, and taught.

15 And the Jews marvelled, saying, How knoweth this man letters, having never learned?

16 Jesus answered them, and said, My doctrine is not mine, but his that sent me.

17 If any man will do his will, he shall know of the doctrine, whether it be of God, or *whether* I speak of myself.

18 He that speaketh of himself seeketh his own glory: but he that seeketh his glory that sent him, the same is true, and no unrighteousness is in him.

19 Did not Moses give you the law, and *yet* none of you keepeth the law? Why go ye about to kill me?

20 The people answered and said, Thou hast a devil: who goeth about to kill thee?

21 Jesus answered and said unto them, I have done one work, and ye all marvel.

22 Moses therefore gave unto you circumcision; (not because it is of Moses, but of the fathers;) and ye on the sabbath day circumcise a man.

23 If a man on the sabbath day receive circumcision, that the law of Moses should not be broken; are ye angry at me, because I have made a man every whit whole on the sabbath day?

24 Judge not according to ~~the appearance~~ **your traditions**, but judge righteous judgment.

25 Then said some of them of Jerusalem, Is not this he, whom they seek to kill?

26 But, lo, he speaketh boldly, and they say nothing unto him. Do the rulers know indeed that this is the very Christ?

27 Howbeit we know this man whence he is: but when Christ cometh, no man knoweth whence he is.

28 Then cried Jesus in the temple as he taught, saying, Ye both know me, and ye know whence I am: and I am not come of myself, but he that sent me is true, whom ye know not.

29 But I know him: for I am from him, and he hath sent me.

30 Then they sought to take him: but no man laid hands on him, because his hour was not yet come.

31 And many of the people believed on him, and said, When Christ cometh, will he do more miracles than these which this *man* hath done?

32 The Pharisees heard that the people murmured such things concerning him; and the Pharisees and the chief priests sent officers to take him.

33 Then said Jesus unto them, Yet a little while ~~am~~ I **am** with you, and *then* I go unto him that sent me.

34 Ye shall seek me, and shall not find *me*: and where I am, *thither* ye cannot come.

35 Then said the Jews among themselves, Whither will he go, that we shall not find him? will he go unto the dispersed among the Gentiles, and teach the Gentiles?

36 What *manner of* saying is this that he said, Ye shall seek me, and shall not find *me*: and where I am, *thither* ye cannot come?

37 In the last day, that great *day* of the feast, Jesus stood and cried, saying, If any man thirst, let him come unto me, and drink.

38 He that believeth on me, as the scripture hath said, out of his belly shall flow rivers of living water.

39 (But this spake he of the Spirit, which they that believe on him should receive; for the Holy Ghost was ~~not yet given; because~~ **promised unto them who believe, after** that Jesus was ~~not yet~~ glorified.)

40 Many of the people therefore, when they heard this saying, said, Of a truth this is the Prophet.

41 Others said, This is the Christ. But some said, Shall Christ come out of Galilee?

42 Hath not the scripture said, That Christ cometh of the seed of David, and out of the town of Bethlehem, where David was?

43 So there was a division among the people because of him.

44 And some of them would have taken him; but no man laid hands on him.

45 Then came the officers to the chief priests and Pharisees; and they said unto them, Why have ye not brought him?

46 The officers answered, Never man spake like this man.

47 Then answered them the Pharisees, Are ye also deceived?

48 Have any of the rulers or of the Pharisees believed on him?

49 But this people who knoweth not the law are cursed.

50 Nicodemus saith unto them, (he that came to Jesus by night, being one of them,)

51 Doth our law judge *any* man, before it hear him, and know what he doeth?

52 They answered and said unto him, Art thou also of Galilee? Search, and look: for out of Galilee ariseth no prophet.

53 And every man went unto his own house.

Chapter 8

1 **And** Jesus went unto the mount of Olives.

2 ~~And~~ Early in the morning he came again into the temple, and all the people came unto him; and he sat down, and taught them.

3 And the scribes and Pharisees brought unto him a woman taken in adultery; and when they had set her in the midst **of the people**,

4 They say unto him, Master, this woman was taken in adultery, in the very act.

5 Now Moses in the law commanded us, that such should be stoned: but what sayest thou?

6 This they said, tempting him, that they might have to accuse him. But Jesus stooped down, and with *his* finger wrote on the ground, *as though he heard them not.*

7 So when they continued asking him, he lifted up himself, and said unto them, He that is without sin among you, let him first cast a stone at her.

8 And again he stooped down, and wrote on the ground.

9 And they which heard *it*, being convicted by *their own* conscience, went out one by one, beginning at the eldest, *even* unto the last; and Jesus was left alone, and the woman standing in the midst **of the temple**.[31]

10 When Jesus had ~~lifted~~ **raised** up himself, and saw none **of her accusers**, ~~but~~ **and** the woman **standing**, he said unto her, Woman, where are those thine accusers? hath no man condemned thee?

11 She said, No man, Lord. And Jesus said unto her, Neither do I condemn thee; go, and sin no more. **And the woman glorified God from that hour, and believed on his name.**

12 Then spake Jesus again unto them, saying, I am the light of the world: he that followeth me shall not walk in darkness, but shall have the light of life.

13 The Pharisees therefore said unto him, Thou bearest record of thyself; thy record is not true.

14 Jesus answered and said unto them, Though I bear record of myself, *yet* my record is true: for I know whence I came, and whither I go; but ye cannot tell whence I come, and whither I go.

15 Ye judge after the flesh; I judge no man.

16 And yet if I judge, my judgment is true: for I am not alone, but I and the Father that sent me.

17 It is also written in your law, that the testimony of two men is true.

18 I am one that bear witness of myself, and the Father that sent me beareth witness of me.

19 Then said they unto him, Where is thy Father? Jesus answered, Ye neither know me, nor my Father: if ye had known me, ye should have known my Father also.

20 These words spake Jesus in the treasury, as he taught in the temple: and no man laid hands on him; for his hour was not yet come.

21 Then said Jesus again unto them, I go my way, and ye shall seek me, and shall die in your sins: whither I go, ye cannot come.

22 Then said the Jews, Will he kill himself? because he saith, Whither I go, ye cannot come.

23 And he said unto them, Ye are from beneath; I am from above: ye are of this world; I am not of this world.

24 I said therefore unto you, that ye shall die in your sins: for if ye believe not that I am *he*, ye shall die in your sins.

25 Then said they unto him, Who art thou? And Jesus saith unto them, Even *the same* that I said unto you from the beginning.

26 I have many things to say and to judge of you: but he that sent me is true; and I speak to the world those things which I have heard of him.

27 They understood not that he spake to them of the Father.

28 Then said Jesus unto them, When ye have lifted up the Son of man, then shall ye know that I am *he*, and *that* I do nothing of myself; but as my Father hath taught me, I speak these things.

29 And he that sent me is with me: the Father hath not left me alone; for I do always those things that please him.

30 As he spake these words, many believed on him.

31 Then said Jesus to those Jews which believed on him, If ye continue in my word, *then* are ye my disciples indeed;

32 And ye shall know the truth, and the truth shall make you free.

33 They answered him, We be Abraham's seed, and were never in bondage to any man: how sayest thou, Ye shall be made free?

34 Jesus answered them, Verily, verily, I say unto you, Whosoever committeth sin is the servant of sin.

35 And the servant abideth not in the house for ever: *but* the Son abideth ever.

36 If the Son therefore shall make you free, ye shall be free indeed.

37 I know that ye are Abraham's seed; but ye seek to kill me, because my word hath no place in you.

38 I speak that which I have seen with my Father: and ye do that which ye have seen with your father.

39 They answered and said unto him, Abraham is our father. Jesus saith unto them, If ye were Abraham's children, ye would do the works of Abraham.

40 But now ye seek to kill me, a man that hath told you the truth, which I have heard of God: this did not Abraham.

41 Ye do the deeds of your father. Then said they to him, We be not born of fornication; we have one Father, *even* God.

42 Jesus said unto them, If God were your Father, ye would love me: for I proceeded forth and came from God; neither came I of myself, but he sent me.

43 Why do ye not understand my speech? *even* because ye cannot ~~hear~~ **bear** my word.

44 Ye are of *your* father the devil, and the lusts of your father ye will do. He was a murderer from the beginning, and abode not in the truth, because there is no truth in him. When he speaketh a lie, he speaketh of his own: for he is a liar, and the father of it.

45 And because I tell *you* the truth, ye believe me not.

46 Which of you convinceth me of sin? And if I say the truth, why do ye not believe me?

47 He that is of God ~~heareth~~ **receiveth** God's words; ye therefore ~~hear~~ **receive** *them* not, because ye are not of God.

48 Then answered the Jews, and said unto him, Say we not well that thou art a Samaritan, and hast a devil?

49 Jesus answered, I have not a devil; but I honour my Father, and ye do dishonour me.

50 And I seek not mine own glory: there is one that seeketh and judgeth.

51 Verily, verily, I say unto you, If a man keep my saying, he shall never see death.

52 Then said the Jews unto him, Now we know that thou hast a devil. Abraham is dead, and the prophets; and thou sayest, If a man keep my saying, he shall never taste of death.

53 Art thou greater than our father Abraham, which is dead? and the prophets are dead: whom makest thou thyself?

54 Jesus answered, If I honour myself, my honour is nothing: it is my Father that honoureth me; of whom ye say, that he is your God:

55 Yet ye have not known him; but I know him: and if I should say, I know him not, I shall be a liar like unto you: but I know him, and keep his saying.

56 Your father Abraham rejoiced to see my day: and he saw *it*, and was glad.

57 Then said the Jews unto him, Thou art not yet fifty years old, and hast thou seen Abraham?

58 Jesus said unto them, Verily, verily, I say unto you, Before Abraham was, I am.

59 Then took they up stones to cast at him: but Jesus hid himself, and went out of the temple, going through the midst of them, and so passed by.

CHAPTER 9

1 And as *Jesus* passed by, he saw a man which was blind from *his* birth.

2 And his disciples asked him, saying, Master, who did sin, this man, or his parents, that he was born blind?

3 Jesus answered, Neither hath this man sinned, nor his parents: but that the works of God should be made manifest in him.

4 I must work the works of him that sent me, while ~~it is day~~ **I am with you;** the ~~night~~ **time** cometh when ~~no man can~~ **I shall have finished my** work, **then I go unto the Father.**

5 As long as I am in the world, I am the light of the world.

6 When he had thus spoken, he spat on the ground, and made clay of the spittle, and he anointed the eyes of the blind man with the clay,

7 And said unto him, Go, wash in the pool of Siloam, (which is by interpretation, Sent.) He went his way therefore, and washed, and came seeing.

8 The neighbours therefore, and they which before had seen him that he was blind, said, Is not this he that sat and begged?

9 Some said, This is he: others *said*, He is like him: *but* he said, I am *he*.

10 Therefore said they unto him, How were thine eyes opened?

11 He answered and said, A man that is called Jesus made clay, and anointed mine eyes, and said unto me, Go to the pool of Siloam, and wash: and I went and washed, and I received sight.

12 Then said they unto him, Where is he? He said, I know not.

13 **And** they brought ~~to the Pharisees~~ him ~~that aforetime was~~ **who had been** blind **to the Pharisees**.

14 And it was the sabbath day when Jesus made the clay, and opened his eyes.

15 Then again the Pharisees also asked him how he had received his sight. He said unto them, He put clay upon mine eyes, and I washed, and do see.

16 Therefore said some of the Pharisees, This man is not of God, because he keepeth not the sabbath day. Others said, How can a man that is a sinner do such miracles? And there was a division among them.

17 They say unto the blind man again, What sayest thou of him ~~that~~ **who** ~~he~~ hath opened thine eyes? He said, He is a prophet.

18 But the Jews did not believe concerning him, that he had been blind, and received his sight, until they called the parents of him that had received his sight.

19 And they asked them, saying, Is this your son, who ye say was born blind? how then doth he now see?

20 His parents answered them and said, We know that this is our son, and that he was born blind:

21 But by what means he now seeth, we know not; or who hath opened his eyes, we know not: he is of age; ask him: he shall speak for himself.

22 These *words* spake his parents, because they feared the Jews: for the Jews had agreed already, that if any man did confess that he was Christ, he should be put out of the synagogue.

23 Therefore said his parents, He is of age; ask him.

24 Then again called they the man that was blind, and said unto him, Give God the praise: we know that this man is a sinner.

25 He answered and said, Whether he be a sinner *or no*, I know not: one thing I know, that, whereas I was blind, now I see.

26 Then said they to him again, What did he to thee? how opened he thine eyes?

27 He answered them, I have told you already, and ye did not ~~hear~~ **believe;** wherefore would ~~ye~~ **you** ~~hear it~~ **believe if I should tell you** again? **and** ~~will~~ **would** ~~ye~~ **you** ~~also~~ be his disciples?

28 Then they reviled him, and said, Thou art his disciple; but we are Moses' disciples.

29 We know that God spake unto Moses; *as for* this ~~fellow~~ **man** we know not from whence he is.

30 The man answered and said unto them, Why herein is a marvellous thing, that ye know not from whence he is, and *yet* he hath opened mine eyes.

31 Now we know that God heareth not sinners: but if any man be a worshipper of God, and doeth his will, him he heareth.

32 Since the world began was it not heard that any man opened the eyes of one that was born blind, **except he be of God.**

33 If this man were not of God, he could do nothing.

34 They answered and said unto him, Thou wast altogether born in sins, and dost thou teach us? And they cast him out.

35 Jesus heard that they had cast him out; and when he had found him, he said unto him, Dost thou believe on the Son of God?

36 He answered and said, Who is he, Lord, that I might believe on him?

37 And Jesus said unto him, Thou hast both seen him, and it is he that talketh with thee.

38 And he said, Lord, I believe. And he worshipped him.

39 And Jesus said, For judgment I am come into this world, that they which see not might see; and that they which see might be made blind.

40 And *some* of the Pharisees which were with him heard these words, and said unto him, Are we blind also?

41 Jesus said unto them, If ye were blind, ye should have no sin: but now ye say, We see; therefore your sin remaineth.

CHAPTER 10

1 Verily, verily, I say unto you, He that entereth not by the door into the sheepfold, but climbeth up some other way, the same is a thief and a robber.

2 But he that entereth in by the door is the shepherd of the sheep.

3 To him the porter openeth; and the sheep hear his voice: and he calleth his own sheep by name, and leadeth them out.

4 And when he putteth forth his own sheep, he goeth before them, and the sheep follow him: for they know his voice.

5 And a stranger will they not follow, but will flee from him: for they know not the voice of strangers.

6 This parable spake Jesus unto them: but they understood not what things they were which he spake unto them.

7 Then said Jesus unto them again, Verily, verily, I say unto you, I am the door of the ~~sheep~~ **sheepfold**.

8 All that ever came before me **who testified not of me** are thieves and robbers; but the sheep did not hear them.

9 I am the door: by me if any man enter in, he shall be saved, and shall go in and out, and find pasture.

10 The thief cometh not, but for to steal, and to kill, and to destroy: I am come that they might have life, and that they might have *it* more abundantly.

11 I am the good shepherd; the good shepherd giveth his life for ~~the~~ **his** sheep.

12 ~~But~~ **And** ~~he~~ **the shepherd** ~~that~~ is ~~an hireling, and~~ not ~~the shepherd~~ **as a hireling**, whose own the sheep are not, **who** seeth the wolf coming, and leaveth the sheep, and fleeth; and the wolf catcheth ~~them~~ **the sheep** and scattereth ~~the sheep~~ **them**.

~~13~~ 14 **For** I am the good shepherd, and know my *sheep*, and am known of mine.

~~14~~ 13 **But he who is a** ~~the~~ hireling fleeth, because he is ~~an~~ **a** hireling, and careth not for the sheep.

15 As the Father knoweth me, even so know I the Father: and I lay down my life for the sheep.

16 And other sheep I have, which are not of this fold: them also I must bring, and they shall hear my voice; and there shall be one fold, *and* one shepherd.

17 Therefore doth my Father love me, because I lay down my life, that I might take it again.

18 No man taketh it from me, but I lay it down of myself. I have power to lay it down, and I have power to take it again. This commandment have I received of my Father.

19 There was a division therefore again among the Jews for these sayings.

20 And many of them said, He hath a devil, and is mad; why hear ye him?

21 Others said, These are not the

words of him that hath a devil. Can a devil open the eyes of the blind?

22 And it was at Jerusalem the feast of the dedication, and it was winter.

23 And Jesus walked in the temple in Solomon's porch.

24 Then came the Jews round about him, and said unto him, How long dost thou make us to doubt? If thou be the Christ, tell us plainly.

25 Jesus answered them, I told you, and ye believed not: the works that I do in my Father's name, they bear witness of me.

26 But ye believe not, because ye are not of my sheep, as I said unto you.

27 My sheep hear my voice, and I know them, and they follow me:

28 And I give unto them eternal life; and they shall never perish, neither shall any *man* pluck them out of my hand.

29 My Father, which gave *them* me, is greater than all; and no *man* is able to pluck *them* out of my Father's hand.

30 I and *my* Father are one.

31 Then the Jews took up stones again to stone him.

32 Jesus answered them, Many good works have I shewed you from my Father; for which of those works do ye stone me?

33 The Jews answered him, saying, For a good work we stone thee not; but for blasphemy; and because that thou, being a man, makest thyself God.

34 Jesus answered them, Is it not written in your law, I said, Ye are gods?

35 If he called them gods, unto whom the word of God came, and the scripture cannot be broken;

36 Say ye of him, whom the Father hath sanctified, and sent into the world, Thou blasphemest; because I said, I am the Son of God?

37 If I do not the works of my Father, believe me not.

38 But if I do, though ye believe not me, believe the works: that ye may know, and believe, that the Father *is* in me, and I in him.

39 Therefore they sought again to take him: but he escaped out of their hand,

40 And went away again beyond Jordan into the place where John at first baptized; and there he abode.

41 And many resorted unto him, and said, John did no miracle: but all things that John spake of this man were true.

42 And many believed on him there.

CHAPTER 11

1 Now a certain *man* was sick, ~~named~~ **whose name was** Lazarus, of **the town of** Bethany**;** ~~the town of Mary and her sister Martha~~

2 ~~It was *that*~~ **And** Mary, **his sister** ~~which~~ **who** anointed the Lord with ointment and wiped his feet with her hair, **lived with her sister Martha, in** whose **house her** brother Lazarus was sick.

3 Therefore his sisters sent unto him, saying, Lord, behold, he whom thou lovest is sick.

4 **And** when Jesus heard ~~that~~ **he was sick**, he said, This sickness is not unto death, but for the glory of God, that the Son of God might be glorified thereby.

5 Now Jesus loved Martha, and her sister, and Lazarus.

6 ~~When~~ **And Jesus tarried two days, after** he ~~had~~ heard ~~therefore~~ that ~~he~~ **Lazarus** was sick, ~~he abode two days still~~ in the same place where he was.

7 ~~Then~~ After that **he** ~~saith~~ **said** ~~he to~~ **unto** *his* disciples, Let us go into ~~Judaea~~ **Judea** again.

8 **But** *his* disciples ~~say~~ **said** unto him, Master, the Jews of late sought to stone thee; and goest thou thither again?

9 Jesus answered, Are there not twelve hours in the day? If any man walk in the day, he stumbleth not, because he seeth the light of this world.

10 But if a man walk in the night, he stumbleth, because there is no light in him.

11 These things said he: and after that he saith unto them, Our friend Lazarus sleepeth; but I go, that I may awake him out of sleep.

12 Then said his disciples, Lord, if he sleep, he shall do well.

13 Howbeit Jesus spake of his death: but they thought that he had spoken of taking of rest in sleep.

14 Then said Jesus unto them plainly, Lazarus is dead.

15 And I am glad for your sakes that I was not there, to the intent ye may believe; nevertheless let us go unto him.

16 Then said Thomas, which is called Didymus, unto his fellow disciples, Let us also go, that we may die with him**; for they feared lest the Jews should take Jesus and put him to death, for as yet they did not understand the power of God**.

17 ~~Then~~ **And** when Jesus came **to Bethany, to Martha's house,** ~~he found that he~~ **Lazarus** had *~~lain~~* **already been** in the grave four days ~~already~~.

18 Now Bethany was nigh unto Jerusalem, about fifteen furlongs off:

19 And many of the Jews came to Martha and Mary, to comfort them concerning their brother.

20 Then Martha, as soon as she heard that Jesus was coming, went and met him: but Mary sat *still* in the house.

21 Then said Martha unto Jesus, Lord, if thou hadst been here, my brother had not died.

22 But I know, that even now, whatsoever thou wilt ask of God, God will give *it* thee.

23 Jesus saith unto her, Thy brother shall rise again.

24 Martha saith unto him, I know that he shall rise again in the resurrection at the last day.

25 Jesus said unto her, I am the resurrection, and the life: he that believeth in me, though he were dead, yet shall he live:

26 And whosoever liveth and believeth in me shall never die. Believest thou this?

27 She saith unto him, Yea, Lord: I believe that thou art the Christ, the Son of God, which should come into the world.

28 And when she had so said, she went her way, and called Mary her sister secretly, saying, The Master is come, and calleth for thee.

29 As soon as ~~she~~ **Mary** heard *that* **Jesus was come**, she arose quickly, and came unto him.

30 Now Jesus was not yet come into the town, but was in ~~that~~ **the** place where Martha met him.

31 The Jews then which were with her in the house, and comforted her, when they saw Mary, that she rose up hastily and went out, followed her, saying, She goeth unto the grave to weep there.

32 Then when Mary was come where Jesus was, and saw him, she fell down at his feet, saying unto him, Lord, if thou hadst been here, my brother had not died.

33 When Jesus therefore saw her weeping, and the Jews also weeping which came with her, he groaned in the spirit, and was troubled,

34 And said, Where have ye laid him? They said unto him, Lord, come and see.

35 Jesus wept.

36 Then said the Jews, Behold how he loved him!

37 And some of them said, Could not this man, which opened the eyes of the blind, have caused that even this man should not have died?

38 Jesus therefore again groaning in himself cometh to the grave. It was a cave, and a stone lay upon it.

39 Jesus said, Take ye away the stone. Martha, the sister of him that was dead, saith unto him, Lord, by this time he stinketh: for he hath been *dead* four days.

40 Jesus saith unto her, Said I not unto thee, that, if thou wouldest believe, thou shouldest see the glory of God?

41 Then they took away the stone *from the place* where the dead was laid. And Jesus lifted up *his* eyes, and said, Father, I thank thee that thou hast heard me.

42 And I knew that thou hearest me always: but because of the people which stand by I said *it*, that they may believe that thou hast sent me.

43 And when he thus had spoken, he cried with a loud voice, Lazarus, come forth.

44 And he that was dead came forth, bound hand and foot with graveclothes: and his face was bound about with a napkin. Jesus saith unto them, Loose him, and let him go.

45 Then many of the Jews which came to Mary, and had seen the things which Jesus did, believed on him.

46 But some of them went their ways to the Pharisees, and told them what things Jesus had done.

47 Then gathered the chief priests and the Pharisees a council, and said, What **shall we** do we? for this man doeth many miracles.

48 If we let him thus alone, all *men* will believe on him: and the Romans shall come and take away both our place and nation.

49 And one of them, *named* Caiaphas, being the high priest that same year, said unto them, Ye know nothing at all,

50 Nor consider that it is expedient for us, that one man should die for the people, and that the whole nation perish not.

51 And this spake he not of himself: but being high priest that year, he prophesied that Jesus should die for that nation;

52 And not for that nation only, but that also he should gather together in one the children of God that were scattered abroad.

53 Then from that day forth they took counsel together for to put him to death.

54 Jesus therefore walked no more openly among the Jews; but went thence unto a country near to the wilderness, into a city called Ephraim, and there continued with his disciples.

55 And the Jews' passover was nigh at hand: and many went out of the country up to Jerusalem before the passover, to purify themselves.

56 Then sought they for Jesus, and spake among themselves, as they stood in the temple, What think ye that he **of Jesus?** Will **he** not come to the feast?

57 Now both the chief priests and

the Pharisees had given a commandment, that, if any man knew where he
~~were~~ **was**, he should show ~~it~~ **them**,
that they might take him.

1 Then Jesus six days before the
passover came to Bethany, where
Lazarus was which had been dead,
whom he raised from the dead.
2 There they made him a supper;
and Martha served: but Lazarus was
one of them that sat at the table with
him.
3 Then took Mary a pound of ointment of spikenard, very costly, and
anointed the feet of Jesus, and wiped
his feet with her hair: and the house
was filled with the odour of the ointment.
4 Then saith one of his disciples, Judas Iscariot, Simon's *son*, which should
betray him,
5 Why was not this ointment sold
for three hundred pence, and given to
the poor?
6 This he said, not that he cared for
the poor; but because he was a thief,
and had the bag, and bare what was
put therein.
7 Then said Jesus, Let her alone;
~~against the day of my burying~~ **for**
~~hath~~ she **hath** ~~kept~~ **preserved** this
**ointment until now, that she might
anoint me in token of my burial.**
8 For the poor always ye have with
you; but me ye have not always.
9 Much people of the Jews therefore
knew that he was there: and they came
not for Jesus' sake only, but that they
might see Lazarus also, whom he had
raised from the dead.
10 But the chief priests consulted
that they might put Lazarus also to
death;
11 Because that by reason of him

many of the Jews went away, and believed on Jesus.
12 On the next day much people
that were come to the feast, when they
heard that Jesus was coming to Jerusalem,
13 Took branches of palm trees, and
went forth to meet him, and cried,
Hosanna: Blessed *is* the King of Israel
that cometh in the name of the
Lord.
14 And Jesus, when he had ~~found~~
sent two of his disciples and got a
young ass, sat thereon; as it is written,
15 Fear not, daughter of Sion: behold, thy King cometh, sitting on an
ass's colt.
16 These things understood not his
disciples at the first: but when Jesus
was glorified, then remembered they
that these things were written of him,
and *that* they had done these things
unto him.
17 The people therefore that was
with him when he called Lazarus out
of his grave, and raised him from the
dead, bare record.
18 For this cause the people also met
him, for that they heard that he had
done this miracle.
19 The Pharisees therefore said
among themselves, Perceive ye how ye
prevail nothing? behold, the world is
gone after him.
20 And there were certain Greeks
among them that came up to worship
at the feast:
21 The same came therefore to
Philip, which was of Bethsaida of Galilee, and desired him, saying, Sir, we
would see Jesus.
22 Philip cometh and telleth Andrew: and again Andrew and Philip
tell Jesus.
23 And Jesus answered them, saying,

The hour is come, that the Son of man should be glorified.

24 Verily, verily, I say unto you, Except a corn of wheat fall into the ground and die, it abideth alone: but if it die, it bringeth forth much fruit.

25 He that loveth his life shall lose it; and he that hateth his life in this world shall keep it unto life eternal.

26 If any man serve me, let him follow me; and where I am, there shall also my servant be: if any man serve me, him will *my* Father honour.

27 Now is my soul troubled; and what shall I say? Father, save me from this hour: but for this cause came I unto this hour.

28 Father, glorify thy name. Then came there a voice from heaven, *saying*, I have both glorified *it*, and will glorify *it* again.

29 The people therefore, that stood by, and heard *it*, said that it thundered: others said, An angel spake to him.

30 Jesus answered and said, This voice came not because of me, but for your sakes.

31 Now is the judgment of this world: now shall the prince of this world be cast out.

32 And I, if I be lifted up from the earth, will draw all *men* unto me.

33 This he said, signifying what death he should die.

34 The people answered him, We have heard out of the law that Christ abideth for ever: and how sayest thou, The Son of man must be lifted up? who is this Son of man?

35 Then Jesus said unto them, Yet a little while is the light with you. Walk while ye have the light, lest darkness come upon you: for he that walketh in darkness knoweth not whither he goeth.

36 While ye have light, believe in the light, that ye may be the children of light. These things spake Jesus, and departed, and did hide himself from them.

37 But though he had done so many miracles before them, yet they believed not on him:

38 That the saying of Esaias the prophet might be fulfilled, which he spake, Lord, who hath believed our report? and to whom hath the arm of the Lord been revealed?

39 Therefore they could not believe, because that Esaias said again,

40 He hath blinded their eyes, and hardened their heart; that they should not see with *their* eyes, nor understand with *their* heart, and be converted, and I should heal them.

41 These things said Esaias, when he saw his glory, and spake of him.

42 Nevertheless among the chief rulers also many believed on him; but because of the Pharisees they did not confess *him*, lest they should be put out of the synagogue:

43 For they loved the praise of men more than the praise of God.

44 Jesus cried and said, He that believeth on me, believeth not on me, but on him that sent me.

45 And he that seeth me seeth him that sent me.

46 I am come a light into the world, that whosoever believeth on me should not abide in darkness.

47 And if any man hear my words, and believe not, I judge him not: for I came not to judge the world, but to save the world.

48 He that rejecteth me, and receiveth not my words, hath one that judgeth him: the word that I have spoken, the same shall judge him in the last day.

49 For I have not spoken of myself; but the Father which sent me, he gave me a commandment, what I should say, and what I should speak.

50 And I know that his commandment is life everlasting: whatsoever I speak therefore, even as the Father said unto me, so I speak.

CHAPTER 13

1 Now before the feast of the passover, when Jesus knew that his hour was come that he should depart out of this world unto the Father, having loved his own which were in the world, he loved them unto the end.

2 And supper being ended, the devil having now put into the heart of Judas Iscariot, Simon's *son*, to betray him;

3 Jesus knowing that the Father had given all things into his hands, and that he was come from God, and went to God;

4 He riseth from supper, and laid aside his garments; and took a towel, and girded himself.

5 After that he poureth water into a bason, and began to wash the disciples' feet, and to wipe *them* with the towel wherewith he was girded.

6 Then cometh he to Simon Peter: and Peter saith unto him, Lord, dost thou wash my feet?

7 Jesus answered and said unto him, What I do thou knowest not now; but thou shalt know hereafter.

8 Peter saith unto him, Thou ~~shalt never~~ **needest not to** wash my feet. Jesus answered him, If I wash thee not, thou hast no part with me.

9 Simon Peter saith unto him, Lord, not my feet only, but also *my* hands and *my* head.

10 Jesus saith to him, He that ~~is~~ **has** washed **his hands and his head,**

needeth not save to wash *his* feet, but is clean every whit; and ye are clean, but not all. **Now this was the custom of the Jews under their law; wherefore, Jesus did this that the law might be fulfilled.**

11 For he knew who should betray him; therefore said he, Ye are not all clean.

12 So after he had washed their feet, and had taken his garments, and was set down again, he said unto them, Know ye what I have done to you?

13 Ye call me Master and Lord: and ye say well; for *so* I am.

14 If I then, *your* Lord and Master, have washed your feet; ye also ought to wash one another's feet.

15 For I have given you an example, that ye should do as I have done to you.

16 Verily, verily, I say unto you, The servant is not greater than his lord; neither he that is sent greater than he that sent him.

17 If ye know these things, happy are ye if ye do them.

18 I speak not of you all: I know whom I have chosen: but that the scripture may be fulfilled, He that eateth bread with me hath lifted up his heel against me.

19 Now I tell you before it come, that, when it is come to pass, ye may believe that I am ~~he~~ **the Christ**.

20 Verily, verily, I say unto you, He that receiveth whomsoever I send receiveth me; and he that receiveth me receiveth him that sent me.

21 When Jesus had thus said, he was troubled in spirit, and testified, and said, Verily, verily, I say unto you, that one of you shall betray me.

22 Then the disciples looked one on another, doubting of whom he spake.

23 Now there was leaning on Jesus'

bosom one of his disciples, whom Jesus loved.

24 Simon Peter therefore beckoned to him, that he should ask who it should be of whom he spake.

25 He then lying on Jesus' breast saith unto him, Lord, who is it?

26 Jesus answered, He it is, to whom I shall give a sop, when I have dipped *it*. And when he had dipped the sop, he gave *it* to Judas Iscariot, *the son* of Simon.

27 And after the sop Satan entered into him. Then said Jesus unto him, That thou doest, do quickly.

28 Now no man at the table knew for what intent he spake this unto him.

29 For some *of them* thought, because Judas had the bag, that Jesus had said unto him, Buy *those things* that we have need of against the feast; or, that he should give something to the poor.

30 He then having received the sop went immediately out: and it was night.

31 Therefore, when he was gone out, Jesus said, Now is the Son of man glorified, and God is glorified in him.

32 If God be glorified in him, God shall also glorify him in himself, and shall straightway glorify him.

33 Little children, yet a little while I am with you. Ye shall seek me: and as I said unto the Jews, Whither I go, ye cannot come; so now I say to you.

34 A new commandment I give unto you, That ye love one another; as I have loved you, that ye also love one another.

35 By this shall all *men* know that ye are my disciples, if ye have love one to another.

36 Simon Peter said unto him, Lord, whither goest thou? Jesus answered him, Whither I go, thou canst not follow me now; but thou shalt follow me afterwards.

37 Peter said unto him, Lord, why cannot I follow thee now? I will lay down my life for thy sake.

38 Jesus answered him, Wilt thou lay down thy life for my sake? Verily, verily, I say unto thee, The cock shall not crow, till thou hast denied me thrice.

CHAPTER 14

1 Let not your heart be troubled: ye believe in God, believe also in me.

2 In my Father's house **kingdom**[32] are many mansions: if *it were* not *so*, I would have told you. I go to prepare a place for you.

3 And if **when** I go and, I will prepare a place for you, I will **and** come again, and receive you unto myself; that where I am, there ye may be also.

4 And whither I go ye know, and the way ye know.

5 Thomas saith unto him, Lord, we know not whither thou goest; and how can we know the way?

6 Jesus saith unto him, I am the way, the truth, and the life: no man cometh unto the Father, but by me.

7 If ye had known me, ye should have known my Father also: and from henceforth ye know him, and have seen him.

8 Philip saith unto him, Lord, shew us the Father, and it sufficeth us.

9 Jesus saith unto him, Have I been so long time with you, and yet hast thou not known me, Philip? he that hath seen me hath seen the Father; and how sayest thou *then*, Shew us the Father?

10 Believest thou not that I am in the Father, and the Father in me? the words that I speak unto you I speak not of myself: but the Father that

dwelleth in me, he doeth the works.

11 Believe me that I *am* in the Father, and the Father in me: or else believe me for the very works' sake.

12 Verily, verily, I say unto you, He that believeth on me, the works that I do shall he do also; and greater *works* than these shall he do; because I go unto my Father.

13 And whatsoever ye shall ask in my name, that will I do, that the Father may be glorified in the Son.

14 If ye shall ask any thing in my name, I will do *it*.

15 If ye love me, keep my commandments.

16 And I will pray the Father, and he shall give you another Comforter, that he may abide with you for ever;

17 *Even* the Spirit of truth; whom the world cannot receive, because it seeth him not, neither knoweth him: but ye know him; for he dwelleth with you, and shall be in you.

18 I will not leave you comfortless: I will come to you.

19 Yet a little while, and the world seeth me no more; but ye see me: because I live, ye shall live also.

20 At that day ye shall know that I *am* in my Father, and ye in me, and I in you.

21 He that hath my commandments, and keepeth them, he it is that loveth me: and he that loveth me shall be loved of my Father, and I will love him, and will manifest myself to him.

22 Judas saith unto him, (not Iscariot,) Lord, how is it ~~that~~ thou wilt manifest thyself unto us, and not unto the world?

23 Jesus answered and said unto him, If a man love me, he will keep my words: and my Father will love him, and we will come unto him, and make our abode with him.

24 He that loveth me not keepeth not my sayings: and the word which ye hear is not mine, but the Father's which sent me.

25 These things have I spoken unto you, being *yet* present with you.

26 But the Comforter, *which is* the Holy Ghost, whom the Father will send in my name, he shall teach you all things, and bring all things to your remembrance, whatsoever I have said unto you.

27 Peace I leave with you, my peace I give unto you: not as the world giveth, give I unto you. Let not your heart be troubled, neither let it be afraid.

28 Ye have heard how I said unto you, I go away, and come *again* unto you. If ye loved me, ye would rejoice, because I said, I go unto the Father: for my Father is greater than I.

29 And now I have told you before it come to pass, that, when it is come to pass, ye might believe.

30 Hereafter I will not talk much with you; for the prince of **darkness, who is of** this world**,** cometh, ~~and~~ **but** hath ~~nothing in~~ **no power over** me**, but he hath power over you.**

31 ~~But~~ **And I tell you these things,** that ~~the world~~ **ye** may know that I love the Father; and as the Father gave me commandment, even so I do. Arise, let us go hence.

CHAPTER 15

1 I am the true vine, and my Father is the husbandman.

2 Every branch in me that beareth not fruit he taketh away: and every *branch* that beareth fruit, he purgeth it, that it may bring forth more fruit.

3 Now ye are clean through the word which I have spoken unto you.

4 Abide in me, and I in you. As the

branch cannot bear fruit of itself, except it abide in the vine; no more can ye, except ye abide in me.

5 I am the vine, ye *are* the branches: He that abideth in me, and I in him, the same bringeth forth much fruit: for without me ye can do nothing.

6 If a man abide not in me, he is cast forth as a branch, and is withered; and men gather them, and cast *them* into the fire, and they are burned.

7 If ye abide in me, and my words abide in you, ye shall ask what ye will, and it shall be done unto you.

8 Herein is my Father glorified, that ye bear much fruit; so shall ye be my disciples.

9 As the Father hath loved me, so have I loved you: continue ye in my love.

10 If ye keep my commandments, ye shall abide in my love; even as I have kept my Father's commandments, and abide in his love.

11 These things have I spoken unto you, that my joy might remain in you, and *that* your joy might be full.

12 This is my commandment, That ye love one another, as I have loved you.

13 Greater love hath no man than this, that a man lay down his life for his friends.

14 Ye are my friends, if ye do whatsoever I command you.

15 Henceforth I call you not servants; for the servant knoweth not what his lord doeth: but I have called you friends; for all things that I have heard of my Father I have made known unto you.

16 Ye have not chosen me, but I have chosen you, and ordained you, that ye should go and bring forth fruit, and *that* your fruit should remain: that whatsoever ye shall ask of the Father in my name, he may give it you.

17 These things I command you, that ye love one another.

18 If the world hate you, ye know that it hated me before *it hated* you.

19 If ye were of the world, the world would love his own: but because ye are not of the world, but I have chosen you out of the world, therefore the world hateth you.

20 Remember the word that I said unto you, The servant is not greater than his lord. If they have persecuted me, they will also persecute you; if they have kept my saying, they will keep yours also.

21 But all these things will they do unto you for my name's sake, because they know not him that sent me.

22 If I had not come and spoken unto them, they had not had sin: but now they have no cloke for their sin.

23 He that hateth me hateth my Father also.

24 If I had not done among them the works which none other man did, they had not had sin: but now have they both seen and hated both me and my Father.

25 But *this cometh to pass*, that the word might be fulfilled that is written in their law, They hated me without a cause.

26 But when the Comforter is come, whom I will send unto you from the Father, *even* the Spirit of truth, which proceedeth from the Father, he shall testify of me:

27 And ye also shall bear witness, because ye have been with me from the beginning.

CHAPTER 16

1 These things have I spoken unto you, that ye should not be offended.

2 They shall put you out of the synagogues: yea, the time cometh, that whosoever killeth you will think that he doeth God service.

3 And these things will they do unto you, because they have not known the Father, nor me.

4 But these things have I told you, that when the time shall come, ye may remember that I told you of them. And these things I said not unto you at the beginning, because I was with you.

5 But now I go my way to him that sent me; and none of you asketh me, Whither goest thou?

6 But because I have said these things unto you, sorrow hath filled your heart.

7 Nevertheless I tell you the truth; It is expedient for you that I go away: for if I go not away, the Comforter will not come unto you; but if I depart, I will send him unto you.

8 And when he is come, he will re-prove **remind**[33] the world of sin, and of righteousness, and of judgment:

9 Of sin, because they believe not on me;

10 Of righteousness, because I go to my Father, and ye **they** see me no more;

11 Of judgment, because the prince of this world is judged.

12 I have yet many things to say unto you, but ye cannot bear them now.

13 Howbeit when he, the Spirit of truth, is come, he will guide you into all truth: for he shall not speak of himself; but whatsoever he shall hear, *that* shall he speak: and he will shew you things to come.

14 He shall glorify me: for he shall receive of mine, and shall shew *it* unto you.

15 All things that the Father hath are mine: therefore said I, that he shall take of mine, and shall shew *it* unto you.

16 A little while, and ye shall not see me: and again, a little while, and ye shall see me, because I go to the Father.

17 Then said *some* of his disciples among themselves, What is this that he saith unto us, A little while, and ye shall not see me: and again, a little while, and ye shall see me: and, Because I go to the Father?

18 They said therefore, What is this that he saith, A little while? we cannot tell what he saith.

19 Now Jesus knew that they were desirous to ask him, and said unto them, Do ye enquire among yourselves of that I said, A little while, and ye shall not see me: and again, a little while, and ye shall see me?

20 Verily, verily, I say unto you, That ye shall weep and lament, but the world shall rejoice: and ye shall be sorrowful, but your sorrow shall be turned into joy.

21 A woman when she is in travail hath sorrow, because her hour is come: but as soon as she is delivered of the child, she remembereth no more the anguish, for joy that a man is born into the world.

22 And ye now therefore have sorrow: but I will see you again, and your heart shall rejoice, and your joy no man taketh from you.

23 And in that day ye shall ask me nothing **but it shall be done unto you**. Verily, verily, I say unto you, Whatsoever ye shall ask the Father in my name, he will give *it* you.

24 Hitherto have ye asked nothing in my name: ask, and ye shall receive, that your joy may be full.

25 These things have I spoken unto you in proverbs: but the time cometh, when I shall no more speak unto you in proverbs, but I shall shew you plainly of the Father.

26 At that day ye shall ask in my name: and I say not unto you, that I will pray the Father for you:

27 For the Father himself loveth you, because ye have loved me, and have believed that I came out from God.

28 I came forth from the Father, and am come into the world: again, I leave the world, and go to the Father.

29 His disciples said unto him, Lo, now speakest thou plainly, and speakest no proverb.

30 Now are we sure that thou knowest all things, and needest not that any man should ask thee: by this we believe that thou camest forth from God.

31 Jesus answered them, Do ye now believe?

32 Behold, the hour cometh, yea, is now come, that ye shall be scattered, every man to his own, and shall leave me alone: and yet I am not alone, because the Father is with me.

33 These things I have spoken unto you, that in me ye might have peace. In the world ye shall have tribulation: but be of good cheer; I have overcome the world.

CHAPTER 17

1 These words spake Jesus, and lifted up his eyes to heaven, and said, Father, the hour is come; glorify thy Son, that thy Son also may glorify thee:

2 As thou hast given him power over all flesh, that he should give eternal life to as many as thou hast given him.

3 And this is life eternal, that they might know thee the only true God, and Jesus Christ, whom thou hast sent.

4 I have glorified thee on the earth: I have finished the work which thou gavest me to do.

5 And now, O Father, glorify thou me with thine own self with the glory which I had with thee before the world was.

6 I have manifested thy name unto the men which thou gavest me out of the world: thine they were, and thou gavest them me; and they have kept thy word.

7 Now they have known that all things whatsoever thou hast given me are of thee.

8 For I have given unto them the words which thou gavest me; and they have received *them*, and have known surely that I came out from thee, and they have believed that thou didst send me.

9 I pray for them: I pray not for the world, but for them which thou hast given me; for they are thine.

10 And all mine are thine, and thine are mine; and I am glorified in them.

11 And now I am no more in the world, but these are in the world, and I come to thee. Holy Father, keep through thine own name those whom thou hast given me, that they may be one, as we *are*.

12 While I was with them in the world, I kept them in thy name: those that thou gavest me I have kept, and none of them is lost, but the son of perdition; that the scripture might be fulfilled.

13 And now come I to thee; and these things I speak in the world, that they might have my joy fulfilled in themselves.

14 I have given them thy word; and the world hath hated them, because

they are not of the world, even as I am not of the world.

15 I pray not that thou shouldest take them out of the world, but that thou shouldest keep them from the evil.

16 They are not of the world, even as I am not of the world.

17 Sanctify them through thy truth: thy word is truth.

18 As thou hast sent me into the world, even so have I also sent them into the world.

19 And for their sakes I sanctify myself, that they also might be sanctified through the truth.

20 Neither pray I for these alone, but for them also which shall believe on me through their word;

21 That they all may be one; as thou, Father, *art* in me, and I in thee, that they also may be one in us: that the world may believe that thou hast sent me.

22 And the glory which thou gavest me I have given them; that they may be one, even as we are one:

23 I in them, and thou in me, that they may be made perfect in one; and that the world may know that thou hast sent me, and hast loved them, as thou hast loved me.

24 Father, I will that they also, whom thou hast given me, be with me where I am; that they may behold my glory, which thou hast given me: for thou lovedst me before the foundation of the world.

25 O righteous Father, the world hath not known thee: but I have known thee, and these have known that thou hast sent me.

26 And I have declared unto them thy name, and will declare *it*: that the love wherewith thou hast loved me may be in them, and I in them.

CHAPTER 18

1 When Jesus had spoken these words, he went forth with his disciples over the brook Cedron, where was a garden, into the which he entered, and his disciples.

2 And Judas also, which betrayed him, knew the place: for Jesus ofttimes resorted thither with his disciples.

3 Judas then, having received a band *of men* and officers from the chief priests and Pharisees, cometh thither with lanterns and torches and weapons.

4 Jesus therefore, knowing all things that should come upon him, went forth, and said unto them, Whom seek ye?

5 They answered him, Jesus of Nazareth. Jesus saith unto them, I am *he*. And Judas also, which betrayed him, stood with them.

6 As soon then as he had said unto them, I am *he*, they went backward, and fell to the ground.

7 Then asked he them again, Whom seek ye? And they said, Jesus of Nazareth.

8 Jesus answered, I have told you that I am *he*: if therefore ye seek me, let these go their way:

9 That the saying might be fulfilled, which he spake, Of them which thou gavest me have I lost none.

10 Then Simon Peter having a sword drew it, and smote the high priest's servant, and cut off his right ear. The servant's name was Malchus.

11 Then said Jesus unto Peter, Put up thy sword into the sheath: the cup which my Father hath given me, shall I not drink it?

12 Then the band and the captain and officers of the Jews took Jesus, and bound him,

13 And led him away to Annas first; for he was father in law to Caiaphas, which was the high priest that same year.

14 Now Caiaphas was he, which gave counsel to the Jews, that it was expedient that one man should die for the people.

15 And Simon Peter followed Jesus, and *so did* another disciple: that disciple was known unto the high priest, and went in with Jesus into the palace of the high priest.

16 But Peter stood at the door without. Then went out that other disciple, which was known unto the high priest, and spake unto her that kept the door, and brought in Peter.

17 Then saith the damsel that kept the door unto Peter, Art not thou also *one* of this man's disciples? He saith, I am not.

18 And the servants and officers stood there, who had made a fire of coals; for it was cold: and they warmed themselves: and Peter stood with them, and warmed himself.

19 The high priest then asked Jesus of his disciples, and of his doctrine.

20 Jesus answered him, I spake openly to the world; I ever taught in the synagogue, and in the temple, whither the Jews always resort; and in secret have I said nothing.

21 Why askest thou me? ask them which heard me, what I have said unto them: behold, they know what I said.

22 And when he had thus spoken, one of the officers which stood by struck Jesus with the palm of his hand, saying, Answerest thou the high priest so?

23 Jesus answered him, If I have spoken evil, bear witness of the evil: but if well, why smitest thou me?

24 Now Annas had sent him bound unto Caiaphas the high priest.

25 And Simon Peter stood and warmed himself. They said therefore unto him, Art not thou also *one* of his disciples? He denied *it*, and said, I am not.

26 One of the servants of the high priest, being *his* kinsman whose ear Peter cut off, saith, Did not I see thee in the garden with him?

27 Peter then denied again: and immediately the cock crew.

28 Then led they Jesus from Caiaphas unto the hall of judgment: and it was early; and they themselves went not into the judgment hall, lest they should be defiled; but that they might eat the passover.

29 Pilate then went out unto them, and said, What accusation bring ye against this man?

30 They answered and said unto him, If he were not a malefactor, we would not have delivered him up unto thee.

31 Then said Pilate unto them, Take ye him, and judge him according to your law. The Jews therefore said unto him, It is not lawful for us to put any man to death:

32 That the saying of Jesus might be fulfilled, which he spake, signifying what death he should die.

33 Then Pilate entered into the judgment hall again, and called Jesus, and said unto him, Art thou the King of the Jews?

34 Jesus answered him, Sayest thou this thing of thyself, or did others tell it thee of me?

35 Pilate answered, Am I a Jew? Thine own nation and the chief priests have delivered thee unto me: what hast thou done?

36 Jesus answered, My kingdom is not of this world: if my kingdom were

of this world, then would my servants fight, that I should not be delivered to the Jews: but now is my kingdom not from hence.

37 Pilate therefore said unto him, Art thou a king then? Jesus answered, Thou sayest that I am a king. To this end was I born, and for this cause came I into the world, that I should bear witness unto the truth. Every one that is of the truth heareth my voice.

38 Pilate saith unto him, What is truth? And when he had said this, he went out again unto the Jews, and saith unto them, I find in him no fault *at all*.

39 But ye have a custom, that I should release unto you one at the passover: will ye therefore that I release unto you the King of the Jews?

40 Then cried they all again, saying, Not this man, but Barabbas. Now Barabbas was a robber.

CHAPTER 19

1 Then Pilate therefore took Jesus, and scourged *him*.

2 And the soldiers platted a crown of thorns, and put *it* on his head, and they put on him a purple robe,

3 And said, Hail, King of the Jews! and they smote him with their hands.

4 Pilate therefore went forth again, and saith unto them, Behold, I bring him forth to you, that ye may know that I find no fault in him.

5 Then came Jesus forth, wearing the crown of thorns, and the purple robe. And *Pilate* saith unto them, Behold the man!

6 When the chief priests therefore and officers saw him, they cried out, saying, Crucify *him*, crucify *him*. Pilate saith unto them, Take ye him, and crucify *him*: for I find no fault in him.

7 The Jews answered him, We have a law, and by our law he ought to die, because he made himself the Son of God.

8 When Pilate therefore heard that saying, he was the more afraid;

9 And went again into the judgment hall, and saith unto Jesus, Whence art thou? But Jesus gave him no answer.

10 Then saith Pilate unto him, Speakest thou not unto me? knowest thou not that I have power to crucify thee, and have power to release thee?

11 Jesus answered, Thou couldest have no power *at all* against me, except it were given thee from above; therefore he that delivered me unto thee hath the greater sin.

12 And from thenceforth Pilate sought to release him: but the Jews cried out, saying, If thou let this man go, thou art not Caesar's friend: whosoever maketh himself a king speaketh against Caesar.

13 When Pilate therefore heard that saying, he brought Jesus forth, and sat down in the judgment seat in a place that is called the Pavement, but in the Hebrew, Gabbatha.

14 And it was the preparation of the passover, and about the sixth hour: and he saith unto the Jews, Behold your King!

15 But they cried out, Away with *him*, away with *him*, crucify him. Pilate saith unto them, Shall I crucify your King? The chief priests answered, We have no king but Caesar.

16 Then delivered he him therefore unto them to be crucified. And they took Jesus, and led *him* away.

17 And he bearing his cross went forth into a place called *the place* of a skull **burial;** which is called in the Hebrew Golgotha;

18 Where they crucified him, and

two other with him, on either side one, and Jesus in the midst.

19 And Pilate wrote a title, and put *it* on the cross. And the writing was, Jesus of Nazareth the King of the Jews.

20 This title then read many of the Jews: for the place where Jesus was crucified was nigh to the city: and it was written in Hebrew, *and* Greek, *and* Latin.

21 Then said the chief priests of the Jews to Pilate, Write not, The King of the Jews; but that he said, I am King of the Jews.

22 Pilate answered, What I have written I have written.

23 Then the soldiers, when they had crucified Jesus, took his garments, and made four parts, to every soldier a part; and also *his* coat: now the coat was without seam, woven from the top throughout.

24 They said therefore among themselves, Let us not rend it, but cast lots for it, whose it shall be: that the scripture might be fulfilled, which saith, They parted my raiment among them, and for my vesture they did cast lots. These things therefore the soldiers did.

25 Now there stood by the cross of Jesus his mother, and his mother's sister, Mary the *wife* of Cleophas, and Mary Magdalene.

26 When Jesus therefore saw his mother, and the disciple standing by, whom he loved, he saith unto his mother, Woman, behold thy son!

27 Then saith he to the disciple, Behold thy mother! And from that hour that disciple took her unto his own *home.*

28 After this, Jesus knowing that all things were now accomplished, that the scripture might be fulfilled, saith, I thirst.

29 Now there was set a vessel full of vinegar, **mingled with gall,** and they filled a spunge sponge with vinegar it, and put *it* upon hyssop, and put *it* to his mouth.

30 When Jesus therefore had received the vinegar, he said, It is finished: and he bowed his head, and gave up the ghost.

31 The Jews therefore, because it was the preparation, that the bodies should not remain upon the cross on the sabbath day, (for that sabbath day was an high day,) besought Pilate that their legs might be broken, and *that* they might be taken away.

32 Then came the soldiers, and brake the legs of the first, and of the other which was crucified with him.

33 But when they came to Jesus, and saw that he was dead already, they brake not his legs:

34 But one of the soldiers with a spear pierced his side, and forthwith came there out blood and water.

35 And he that saw *it* bare record, and his record is true: and he knoweth that he saith true, that ye might believe.

36 For these things were done, that the scripture should be fulfilled, A bone of him shall not be broken.

37 And again another scripture saith, They shall look on him whom they pierced.

38 And after this Joseph of Arimathaea, being a disciple of Jesus, but secretly for fear of the Jews, besought Pilate that he might take away the body of Jesus: and Pilate gave *him* leave. He came therefore, and took the body of Jesus.

39 And there came also Nicodemus, which at the first came to Jesus by night, and brought a mixture of myrrh and aloes, about an hundred pound *weight.*

40 Then took they the body of Jesus, and wound it in linen clothes with the spices, as the manner of the Jews is to bury.

41 Now in the place where he was crucified there was a garden; and in the garden a new sepulchre, wherein was never man yet laid.

42 There laid they Jesus therefore because of the Jews' preparation *day*; for the sepulchre was nigh at hand.

Chapter 20

1 The first *day* of the week cometh Mary Magdalene early, when it was yet dark, unto the sepulchre, and seeth the stone taken away from the sepulchre, **and two angels sitting thereon**.

2 Then she runneth, and cometh to Simon Peter, and to the other disciple, whom Jesus loved, and saith unto them, They have taken away the Lord out of the sepulchre, and we know not where they have laid him.

3 Peter therefore went forth, and that other disciple, and came to the sepulchre.

4 So they ran both together: and the other disciple did outrun Peter, and came first to the sepulchre.

5 And he stooping down, *and looking in*, saw the linen clothes lying; yet went he not in.

6 Then cometh Simon Peter following him, and went into the sepulchre, and seeth the linen clothes lie,

7 And the napkin, that was about his head, not lying with the linen clothes, but wrapped together in a place by itself.

8 Then went in also that other disciple, which came first to the sepulchre, and he saw, and believed.

9 For as yet they knew not the scripture, that he must rise again from the dead.

10 Then the disciples went away again unto their own ~~home~~ **homes**.

11 But Mary stood without at the sepulchre weeping: and as she wept, she stooped down, *and looked* into the sepulchre,

12 And seeth two angels in white sitting, the one at the head, and the other at the feet, where the body of Jesus had lain.

13 And they say unto her, Woman, why weepest thou? She saith unto them, Because they have taken away my Lord, and I know not where they have laid him.

14 And when she had thus said, she turned herself back, and saw Jesus standing, and knew not that it was Jesus.

15 Jesus saith unto her, Woman, why weepest thou? whom seekest thou? She, supposing him to be the gardener, saith unto him, Sir, if thou have borne him hence, tell me where thou hast laid him, and I will take him away.

16 Jesus saith unto her, Mary. She turned herself, and saith unto him, Rabboni; which is to say, Master.

17 Jesus saith unto her, ~~touch~~ **Hold**[34] me not; for I am not yet ascended to my Father; but go to my brethren, and say unto them, I ascend unto my Father, and your Father; and *to* my God, and your God.

18 Mary Magdalene came and told the disciples that she had seen the Lord, and *that* he had spoken these things unto her.

19 Then the same day at evening, being the first *day* of the week, when the doors were shut where the disciples were assembled for fear of the Jews, came Jesus and stood in the midst, and saith unto them, Peace *be* unto you.

20 And when he had so said, he shewed unto them *his* hands and his side. Then were the disciples glad, when they saw the Lord.

21 Then said Jesus to them again, Peace *be* unto you: as *my* Father hath sent me, even so send I you.

22 And when he had said this, he breathed on *them*, and saith unto them, Receive ye the Holy Ghost:

23 Whose soever sins ye remit, they are remitted unto them; *and* whose soever *sins* ye retain, they are retained.

24 But Thomas, one of the twelve, called Didymus, was not with them when Jesus came.

25 The other disciples therefore said unto him, We have seen the Lord. But he said unto them, Except I shall see in his hands the print of the nails, and put my finger into the print of the nails, and thrust my hand into his side, I will not believe.

26 And after eight days again his disciples were within, and Thomas with them: *then* came Jesus, the doors being shut, and stood in the midst, and said, Peace *be* unto you.

27 Then saith he to Thomas, Reach hither thy finger, and behold my hands; and reach hither thy hand, and thrust *it* into my side: and be not faithless, but believing.

28 And Thomas answered and said unto him, My Lord and my God.

29 Jesus saith unto him, Thomas, because thou hast seen me, thou hast believed: blessed *are* they that have not seen, and *yet* have believed.

30 And many other signs truly did Jesus in the presence of his disciples, which are not written in this book:

31 But these are written, that ye might believe that Jesus is the Christ, the Son of God; and that believing ye might have life through his name.

CHAPTER 21

1 After these things Jesus shewed himself again to the disciples at the sea of Tiberias; and on this wise shewed he *himself.*

2 There were together Simon Peter, and Thomas called Didymus, and Nathanael of Cana in Galilee, and the *sons* of Zebedee, and two other of his disciples.

3 Simon Peter saith unto them, I go a fishing. They say unto him, We also go with thee. They went forth, and entered into a ship immediately; and that night they caught nothing.

4 But when the morning was now come, Jesus stood on the shore: but the disciples knew not that it was Jesus.

5 Then Jesus saith unto them, Children, have ye any meat? They answered him, No.

6 And he said unto them, Cast the net on the right side of the ship, and ye shall find. They cast therefore, and now they were not able to draw it for the multitude of fishes.

7 Therefore that disciple whom Jesus loved saith unto Peter, It is the Lord. Now when Simon Peter heard that it was the Lord, he girt *his* fisher's coat *unto him,* (for he was naked,) and did cast himself into the sea.

8 And the other disciples came in a little ship; (for they were not far from land, but as it were two hundred cubits,) dragging the net with fishes.

9 As soon then as they were come to land, they saw a fire of coals there, and fish laid thereon, and bread.

10 Jesus saith unto them, Bring of the fish which ye have now caught.

11 Simon Peter went up, and drew the net to land full of great fishes, an hundred and fifty and three: and for all there were so many, yet was not the net broken.

12 Jesus saith unto them, Come *and* dine. And none of the disciples durst ask him, Who art thou? knowing that it was the Lord.

13 Jesus then cometh, and taketh bread, and giveth them, and fish likewise.

14 This is now the third time that Jesus shewed himself to his disciples, after that he was risen from the dead.

15 So when they had dined, Jesus saith to Simon Peter, Simon, *son* of Jonas, lovest thou me more than these? He saith unto him, Yea, Lord; thou knowest that I love thee. He saith unto him, Feed my lambs.

16 He saith to him again the second time, Simon, *son* of Jonas, lovest thou me? He saith unto him, Yea, Lord; thou knowest that I love thee. He saith unto him, Feed my sheep.

17 He saith unto him the third time, Simon, *son* of Jonas, lovest thou me? Peter was grieved because he said unto him the third time, Lovest thou me? And he said unto him, Lord, thou knowest all things; thou knowest that I love thee. Jesus saith unto him, Feed my sheep.

18 Verily, verily, I say unto thee, When thou wast young, thou girdedst thyself, and walkedst whither thou wouldest: but when thou shalt be old, thou shalt stretch forth thy hands, and another shall gird thee, and carry *thee* whither thou wouldest not.

19 This spake he, signifying by what death he should glorify God. And when he had spoken this, he saith unto him, Follow me.

20 Then Peter, turning about, seeth the disciple whom Jesus loved following; which also leaned on his breast at supper, and said, Lord, which is he that betrayeth thee?

21 Peter seeing him saith to Jesus, Lord, and what *shall* this man *do?*

22 Jesus saith unto him, If I will that he tarry till I come, what *is that* to thee? follow thou me.

23 Then went this saying abroad among the brethren, that that disciple should not die: yet Jesus said not unto him, He shall not die; but, If I will that he tarry till I come, what *is that* to thee?

24 This is the disciple which testifieth of these things, and wrote these things: and we know that his testimony is true.

25 And there are also many other things which Jesus did, the which, if they should be written every one, I suppose that even the world itself could not contain the books that should be written. Amen.

[Only verses with number or text revisions are included in the remainder of the New Testament.]

THE ACTS OF THE APOSTLES

CHAPTER 1

3 To whom also he showed himself alive after his ~~passion~~ **sufferings** by many infallible proofs, being seen of them forty days, and speaking of the things pertaining to the kingdom of God;

4 And, being **with them when they were** assembled together ~~with them~~, commanded them that they should not depart from Jerusalem, but wait for the promise of the Father, which, *saith he*, ye have heard of me.

CHAPTER 2

3 And there appeared unto them cloven tongues like as of fire, and it ~~sat~~ **rested** upon each of them.

27 Because thou wilt not leave my soul in ~~hell~~ **prison**, neither wilt thou suffer thine Holy One to see corruption.

CHAPTER 3

1 Now Peter and John went up together into the temple at the ~~hour of prayer, being the~~ ninth *hour*, **for prayer**.

4 And Peter **and John**, fastening ~~his~~ **their** eyes upon him ~~with John~~, said, Look on us.

12 And when Peter saw *it* **this**, he answered **and said** unto the people, Ye men of Israel, why marvel ye at this? or why look ye so earnestly on us, as though by our own power or holiness we had made this man to walk?

16 And ~~his name~~ **this man,** through faith in his name, hath **been** made ~~this man~~ strong, whom ye see and know; yea, the faith which is ~~by~~ **in**

him hath given him this perfect soundness in the presence of you all.

17 And now, brethren, I ~~wot~~ **know** that through ignorance ye ~~did~~ **have done** ~~it~~ **this**, as ~~did~~ also your rulers.

20 And he shall send Jesus Christ, which before was preached unto you, **whom ye have crucified;**

21 Whom the ~~heaven~~ **heavens** must receive until the times of restitution of all things which God hath spoken by the mouth of all his holy prophets since the world began.

CHAPTER 4

21 So when they had further threatened them, they let them go, finding nothing how they might punish them, because of the people; for ~~all men~~ **many** glorified God for that which was done.

CHAPTER 5

13 And of the ~~rest~~ **rulers** durst no man join himself to them; but the people magnified them.

39 But if it be of God, ye cannot overthrow it; **be careful, therefore,** lest ~~haply~~ ye be found even to fight against God.

CHAPTER 6

9 Then there arose certain of the synagogue, ~~which~~ **who** ~~is~~ **are** called ~~the synagogue of the~~ Libertines, and **also** Cyrenians, and Alexandrians, and of them of Cilicia, and of Asia, disputing with Stephen.

CHAPTER 7

39 ~~To~~ Whom our fathers would not obey, but thrust *him* from them, and

in their hearts turned back again into Egypt,

40 Saying unto Aaron, Make us gods to go before us; for *as for* this Moses, which brought us out of the land of Egypt, we ~~wot~~ **know** not what is become of him.

44 Our fathers had the tabernacle of witness in the wilderness, as he had appointed, speaking unto Moses, that he should make it according to the ~~fashion~~ **pattern** that he had seen.

59 And they stoned Stephen; **and he,** calling upon *God,* ~~and saying~~ **said**, Lord Jesus, receive my spirit.

CHAPTER 9

7 And ~~the men~~ **they** ~~which~~ **who** ~~journeyed~~ **were journeying** with him ~~stood speechless~~ **saw indeed the light, and were afraid; but they** ~~hearing~~ **heard not** ~~a~~ **the** voice **of him who spake to him** ~~but seeing no man~~.

24 But their ~~laying~~ **lying** ~~await~~ **in wait** was known of Saul. And they watched the gates day and night to kill him.

30 ~~Which~~ When the brethren knew **this**, they brought him down to Caesarea, and sent him forth to Tarsus.

32 And it came to pass, as Peter passed throughout all ~~quarters~~ **these regions**, he came down also to the saints which dwelt at Lydda.

38 And forasmuch as Lydda was nigh to Joppa, and the disciples had heard that Peter was there, they sent unto him two men, desiring ~~him~~ that he would not delay to come to them.

CHAPTER 12

7 And, behold, the angel of the Lord came ~~upon~~ **unto** *him*, and a light shined in the prison; and he smote Peter on the side, and raised him up, saying, Arise up quickly. And his chains fell off from *his* hands.

CHAPTER 13

48 And when the Gentiles heard this, they were glad, and glorified the word of the Lord; and as many as **believed** were ordained ~~to~~ **unto** eternal life ~~believed~~.

CHAPTER 14

14 ~~Which~~ When the apostles, Barnabas and Paul, heard ~~of~~ **this**, they rent their clothes, and ran in among the people, crying out,

CHAPTER 15

24 Forasmuch as we have heard, that certain **men** which went out from us have troubled you with words, subverting your souls, saying, *Ye must* be circumcised, and keep the law; to whom we gave no *such* commandment:

CHAPTER 16

13 And on the Sabbath we went out of the city by a river side, where **the people resorted for** prayer ~~was wont~~ to be made; and we sat down, and spake unto the women which resorted *thither*.

CHAPTER 17

19 And they took him and **they** brought him unto **the** Areopagus, saying, May we know what this new doctrine **is**, whereof thou speakest ~~is~~?

27 That they should seek the Lord, if ~~haply~~ they ~~might feel after him, and~~ **are willing to** find him, ~~though~~ **for** he ~~be~~ **is** not far from everyone of us;

31 Because he hath appointed a day, in the which he will judge the world in righteousness by ~~that man~~ **him** whom he hath ordained; ~~whereof~~ **and** he hath given assurance **of this** unto all *men*, in that he hath raised him from the dead.

CHAPTER 20

13 And ~~we~~ **he**˙ went before to ship, and sailed unto Assos, there intending to take in Paul; for so had he appointed, minding himself to go afoot.

21 Testifying both to the Jews, and also to the Greeks, repentance toward God, and faith ~~toward~~ **on the name of** our Lord Jesus Christ.

CHAPTER 21

25 As touching the Gentiles which believe, we have written *and* concluded that they observe no such thing, save only that they keep themselves from *things* offered to idols, and from blood, and from **things** strangled, and from fornication.

CHAPTER 22

10 And I said, What shall I do, Lord? And the Lord said unto me, Arise, and go into Damascus; and there it shall be told thee of all things which are appointed ~~for~~ **of** thee to do.

29 Then straightway they departed from him which should have examined him, and the chief captain also was afraid, after he knew that he was a Roman, ~~and~~ because he had bound him, **and he loosed him from his bands.**[35]

30 On the morrow, because he would have known the certainty wherefore he was accused of the Jews, he ~~loosed him from *his* bands, and~~ commanded the chief priests and all their council to appear, and brought Paul down, and set him before them.

CHAPTER 23

5 Then said Paul, I ~~wist~~ **did** not **know**, brethren, that he was the high priest; for it is written, Thou shalt not speak evil of the ruler of thy people.

15 Now therefore ye with the council signify to the chief captain that he bring him down unto you tomorrow, as though ~~ye~~ **you** would inquire something more perfectly concerning him; and we, ~~or ever~~ **before** he come near, are ready to kill him.

27 This man was taken of the Jews, and ~~should~~ **would** have been killed of them; then came I with an army, and rescued him, having understood that he was a Roman.

CHAPTER 25

17 Therefore, when they were come hither, without any delay on the ~~morrow~~ **day following** I sat on the judgment seat, and commanded the man to be brought forth.

CHAPTER 27

35 And when he had thus spoken, he took bread, and gave thanks to God in **the**˙ presence of them all; and when he had broken *it*, he began to eat.

The Epistle of Paul the Apostle to the
ROMANS

CHAPTER 1

1 Paul, **an apostle,** a servant of ~~Jesus Christ~~ **God**, called ~~to be an apostle~~ **of Jesus Christ, and** separated ~~unto~~ **to** preach the gospel ~~of God~~,

2 (Which he had promised ~~afore~~ **before** by his prophets in the holy scriptures,)

4 And declared ~~to be~~ the Son of God with power, ~~according to~~ **by** the Spirit ~~of holiness, by~~ **according to the truth through** the resurrection from the dead;

5 By whom we have received grace and apostleship, ~~for~~ **through** obedience ~~to the,~~ **and** faith **in his name, to preach the gospel** among all nations ~~for his name;~~

6 Among whom ~~are~~ ye also **are** ~~the~~ called of Jesus Christ;

7 **Wherefore I write** to all ~~that~~ **who** ~~be~~ **are** in Rome, beloved of God, called ~~to be~~ saints; Grace to you, and peace, from God our Father, and the Lord Jesus Christ.

8 First, I thank my God through Jesus Christ, ~~for~~ **that** you all **are steadfast, and** ~~that~~ your faith is spoken of throughout the ~~whole~~ world.

9 For God is my witness, whom I serve ~~with my spirit in the gospel of his Son~~, that without ceasing I make mention of you always in my prayers, **that you may be kept through the Spirit, in the gospel of his Son,**

10 Making request **of you, to remember me in your prayers, I now write unto you, that you will ask him in faith, that** if by any means ~~now,~~ at length, **I may serve you with my labors, and** ~~might~~ **may** have a prosperous journey by the will of God, to come unto you.

11 For I long to see you, that I may impart unto you some spiritual gift, ~~to the end ye~~ **that it** may be established **in you to the end**;

12 That ~~is, that~~ I may be comforted together with you by the mutual faith both of you and me.

13 Now I would not have you ignorant brethren, that oftentimes I purposed to come unto you, (but was ~~let~~ **hindered** hitherto,) that I might have some fruit among you also, even as among other Gentiles.

15 ~~So~~ **And**, as much as in me is, I am ready to preach the gospel to you that are at Rome also.

17 For therein is the righteousness of God revealed ~~from faith to faith~~ **through faith on his name;** as it is written, The just shall live by faith.

18 For the wrath of God is revealed from heaven against all ungodliness and unrighteousness of men; who ~~hold~~ **love not** the truth, **but remain** in unrighteousness,

19 ~~Because~~ **After** that which may be known of God is manifest ~~in~~ **to** them.

20 19 For God hath ~~shewed it~~ **revealed** unto them ~~For~~ the invisible things of him, from the creation of the world, **which** are clearly seen; **things which are not seen** being understood by the things that are made, ~~even~~ **through** his eternal power and Godhead; so that they are without excuse;

21 Because that, when they knew God, they glorified *him* not as God, neither were **they** thankful, but became vain in their imaginations, and their foolish ~~heart~~ **hearts** ~~was~~ **were** darkened.

28 And even as they did not like to retain God ~~in their~~ **according to some**[*] knowledge, God gave them over to a reprobate mind, to do those things which are not convenient;

32 **And some** who knowing the judgment of God, that they which commit such things are worthy of death **are inexcusable**, not only do the same, but have pleasure in them that do them.

CHAPTER 2

1 Therefore thou art inexcusable, O man, whosoever thou art that **thus**

judgest, for wherein thou judgest another, thou condemnest thyself; for thou that judgest doest the same things.

16 In the day when God shall judge the secrets of men by Jesus Christ according to ~~my~~ **the** gospel.

CHAPTER 3

1 What advantage then hath the Jew **over the Gentile?** or what profit *is there* of circumcision, **who is not a Jew from the heart?**

2 **But he who is a Jew from the heart, I say hath** much every way; chiefly because that unto them were committed the oracles of God.

5 But if **we remain in** our unrighteousness **and** commend the righteousness of God, ~~what shall~~ **how dare** we say, ~~Is~~ God **is** unrighteous who taketh vengeance? (I speak as a man **who fears God,**)

7 7–8 For if the truth of God hath more abounded through my lie, **(as it is called of the Jews,)** unto his glory; why yet am I also judged as a sinner? and not ~~rather~~ **received?** ~~as~~ **Because** we ~~be~~ **are** slanderously reported;

8 And ~~as~~ some affirm that we say, **(whose damnation is just,)** Let us do evil that good may come. ~~whose damnation is just~~ **But this is false.**

9 **If not so;** what then are we better *than they?* No, in no wise; for we have ~~before~~ proved ~~both~~ **before, that** Jews and Gentiles ~~that they~~ are all under sin.

20 **For by the law is the knowledge of sin;** therefore by the deeds of the law ~~there~~ shall no flesh be justified in his sight ~~for by the law is the knowledge of sin.~~

24 **Therefore** being justified ~~freely~~ **only**[36] by his grace through the redemption that is in Christ Jesus;

28 Therefore we conclude that a man is justified by faith **alone** without the deeds of the law.

30 Seeing ~~it is one~~ **that** God ~~which shall~~ **will** justify the circumcision by faith, and uncircumcision through faith.

CHAPTER 4

2 For if Abraham were justified by **the law of** works, he hath ~~whereof~~ to glory **in himself;** but not ~~before~~ **of** God.

4 Now to him ~~that~~ **who** ~~worketh~~ **is justified by the law of works,** is the reward ~~not~~ reckoned, **not** of grace, but of debt.

5 But to him that ~~worketh~~ **seeketh** not **to be justified by the law of works,** but believeth on him ~~that~~ **who** justifieth **not** the ungodly, his faith is counted for righteousness.

6 Even as David also describeth the blessedness of the man, unto whom God imputeth righteousness without **the law of** works,

7 *Saying,* Blessed *are* they **through faith** whose iniquities are forgiven, and whose sins are covered.

16 Therefore ~~it is~~ **ye are justified of** faith **and works,** ~~that it might be by~~ **through** grace, to the end the promise might be sure to all the seed; not to ~~that~~ **them** only ~~which~~ **who** ~~is~~ **are** of the law, but to ~~that~~ **them** also ~~which~~ **who** ~~is~~ **are** of the faith of Abraham; who is the father of us all,

CHAPTER 5

3 And not only ~~so~~ **this,** but we glory in tribulations also; knowing that tribulation worketh patience;

13 (For, ~~until~~ **before** the law, sin was in the world; ~~but~~ **yet** sin is not imputed ~~when there is~~ **to those who have** no law.

14 Nevertheless death reigned from

Adam to Moses, even over them that had not sinned after the similitude of Adam's transgression, who is the figure of him that was to come. **For I say that through the offense, death reigned over all.**

15 But ~~not as~~ the offense ~~so also~~ *is* **not as** the free gift**, for the gift aboundeth**. For, if through the offense of one**,** many be dead**;** much more the grace of God, and the gift by grace, *~~which is~~* ~~by one man, Jesus Christ~~ hath abounded **by one man, Jesus Christ,** unto many.

16 And not as *~~it was~~* by one that sinned, *~~so~~*˚ *is* the gift**;** for the judgment ~~was~~ **is** by one to condemnation, but the free gift *is* of many offenses unto justification.

CHAPTER 6

7 For he that is dead **to sin** is freed from sin.

14 For **in so doing** sin shall not have dominion over you**;** for ye are not under the law, but under grace.

17 But God be thanked, that ye ~~were~~ **are not** the servants of sin, ~~but~~ **for** ye have obeyed from the heart that form of doctrine which was delivered you.

19 I speak after the manner of men because of the infirmity of your flesh**;** for as ye have **in times past** yielded your members servants to uncleanness and to iniquity unto iniquity; even so now yield your members servants to righteousness unto holiness.

CHAPTER 7

1 Know ye not, brethren, (for I speak to them that know the law,) how that the law hath dominion over a man **only** as long as he liveth?

2 For the woman which hath ~~an~~ **a** husband is bound by the law to *her* husband ~~so~~ **only as** long as he liveth; ~~but~~ **for** if the husband be dead, she is loosed from the law of *her* husband.

5 For when we were in the flesh, the motions of sins, which were ~~by~~ **not according to** the law, did work in our members to bring forth fruit unto death.

6 But now we are delivered from the law ~~that being dead~~ wherein we were held**, being dead to the law,** that we should serve in newness of spirit, and not *in* the oldness of the letter.

9 For **once** I was alive without **transgression of** the law ~~once,~~ but when the commandment **of Christ** came, sin revived, and I died.

10 And **when I believed not** the commandment **of Christ which came**, which *was ordained* to life, I found ~~to be~~ it **condemned me** unto death.

11 For sin, taking occasion, ~~by~~ **denied** the commandment, **and** deceived me**;** and by it ~~slew~~ *~~me~~* **I was slain**.

12 ~~Wherefore~~ **Nevertheless, I found** the law *is* **to be** holy, and the commandment **to be** holy, and just, and good.

13 Was then that which is good made death unto me? God forbid. But sin, that it might appear sin **by that which is good** working death in me ~~by that which is good~~; that sin**,** by the commandment**,** might become exceeding sinful.

14 For we know that the ~~law~~ **commandment** is spiritual**;** but **when I was under law,** I ~~am~~ **was yet** carnal, sold under sin.

15 **But now I am spiritual;** for that which **I am commanded to do,** I do; **and that which I am commanded not to allow,** I allow not.

16 15 For what **I know is not right,**

I would ~~that do I~~ not **do**; ~~but what~~ **for that which is sin**, I hate ~~that do I~~.

17 16 If then I do **not** that which I would not **allow**, I consent unto the law, that *it is* good; **and I am not condemned.**

18 17 Now then, it is no more I that do ~~it~~ **sin**; but **I seek to subdue that** sin ~~that~~ **which** dwelleth in me.

19 18 For I know that in me, that is, in my flesh, dwelleth no good thing; for to will is present with me, but ~~how~~ to perform that which is good I find not, **only in Christ.**

20 19 For the good that I would **have done when under the law, I find not to be good; therefore,** I do **it** not.

21 19 But the evil which I would not **do under the law, I find to be good;** that, I do.

22 20 Now if I do that, **through the assistance of Christ,** I would not **do under the law, I am not under the law; and** it is no more **that** I ~~that~~ **seek to** do ~~it~~ **wrong,** but **to subdue** sin that dwelleth in me.

23 21–22 I find then **that under** ~~a~~ **the** law, that when I would do good evil ~~is~~ **was** present with me; for I delight in the law of God after the inward man.

24 23 ~~But~~ **And now** I see another law, **even the commandment of Christ, and it is imprinted in my mind.**

25 23 ~~in~~ **But** my members **are** warring against the law of my mind, and bringing me into captivity to the law of sin which is in my members.

26 24 **And if I subdue not the sin which is in me, but with the flesh serve the law of sin;** O wretched man that I am! who shall deliver me from the body of this death?

27 25 I thank God through Jesus Christ our Lord**, then, that** so ~~then~~ with the mind I myself serve the law of God ~~but with the flesh the law of sin~~.

8 So then they that are ~~in~~ **after** the flesh cannot please God.

9 But ye are not ~~in~~ **after** the flesh, but ~~in~~ **after** the Spirit, if so be that the Spirit of God dwell in you. Now if any man have not the Spirit of Christ, he is none of his.

10 And if Christ *be* in you, **though** the body ~~is dead~~ **shall die** because of sin, ~~but~~ **yet** the Spirit *is* life, because of righteousness.

11 ~~But~~ **And** if the Spirit of him that raised up Jesus from the dead**, dwell** in you, he that raised up Christ from the dead shall also quicken your mortal bodies by his Spirit that dwelleth in you.

13 For if ye live after the flesh, **unto sin,** ye shall die; but if ye through the Spirit do mortify the deeds of the body, ye shall live **unto Christ**.

18 For I reckon that the sufferings of this present time *are* not worthy *to be* ~~compared~~ **named** with the glory which shall be revealed in us.

20 For the creature was made subject to ~~vanity~~ **tribulation** not willingly, but by reason of him who hath subjected ~~the same~~ **it** in hope;

25 But if we hope for that we see not, *then* ~~do we~~ with patience **we do** wait for *it*.

26 Likewise the Spirit also helpeth our infirmities; for we know not what we should pray for as we ought; but the Spirit itself maketh intercession for us with ~~groanings~~ **striving** which cannot be ~~uttered~~ **expressed**.[37]

29 For **him** whom he did foreknow, he also did predestinate *to be* conformed to ~~the~~ **his own** image ~~of his~~

~~Son~~, that he might be the firstborn among many brethren.

30 Moreover**, him** whom he did predestinate, ~~them~~ **him** he also called**;** and **him** whom he called, ~~them~~ **him** he also ~~justified~~ **sanctified;** and **him** whom he ~~justified~~ **sanctified**, ~~them~~ **him** he also glorified.

31 What shall we then say to these things? If God *be* for us, who *can ~~be~~* **prevail** against us?

CHAPTER 9

3 (For **once** I could **have** ~~wish~~ **wished** that myself were accursed from Christ**,**) for my brethren, my kinsmen according to the flesh**;**

4 Who are Israelites; ~~to~~ **of** whom ~~pertaineth~~ **are** the adoption, and the glory, and the covenants, and the giving of the law, and the service *of God,*

5 4–5 And the promises ~~Whose~~ **which** *are* **made unto** the fathers**;** and of whom**,** as concerning the flesh**,** Christ ~~came~~ **was**, who is **God** over all, ~~God~~ blessed forever. Amen.

7 Neither, because they are ~~the seed~~ **all children** of Abraham, *are they* ~~all children~~ **the seed;** but, In Isaac shall thy seed be called.

10 And not only ~~this~~ **Sarah**; but when Rebecca also had conceived by one, ~~even by~~ our father Isaac**,**

23 And that he might make known the riches of his glory on the vessels of mercy, which he had ~~afore~~ **before** prepared unto glory,

25 As he saith also in ~~Osee~~ **Hosea**, I will call them my people, which were not my people; and her beloved, which was not beloved.

32 Wherefore ~~Because~~ *they ~~sought it~~* **stumbled at that stumbling stone,** not by faith, but as it were by the works of the law ~~For they stumbled at that stumblingstone;~~

CHAPTER 10

16 17 So then faith ~~cometh~~ **comes** by hearing ~~and hearing by~~[38] the word of God.

17 18 But I say, Have they not heard? Yes verily, their sound went into all the earth, and their words unto the ends of the world.

18 16 But they have not all obeyed the gospel. For Esaias saith, Lord, who hath believed our report?

19 But I say, Did not Israel know? ~~First~~ **Now** Moses saith, I will provoke you to jealousy by *them that are* no people, *and* by a foolish nation I will anger you.

CHAPTER 11

2 God hath not cast away his people which he foreknew. ~~Wot~~ **Know** ye not what the scripture saith of Elias? how he maketh ~~intercession~~ **complaint** to God against Israel, saying,

7 What then? Israel hath not obtained that which ~~he~~ **they** ~~seeketh~~ **seek** for; but the election hath obtained it, ~~and~~ the rest were blinded.

12 Now if the fall of them ~~be~~ **is** the riches of the world, and the diminishing of them the riches of the Gentiles; how much more their fullness?

15 For if the casting away of them ~~be~~ **is** the reconciling of the world, what *shall* the ~~receiving~~ **restoring** *of them be*, but life from the dead?

16 For if the firstfruit ~~be~~ **is** holy, the lump *is* also *holy*; and if the root ~~be~~ **is** holy, so *are* the branches.

17 And if some of the branches be broken off, and thou, being a wild olive tree, ~~wert~~ **wast** ~~graffed~~ **grafted** in among them, and with them partakest of the root and fatness of the olive tree;

18 Boast not against the branches**,** ~~But~~ **for** ~~if thou boast~~ thou bearest not the root, but the root thee.

19 **For if thou boast**, thou wilt say ~~then~~, The branches were broken off, that ~~I~~ **we** might be ~~graffed~~ **grafted*** in.

24 For if thou ~~wert~~ **wast** cut out of the olive tree which is wild by nature, and ~~wert~~ **wast** ~~graffed~~ **grafted*** contrary to nature into a good olive tree; how much more shall these, which be the natural *branches*, be ~~graffed~~ **grafted*** into their own olive tree?

26 And ~~so~~ **then** all Israel shall be saved; as it is written, There shall come out of Sion the Deliverer, and shall turn away ungodliness from Jacob;

CHAPTER 12

2 And be not conformed to this world; but be ye transformed by the renewing of your mind, that ye may prove what *is* that good, and acceptable, and perfect will of God **is**.

9 *Let* love be without dissimulation. Abhor that which is evil **and** cleave to that which is good.

CHAPTER 13

1 Let every soul be subject unto the higher powers. For there is no power **in the church** but of God; the powers that be are ordained of God.

2 Whosoever therefore resisteth the power, resisteth the ordinance of God; and they that resist shall receive to themselves ~~damnation~~ **punishment**.

4 For he is the minister of God to thee for good. But if thou do that which is evil be afraid; for he beareth not the ~~sword~~ **rod** in vain; for he is the minister of God, a revenger to *execute* wrath upon him that doeth evil.

6 For, for this cause pay ye ~~tribute~~ **your consecrations** also **unto them;** for they are God's ministers, attending continually upon this very thing.

7 **But first,** render ~~therefore~~ to all

their dues**, according to custom,** tribute to whom tribute ~~is due~~, custom to whom custom, **that your consecrations may be done in** fear **of him** to whom fear **belongs, and in** honor **of him** to whom honor **belongs**.

8 **Therefore** owe no man anything, but to love one another; for he that loveth another hath fulfilled the law.

14 But put ye on the Lord Jesus Christ, and make not provision for the flesh, to ~~fulfil~~ **gratify** the lusts *thereof.*

CHAPTER 14

11 For ~~it is written,~~ *As* I live saith the Lord, **as it is written. And** every knee shall bow to me, and every tongue shall ~~confess~~ **swear** to God.

15 But if thy brother be grieved with *thy* meat, ~~now~~ **thou** walkest ~~thou~~ not charitably **if thou eatest. Therefore** destroy not him with thy meat, for whom Christ died.

23 And he that doubteth is ~~damned~~ **condemned** if he eat, because ~~he eateth~~ **it is** not of faith; for whatsoever *is* not of faith is sin.

CHAPTER 15

5 Now the God of patience and consolation grant you to be likeminded one toward another according ~~to~~ **as was** Christ Jesus;

24 Whensoever I take my journey into Spain, I will come to you; for I trust to see you in my journey, and to be brought on my way thitherward by you, if first I be somewhat filled with your ~~company~~ **prayers**.

CHAPTER 16

10 Salute Apelles approved in Christ. Salute them which are of Aristobulus' ~~household~~ **church**.

11 Salute Herodian my kinsman.

Greet them that be of the ~~household~~ **church** of Narcissus, which are in the Lord.

16 Salute one another with ~~an~~ **a** holy ~~kiss~~ **salutation**. The churches of Christ salute you.

25 Now to him that is of power to stablish you according to ~~my~~ **the** gospel, and the preaching of Jesus Christ, according to the revelation of the mystery, which was kept secret since the world began,

The First Epistle of Paul the Apostle to the
CORINTHIANS

CHAPTER 1

1 Paul, **an apostle,** called ~~to be an apostle~~ of Jesus Christ through the will of God; and Sosthenes *our* brother,

4 I thank my God always on your behalf, for the grace of God **of** which is given you ~~by~~ **of** Jesus Christ;

10 Now I beseech you, brethren, ~~by~~ **in** the name of our Lord Jesus Christ, that ye all speak the same thing, and *that* there be no divisions among you; but *that* ye be perfectly joined together in the same mind and in the same judgment.

12 Now this I say, that ~~every one~~ **many** of you saith, I am of Paul; and I of Apollos; and I of Cephas; and I of Christ.

24 But unto them ~~which are called~~ **who believe,**[39] both Jews and Greeks, Christ the power of God, and the wisdom of God.

26 For ye see your calling, brethren, how that not many wise men after the flesh, not many mighty, not many noble, *are* ~~called~~ **chosen;**

27 ~~But~~ **For** God hath chosen the foolish things of the world to confound the wise; and God hath chosen the weak things of the world to confound the things which are mighty;

28 And base things of the world, and the things which are despised, hath God chosen, *yea,* and things which are not, to bring to ~~nought~~ **naught** things that are **mighty;**

CHAPTER 2

11 For what man knoweth the things of a man, save the spirit of man which is in him? even so the things of God knoweth no man, ~~but~~ **except he has** the Spirit of God.

CHAPTER 3

2 I have fed you with milk, and not with meat; for hitherto ye were not able *to* ~~bear~~ **receive** *it*, neither yet now are ye able.

15 If any man's work shall be burned, he shall suffer loss; but he himself ~~shall~~ **may** be saved; yet so as by fire.

CHAPTER 4

2 Moreover it is required ~~in~~ **of** stewards, that a man be found faithful.

4 For **though** I know nothing ~~by~~ **against** myself; yet ~~am~~ I **am** not hereby justified; but he ~~that~~ **who** judgeth me is the Lord.

5 Therefore **I** judge nothing before the time, until the Lord come, who both will bring to light the hidden things of darkness, and will make

manifest the counsels of the hearts; and then shall every man have praise of God.

Chapter 5

3 For ~~I~~ verily, as absent in body but present in spirit, **I** have judged already **him who hath so done this deed**, as though I were present, ~~concerning~~ him ~~that hath so done this deed~~

4 In the name of our Lord Jesus Christ, when ye are gathered together, and **have** ~~my~~ **the** Spirit, with the power of our Lord Jesus Christ,

12 For what have I to do to judge them also that are without? do not ~~ye~~ **they** judge them that are within?

Chapter 6

12 All these things are **not** lawful unto me, ~~but~~ **and** all **these** things are not expedient. All things are **not** lawful for me, ~~but~~ **therefore** I will not be brought under the power of any.

18 Flee fornication. Every sin that a man ~~doeth~~ **committeth** is ~~without~~ **against** the body **of Christ,** ~~but~~ **and** he ~~that~~ **who** committeth fornication sinneth against his own body.

Chapter 7

1 Now concerning the things whereof ye wrote unto me, **saying,** *It is* good for a man not to touch a woman.

2 Nevertheless, **I say,** *to avoid* fornication, let every man have his own wife, and let every woman have her own husband.

5 ~~Defraud~~ **Depart** ye not one **from** the other, except *it be* with consent for a time, that ye may give yourselves to fasting and prayer; and come together again, that Satan tempt you not for your incontinency.

6 ~~But~~ **And now what** I speak ~~this~~ **is** by permission, *and* not ~~of~~ **by** commandment.

7 For I would that all men were even as ~~I~~ myself. But every man hath his proper gift of God, one after this manner, and another after that.

9 But if they cannot ~~contain~~ **abide**, let them marry; for it is better to marry than ~~to burn~~ **that any should commit sin**.

11 But and if she depart, let her remain unmarried, or be reconciled to *her* husband; ~~and~~ **but** let not the husband put away *his* wife.

26 I suppose therefore that this is good for the present distress, ~~I say,~~ ~~that~~ *it is* ~~good~~ for a man so to ~~be~~ **remain that he may do greater good**.

28 But ~~and~~ if thou marry, thou hast not sinned; and if a virgin marry, she hath not sinned. Nevertheless, such shall have trouble in the flesh. ~~but~~ **For** I spare you **not**.

29 **But I speak unto you who are called unto the ministry.** ~~But~~ **For** this I say, brethren, the time **that remaineth** *is* but short, ~~it remaineth~~ that **ye shall be sent forth unto the ministry. Even** ~~both~~ they ~~that~~ **who** have wives, **shall** be as though they had none; **for ye are called and chosen to do the Lord's work.**

30 And **it shall be with** ~~they~~ **them** ~~that~~ **who** weep, as though they wept not; and ~~they~~ **them** ~~that~~ **who** rejoice, as though they rejoiced not, and ~~they~~ **them** ~~that~~ **who** buy, as though they possessed not;

31 And ~~they~~ **them** ~~that~~ **who** use this world, as not ~~abusing~~ **using** *it*; for the fashion of this world passeth away.

32 But **I would, brethren, that ye magnify your calling.** I would have you without carefulness. **For** he ~~that~~ **who** is unmarried, careth for the things that belong to the Lord, how he may please the Lord; **therefore he prevaileth.**

33 But he ~~that~~ **who** is married, careth for the things that are of the world, how he may please *his* wife; **therefore there is a difference, for he is hindered.**

36 But if any man think that he behaveth himself uncomely toward his virgin **whom he hath espoused**, if she pass the flower of *her* age, and need so require, let him do what he ~~will~~ **hath promised**, he sinneth not; let them marry.

38 So then he that giveth *her* **himself** in marriage doeth well; but he that giveth *her* **himself** not in marriage doeth better.

CHAPTER 8

4 As concerning therefore the eating of those things ~~that~~ **which** are **in the world** offered in sacrifice unto idols, we know that an idol *is* nothing ~~in the world~~, and that *there is* none other God but one.

CHAPTER 9

24 Know ye not that they which run in a race **all** run ~~all~~, but **only** one receiveth the prize? So run, that ye may obtain.

CHAPTER 10

11 Now**,** all these things happened unto them for ensamples; and they are written for our admonition **also, and for an admonition for those** upon whom the ~~ends~~ **end** of the world ~~are~~ **shall** come.

23 All things are **not** lawful for me, ~~but~~ **for** all things are not expedient; all things are **not** lawful ~~for me~~, ~~but~~ **for** all things edify not.

24 Let no man seek **therefore** his own, but every man another's *wealth* **good**.

27 If any of them that believe not bid you *to a feast*, and ye be disposed

to ~~go~~ **eat**; whatsoever is set before you, eat, asking no ~~question~~ **questions** for ~~conscience~~ **conscience'** sake.

33 Even as I please all *men* in all *things*, not seeking mine own profit, but **of** the ~~profit of~~ many, that they may be saved.

CHAPTER 11

10 For this cause ought the woman to have ~~power~~ **a covering** on *her* head because of the angels.

19 For there must be also ~~heresies~~ **divisions** among you, that they which are approved may be made manifest among you.

20 When ye come together ~~therefore~~ ~~into~~ **unto** one place, ~~this~~ is **it** not to eat the Lord's supper?

21 ~~For~~ **But** in eating everyone taketh before ~~other~~ his own supper; and one is hungry, and another is drunken.

29 For he that eateth and drinketh unworthily, eateth and drinketh ~~damnation~~ **condemnation** to himself, not discerning the Lord's body.

CHAPTER 12

1 Now concerning spiritual ~~gifts~~ **things**, brethren, I would not have you ignorant.

3 Wherefore I give you to understand, that no man speaking by the Spirit of God calleth Jesus accursed; and *that* no man can ~~say~~ **know**[40] that Jesus is the Lord, but by the Holy Ghost.

31 **I say unto you, Nay; for I have shown unto you a more excellent way,** ~~But~~ **therefore** covet earnestly the best gifts. ~~and yet shew I unto you a more excellent way~~

CHAPTER 14

2 For he that speaketh in ~~an unknown~~ **another** tongue speaketh not

unto men, but unto God; for no man understandeth him; howbeit in the spirit he speaketh mysteries.

4 He that speaketh in ~~an unknown~~ **another** tongue edifieth himself; but he that prophesieth edifieth the church.

13 Wherefore let him that speaketh in ~~an unknown~~ **another** tongue pray that he may interpret.

14 For if I pray in ~~an unknown~~ **another** tongue, my spirit prayeth, but my understanding is unfruitful.

19 Yet in the church I had rather speak five words with my understanding, that *by my voice* I might teach others also, than ten thousand words in ~~an unknown~~ **another** tongue.

27 If any man speak in ~~an unknown~~ **another** tongue, *let it be* by two, or at the most *by* three, and *that* by course; and let one interpret.

34 Let your women keep silence in the churches; for it is not permitted unto them to ~~speak~~ **rule**; but ~~they are commanded~~ to be under obedience, as also saith the law.

35 And if they will learn anything, let them ask their husbands at home; for it is a shame for women to ~~speak~~ **rule** in the church.

CHAPTER 15

10 But by the grace of God I am what I am; and his grace which *was bestowed* upon me was not in vain; ~~but~~ **for** I labored more abundantly than they all; yet not I, but the grace of God which was with me.

24 ~~Then~~ **Afterward** *cometh* the end, when he shall have delivered up the kingdom to God, even the Father;

when he shall have put down all rule, and all authority and power.

26 The last enemy, **death,** ~~that~~ shall be destroyed ~~is death~~.

27 For **he saith, When it is manifest that** he hath put all things under his feet, ~~But when he saith~~ **and that** all things are put under *him,* ~~it is manifest that~~ he is excepted **of the Father** ~~which~~ **who** did put all things under him.

31 I protest ~~by~~ **unto you the resurrection of the dead; and this is** ~~your~~ **my** rejoicing which I have in Christ Jesus our Lord **daily,** **though** I die ~~daily~~.

37 And that which thou sowest, thou sowest not that body ~~that~~ **which** shall be, but ~~bare~~ grain, it may ~~chance~~ **be** of wheat, or ~~of~~ some other ~~grain~~;

40 ~~There are~~ **Also** celestial bodies, and bodies terrestrial, **and bodies telestial;** but the glory of the celestial ~~is,~~ one; and ~~glory of~~ the terrestrial ~~is,~~ another; **and the telestial, another.**

46 Howbeit, that ~~was not first~~ which is ~~spiritual~~ **natural first, and not** ~~but~~ that which is ~~natural~~ **spiritual**; ~~and~~ **but** ~~afterward~~ **afterwards,** that which is spiritual;

52 In a moment, in the twinkling of an eye, at the **sound of the** last trump; for the trumpet shall sound, and the dead shall be raised incorruptible, and we shall be changed.

CHAPTER 16

9 For a great door and effectual is opened unto me, ~~and~~ **but** *there are* many adversaries.

20 All the brethren greet you. Greet ye one another with ~~an~~ **a** holy ~~kiss~~ **salutation.**

The Second Epistle of Paul the Apostle to the
CORINTHIANS

CHAPTER 1

17 When I therefore was thus minded, did I use lightness? or the things that I purpose, do I purpose according to the flesh, that with me there ~~should~~ **shall** be yea, yea, and nay, nay?

CHAPTER 2

10 To whom ye forgive anything, I *forgive* also; for if I forgave anything, to whom I forgave *it*, for your sakes ~~forgave~~ **forgive** *I it* in the person of Christ;

CHAPTER 3

3 *Forasmuch as ye are* manifestly declared to be the epistle of Christ ministered by us, written not with ink, but with the Spirit of the living God; not in tables of stone, but in ~~fleshy~~ **fleshly** tables of the heart.

4 And such trust have we through Christ ~~to~~ **toward** ~~God-ward~~ **God.**

16 Nevertheless, when ~~it~~ **their heart** shall turn to the Lord, the ~~vail~~ **veil** shall be taken away.

CHAPTER 4

12 So then ~~death~~ **it** worketh **death** ~~in~~ **unto** us, but life ~~in~~ **unto** you.

15 For **we bear** all things ~~are~~ for your sakes, that the abundant grace might, through the thanksgiving of many, redound to the glory of God.

CHAPTER 5

10 For we must all appear before the judgment seat of Christ, that everyone may receive **a reward of** the ~~things~~ **deeds** *done* in ~~his~~ **the** body; **things** according to ~~that~~ **what** he hath done, whether ~~it be~~ good or bad.

13 For ~~whether~~ **we bear record that** we ~~be~~ **are not** beside ourselves; **for whether we glory**, *it is* to God**,** or whether we be sober, *it is* for your ~~cause~~ **sakes**.

14 For the love of Christ constraineth us; because we thus judge, that if one died for all, then ~~were~~ **are** all dead;

15 And ~~that~~ he died for all, that they which live should not henceforth live unto themselves, but unto him which died for them, and rose again.

16 Wherefore**,** henceforth ~~know~~ **live** we no ~~man~~ **more** after the flesh; yea, though **we once lived after the flesh, yet since** we have known Christ ~~after the flesh,~~ ~~yet~~ now henceforth ~~know~~ **live** we ~~him~~ no more **after the flesh**.

17 Therefore if any man ~~be~~ **live** in Christ, *he is* a new creature; old things are passed away; behold, all things are become new**,**

18 And **receiveth** all the things ~~are~~ of God, who hath reconciled us to himself by Jesus Christ, and hath given to us the ministry of reconciliation;

19 To wit, that God ~~was~~ **is** in Christ, reconciling the world unto himself, not imputing their trespasses unto them; and hath committed unto us the word of reconciliation.

CHAPTER 6

1 We then, *as* workers together *with* ~~him~~ **Christ**, beseech *you* also that ye receive not the grace of God in vain.

CHAPTER 8

1 Moreover, brethren, we ~~do~~ **would have** you to ~~wit~~ **know** of the grace of God bestowed on the churches of Macedonia;

5 And *this they did*, not as we ~~hoped~~ **required**, but first gave their own selves to the Lord, and unto us by the will of God.

22 And we have sent with them our brother, whom we have ~~oftentimes~~ proved diligent in many things, but now much more diligent,

23 22–23 **Therefore we send him unto you**, ~~upon~~ **in consequence of** the great confidence which ~~I~~ **we** *have* in you, ~~Whether~~ *any do enquire* of ~~Titus,~~ *he is* ~~my~~ partner and fellow-helper **that you will receive the things** concerning you**, to the glory of Christ; whether we send by the hand of Titus, my partner and fellow laborer,** or our brethren, *be en-quired of, they are* the messengers of the churches *and the glory of Christ.*

CHAPTER 11

4 For if he that cometh preacheth another Jesus, whom we have not preached, or *if* ye receive another spirit, which ye have not received, or another gospel, which ye have not accepted, ye might well bear with ~~him~~ **me**.

23 Are they ministers of Christ? (I speak as a fool,) ~~I~~ **so** *am* **I** ~~more~~; in labors more abundant, in stripes above measure, in prisons more frequent, in deaths oft.

29 Who is weak, and I am not weak? who is offended, and I ~~burn~~ **anger** not?

CHAPTER 12

6 For though I would desire to glory, I shall not be a fool; for I will say the truth**;** but *now* I forbear, lest any man should think of me above that which he seeth **of** me ~~to be~~, or *that* he heareth of me.

CHAPTER 13

12 Greet one another with ~~an~~ **a** holy ~~kiss~~ **salutation**.

The Epistle of Paul the Apostle to the
GALATIANS

CHAPTER 1

10 For do I now ~~persuade~~ **please** men, or God? or do I seek to please men? for if I yet pleased men, I should not be the servant of Christ.

24 And they glorified God ~~in~~ **on account of** me.

CHAPTER 2

4 ~~And that because of~~ **Notwithstanding,** there were some **brought in by** false brethren unwares ~~brought in~~, who came in privily to spy out our liberty which we have in Christ Jesus, that they might bring us into bondage**;**

CHAPTER 3

14 That the blessing of Abraham might come on the Gentiles through Jesus Christ; that ~~we~~ **they** might receive the promise of the Spirit through faith.

15 Brethren, I speak after the manner of men; Though *it be* but a man's covenant, yet ~~if~~ **when** *it be* confirmed, no man disannulleth, or addeth thereto.

18 For if the inheritance ~~be~~ **is** of the law, **then** *it is* no more of promise; but God gave *it* to Abraham by promise.

19 Wherefore then ~~serveth~~, the law ~~It~~ was added because of transgressions, till the seed should come to whom the promise was made **in the law given to Moses,** ~~and it was~~ **who was** ordained by **the hand of** angels ~~in the hand of~~ **to be** a mediator **of this first covenant, (the law.)**

20 Now ~~a~~ **this** mediator ~~is~~ **was** not *a mediator* of ~~one~~ **the new covenant;** but **there** ~~God~~ is one **mediator of the new covenant, who is Christ, as it is written in the law concerning the promises made to Abraham and his seed. Now Christ is the mediator of** life; **for this is the promise which God made unto Abraham.**

24 Wherefore the law was our schoolmaster ~~to bring us~~ ~~unto~~ **until** Christ, that we might be justified by faith.

26 For ye are all the children of God by faith in **Jesus** Christ ~~Jesus~~.

29 And if ye ~~be~~ **are** Christ's, then are ye Abraham's seed, and heirs according to the promise.

<h3 style="text-align:center">CHAPTER 4</h3>

12 Brethren, I beseech you **to** be **perfect** as I *am* **perfect**; for I *am* persuaded as ye ~~are~~ **have a knowledge of me,** ye have not injured me at all **by your sayings**.

<h1 style="text-align:center">The Epistle of Paul the Apostle to the
EPHESIANS</h1>

<h3 style="text-align:center">CHAPTER 2</h3>

8 For by grace are ye saved through faith; and that not of yourselves; **but** *it is* the gift of God;

11 Wherefore remember, that ye ~~being~~ **were** in ~~time~~ **times** past Gentiles in the flesh, who are called Uncircumcision by that which is called the Circumcision in the flesh made by hands;

<h3 style="text-align:center">CHAPTER 3</h3>

1 For this cause, I, Paul, **am** the prisoner of Jesus Christ ~~for~~ **among** you Gentiles.

2 ~~If ye have heard of~~ **For** the dispensation of the grace of God which is given me to you-ward;

3 ~~How~~ **As ye have heard** that by revelation he made known unto me the mystery **of Christ**; as I wrote ~~afore~~ **before** in few words;

<h3 style="text-align:center">CHAPTER 4</h3>

4 ~~There is~~ **In** one body, and one Spirit, even as ye are called in one hope of your calling;

10 He ~~that~~ **who** descended**,** is the same also ~~that~~ **who** ascended up ~~far above~~ **into heaven, to glorify him who reigneth over** all heavens, that he might fill all things.)

13 Till we ~~all come,~~ in the unity of the faith, ~~and of~~ **all come to** the knowledge of the Son of God, unto a perfect man, unto the measure of the stature of the fullness of Christ;

21 If so be that ye have ~~heard~~ **learned** him, and have been taught by him, as the truth is in Jesus;

22 ~~That ye put off~~ **And now I speak unto you** concerning the former conversation, **by exhortation, that ye put off** the old man, which is corrupt according to the deceitful lusts;

23 And be renewed in the ~~spirit~~ **mind** of ~~your mind~~ **the Spirit**;

26 ~~Be~~ **Can** ye be angry, and **not** sin ~~not~~? let not the sun go down upon your wrath;

28 Let him that stole steal no more; but rather let him labor, working with *his* hands **for** the ~~thing~~ **things** which ~~is~~ **are** good, that he may have to give to him that needeth.

<h3 style="text-align:center">Chapter 5</h3>

17 Wherefore be ye not unwise, but understanding what **is** the will of the Lord ~~is~~.

<h1 style="text-align:center">The Epistle of Paul the Apostle to the
PHILIPPIANS</h1>

<h3 style="text-align:center">Chapter 1</h3>

4 Always in every prayer of mine, for **the steadfastness of** you all, making request with joy,

21 22 But if I live in the flesh, ~~this is~~ **ye are** the fruit of my labor. **Yet** what I shall choose I ~~wot~~ **know** not.

22 21 For **me** to ~~me to~~ live, *is* **to do the will of** Christ; and to die, *is* **my** gain.

23 ~~For~~ **Now** I am in a strait betwixt two, having a desire to depart, and to be with Christ; which is far better;

26 That your rejoicing **with me** may be more abundant in Jesus Christ, for ~~me by~~ my coming to you again.

27 ~~Only~~ **Therefore** let your conversation be as it becometh the gospel of Christ; that whether I come and see you, or else be absent, I may hear of your affairs, that ye stand fast in one spirit, with one mind striving together for the faith of the gospel;

28 And in nothing terrified by your adversaries, **who reject the gospel,** which ~~is to them an evident token of perdition~~ **bringeth on them destruction;** but ~~to~~ you ~~of~~ **who receive the gospel,** salvation; and that of God.

30 Having the same conflict which ye saw in me, and now ~~hear~~ **know** *to be* in me.

<h3 style="text-align:center">Chapter 2</h3>

17 Yea, and if I be offered ~~upon the~~ **a** sacrifice ~~and~~ **upon the** service of your faith, I joy, and rejoice with you all.

<h3 style="text-align:center">Chapter 3</h3>

1 Finally, my brethren, rejoice in the Lord. To write the same things to you, to me indeed *is* not grievous, ~~but~~ **and** for you *it is* safe.

11 If by any means I might attain unto the resurrection of the ~~dead~~ **just.**

18 (For many walk, of whom I have told you often, and now tell you even weeping, ~~that they are~~ **as** the enemies of the cross of Christ;

19 Whose end *is* destruction, whose God *is their* belly, and ~~whose~~ **who** glory ~~is~~ in their shame, who mind earthly things.)

<h3 style="text-align:center">Chapter 4</h3>

6 Be ~~careful~~ **afflicted** for nothing; but in everything by prayer and supplication with thanksgiving let your requests be made known unto God.

The Epistle of Paul the Apostle to the
COLOSSIANS

CHAPTER 1

4 Since we heard of your faith in Christ Jesus, and of ~~the~~ **your** love ~~which ye have~~ to all the saints,

6 Which is come unto you, as ~~it is~~ in all **generations of** the world; and bringeth forth fruit, as *it doth* also in you, since the day ye heard *of it,* and knew the grace of God in truth;

CHAPTER 2

2 That their hearts might be comforted, being knit together in love, and unto all riches of the full assurance of understanding, to the acknowledgment of the mystery of ~~God~~ **Christ** ~~and of~~, **who is of God, even** the Father ~~and of Christ~~;

7 Rooted and built up in him, and ~~stablished~~ **established** in the faith, as ye have been taught, abounding therein with thanksgiving.

20 Wherefore if ye be dead with Christ from the rudiments of the world, why, as though living in the world, are ye subject to ordinances,

21 21–22 **Which are after the doctrines and commandments of men, who teach you to** touch not; taste not; handle not; **all those things** which ~~all~~ are to perish with the using ~~after the commandments and doctrines of men~~?

22 23 Which things have indeed a show of wisdom in will worship, and humility, and neglecting ~~of~~ the body **as to the satisfying the flesh,** not in any honor to **God** ~~the satisfying of the flesh~~.

CHAPTER 4

11 And Jesus, which is called Justus, who are of the circumcision. These only *are my* fellow workers ~~unto~~ **in** the kingdom of God, which have been a comfort unto me.

The First Epistle of Paul the Apostle to the
THESSALONIANS

CHAPTER 1

1 Paul, and Silvanus, and Timotheus, **servants of God the Father and the Lord Jesus Christ,** unto the church of the Thessalonians ~~which is~~ in ~~God the Father and in~~ the Lord ~~Jesus Christ~~; grace *be* unto you, and peace from God our Father, and the Lord Jesus Christ.

2 We give thanks ~~to God~~ always ~~for you all~~, making mention of you **all,** in our prayers **to God for you**.

8 For from you sounded out the word of the Lord not only in Macedonia and Achaia, but also in every place your faith ~~to~~ **toward**[*] ~~God-ward~~ **God** is spread abroad; so that we need not to speak anything.

CHAPTER 2

16 Forbidding us to speak to the Gentiles that they might be saved, to fill up their sins ~~alway~~ **always;** for the wrath is ~~come~~ **coming** upon them to the uttermost.

CHAPTER 4

15 For this we say unto you by the word of the Lord, that ~~we~~ **they** ~~which~~ **who** are alive ~~and remain unto~~ **at** the coming of the Lord**,** shall not prevent them ~~which~~ **who remain unto the coming of the Lord, who** are asleep.

17 Then ~~we~~ **they** ~~which~~ **who** are alive ~~and remain~~, shall be caught up together ~~with them in~~ **into** the clouds **with them who remain**, to meet the Lord in the air**;** and so shall we **be** ever ~~be~~ with the Lord.

CHAPTER 5

26 Greet all the brethren with ~~an~~ **a** holy ~~kiss~~ **salutation**.

The Second Epistle of Paul the Apostle to the
THESSALONIANS

CHAPTER 1

1 Paul, and Sylvanus, and Timotheus, **the servants of God the Father and our Lord Jesus Christ,** unto the church of the Thessalonians ~~in God our Father and the Lord Jesus Christ;~~

9 Who shall be punished with ~~everlasting~~ destruction from the presence of the Lord, and from the glory of his **everlasting** power;

CHAPTER 2

2 That ye be not soon shaken in mind, or be troubled **by letter, except ye receive it from us;** neither by spirit, nor by word, ~~nor by letter as from us~~ as that the day of Christ is at hand.

3 Let no man deceive you by any means**;** for *~~that day shall not come, except~~* there **shall** come a falling away first, and that man of sin be revealed, the son of perdition;

7 For the mystery of iniquity doth already work**,** ~~only~~ **and** he **it is** who now ~~letteth~~ *~~will let~~* **worketh, and Christ suffereth him to work,** until **the time is fulfilled that** he **shall** be taken out of the way.

8 And then shall that wicked **one** be revealed, whom the Lord shall consume with the spirit of his mouth, and shall destroy with the brightness of his coming**.**

9 **Yea, the Lord**, *even ~~him~~* **Jesus**, whose coming is ~~after~~ **not until after there cometh a falling away, by** the working of Satan with all power, and signs and lying wonders,

The First Epistle of Paul the Apostle to
TIMOTHY

CHAPTER 1

1 Paul, an apostle of Jesus Christ by the commandment of God ~~our Saviour~~ and **the** Lord Jesus Christ, **our** Savior ~~which is~~ **and** our hope;

CHAPTER 2

4 Who ~~will~~ **is willing to** have all men to be saved, and to come unto the knowledge of the truth **which is in Christ Jesus, who is the Only Begotten Son of God, and ordained to be a Mediator between God and man; who is one God, and hath power over all men.**

9 In like manner also, that women adorn themselves in modest apparel, with shamefacedness and sobriety; not with ~~broided~~ **braided** hair, or gold, or pearls, or costly array;

12 ~~But~~ **For** I suffer not a woman to teach, nor to usurp authority over the man, but to be in silence.

15 Notwithstanding ~~she~~ **they** shall be saved in childbearing, if they continue in faith and charity and holiness with sobriety.

CHAPTER 3

8 Likewise ~~must~~ the deacons **must** *be* grave, not doubletongued, not given to much wine, not greedy of filthy lucre;

15 But if I tarry long, that thou mayest know how thou oughtest to behave thyself in the house of God, which is the church of the living God,

16 15–16 The pillar and ground of the truth **is,** (and without controversy,

great is the mystery of godliness**,**) God was manifest in the flesh, justified in the Spirit, seen of angels, preached unto the Gentiles, believed on in the world, received up into glory.

CHAPTER 4

2 Speaking lies in hypocrisy; having their conscience seared **as** with a hot iron;

CHAPTER 5

10 Well reported of for good works; if she have brought up children, if she have lodged strangers, if she have washed the saints' ~~feet~~ **clothes**, if she have relieved the afflicted, if she have diligently followed every good work.

23 24 Some men's sins are open beforehand, going before to judgment; and some *men* they follow after.

24 25 Likewise also the good works *of some* are manifest beforehand; and they that are otherwise cannot be hid.

CHAPTER 6

15 Which in his times he shall show, *who is* the blessed and only Potentate, the King of kings, and Lord of lords**, to whom be honor and power everlasting;**

16 ~~Who only hath immortality, dwelling in the light which no man can approach unto~~ Whom no man hath seen, nor can see, ~~to whom *be* honour and power everlasting. Amen~~ **unto whom no man can approach, only he who hath the light and the hope of immortality dwelling in him.**

The Second Epistle of Paul the Apostle to
TIMOTHY

CHAPTER 2

5 And if a man also strive for masteries, ~~yet~~ **he** is ~~he~~ not crowned, except he strive lawfully.

8 Remember that Jesus Christ of the seed of David was raised from the dead, according to ~~my~~ **the** gospel;

11 **For** ~~It~~ **this** *is* a faithful saying, ~~For~~ If we be dead with *him*, we shall also live with *him*;

CHAPTER 3

13 ~~But~~ **For** evil men and seducers shall wax worse and worse, deceiving, and being deceived.

16 **And** all scripture ~~is~~ given by inspiration of God, ~~and~~ *is* profitable for doctrine, for reproof, for correction, for instruction in righteousness;

CHAPTER 4

1 I charge *thee* therefore before God, and the Lord Jesus Christ, who shall judge the quick and the dead at his appearing and **in** his kingdom;

2 Preach the word: be instant in season; **those**[41] **who are** out of season reprove, rebuke, exhort with all longsuffering and doctrine.

15 Of whom be thou ware ~~also~~; for he hath greatly withstood our words.

22 The Lord Jesus Christ *be* with ~~thy spirit~~ **you, and** grace *be* with you **all**. Amen.

The Epistle of Paul to
TITUS

CHAPTER 1

15 Unto the pure, **let** all things ~~are~~ **be** pure; but unto them ~~that~~ **who** are defiled and unbelieving, ~~is~~ nothing **is** pure; but even their mind and conscience is defiled.

CHAPTER 2

11 For the grace of God ~~that~~ **which** bringeth salvation **to all men,** hath appeared ~~to all men~~;

The Epistle of Paul to
PHILEMON

CHAPTER 1

25 The grace of our Lord Jesus Christ *be* with ~~your spirit~~ **you**. Amen.

The Epistle of Paul the Apostle to the
HEBREWS

CHAPTER 1

6 And again, when he bringeth in the first begotten into the world, he saith, And let all the angels of God worship him, **who maketh his ministers as a flame of fire.**

7 And of the angels he saith, ~~Who maketh his angels spirits, and his ministers a flame of fire~~ **Angels are ministering spirits.**

CHAPTER 2

16 For verily, he took not on *him* the *~~nature~~* **likeness** *of* angels; but he took on *him* the seed of Abraham.

CHAPTER 3

3 For ~~this *man*~~ **he** was counted worthy of more glory than Moses, inasmuch as he who hath builded the house hath more honor than the house.

CHAPTER 4

2 For unto us was the ~~gospel~~ **rest** preached, as well as unto them; but the word preached did not profit them, not being mixed with faith in them that heard *it*.

3 For we ~~which~~ **who** have believed do enter into rest, as he said, As I have sworn in my wrath, If they **harden their hearts they** shall **not** enter into my rest; **also, I have sworn, If they will not harden their hearts, they shall enter into my rest;** although the works **of God** were **prepared, (or** finished,**)** from the foundation of the world.

5 And in this *place* again, If they **harden not their hearts they** shall enter into my rest.

12 For the word of God *is* quick, and powerful, and sharper than any two-edged sword, piercing even to the dividing asunder of ~~soul~~ **body** and spirit, and of the joints and marrow, and *is* a discerner of the thoughts and intents of the heart.

CHAPTER 6

1 Therefore **not** leaving the principles of the doctrine of Christ, let us go on unto perfection; not laying again the foundation of repentance from dead works, and of faith toward God.

3 And ~~this~~ **we** will ~~we do~~ **go on unto perfection** if God permit.

4 For ~~it is~~ **he hath made it** impossible for those who were once enlightened, and have tasted of the heavenly gift, and were made partakers of the Holy Ghost,

6 If they shall fall away, to ~~renew them~~ **be renewed** again unto repentance; seeing they crucify ~~to~~ **unto** themselves the Son of God afresh, and put *him* to an open shame.

7 For **the day cometh that** the earth which drinketh in the rain that cometh oft upon it, and bringeth forth herbs meet for them **who dwelleth thereon,** by whom it is dressed, **who now** receiveth ~~blessing~~ **blessings** from God, **shall be cleansed with fire.**

8 ~~But~~ **For** that which beareth thorns and briers *is* rejected, and *is* nigh unto cursing; **therefore they who bring not forth good fruits, shall be cast into the fire; for** ~~whose~~ **their** end *is* to be burned.

9 But, beloved, we are persuaded **of** better things of you, and things that

accompany salvation, though we thus speak.

10 For God *is* not unrighteous ~~to,~~ **therefore he will not** forget your work and labor of love, which ye have showed toward his name, in that ye have ministered to the saints, and do minister.

CHAPTER 7

3 **For this Melchizedek**[*] **was ordained a priest after the order of the Son of God, which order was** without father, without mother, without descent, having neither beginning of days, nor end of life. ~~but~~ **And all those who are ordained unto this priesthood are** made like unto the Son of God, ~~abideth~~ **abiding** a priest continually.

19 For the law **was administered without an oath and** made nothing perfect, but **was only** the bringing in of a better hope ~~did~~; by the which we draw nigh unto God.

20 ~~And~~ Inasmuch as **this high priest was** not without an oath, **by so much** ~~he was~~ **Jesus** *made* ~~priest~~ **the surety of a better testament.**

25 26 For such an high priest became us, *who is* holy, harmless, undefiled, separate from sinners, and made ~~higher~~ **ruler** ~~than~~ **over** the heavens;

26 27 ~~Who needeth~~ **And** not ~~daily~~ as those high priests ~~to~~ **who** ~~offer~~ **offered** up sacrifice **daily,** first for ~~his~~ **their** own sins, and then for the ~~people's~~ **sins of the people;** for **he needeth not offer sacrifice for his own sins, for he knew no sins; but for the sins of the people. And** this he did once, when he offered up himself.

CHAPTER 8

4 ~~For if~~ **Therefore while** he ~~were~~ **was** on **the** earth, he ~~should not be a priest, seeing that there are priests that~~ **offered for a sacrifice his own life for the sins of the people. Now every priest under the law, must needs** offer gifts, **or sacrifices,** according to the law.

CHAPTER 9

8 The Holy Ghost ~~this~~ signifying **this,**[*] that the way into the holiest of all was not yet made manifest, while as **yet** the first tabernacle was ~~yet~~ standing;

10 *Which* ~~stood~~ **consisted** only in meats and drinks, and divers washings, and carnal ordinances, imposed *on them* until the time of reformation.

15 And for this cause he is the mediator of the new ~~testament~~ **covenant,** that by means of death, for the redemption of the transgressions *that were* under the first ~~testament~~ **covenant,** they which are called might receive the promise of eternal inheritance.

16 For where a ~~testament~~ **covenant** *is,* there must also of necessity be the death of the ~~testator~~ **victim.**

17 For a ~~testament~~ **covenant** *is* of force after ~~men~~ **the victim** ~~are~~ **is** dead; otherwise it is of no strength at all while the ~~testator~~ **victim** liveth.

18 Whereupon neither the first ~~testament~~ **covenant** was dedicated without blood.

20 Saying, This *is* the blood of the ~~testament~~ **covenant** which God hath enjoined unto you.

21 Moreover he sprinkled **likewise** with blood both the tabernacle, and all the vessels of the ministry.

26 For then must he often have suffered since the foundation of the world; but now once in the ~~end~~ **meridian** of ~~the world~~ **time** hath he appeared to put away sin by the sacrifice of himself.

28 So Christ was once offered to bear the sins of many; and ~~unto them~~

~~that look for him~~ **he** shall ~~he~~ appear the second time, without sin unto salvation **unto them that look for him**.

CHAPTER 10

1 For the law having a shadow of good things to come, *and* not the very image of the things, can never with those sacrifices, which they offered ~~year by year~~ continually, make the comers thereunto perfect.

10 By ~~the~~ which will we are sanctified through the offering **once** of the body of Jesus Christ ~~once for all~~.

13 From henceforth ~~expecting~~ **to reign** ~~till~~ **until** his enemies be made his footstool.

21 And *having* **such** an high priest over the house of God;

CHAPTER 11

1 Now faith is the ~~substance~~ **assurance** of things hoped for, the evidence of things not seen.

12 Therefore sprang there even of one, and him as good as dead, ~~so~~ **as** *many* as the stars of the sky in multitude, and as the sand which is by the seashore innumerable.

23 By faith Moses, when he was born, was hid three months of his parents, because they saw **that** *he was* a ~~proper~~ **peculiar** child; and they were not afraid of the king's commandment.

24 By faith Moses, when he was come to years **of discretion**, refused

to be called the son of Pharaoh's daughter;

35 Women received their dead raised to life again; and others were tortured, not accepting deliverance; that they might obtain ~~a~~ **the** ~~better~~ **first** resurrection;

39 And these all, having obtained a good report through faith, received not the ~~promise~~ **promises:**

40 God having provided some better ~~thing~~ **things** for ~~us, that~~ **them through their sufferings, for without sufferings** they ~~without us should~~ **could** not be made perfect.

CHAPTER 12

12 Wherefore lift up the hands which hang down, and **strengthen** the feeble knees;

28 Wherefore we receiving a kingdom which cannot be moved, ~~let us~~ **should˙** have grace, whereby we may serve God acceptably with reverence and godly fear;

CHAPTER 13

3 Remember them that are in bonds, as bound with them; *and* them which suffer adversity, as being yourselves also ~~in~~ **of** the body.

5 *Let your* ~~conversation~~ **consecrations** *be* without covetousness; *and be* content with **giving** such things as ye have; for he hath said, I will never leave thee, nor forsake thee.

The General Epistle of

JAMES

CHAPTER 1

2 My brethren, count it all joy when ye fall into ~~divers~~ **many** ~~temptations~~ **afflictions**;

4 But let patience have *her* **its** perfect work, that ye may be perfect and entire, wanting nothing.

12 Blessed *is* the man that ~~endureth~~ **resisteth** temptation; for when he is tried, he shall receive the crown of life, which the Lord hath promised to them that love him.

21 Wherefore lay ~~apart~~ **aside** all filthiness and superfluity of naughtiness, and receive with meekness, the engrafted word, which is able to save your souls.

27 Pure religion and undefiled before God and the Father is this, To visit the fatherless and widows in their affliction, *and* to keep himself unspotted from the **vices of the** world.

CHAPTER 2

1 My brethren, **ye cannot** have ~~not~~ the faith of our Lord Jesus Christ, *the Lord* of glory, ~~with~~ **and yet have** respect ~~of~~ **to** persons.

2 ~~For~~ **Now** if there come unto your assembly a man with a gold ring, in goodly apparel, and there come in also a poor man in vile raiment;

4 Are ye not then ~~partial~~ in yourselves **partial judges**, and ~~are~~ become ~~judges of~~ evil **in your** thoughts?

10 For whosoever shall, **save in one point,** keep the whole law, ~~and yet offend in one *point*~~ he is guilty of all.

14 What ~~doth it~~ profit **is it**, my brethren, ~~though~~ **for** a man **to** say he hath faith, and ~~have~~ **hath** not works? can faith save him?

15 18 Yea, a man may say, ~~Thou hast faith, and~~ **I will show thee** I have **faith without** works; **but I say,** Show me thy faith without ~~thy~~ works, and I will show thee my faith by my works.

16 15–16 **For** if a brother or sister be naked and destitute ~~of daily food~~, and one of you say ~~unto them~~, Depart in peace, be ~~ye~~ warmed and filled; notwithstanding ~~ye~~ **he** give ~~them~~ not those things which are needful to the body; what ~~doth it~~ profit **is your faith unto such**?

17 Even so faith, if it ~~hath~~ **have** not works is dead, being alone.

18 20 ~~But~~ **Therefore** wilt thou know, O vain man, that faith without works is dead **and cannot save you**?

19 Thou believest ~~that~~ there is one God; thou doest well; the devils also believe, and tremble; **thou hast made thyself like unto them, not being justified**.

21 22 Seest thou how ~~faith~~ **works** wrought with his ~~works~~ **faith**, and by works was faith made perfect?

23 24 Ye see then ~~how~~ that by works a man is justified, and not by faith only.

24 25 Likewise also ~~was not~~ Rahab the harlot **was** justified by works, when she had received the messengers and ~~had~~ sent *them* out another way.

25 26 For, as the body without the spirit is dead, so faith without works is dead ~~also~~.

CHAPTER 3

1 My brethren, ~~be~~ **strive** not ~~many masters~~ **for the mastery**, knowing that **in so doing** we shall receive the greater condemnation.

The First Epistle General of
PETER

CHAPTER 1

9 Receiving the ~~end~~ **object** of your faith, *even* the salvation of *your* souls.

10 ~~Of~~ **Concerning** which salvation the prophets **who prophesied of the grace bestowed upon you,** ~~have~~ inquired and searched diligently; ~~who prophesied of the grace *that should come* unto you~~

11 Searching what **time,** ~~or~~ **and** what manner of ~~time~~ **salvation** the Spirit of Christ which was in them did signify, when it testified beforehand the sufferings of Christ, and the glory ~~that~~ **which** should follow.

CHAPTER 2

7 **7–8** Unto you therefore ~~which~~ **who** believe, *he is* precious; but unto them ~~which~~ **who** ~~be~~ **are** disobedient, ~~And a stone of stumbling, and a rock of offence, *even to them* which~~ **who** stumble at the word, ~~being~~ **through** ~~disobedient~~ **disobedience**, whereunto ~~also~~ they were appointed, **a stone of stumbling, and a rock of offense.**

8 **7 For** the stone which the builders disallowed, ~~the same~~ is ~~made~~ **become** the head of the corner.

12 Having your ~~conversation~~ **conduct** honest among the Gentiles; that, whereas they speak against you as evildoers, they may by *your* good works, which they shall behold, glorify God in the day of visitation.

CHAPTER 3

1 Likewise, ye wives, *be* in subjection to your own husbands; that, if any obey not the word, they also may without the word be won by the ~~conversation~~ **conduct** of the wives;

2 While they behold your chaste ~~conversation~~ **conduct** *coupled* with fear.

3 ~~Whose~~ **Let your** adorning ~~let it~~ **be** not ~~be~~ that outward *adorning* of plaiting the hair, and ~~of~~ wearing of gold, or ~~of~~ putting on of apparel;

5 For after this manner in ~~the~~ old ~~time~~ **times** the holy women ~~also,~~ who trusted in God, adorned themselves, being in subjection unto their own husbands;

15 But sanctify the Lord God in your hearts; and *be* ready always to *give* an answer **with meekness and fear** to every man that asketh ~~of~~ you a reason ~~of~~ **for** the hope that is in you ~~with meekness and fear;~~

16 Having a good conscience; that, whereas they speak evil of you, as of evildoers, they may be ashamed that falsely accuse your good ~~conversation~~ **conduct** in Christ.

18 For Christ also ~~hath~~ once suffered for sins, the just for the unjust, ~~that he might bring us to God~~ being put to death in the flesh, but quickened by the Spirit**, that he might bring us to God.**

19 ~~By~~ **For** which **cause** also, he went and preached unto the spirits in prison;

20 ~~Which sometime~~ **Some of whom** were disobedient **in the days of Noah,** ~~when once~~ **while** the longsuffering of God waited ~~in the days of Noah~~, while the ark was ~~a~~ preparing, wherein few, that is, eight souls were saved by water.

CHAPTER 4

1 Forasmuch then as Christ hath suffered for us in the flesh, arm yourselves likewise with the same mind:

2 1–2 For ~~he~~ **you** ~~that~~ **who** ~~hath~~ **have** suffered in the flesh ~~hath~~ **should** ~~ceased~~ **cease** from sin, that ~~he~~ **you** no longer ~~should live~~ the rest of ~~his~~ **your** time in the flesh, **should live** to the lusts of men, but to the will of God.

3 For the time past of ~~our~~ life may suffice ~~us~~ to have wrought the will of the Gentiles, when ~~we~~ **ye** walked in lasciviousness, lusts, excess of wine, revellings, banquetings, and abominable idolatries;

4 Wherein they **speak evil of you**, ~~think~~ **thinking** it strange that ~~ye~~ **you** run not with *them* to the same excess of riot; ~~speaking evil of you~~

6 ~~For for~~ **Because of** this ~~cause, was~~ **is** the gospel preached ~~also~~ to them ~~that~~ **who** are dead, that they might be judged according to men in the flesh,

but live **in the spirit** according to **the will of** God ~~in the spirit~~.

7 But **to you,** the end of all things is at hand; be ye therefore sober, and watch unto prayer.

8 And above all things have fervent charity among yourselves; for charity ~~shall cover~~ **preventeth** ~~the~~ **a** multitude of sins.

11 If any man speak, *let him speak* as ~~the~~ **an** ~~oracles~~ **oracle** of God; if any man minister, *let him do it* as of the ability which God giveth; that God in all things may be glorified through Jesus Christ; to whom be praise and dominion forever and ever. Amen.

Chapter 5

13 ~~The *church that is*~~ **They** at Babylon, elected together with *you,* saluteth you; and *so doth* Marcus my son.

The Second Epistle General of
PETER

Chapter 1

19 We have ~~also~~ **therefore** a more sure **knowledge of the** word of prophecy, ~~whereunto~~ **to which word of prophecy** ye do well that ye take heed, as unto a light ~~that~~ **which** shineth in a dark place, until the day dawn, and the day star arise in your hearts;

20 Knowing this first, that no prophecy of the ~~scripture~~ **scriptures** is **given** of any private ~~interpretation~~ **will of man.**

Chapter 2

1 But there were false prophets also among the people, even as there shall be false teachers among you, who privily shall bring in ~~damnable~~ **abom-**

inable heresies, even denying the Lord that bought them, and bring upon themselves swift destruction.

3 And through covetousness shall they with feigned words make merchandise of you; whose judgment now of a long time lingereth not, and their ~~damnation~~ **destruction** slumbereth not.

19 While they promise them liberty, they themselves are the servants of corruption; for of whom a man is overcome, of the same is he brought ~~in~~ **into** bondage.

Chapter 3

1 This second epistle, beloved, I now

write unto you; in ~~both~~ which I stir up your pure minds by way of remembrance;

3 Knowing this first, that **in the last days** there shall come ~~in the last days~~ scoffers, walking after their own lusts.

4 **Denying the Lord Jesus Christ,** and saying, Where is the promise of his coming? for since the fathers fell asleep, all things **must** continue as *they* ~~*were*~~ **are, and have continued as they are** from the beginning of the creation.

5 For this they willingly are ignorant of, ~~that by the word of God the heavens were of old~~ **that of old the heavens,** and the earth standing ~~out of~~ **in** the water and ~~in~~ **out of** the water, **were created by the word of God;**

6 ~~Whereby~~ **And by the word of God,** the world that then was, being overflowed with water perished;

7 But the heavens, and the earth which are now, ~~by the same word~~ are kept in store **by the same word**, reserved unto fire against the day of judgment and perdition of ungodly men.

8 But **concerning the coming of the Lord,** beloved, ~~be~~ **I would** not **have you** ignorant of this one thing, that one day *is* with the Lord as a thousand years, and a thousand years as one day.

9 The Lord is not slack concerning his promise **and coming**, as some men count slackness; but ~~is~~ longsuffering ~~to~~ **toward** ~~us-ward~~ **us**, not willing that any should perish, but that all should come to repentance.

10 But the day of the Lord will come as a thief in the night, in the which the heavens shall **shake, and the earth also shall tremble, and the mountains**

shall melt, and pass away with a great noise, and the elements shall **be filled** ~~melt~~ with fervent heat; the earth also **shall be filled,** and the **corruptible** works ~~that~~ **which** are therein shall be burned up.

11 ~~Seeing~~ **If** then ~~that~~ all these things shall be ~~dissolved~~ **destroyed**, what manner *of persons* ought ye to be in ~~all~~ holy ~~conversation~~ **conduct** and godliness,

12 Looking ~~for~~ **unto**, and ~~hasting~~ **preparing** ~~unto~~ **for** the ~~coming of the~~ day **of the coming** of ~~God~~ **the Lord** wherein the **corruptible things of the** heavens being on fire, shall be dissolved, and the ~~elements~~ **mountains** shall melt with fervent heat?

13 Nevertheless, **if we shall endure,** we **shall be kept** according to his promise. **And we** look for new heavens, and a new earth wherein dwelleth righteousness.

15 And account ~~that~~ ~~the longsuffering of our Lord *is* salvation,~~ even as our beloved brother Paul also, according to the wisdom given unto him, hath written unto you, **the longsuffering and waiting of our Lord, for salvation.**

16 As also in all *his* epistles, speaking in them of these things, in which are some things hard to be understood, which they ~~that~~ **who** are unlearned and unstable wrest, as *they do* also the other scriptures, unto their own destruction.

17 Ye therefore, beloved, seeing ye know ~~these things~~ before **the things which are coming**, beware lest ye also being led away with the error of the wicked, fall from your own ~~stedfastness~~ **steadfastness.**

The First Epistle General of
JOHN

CHAPTER 1

1 **Brethren, this is the testimony which we give of** that which was from the beginning, which we have heard, which we have seen with our eyes, which we have looked upon, and our hands have handled, of the Word of life;

CHAPTER 2

1 My little children, these things write I unto you, that ye sin not. ~~And~~ **But** if any man sin **and repent**, we have an advocate with the Father, Jesus Christ the righteous;

7 Brethren, I write ~~no~~ **a** new commandment unto you, but ~~an old~~ **it is the same** commandment which ye had from the beginning. The old commandment is the word which ye have heard from the beginning.

8 Again, a new commandment I write unto you, which thing **was of old ordained of God; and** is true in him, and in you; because the darkness is past **in you**, and the true light now shineth.

15 Love not the world, neither the things *that are* ~~in~~ **of** the world. If any man love the world, the love of the Father is not in him.

16 For all ~~that is~~ in the world **that is of** the ~~lust~~ **lusts** of the flesh, and the lust of the eyes, and the pride of life, is not of the Father, but is of the world.

24 Let that therefore abide in you, which ye have heard from the beginning. If that which ye have heard from the beginning shall remain in you, ye ~~also~~ shall continue in the Son, and **also** in the Father.

CHAPTER 3

6 Whosoever abideth in him sinneth not; whosoever ~~sinneth~~ **continueth in sin** hath not seen him, neither known him.

8 He that ~~committeth~~ **continueth in** sin is of the devil; for the devil sinneth from the beginning. For this purpose the Son of God was manifested, that he might destroy the works of the devil.

9 Whosoever is born of God doth not ~~commit~~ **continue in** sin; for ~~his seed~~ **the Spirit of God** remaineth in him; and he cannot **continue in** sin, because he is born of God, **having received that holy Spirit of promise**.

16 Hereby perceive we the love *of* ~~God~~ **Christ**, because he laid down his life for us; and we ought to lay down *our* lives for the brethren.

18 My little children, let us not love in word, neither in tongue **only**; but in deed and in truth.

21 Beloved, if our heart condemn us not, *then* **we** have ~~we~~ confidence toward God.

CHAPTER 4

3 And every spirit that confesseth not that Jesus Christ is come in the flesh is not of God; and this is that *spirit* of antichrist, whereof ye have heard that it should come; and even now **it is** already ~~is it~~ in the world.

12 No man hath seen God at any time, **except them who believe**. If we love one another, God dwelleth in us, and his love is perfected in us.

CHAPTER 5

13 These things have I written unto
you that believe on the name of the
Son of God; that ye may know that ye
have eternal life, and that ye may **continue to** believe on the name of the
Son of God.

18 We know that whosoever is born
of God ~~sinneth~~ **continueth** not **in
sin**; but he ~~that~~ **who** is begotten of
God **and** keepeth himself, ~~and~~ that
wicked one ~~toucheth~~ **overcometh**
him not.

The General Epistle of
JUDE

CHAPTER 1

1 Jude, the servant **of God, called** of
Jesus Christ, and brother of James**;** to
them ~~that~~ **who** are sanctified ~~by God~~
of the Father; and preserved in Jesus
Christ ~~and called~~;

11 Woe unto them! for they have
gone in the way of Cain, and ran
greedily after the error of Balaam for
reward, and **shall** ~~perished~~ **perish** in
the gainsaying of Core.

THE REVELATION
of Saint John the Divine

CHAPTER 1

1 The Revelation of ~~Jesus Christ~~
John, a servant of God, which ~~God
gave~~ **was given** unto him **of Jesus
Christ**, to show unto his servants
things which must shortly come to
pass, ~~and~~ **that** he sent and signified ~~it~~
by his angel unto his servant John,

2 Who ~~bare~~ **bore** record of the word
of God, and of the testimony of Jesus
Christ, and of all things that he saw.

3 Blessed ~~is~~ **are** ~~he~~ **they** ~~that~~ **who**
~~readeth~~ **read**, and they ~~that~~ **who** hear
and understand the words of this
prophecy, and keep those things
which are written therein, for the time
of the coming of the Lord ~~is at hand~~
draweth nigh.

4 **Now this is the testimony of** John
to **the seven servants who are over**
the seven churches ~~which are~~ in Asia.
Grace ~~be~~ unto you, and peace from
him ~~which~~ **who** is, and ~~which~~ **who**
was, and ~~which~~ **who** is to come; ~~and~~
who hath sent forth his angel from
~~the seven Spirits which are~~ before his
throne, **to testify unto those who are
the seven servants over the seven
churches.**

5 ~~And from Jesus Christ, who is~~
Therefore, I, John, the faithful witness, **bear record of the things which
were delivered me of the angel,** *and*
from Jesus Christ the first begotten
of the dead, and the Prince of the
kings of the earth.

6 5–6 **And** unto him ~~that~~ **who** loved us, **be glory;** ~~and~~ **who** washed us from our sins in his own blood, and hath made us kings and priests unto God**,** ~~and~~ his Father**.** To him *be* glory and dominion, forever and ever. Amen.

7 **For** behold, he cometh ~~with~~ **in the** clouds **with ten thousands of his saints in the kingdom, clothed with the glory of his Father.** And every eye shall see him**;** and they ~~also~~ ~~which~~ **who** pierced him**,** and all kindreds of the earth shall wail because of him. Even so, Amen.

8 **For he saith,** I am Alpha and Omega, the beginning and the ending, ~~saith~~ the Lord, ~~which~~ **who** is, and ~~which~~ **who** was, and ~~which~~ **who** is to come, the Almighty.

12 And I turned to see **from whence** the voice **came** that spake ~~with~~ **to** me**;** and being turned, I saw seven golden candlesticks;

16 And he had in his right hand seven stars; and out of his mouth went a sharp twoedged sword**;** and his countenance *was* as the sun ~~shineth~~ **shining** in his strength.

20 **This is** the mystery of the seven stars which thou sawest in my right hand, and the seven golden candlesticks. The seven stars are the ~~angels~~ **servants** of the seven churches**;** and the seven candlesticks which thou sawest are the seven churches.

CHAPTER 2

1 Unto the ~~angel~~ **servant** of the church of Ephesus write; These things saith he that holdeth the seven stars in his right hand, who walketh in the midst of the seven golden candlesticks;

8 And unto the ~~angel~~ **servant** of the church in Smyrna write; These things saith the first and the last, which was dead, and is alive;

12 And to the ~~angel~~ **servant** of the church in Pergamos write; These things saith he which hath the sharp sword with two edges;

18 And unto the ~~angel~~ **servant** of the church in Thyatira write; These things saith the Son of God, who hath his eyes like unto a flame of fire, and his feet *are* like fine brass;

21 And I gave her space to repent of her ~~fornication~~ **fornications**; and she repented not.

22 Behold, I will cast her into ~~a bed~~ **hell**, and them that commit adultery with her into great tribulation, except they repent of their deeds.

26 And **to** ~~he~~ **him** ~~that~~ **who** overcometh, and keepeth my ~~works~~ **commandments** unto the end, ~~to him~~ will I give power over ~~the nations~~ **many kingdoms;**

27 And he shall rule them with ~~a rod of iron~~ **the word of God**; **and they shall be in his hands** as the vessels of **clay in the hands of** a potter, **and he** shall ~~they be broken to shivers~~ **govern them by faith, with equity and justice,** even as I received of my Father.

CHAPTER 3

1 And unto the ~~angel~~ **servant** of the church in Sardis**,** write; These things saith he ~~that~~ **who** hath the seven **stars, which are the seven** ~~Spirits~~ **servants** of God; ~~and the seven stars~~ I know thy works, that thou hast a name that thou livest, and art not dead.

2 Be watchful **therefore**, and strengthen ~~the things~~ **those** ~~which~~ **who** remain, ~~that~~ **who** are ready to die**;** for I have not found thy works perfect before God.

7 And to the ~~angel~~ **servant** of the church in Philadelphia write; These things saith he that is holy, he that is true, he that hath the key of David, he

that openeth, and no man shutteth; and shutteth, and no man openeth;

12 Him that overcometh will I make a pillar in the temple of my God, and he shall go no more out; and I will write upon him the name of my God; and the name of the city of my God, ~~which~~ **this**‡ *is* New Jerusalem, which cometh down out of heaven from my God; and *I will write upon him* my new name.

14 And unto the ~~angel~~ **servant** of the church of the Laodiceans write; These things saith the Amen, the faithful and true witness, the beginning of the creation of God;

CHAPTER 4

1 After this I looked, and behold, a door *was* opened ~~in~~ **into** heaven; and the first voice which I heard *was* as it were of a trumpet talking with me; which said, Come up hither, and I will show thee things which must be hereafter.

3 And he that sat **there** was to look upon like a jasper and a sardine stone; and *there was* a rainbow round about the throne, in sight like unto an emerald.

4 And ~~round about~~ **in the midst of** the throne *were* four and twenty seats; and upon the seats I saw four and twenty elders sitting, clothed in white raiment, and they had on their heads crowns ~~of~~ **like** gold.

5 And out of the throne proceeded lightnings and thunderings and voices; and *there were* seven lamps of fire burning before the throne, which are the seven ~~Spirits~~ **servants** of God.

6 And before the throne *there was* a sea of glass like unto crystal; and in the midst of the throne **were the four and twenty elders;** and round about

the throne, *were* four beasts full of eyes before and behind.

9 And when those beasts give glory and honor and thanks to him that ~~sat~~ **sits** on the throne, who liveth forever and ever,

10 The four and twenty elders fall down before him that ~~sat~~ **sits** on the throne, and worship him that liveth forever and ever, and cast their crowns before the throne, saying,

CHAPTER 5

1 And I saw in the right hand of him that ~~sat~~ **sits** on the throne a book written within and on the back side, sealed with seven seals.

2 And I saw a strong angel**, and heard him** proclaiming with a loud voice, Who is worthy to open the book, and ~~to~~ loose the seals thereof?

6 And I beheld, and, lo, in the midst of the throne and of the four beasts, and in the midst of the elders, stood a Lamb as it had been slain, having ~~seven~~ **twelve** horns and ~~seven~~ **twelve** eyes, which are the ~~seven~~ **twelve** ~~Spirits~~ **servants** of God, sent forth into all the earth.

CHAPTER 6

1 And I saw when the Lamb opened one of the seals, **one of the four beasts,** and I heard, as it were**,** the noise of thunder, ~~one of the four beasts~~ saying, Come and see.

6 And I heard a voice in the midst of the four beasts say, A measure of wheat for a penny, and three measures of barley for a penny; and ~~see thou~~ hurt not **thou** the oil and the wine.

14 And the ~~heaven~~ **heavens** ~~departed~~ **opened** as a scroll **is opened** when it is rolled together; and every mountain, and island, ~~were~~ **was** moved out of ~~their~~ **its** ~~places~~ **place.**

CHAPTER 7

2 And I saw another angel ascending from the east, having the seal of the living God; and ~~he cried~~ **I heard him cry** with a loud voice to the four angels, to whom it was given to hurt the earth and the sea,

4 And ~~I heard~~ the number of them ~~which~~ **who** were sealed, *~~and there~~ were ~~sealed~~* an hundred *and* forty *and* four thousand of all the tribes of the children of Israel.

CHAPTER 8

12 And the fourth angel sounded, and the third part of the sun was smitten, and the third part of the moon, and the third part of the stars; so ~~as~~ **that** the third part of them was darkened, and the day shone not for a third part of it, and the night likewise.

CHAPTER 9

14 Saying to the sixth angel which had the trumpet, Loose the four angels which are bound in the ~~great river Euphrates~~ **bottomless pit**.

16 And the number of the army of the horsemen *were* two hundred thousand thousand; and I ~~heard~~ **saw** the number of them.

CHAPTER 10

4 And when the seven thunders had uttered their voices, I was about to write; and I heard a voice from heaven saying unto me, ~~Seal up~~ Those things **are sealed up** which the seven thunders uttered, and write them not.

CHAPTER 11

15 And the seventh angel sounded; and there were great voices in heaven, saying, The kingdoms of this world are become *the ~~kingdoms~~* **kingdom** of our Lord, and of his Christ; and he shall reign forever and ever.

CHAPTER 12

1 And there appeared a great ~~wonder~~ **sign** in heaven, **in the likeness of things on the earth;** a woman clothed with the sun, and the moon under her feet, and upon her head a crown of twelve stars**.**

2 And ~~she~~ **the woman** being with child**,** cried, travailing in birth, and pained to be delivered.

3 5 And she brought forth a man child, who was to rule all nations with a rod of iron; and her child was caught up unto God and ~~to~~ his throne.

4 3–4 And there appeared another ~~wonder~~ **sign** in heaven; and behold**,** a great red dragon, having seven heads and ten horns, and seven crowns upon his heads. And his tail drew the third part of the stars of heaven, and did cast them to the earth**.** And the dragon stood before the woman which was ~~ready to be~~ delivered, ~~for~~ **ready** to devour her child ~~as soon as~~ **after** it was born.

5 6 And the woman fled into the wilderness, where she ~~hath~~ **had** a place prepared of God, that they should feed her there a thousand **and** two hundred *and* threescore ~~days~~ **years**.

6 7 And there was war in heaven; Michael and his angels fought against the dragon; and the dragon **and his angels** fought ~~and his angels~~ **against Michael;**

7 8 And **the dragon** prevailed not **against Michael, neither the child, nor the woman which was the church of God, who had been delivered of her pains, and brought forth the kingdom of God and his Christ**.

8 8–9 Neither was ~~their~~ **there** place found ~~any more~~ in heaven ~~and~~ **for** the great dragon, **who** was cast out; that old serpent called the devil, and **also**

called Satan, which deceiveth the whole world; he was cast out into the earth; and his angels were cast out with him.

9 10 And I heard a loud voice saying in heaven, Now is come salvation, and strength, and the kingdom of our God, and the power of his Christ:

10 For the accuser of our brethren is cast down, which accused them before our God day and night.

11 11–12 ~~And~~ **For** they ~~overcame~~ **have overcome** him by the blood of the Lamb, and by the word of their testimony; ~~and~~ **for** they loved not their **own** lives, **but kept the testimony even** unto ~~the~~ death. **Therefore,** rejoice **O** ~~ye~~ heavens, and ye that dwell in them.

12 **And after these things I heard another voice saying,** Woe to the inhabiters of the earth, **yea,** and **they who dwell upon the islands** of the sea! for the devil is come down unto you, having great wrath, because he knoweth that he hath but a short time.

13 ~~And~~ **For** when the dragon saw that he was cast unto the earth, he persecuted the woman which brought forth the man *child*.

14 ~~And~~ **Therefore,** to the woman were given two wings of a great eagle, that she might ~~fly~~ **flee** into the wilderness, into her place, where she is nourished for a time, and times, and half a time, from the face of the serpent.

15 And the serpent ~~cast~~ **casteth** out of his mouth water as a flood after the woman, that he might cause her to be carried away of the flood.

16 And the earth ~~helped~~ **helpeth** the woman, and the earth ~~opened~~ **openeth** her mouth, and ~~swallowed~~ **swalloweth** up the flood which the dragon ~~cast~~ **casteth** out of his mouth.

17 ~~And~~ **Therefore,** the dragon was wroth with the woman, and went to make war with the remnant of her seed, which keep the commandments of God, and have the testimony of Jesus Christ.

CHAPTER 13

1 And I ~~stood upon the sand of the sea, and~~ saw **another sign, in the likeness of the kingdoms of the earth;** a beast rise up out of the sea, **and he stood upon the sand of the sea,** having seven heads and ten horns; and upon his horns ten crowns; and upon his heads the name of blasphemy.

2 And the beast which I saw was like unto a leopard, and his feet were as *the feet* of a bear, and his mouth as the mouth of a lion; and the ~~dragon~~ **devil**[42] gave him his power, and his seat, and great authority.

CHAPTER 14

13 And I heard a voice from heaven saying unto me, Write, Blessed *are* the dead which die in the Lord from henceforth; Yea, saith the Spirit, that they may rest from their labors; and ~~their works do follow them~~ **they shall continue their work**.[43]

20 And the winepress was trodden without the city, and blood came out of the winepress, even unto the ~~horse~~ **horses'** bridles, by the space of a thousand *and* six hundred furlongs.

CHAPTER 16

7 And I heard another **angel who came** out ~~of~~ **from** the altar ~~say~~ **saying,** Even so, Lord God Almighty, true and righteous *are* thy judgments.

CHAPTER 17

17 For God hath put in their hearts to fulfill his will, and to agree, and

give their kingdom unto the beast, until the words of God shall be **are** fulfilled.

Chapter 19

2 For true and righteous *are* his judgments; for he hath judged the great whore, which did corrupt the earth with her fornication, and hath avenged the blood of his servants **saints** at her hand.

5 And a voice came out of the throne, saying, Praise our God, all ye his servants **saints**, and ye that fear him, both small and great.

10 And I fell at his feet to worship him. And he said unto me, See **that** *thou do it* not; I am thy fellow servant, and of thy brethren that have the testimony of Jesus; worship God; for the testimony of Jesus is the spirit of prophecy.

11 And I saw heaven opened, and behold a white horse; and he that sat upon him was **is** called Faithful and True, and in righteousness he doth judge and make war;

12 His eyes were as a flame of fire; and **he had** on his head were many crowns; and he had a name written, that no man knew, but he himself.

13 And he was **is** clothed with a vesture dipped in blood; and his name is called The Word of God.

15 And out of his mouth goeth a sharp sword **proceedeth the word of God**, that **and** with it he should **will** smite the nations; and he shall **will** rule them with a rod of iron **the word**

of his mouth; and he treadeth the winepress of **in** the fierceness and wrath of Almighty God.

16 And he hath on his **a** vesture, and on his thigh a name written, KING OF KINGS, AND LORD OF LORDS.

18 That ye may eat the flesh of kings, and the flesh of captains, and the flesh of mighty men, and the flesh of horses, and of them that sit on them, and the flesh of all **who fight against the Lamb**, men *both* free **bond** and bond **free**, both small and great.

21 And the remnant were slain with the sword **word** of him that sat upon the horse, which sword **word** proceeded out of his mouth; and all the fowls were filled with their flesh.

Chapter 20

1 And I saw an angel come down from **out of** heaven, having the key of the bottomless pit and a great chain in his hand.

6 Blessed and holy *is* **are** he **they** that **who** hath **have** part in the first resurrection; on such the second death hath no power, but they shall be priests of God and of Christ, and shall reign with him a thousand years.

Chapter 22

9 Then saith he unto me, See **that** *thou do it* not; for I am thy fellowservant, and of thy brethren the prophets, and of them which keep the sayings of this book; worship God.

New Testament Notes

24. *Plainer*, 155–156.
25. *Plainer*, 204. Bracketed [ ] text is not in Inspired Version.
26. *Plainer,* 204. Same as above.
27. *Plainer*, 204. Same as above.
28. *Plainer*, 306. The original manuscript indicated "purple" as correct.
29. *Plainer*, 202, 203. Bracketed [ ] text is not in Inspired Version.
30. *Words of Joseph*, 211.
31. *Plainer*, 151.
32. *Teachings*, 331.
33. *Words of Joseph*, 68.
34. *Plainer*, 186.
35. *Plainer*, 153. Here as in 1944 & 1991 Inspired Versions. Manuscript unclear on placement; 1867 Inspired Version places phrase after "afraid."
36. *Plainer*, 152.
37. *Teachings*, 278.
38. *Words of Joseph*, 191.
39. *Plainer*, 187.
40. *Teachings*, 223.
41. *Plainer*, 188–189.
42. *Teachings*, 293.
43. *Plainer*, 210. Edward Stevenson's personal journal 1839.

REFERENCES

Doctrine and Covenants. The Church of Jesus Christ of Latter-day Saints, 1979.

Faulring, Scott H., Kent P. Jackson, Robert J. Matthews, eds. *Joseph Smith's New Translation of the Bible,* 2004.

Holy Bible, King James Version.

Holy Scriptures. [Reorganized] Church of Jesus Christ of Latter Day Saints, 1867.

Holy Scriptures Inspired Version. Reorganized Church of Jesus Christ of Latter Day Saints, 1991.

Joseph Smith's "New Translation" of the Bible, 1970.

Matthews, Robert J. *"A Plainer Translation:" Joseph Smith's Translation of the Bible, a History and Commentary,* 1985.

McConkie, Bruce R. *Mormon Doctrine,* 1958.

RLDS Publications Committee Manuscript to the "Inspired Version" of the Bible, 1867.

Skinner, Andrew C. "Restored Light on the Savior's Last Week in Mortality," *Ensign,* June 1999.

Smith, Joseph. *Teachings of the Prophet Joseph Smith,* comp. Joseph Fielding Smith, 1938.

Smith, Joseph, *The Words of Joseph Smith,* comp. Andrew F. Ehat and Lyndon W. Cook, 1996.

About the Compilers

KENNETH O. LUTES was born in Illinois, about two hours from the city Joseph Smith called Nauvoo the Beautiful. More than thirty years passed before he learned the significance of Nauvoo and about the Prophet Joseph. While living in the San Francisco Bay area, Ken was introduced to the missionaries. They left a Book of Mormon with him. While reading it, he gained a testimony of The Church of Jesus Christ of Latter-day Saints and of Joseph Smith, and was baptized a few months later. From that time until today, the restored gospel has been a constant source of excitement and joy to him.

Prior to joining the Church, Ken graduated from West Point and completed a master's degree in electrical engineering at Texas A&M University. During his careers, he has worked for several well-known corporations, owned his own businesses, and lent his talents to the Church as he worked in the Temple, Family History, and Information Systems Departments.

Of his many callings, Ken treasures most the many years of working and serving in the temples of the Lord. He also especially enjoyed the ten years he spent as the director of the Jordan River Temple Grounds Tours, the three years he served on the high council of a Brigham Young University (BYU) married student stake, and serving in several bishoprics.

LYNDELL JOHNSON LUTES was born and raised in the San Francisco Bay area, but did not meet Ken until she was working for the Family History Department of the Church. She earned a bachelor's degree from the University of California at Santa Barbara then a master's degree and a doctorate in instructional psychology and technology from BYU.

Lyndell enjoys reading, singing, playing the piano, skiing, and travel. Her favorite callings have been teaching the Gospel Doctrine class and Relief Society, and serving in the stake Young Women presidency.